THE GOLDEN AGE OF AMERICAN MUSICAL THEATRE

1943–1965

Corinne J. Naden

THE SCARECROW PRESS, INC.
Lanham • Toronto • Plymouth, UK
2011

Published by Scarecrow Press, Inc.
A wholly owned subsidiary of The Rowman & Littlefield Publishing Group, Inc.
4501 Forbes Boulevard, Suite 200, Lanham, Maryland 20706
http://www.scarecrowpress.com

Estover Road, Plymouth PL6 7PY, United Kingdom

British Library Cataloguing in Publication Information Available

Library of Congress Cataloging-in-Publication Data
Naden, Corinne J.
  The golden age of American musical theatre : 1943–1965 / Corinne J.
Naden.
      p. cm.
  Includes bibliographical references and index.
  ISBN 978-0-8108-7733-7 (cloth : alk. paper) — ISBN 978-0-8108-7734-4
(ebook)
  1. Musicals—United States—20th century—History and criticism. 2.
Musicals—Stories, plots, etc. 3. Musical theater—United States—History—
20th century. I. Title.
  ML1711.N22 2011
  792.609747'1—dc22   2010028844

∞™ The paper used in this publication meets the minimum requirements of
American National Standard for Information Sciences—Permanence of Paper
for Printed Library Materials, ANSI/NISO Z39.48-1992.

Printed in the United States of America.

In memory of Rose Blue,
and with thanks to Abby Simon and Trudi Neuhoff
for all their technical and uncomplaining help.

A very special thank you to
my longtime friend and avid theatregoer Harold C. Vaughan
for trusting me with all his original playbills.

CONTENTS

AMERICA'S UNIQUE CONTRIBUTION

The musical, or musical comedy, is America's unique contribution to the world of the theatre. The words *Broadway musical* refer to any performance incorporating music and dance in one of thirty-eight professional theatres that each seat 500 or more people in the Times Square district of the borough of Manhattan, New York City. The Vivian Beaumont at Lincoln Center (uptown at 65th Street) is the thirty-ninth Broadway-class theatre. It is the only one not located in the Times Square district, which is roughly defined as the area between 40th and 53rd streets and 6th and 9th avenues. The district got its name from the Times Tower, headquarters of the *New York Times*, built in 1904, on 43rd Street just off Broadway. Non-musical performances, known as plays or dramas, are also performed in the Broadway theatre district.

To the English-speaking world, Broadway theatre, along with London's West End district, generally represents commercial theatre at its highest level. It is the theatre area most well known to the American general public, the most prestigious for performers, and the most lucrative for all those involved in the business of putting on a show. Historically, the shows that make it to Broadway are seen as more mainstream or less experimental than many of the performances Off- and Off-Off-Broadway or in regional theatres throughout the country.

Off-Broadway refers to plays or musicals performed in New York City in theatres seating 100 to 499 patrons. Originally the term referred to location, not size. These productions are generally less publicized, less expensive, and less well-known. A number of shows that began in these smaller the-atres have made it to Broadway, such as *A Chorus Line*, *Hair*, and *Sunday in the Park with George*. Off-Broadway theatres include the Astor Place on Lafayette Street, the Cherry Lane on Commerce, and the Orpheum on Second Avenue.

Off-Off-Broadway theatres generally have fewer than 100 seats. They began in 1958 as a reaction to Off-Broadway. The term was supposedly first used by Jerry Talmer of the *Village Voice* and referred to coffeehouses in Greenwich Village. There are a number of Off-Off-Broadway theatres scat-tered about the city, including La MaMa on Second Avenue, the Flea on White Street, and the Collapsable Giraffe in Brooklyn.

Off- and Off-Off-Broadway often present cutting-edge or experimental plays or musicals, many by first-time playwrights and performers. In addi-tion to these productions, nearly 2,000 not-for-profit professional theatres operate around the United States, thanks in large measure to the National Endowment for the Arts (NEA). Since 1965, it has offered musicals and modern plays, classics, and new works to a theatre-loving public. The NEA is a public agency established by Congress. It supports new and established arts with the aim of bringing the arts to all Americans. NEA activities range from youth education to increasing access to high quality theatre. For instance, it launched Shakespeare in American Communities in 2003. In addition, it introduced American Masterpieces; theatre companies tour the states with outstanding American musicals.

The musicals that appear on Broadway usually have a longer run than nonmusical plays. *Fiddler on the Roof*, which opened in 1964, ran for a record-setting total of 3,242 performances. It kept the record for the lon-gest-running Broadway musical for almost ten years, until *Grease* topped it. The aim of all Broadway shows is to make a profit for the producers and investors. Early audience response, advertising, the star quality of the leads, and word of mouth all generally contribute to how long a musical will run—and usually, therefore, how financially successful it will be; however, even a fairly long run does not always guarantee that the musical finishes in the profit column. Some Broadway theatre is presented as a regular sub-scription season, such as Lincoln Center Theater, the Roundabout Theatre Company, or Manhattan Theatre Club. In that case, the run of the show is predetermined.

Most Broadway shows are open-ended (with many exceptions), meaning they will run as long as it is profitable to do so. But producers and investors (known as backers or angels) do not necessarily have to make a profit "right now." If the show meets weekly operating expenses, it may stay open in the expectation that it will eventually pay back the initial costs. In addition to a hoped-for long Broadway run, producers often assemble a new cast and crew for a national tour. Some productions have settled down in major U.S. cities for a long run. Others play for one or two weeks. Smaller cities are serviced by "bus and track" tours; the cast usually travels by bus, and the equipment goes by railroad. These tours may play half a week or even a "one-nighter" in a town before moving on to the next.

Most Broadway theatres schedule evening performances Tuesday through Saturday, with an 8 p.m. curtain, and afternoon matinees on Wednesday and Saturday at 2 p.m. and on Sunday at 3 p.m. This schedule gives actors and crew members a Sunday-evening-until-Tuesday-evening weekend. When performances are not scheduled, the theatre is said to be "dark."

The American musical that is today so much a part of the Broadway theatre scene can trace its origins back to Europe in the first decades of the twentieth century, to the immigrants who arrived from the Old World with operalike performances known as operettas. Although the background of the Broadway musical may be in Europe and its antecedents may be traced to burlesque and vaudeville, to minstrels and music halls, the shows that began in the late nineteenth century and still light the marquees of Broadway are mainly all-American. From those decades of building a new art form, this book concentrates on the Golden Age of America's musical theatre. The time span is twenty-two years, from *Oklahoma!* in 1943 to *On a Clear Day You Can See Forever* in 1965.

In the 1920s, as theatre was truly taking hold in the country, it soon faced a troubling challenge—the motion picture. In 1927, *The Jazz Singer*, starring Al Jolson, became the first "talking" film (actually, that first talkie is silent with sequences of music and voices). People began to wonder whether this new art form—which immediately became very popular—might not replace live theatre altogether.

But the theatre survived, and one of the main reasons was the splendid period of the 1920s and 1930s, when Jerome Kern, Cole Porter, and George and Ira Gershwin enchanted crowds with timeless, memorable tunes and sophisticated comedy. And during this time came a giant step—*Show Boat* (December 27, 1927), based on the novel by Edna Ferber, about life on the Mississippi River. It is generally considered to be America's first true musical. *Show Boat* was distinct from the productions that preceded it because it provided a plot with music that was a central part of the narrative. That distinction started a change on Broadway that evolved, after the lean years of the Great Depression, into the 1943 blockbuster production of *Oklahoma!*. In his autobiography, *Musical Stages* (1975), Richard Rodgers said that *Oklahoma!* was significant because all the parts were a complement to each other rather than overshadowing each other. This is part of what makes the American musical and the Golden Age what they still are today.

Other great musicals followed in the same vein, such as *Carousel* (1945) and *South Pacific* (1949), both the work of Richard Rodgers and Oscar Hammerstein II. In 1956, Alan Jay Lerner and Frederick Loewe collaborated on what many consider the finest of all American musical comedies—*My Fair Lady*.

Such musicals continued into the 1960s, with *Fiddler on the Roof* in 1964 considered the last true masterpiece of the Golden Age. But by about mid-decade, the American musical that audiences had grown to know and love had begun to change perceptively. Although some shows continued in the old vein, pure spectacle began to take over with productions that mainly featured extravagant light settings and dramatic staging. Rock and roll provided the music. *Hair* (1967) is a notable example; enter not only stroboscopic lighting and very loud music, but also nudity, which would have shocked theatre audiences in the Golden Age. Broadway also changed in that individual people became more famous than the shows they staged, such as the highly successful works of Andrew Lloyd Webber, among others. Theatre tickets became increasingly expensive; rock music ushered in by the Beatles often drowned out the old melodies; the traditional sentimental composers seemed out of sync; and the new creative direction of Bob Fosse and Stephen Sondheim, among others, began to change the shape of the traditional musical. These new-age musicals were often devoted to the direction and choreography of one person, such as Fosse. So, to mark the distinction of a changing Broadway, we end the twenty-two years of the Golden Age in 1965, with *On a Clear Day You Can See Forever*.

After that, the "old" musicals seemed about to fade into the background, but not so. The musicals of the Golden Age are still with us, revived time and again. Their songs and their incredible variety never die. The magic still lingers. Twenty-first-century audiences are as thrilled when a brassy young woman sings "Diamonds Are a Girl's Best Friend" as were audiences back in 1949, when Carol Channing brought them to their feet in *Gentlemen Prefer Blondes*. It was during this twenty-two-year period that Broadway showed off its greatness time and again, exhibiting some of its finest productions, masterpieces of plot, music, dance, and dialogue.

In *The Golden Age of American Musical Theatre*, chapter 2, "The History of Broadway," traces the beginnings of theatre in New York's Times Square district. It details its growth through the decades of the twentieth century until the end of the twenty-two-year period known as the Golden Age.

Chapter 3, "Golden Age Timeline," lists Broadway productions chronologically between 1943 and 1965. Not noted are operettas, revues, follies, revivals, dance revues, and other shows that can be loosely termed burlesque or vaudeville acts.

"The Golden Age Musicals of Broadway," chapter 4, gives opening dates and theatre production credits, casts, synopses, major songs of the scores, awards, and other pertinent information about these memorable productions. Also noted but not given full data are those musicals designated as flops (marked with an °), which can be difficult to define. The term is somewhat ambiguous because it is not so easy to determine what "flopped" on Broadway either because critics and audiences did not like them or they were not commercial successes. Most would concede that a production lasting not even a week was definitely a flop; even worse, some shows closed on opening night. But there were also instances of musicals running for as long as a year that did not recover their original investments. To the backers and cast members, those might also be considered unsuccessful. Producers aim to entertain, but they also aim to make money. Theatre prices are set before the show opens and according to the capacity of the theatre. At that point, the producers cannot know what the demand for tickets will be. Demand is also influenced by economics and world events. During the 2001–2002 season, for instance, a slowdown in the U.S. economy and terrorist attacks dropped the Broadway attendance figure by 8 percent. Here, the cutoff line to designate a flop is set at fewer than 161 (1–160) performances, or no more than three months.

Chapter 5, "The Golden Age Stars of Broadway," features short biographies and awards for some of the great entertainers during this period. "The Awards of Broadway," chapter 7, highlights the opposite end of the Broadway flop, the special recognition to the best of the theatre. And chapter 6, "The Theatres of Broadway," gives historical data on the buildings that house these memorable productions.

The Golden Age of American Musical Theatre opens with *Oklahoma!*, when as never before, the whole idea of what was musical theatre in New York began to change. It ends with *On a Clear Day You Can See Forever* to mark the distinction of a changing Broadway. For the longtime devotee or the novice just about to fall under the spell of the theatre, this is a look back at a spectacular period on the American stage. For beauty and talent, for glorious costumes and innovative staging, for true magic when the lights went down, this was surely the Golden Age.

2

THE HISTORY OF BROADWAY

Native Americans called it the Wickquasgeck Trail. To the Dutch, it was Breede weg. It is the oldest north–south main street in New York City. It is also one of the longest boulevards in the country, stretching 150 miles from the Battery downtown to the upstate capital of Albany. Although it was renamed in the late nineteenth century, Broadway has come to mean much more than a mere address. To most New Yorkers, to thousands of people throughout the country and the world, Broadway simply means *theatre*.

Although the actual street covers the entire length of Manhattan Island, its most famous area is near Times Square, where Broadway crosses Seventh Avenue in midtown. This is the area, between 42nd and 53rd streets, known as the theatre district or the Great White Way. The nickname comes from a newspaper headline of February 3, 1902, in the *New York Evening Telegram*. It read, "Found on the Great White Way." The inspiration stemmed from the millions of lights on theatre marquees and billboards, especially around Times Square. When *The Red Mill* opened in 1906, theatre owners put colored electric lights in front of the buildings, but colored lights burned out too quickly and were soon replaced with white ones, hence the nickname. As far back as 1880, almost a mile of Broadway was lit by arc lamps, making it one of the first U.S. streets with electric lights.

OPERETTAS, REVUES, AND FOLLIES

The beginnings of what we know as the American musical trace back to Europe and especially England with such works as *The Beggar's Opera* (1728) by John Gay. It created an opera based mainly on folk music. These productions are known as operettas. They are operalike performances with dialogue, a romantically sentimental plot, and elaborate dancing scenes all interspersed with songs and orchestral music. The operetta came from the French *opera comique* in the mid-nineteenth century. Jacques Offenbach is generally regarded as having written the first operettas, for example, *Les deux aveugles* in 1858, although some give the credit to Florimond Ronger, known as Herve, said to have written *L'Ours et le pacha* in 1842; however, Offenbach popularized the musical form. His operettas portray life in a rather grotesque way that borders on the pornographic.

The outstanding composer of operettas in the German language was Austrian Johann Strauss Jr. His *Die Fledermaus* (1874) became the most performed operetta in the world. The fame for operettas in English rests with W. S. Gilbert and Sir Arthur Sullivan. They wrote fourteen such works that remain popular to this day, such as *HMS Pinafore* and *The Pirates of Penzance*. Other noted operetta composers in the United States were Victor Herbert, Sigmund Romberg, and Rudolf Friml.

Besides operettas, revues were very popular in early America, and they are still performed today. This is multiact entertainment with music, sketches, and dance. Its heyday was in the early twentieth century, from about 1916 to 1932. Revues frequently satirized news stories or contemporary figures, usually in an irreverent manner. The first popular American revue (spelled *review* until Florenz Ziegfeld used the French spelling) was *The Passing Show* (1894) by George Lederer. Many well-known entertainers got their start in revues, such as W. C. Fields. Cole Porter wrote for the revue *Hitchy-Koo* in 1919. Richard Rodgers and Lorenz Hart presented *The Garrick Gaieties* in 1925. Today, revues are common as student entertainment in various universities.

Out of the revue grew the stage extravaganza known as the follies made popular by Chicago-born Florenz Ziegfeld, who promoted the beauty of the American girl. His shows included daring costumes, comedy, and burlesque routines. They were a popular form of entertainment from the Follies of 1907 until 1931. By 1908, the Ziegfeld Follies were a fixture on Broadway, and they made stars of the performers, notably Eddie Cantor and Fanny Brice, who made a big hit singing "Rose of Washington Square." Brice last appeared on stage in the Follies of 1936.

THE BEGINNINGS OF MUSICAL COMEDY

Beginning with the operetta, musical theatre was working toward the Golden Age in America for some time. The first musical comedy opened in New York City on September 12, 1866. It was called *The Black Crook*, a sort of melodrama and ballet. Opera buffs went to see it, and so did patrons of burlesque. It did not call itself a musical, but it was the beginning of one, with dance and music added to tell the story. (The first production to actually call itself a musical comedy was *The Black Domino/Between You, Me, and the Post*, which also debuted in 1866.) The opening night performance of *The Black Crook* kept patrons spellbound—and perhaps numb—for five and a half hours, but it was a great hit and ran for more than a year. It would later be revived on Broadway eight times.

The Black Crook opened at Niblo's Garden, a huge place in lower Manhattan that sat 3,200 people. At that time, what theatre there was in New York City—and for that matter in the country—was in the southern end of the island. The first theatre was opened in 1750 by actor-managers Walter Murray and Thomas Kean. It was located on Nassau Street, with seating for about 280. Other theatres followed and, by the 1840s, P. T. Barnum had an entertainment complex in lower Manhattan. The Astor Place Theatre opened in 1847 and two years later was the scene of a riot, fought along class lines.

Some twenty-six years before the Astor Place, the Broadway Theatre had opened in lower Manhattan, catering mostly to working class people. To avoid having to mingle with the "lower class," wealthier theatregoing New Yorkers preferred their productions at the Astor Place, about a twelve-minute walk from the Broadway. The theatre had high ticket prices and a dress code of kid gloves for gentlemen. William Charles Macready was the lead actor at the Astor Place on May 7, 1849, for the opening of Shakespeare's *Macbeth*. In deliberate competition, the Broadway decided to present *Macbeth* on the very same night. Edwin Forrest, a former friend of Macready's and a favorite of the working class, was the lead.

On opening night, a mob stormed the Astor Place and pelted Macready with eggs and old shoes until he got off the stage. An unwilling Macready was convinced—and financially backed—by wealthy patrons to try again. He took the stage once more on May 10. By the time the curtain went up, thousands of people were mingling in the streets around the theatre. Before long, the first window was broken, and the fight was on; in the end, twenty-five died, with at least thirty-eight injured. The National Guard had to be called in, and when the rioters still would not give up, the soldiers fired into the crowd.

Everyone was much calmer in 1878, when Gilbert and Sullivan's *HMS Pinafore* was imported from England. Although known as an operetta, it might more precisely be called a light opera. Works by Gilbert and Sullivan, even though dated by their period, have been constantly revived. And their influence stemmed further than that. In 1973, Max Wilk published a book entitled *They're Playing Our Song*, in which he interviewed composers and lyricists from Broadway and Hollywood. A number of them, including Johnny Mercer and Sammy Cahn, said W. S. Gilbert was their main influence in writing lyrics.

In the late 1890s, George Edwardes came to New York with his London Gaiety Girls, which he said was a musical comedy, not to be confused with a burlesque show. Burlesque was a cousin of vaudeville. With prominently featured music, it was a satire, a parody of almost anything. The performances consisted of one act and lasted about an hour and a quarter.

THE 1900s

By the 1900s, theatre had gradually been moving up to midtown, as owners and producers tried to escape high real estate prices. Theatres did not actually arrive in the Times Square district until the early part of the decade; a large number of them were built in the 1920s and 1930s. As transportation improved, so did street lighting, and more and more people felt it safe to be out at night. That increased theatre attendance and meant that plays could run longer. Theatre attendance was also helped by a decision made in 1900. A series of underground railways—subways—were started by the Interborough Rapid Transit Company. When they neared completion in 1904, the *New York Times* had already moved into the Times Tower, a patch of land north of 42nd Street and bounded on either side by Broadway and Seventh Avenue.

Although most of New York's "theatre" was downtown, between Union Square and 24th Street, producer Rudolf Aronson had his eye on a vacant lot way uptown, at Broadway and 39th Street. His Casino opened in 1882, with the city's first roof garden. Lillian Russell and Marie Dressler appeared at the Casino, among other well-known names.

The popularity of Gilbert and Sullivan and others was followed by the giant of the operetta, Irish-born Victor Herbert, who received his musical training in Germany. When his wife, Therese Foster, got a contract to sing at the Metropolitan Opera in New York City, they both came to the United States. Just before the turn of the century, Herbert began composing the music for a string of some thirty operettas and musicals that brought him lasting fame. Among his biggest successes were *Babes in Toyland* (1903), *Naughty Marietta* (1910), and *Sweethearts* (1913). These sentimental productions set up a tradition of a play that was based on songs and musical numbers.

In 1900, a British production came to town at the Casino Theatre. By this time, theatregoers were paying up to $2.00 a performance. *Florodora*, about lovely ladies and handsome gentlemen in the Philippines, ran for 553 performances. But what was most remembered of that era was not the show but one of the showgirls, although not an original member of the cast. Sixteen-year-old Evelyn Nesbit joined the *Florodora* chorus girls and caught the interest of architect Stanford White, a married man and notorious womanizer. Supposedly, an affair began at White's apartment, which supposedly contained a red velvet swing. (The 1955 movie *The Girl in the Red Velvet Swing* detailed the affair and subsequent tragedy.) Although Nesbit was courted by John Barrymore, she married Harry Kendall Thaw, son of a coal baron and rumored cocaine addict, in 1905. The following year, the couple met White at a Madison Square Garden theatre performance. During the song "I Could Love a Million Girls," Thaw shot White three times in the face. Judged insane, Thaw stayed in prison until 1913. In 1915, he was declared sane. Nesbit got a divorce but no money.

For all its success, *Florodora* was not musical comedy, but it was getting closer in the person of the Yankee Doodle Dandy himself, George M. Cohan from Providence, Rhode Island (1878–1942). In 1905, in his third attempt on Broadway, Cohan presented *Little Johnny Jones*. It was also his third flop. This time, however, he took the show on tour and gave it two new songs. They were "I'm a Yankee Doodle Boy" and "Give My Regards to Broadway," which along with Irving Berlin's "There's No Business Like Show Business" (1940), became the national anthem of the Broadway theatre.

This was just the beginning for the brash young man from Rhode Island. The rest of the decade was his. Cohan's next production, *Forty-Five Minutes from Broadway* (1906), was a hit, and the song "Mary Is a Grand Old Name" became a standard. So did such songs as "You're a Grand Old Flag." He was so successful that at the beginning of the next decade, he opened his own theatre (appropriately named Cohan's) on the corner of Broadway and 43rd Street. Cohan would dominate Broadway for years.

George M. Cohan was arrogant and self-assured. He did not have the talent perhaps of Ira Gershwin or Oscar Hammerstein, but he brought a great gift to the American theatre. For audiences that were used to the extravagance of the operetta on stage, Cohan gave them the start of something new, just the beginning of a story line that was enhanced by—not interrupted by—the music and dancing around it. From these beginnings would emerge Broadway's Golden Age.

In 1904, *The Earl and the Girl*, with Eddie Foy, opened at the Lyric Theatre and transferred to the Casino the following year, where it ran for 148 performances. One of the songs was "How'd You Like to Spoon with Me?" written by a twenty-year-old unknown named Jerome Kern.

By this time, the Broadway area was getting used to what would become household names in the world of theatre. Playwright David Belasco arrived in New York City in 1882. During his long career, he wrote, directed, or produced more than 100 plays and became the most powerful personality in the theatre. A young Mary Pickford appeared in his *The Warrens of Virginia* at the Belasco Theater in 1907. Belasco was known as the "Bishop of Broadway" because he always dressed in black, which made him look like a priest. In 1910, he renamed the Stuyvesant Theater on 44th Street for himself; it is still in operation.

Also gaining fame were the Shubert brothers, Samuel, Lee, and Jacob. In 1900, they leased the Herald Square Theatre at Broadway and 35th Street. Samuel died from injuries suffered in a train wreck in 1905, but the Shuberts established what became the largest theatre empire in the twentieth century. The Sam S. Shubert Theatre on West 44th Street, opened in 1913, is a city landmark and remains in operation today.

Broadway was changing but not always for the better. While most of the theatres were relatively small, the Hippodrome opened in 1905 with a capacity to seat 5,000. It took up an entire block between 43rd and 44th streets on Sixth Avenue. The opening show on April 12 had 280 chorus girls, to say nothing of a parade of elephants and dancing horses. The audience was somewhat overawed, and it wasn't long before the Hippodrome ran into financial trouble. It was eventually taken over by the Shuberts.

But things progressed in other areas. The first "moving" electrical billboard was built in the city in 1906. And in 1907, the first of twenty lavish musical revues appeared on Broadway. They were produced by Ziegfeld, inspired by the Folies Bergere of Paris, and known as the *Ziegfeld Follies*. *The Follies of 1907*, at $2.50 a ticket, began these lavish productions that glorified the American girl with spectacular production numbers. The Follies girls were decked out in elaborate costumes by leading designers, and their clothes became the talk of Broadway. Many of the top entertainers of the time appeared in the Follies. In 1936, the movie *The Great Ziegfeld*, with William Powell, honored Ziegfeld and won an Oscar for Luise Rainer, who played his first wife, Anna Held. The hit song of the show was "A Pretty Girl Is Like a Melody." A second movie, *Ziegfeld Follies*, in 1936, featured

Judy Garland and Fred Astaire. The last of these elaborate reviews on stage appeared at the Winter Garden Theatre in 1957.

THE 1910s

As World War I (1914–1918) occupied much of the decade, changes were occurring in Broadway theatre. A young playwright named Eugene O'Neill was introduced to audiences at a summer theatre in Provincetown, Massachusetts. George and Susan Cook converted a stable in Greenwich Village in downtown Manhattan to the Playwright's Theatre. In 1915, some village residents formed the Washington Square Players, producing some fifty plays. During one of the productions, Katherine Cornell was introduced to the theatre world.

But the decade really belonged to Cohan. He had a string of hits, including *Get Rich Quick Wallingford* and *The Little Millionaire*. In 1917, he published one of his most memorable tunes, "Over There." Years later, he was honored by President Franklin Roosevelt for his contribution to the war effort.

With Cohan and other soon-to-be-famous names, Broadway was slowly changing. To be sure, the European operetta influence was still strong. In fact, another giant of the operetta, Hungarian-born Sigmund Romberg, had a big hit with *Maytime* (1917), to be followed by such productions as *The Student Prince* and *The Desert Song*. Romberg had moved to the United States in 1909. He published a few songs and came to the attention of the Shubert brothers, who hired him to write music for their theatre shows. One of Romberg's early tunes and still a jazz-blues classic is "Lover, Come Back to Me."

As Romberg was enjoying success, other newcomers in a decidedly different musical vein were also entering the Broadway scene. *Alexander's Ragtime Band* (1911), which was really a march, not rag, made Irving Berlin (1888–1989) a songwriting star. He would go on to become one of America's most prolific songwriters, eventually composing some 3,000 tunes, including "White Christmas" and "God Bless America." His first full-length musical stage work was *Watch Your Step* (1914), with Irene and Vernon Castle in the leading roles. In 1917, Berlin enlisted in the army during World War I and staged a musical revue, *Yip Yip Yaphank*. His song "God Bless America" was written for the show as a patriotic tribute, but Berlin decided against using it. The song was released more than twenty years later and remains today one of his most successful, especially as sung by Kate Smith. Berlin's big hit on Broadway was *Annie Get Your Gun* in 1946, but *Miss Liberty* in 1949 did not do well. His second greatest triumph was *Call Me Madam* in 1950 with Ethel Merman. His last show on Broadway, *Mr. President* (1962), did poorly, and after that, Berlin retired.

Between 1914 and 1920, another songwriter was hard at work. Jerome Kern scored sixteen Broadway productions during that period, including the hit song "They Didn't Believe Me" for the musical *The Girl from Utah* (1914). Musical comedy as we know it wasn't quite here yet, but the discerning among the theatregoing public were beginning to get a glimpse of something new, of songs and dances that were an integral part of the plot. As yet, it wasn't fully developed, and it didn't have a name.

THE 1920s

Broadway was a bustling place in the 1920s, with ticket prices as high as $3.50 a seat. World War I was over, and crowds wanted to celebrate. The so-called Roaring Twenties was an era of great social and political change, of recklessness and irresponsibility—and Broadway was no exception. Perhaps as many as seventy theatres were booming on Broadway in that decade, with a record 264 productions in 1928. Another great boost to the theatre world was the emergence of the Theatre Guild, organized in 1919 by Lawrence Langner and others. It evolved from the Washington Square Players group with the purpose of producing noncommercial plays by American and foreign playwrights. The Theatre Guild was especially effective on Broadway from the 1920s through the 1970s.

Productions in the early 1920s were often revues, such as *Frivolities of the 1920s*. It opened in January 1920 with two sets and seventeen scenes. New to theatre in that decade was the emergence of African American actors. Before that time, black performers usually played in revues or other burlesque forms of entertainment. If a black character was called for on Broadway, the face behind the makeup was usually white, but Charles Gilpin, a black actor, opened on Broadway in Eugene O'Neill's *The Emperor Jones* in November 1920. The door was now open for the black performer.

The year 1925 was in some ways also an opening door for the Golden Age of musical comedy in the United States. In that year, four musicals took over Broadway. *No, No Nanette*, with 321 performances and music by Vincent Youmans, was the hit of the decade. The story involved the pretty young ward of a bible salesman who goes off to Atlantic City—*unchaperoned*. Forty-six years later, the Broadway revival ran for 891 performances and brought 1930s film star Ruby Keeler out of retirement to play the bible salesman's wife.

Rudolf Friml's operetta *The Vagabond King* made it for 511 performances with matinee idol Dennis King, who stops a revolt against Louis XI of France. Topping that was *Sunny* (517 performances) with the first of several collaborations for Jerome Kern and lyricists Oscar Hammerstein II and Otto Harbach. It starred popular actress Marilyn Miller as a circus bareback rider who marries a millionaire. Next came the work of Rodgers and Hart in *Dearest Enemy*, with 286 performances about a New York lass and a British officer in the American Revolution.

No story of Broadway in the 1920s can be complete without mention of its chronicler and adopted son, Damon Runyon (1880–1946). Runyon was a newspaperman best known for his stories about the Broadway theatre world, writing of such hustlers, gamblers, and gangsters known as Harry the Horse, Big Jule, or Nathan Detroit. To Runyon, the ladies of Broadway were "daffy dames," "dolls," or "tough Broads." It was Broadway slang as only Runyon knew it. Besides his stories, Runyon left his mark on the Great White Way with the highly successful musical *Guys and Dolls* (1950), based on two of his stories, "The Idyll of Miss Sarah Brown" and "Blood Pressure."

Theatre was making a mark in the 1920s, even facing such challenges as the motion picture. Then came a giant step toward musical comedy as we know it. *Show Boat* opened on December 17, 1927, at the Ziegfeld Theatre. With a score by Jerome Kern and lyrics and book by Oscar Hammerstein II, who also directed, it is generally considered to be America's first true musical, lasting for 572 performances. It set new standards for those who produced shows and those who wrote the scores. *Show Boat* was distinct from the operettas, follies, and revues that preceded it because it was the first to provide a plot with music that was a central part of the narrative. It was significantly different from the operettes or light musical comedies that preceded it. Such songs as "Ol' Man River," "Why Do I Love You?" and "Make Believe" were not only lovely to the ear but a real part of the story line. That distinction started a change on Broadway that would, in 1943, evolve into the first true blockbuster musical of the Golden Age.

The story of *Show Boat* involves the lives of Cap'n Andy Hawks and his wife, Parthy Ann, who live and work on the Mississippi River in their show boat *Cotton Blossom*. It also concerns their daughter Magnolia and Gaylord Ravenal, a gambler. When Julie, mulatto star of the river show, and Steve, the leading man, must leave because of prejudice about their mixed marriage, Magnolia and Gaylord take over. After they marry, they go to Chicago, but Gaylord cannot give up gambling. They break up, and Magnolia begins a career in a café and is eventually reunited with her parents. In all, the time span covers forty-seven years.

Kern had been attracted by Ferber's best-selling 1926 novel about life on the turbulent Mississippi River, but Edna Ferber was less than enthusiastic about having her serious book turned into a musical comedy. With Kern's promise to get the best librettist in the business, Ferber agreed, and Kern got Oscar Hammerstein II. The result is what is often called the first true American musical play and one of the most influential works of the American musical theatre.

The original production of *Show Boat* lasted four and a half hours, but it was trimmed to just more than three hours before reaching Broadway. The role of Joe, the stevedore who sings "Ol' Man River," was especially written for noted black concert singer Paul Robeson, but he had to back out because of his schedule, so the part went to Jules Bledsoe. Robeson later sang the part in four productions (1928 in London, 1932 in New York City, 1936 in Hollywood, and a revival in Los Angeles in 1940), for which he became famous.

Show Boat was the first racially integrated musical comedy, with both black and white performers appearing on the stage together. It was the first to speak of interracial marriage. The show was also criticized because a racial epithet was used in an opening song in the first scene, but it was changed in many productions. However, through the years there have been critics who say that the show is prejudiced because it is based on racial caricatures.

Show Boat closed in 1929, but it has since enjoyed many revivals, the latest productions including two at the Uris Theatre in New York City in 1983 and 1994. A 1983 revival in Washington, D.C., featured Andy Rooney as Cap'n Andy. The musical comedy has also enjoyed many performances in London's West End. It was made into a film in 1929, 1936, and 1951. The stage show won the Tony Award for Best Revival of a Musical in 1995 and the Laurence Olivier Award for Best Musical Revival in 2008.

It would take almost two decades before the triumph of *Show Boat* was finally realized in *Oklahoma!*. Even so, after 1927, Broadway would never be the same again; however, the decade did end on an interesting musical note. Star Jeanette MacDonald appeared in a forgettable production at the Casino called *Boom Boom*. No one paid any attention to a young member of the chorus named Archibald Leach. He later moved to Hollywood and became famous as Cary Grant. Not long after the show ended, the Casino closed to make room for the expanding garment industry in the city. In less than fifty years, the theatre district had expanded so much that the Casino, once the most uptown theatre, was now the most downtown.

THE 1930s

The big word in the 1930s was *Depression*. It affected nearly everything and everyone, and Broadway was no exception. The 1929–1930 theatre season offered 233 productions. The first year of the new decade produced 187; by the end of the decade, the number was down to 98. Producer David Belasco died in 1931, a year after Stephen Sondheim, who would make a big mark on Broadway, was born. Most noteworthy for the musical was the introduction of Ethel Merman in George and Ira Gershwin's *Girl Crazy*. When she held a note for sixteen bars in her rendition of "I Got Rhythm," the audience was astounded. So was George Gershwin, who supposedly told her never to go near a voice teacher. Writer-critic Scott Siegel wrote that she "could hold a note longer than Chase Manhattan."

A Pulitzer Prize winner was *Allison's House* at Eva Le Gallienne's Civic Repertory Theater on 14th Street. After winning the Pulitzer, the play moved uptown. The Theater Guild also produced plays on Broadway, such as Maxwell Anderson's *Elizabeth the Queen*. The second Theatre Guild play proved even more interesting. It was *Green Grow the Lilacs* by Lynn Riggs, with a cast that included a cowboy named Curly. Set in Oklahoma, it was nominated for the Pulitzer Prize but lost out to *Allison's House*. It ran for sixty-four performances, but in 1943 the show began a much brighter history, when Rodgers and Hammerstein transformed it into *Oklahoma!*

George S. Kaufman and Moss Hart began the first of eight collaborations in the early part of the decade. Kaufman and collaborator Morrie Ryskind wrote the book for the first musical to win the Pulitzer Prize for drama. It was *Of Thee I Sing* (1931), with music and lyrics by George and Ira Gershwin.

Kaufman and Ryskind first had the idea of a musical about political parties fighting over a new national anthem, but the result was the first musical that was definitely satiric in tone. Brooks Atkinson, writing in the *New York Times*, said it was, "funnier than the government, and not nearly so dangerous." It concerns John P. Wintergreen, who is running for president on a "love" platform. He will marry the winner of the beautiful girl pageant in Atlantic City, New Jersey. Instead, he falls in love with Mary Turner, who is running the pageant. When he marries her, the pageant winner, Diana, sues, but the court rules for Mary; however, in Act II, Diana is gaining support and Wintergreen is urged to divorce Mary, but Mary announces she is pregnant. Now France gets involved, because Diana is somehow distantly related to Napoleon. In the end, all is well, and Mary gives birth to twins.

Somehow, the audiences liked this, and it ran for 441 performances with budding star George Murphy in the chorus. This was the longest-running Gershwin show during George's lifetime. The story line may have been a bit convoluted, but the music was delightful, with such melodies as "Love Is Sweeping the Country," "Who Could Ask for Anything More?," "Who Cares?," and, of course, "Of Thee I Sing."

The show was revived in 1933 at the Imperial and in 1952 at the Ziegfeld, both directed by Kaufman. It was never made into a movie, but it did appear on television in 1972. A sequel hit Broadway in 1933 as *Let 'Em Eat Cake*, a much darker satire than the first. In this, Wintergreen is defeated for reelection, and he and the vice president form a Fascist movement to take over the government. The critics and public were not impressed, and the show was a flop, with no memorable songs. Besides *Porgy and Bess*, which is often called an opera rather than musical, that was the last Broadway musical for the Gershwins.

THE 1940s

This was not the best of times for Broadway. Still not quite out of the Great Depression, America was soon plunged into war with the rest of the world. One of the victims was the theatre, with only seventy-two productions during 1940–1941. Many of the theatres on Broadway became film houses, and television was looming as real competition. By 1948, the unemployment rate for Broadway actors would reach a shocking 80 percent.

Theatre professionals decided that what audiences needed at the time was an escape from reality, the more lighthearted entertainment the better. Irving Berlin, reigning as the top U.S. composer, did his best with *Louisiana Purchase*, which opened in 1940, and *This Is the Army*, in 1942. Audiences delighted in such tunes as "I Left My Heart at the Stage Door Canteen" and "Oh, How I Hate to Get Up in the Morning," performed by Berlin himself.

Cole Porter was also busy during this period. *Panama Hattie* (1940) starred Ethel Merman and became the first Broadway musical to last more than 500 performances since the 1920s. *Let's Face It* in 1941 showcased Eve Arden and Danny Kaye. Merman was back in 1943 with *Something for the Boys*, a bit of silliness near a military base that ran for more than a year.

But others, such as Richard Rodgers and Lorenz Hart, were looking for a little more than fluff. They presented *Pal Joey*, whose antihero title character is a hustler who gets rich by deceiving a wealthy mistress. New star Gene Kelly was in the title role, and the romantically beautiful "Bewitched,

Bothered, and Bewildered" was the hit song. The subject matter may have been on the seamy side, but audiences flocked to it for a year.

Ira Gershwin returned to Broadway after the death of his brother George for *Lady in the Dark*, which starred Danny Kaye and Gertrude Lawrence in the longest run of her career. In 1942, the longest-running show for Rodgers and Hart opened. It was *By Jupiter*, with Ray Bolger.

By this time, however, Hart was well on the way to becoming lost in alcohol. Rodgers asked him to sober up so they could work on an adaptation for a new musical. Hart turned him down and headed for Mexico. Rodgers began to collaborate with Oscar Hammerstein II. With that step, the Golden Age of musical theatre in America was about to begin. And so it did in 1943, when the curtain went up on the first true musical—*Oklahoma!*

Oklahoma! marks the beginning of *The Golden Age of American Musical Theatre*. It was also the first collaboration between perhaps the most extraordinary musical theatre team of the Golden—or any other—Age: composer Richard Rodgers (1902–1979) and lyricist/librettist Oscar Hammerstein II (1895–1960). Born in New York City, Rodgers already had a string of hits when he teamed with Hammerstein. Born in Pennsylvania, Hammerstein came from a distinguished theatrical family. He first collaborated with Jerome Kern, producing the great hit *Show Boat*. Together, Rodgers and Hammerstein so influenced the theatre world that after 1943, nearly every musical on Broadway incorporated music and dance as part of the story line, not distinct from it.

Oklahoma! was a perfect blend of story, music, and dance as never before. It was so smoothly done that most audiences did not realize at the time they were watching something different. It simply flowed. With a tightly constructed plot, the libretto loosely followed the story line instead of using song and dance as separate elements. In premusical comedy productions, the action of the play would literally stop for a song or dance and then pick up again where the conversation had left off. But now, the song or dance either more fully explained the conversation or extended or changed it. Everything was totally integrated and, for the first time, the choreography (by Agnes de Mille) actually advanced the plot.

The play that Rodgers had first wanted to adapt with Hart was *Green Grow the Lilacs*, which had opened on Broadway in 1931, and closed after sixty-four performances. Named for a popular folk song at the time, it was set in the Indian Territory (Oklahoma) of 1900 and starred rather sophisticated film actor Franchot Tone as a cowboy called "Curly." *Green Grow the Lilacs* is largely forgotten today; *Oklahoma!* is still one of the most popular American musicals of all time.

But in the early 1940s, no one was much interested in investing in this adaptation from Rodgers and his new partner. For one thing, Hammerstein hadn't had a Broadway hit since the 1930s. And there were other drawbacks: *Green Grow the Lilacs* had pretty much been a dud; Rodgers was without Hart for the first time, and this was choreographer de Mille's first musical; the title when the show opened in New Haven, Connecticut, was *Away We Go*, which the critics found boring; there were no racy jokes; and chorus girls did not appear until forty-five minutes into the first act.

Some changes were made during preview performances, including change of title, made in Boston. De Mille staged a dance with the chorus coming right down to the footlights in a V formation. They sang O-K-L-A-H-O-M-A, Oklahoma, and then yelled "yeeeow!" The Boston audience howled with applause. And the show's name was changed. Before it opened for real, an exclamation point was added, making it *Oklahoma!* The musical opened on Broadway on March 31, 1943, with empty seats in the St. James Theater, but Rodgers and Hammerstein did not have to worry for long. By the first act intermission, they knew they had a hit—and so did everyone else.

The reviews were simply raves. The show was a runaway—an astounding 2,212 performances. Compare that to two of the longest-running hits of the 1930s: George and Ira Gerswin's *Of Thee I Sing*, which opened in 1931 and ran for 441 performances, and Cole Porter's *Anything Goes* (1934), which had a string of 440. *Oklahoma!* was the first musical to win a Pulitzer Prize (1944), a Special Citation in Letters given to Rodgers and Hammerstein. The musical also broke all existing box office records.

The story line is straightforward. Set in the territory before statehood, farm girl Laurey must choose to go to a dance with Jud, the farmhand she fears, or Curly, the cowboy she loves. As it turns out, Jud proves to be a murderer whom Curley is forced to kill in self-defense. Murder in a musical? It was unheard of, but it worked.

The choreography by Agnes de Mille helped to make it work. One of the show's most notable features is a fifteen-minute first act ballet, which is often called the dream ballet, during which Laurey tries to make up her mind about which man to choose. And whereas the musicals of the 1920s and 1930s generally presented one or two memorable songs, *Oklahoma!* sent its audiences out into the street with several unforgettable lines running through their heads. There was "Oh, What a Beautiful Mornin'," "The Surrey with the Fringe on Top," "I Cain't Say No," "People Will Say We're in Love," and, of course, "Oklahoma." For the first time, the original cast recorded the album of a Broadway show, a practice that is common today.

The album brought in more than one million sales. The original cast album of *Oklahoma!* is still in print in various electronic forms.

To bolster what looked like poor sales at first, the Theatre Guild wanted a star's name on the marquee, such as Shirley Temple, but Rodgers and Hammerstein were insistent on lesser-known names. They were right, for raves went to the original cast as well. It starred Alfred Drake (beginning his reign as Broadway's top male musical star) as Curley, Joan Roberts as Laurey, Betty Garde as Aunt Eller, Lee Dixon as Will, Celeste Holm as playful Ado Annie (gaining the stardom she would keep into the next century), and Howard Da Silva as Jud. In time, these actors were replaced by others who also made a name on Broadway and in films, including Howard Keel, John Raitt, Shelley Winters, and Florence Henderson. Touring companies of *Oklahoma!* played all over the United States for the next ten years and in foreign countries as well. In fact, it broke all records—with 1,151 performances—at London's Drury Lane Theatre.

On a sad note, amid all the jubilation on opening night, Lorenz Hart was in the audience and sober to see his former partner's triumph. He was said to have been stunned by the audience reaction. After that, Hart agreed to work on a revival of *A Connecticut Yankee* with Rodgers, but on opening night, he showed up drunk again. He was thrown out of the theatre during the second act. A couple of nights later, Frederick Loewe found him sitting on a curbside in the icy November weather. Hart caught pneumonia and died a few days later at the age of forty-eight.

Why was *Oklahoma!* so successful? For the same reason that it opens these twenty-two years of musical comedy on Broadway. All elements of the show—music, lyrics, ballet—were a perfect blending. And all these elements had a definite and close connection with the plot. Usher in the Golden Age.

Rodgers and Hammerstein continued their winning ways in the 1940s. They received an Oscar in 1946 for "It Might as Well Be Spring" in the film version of *State Fair.* (A previous winner, Hammerstein was the only person named Oscar ever to win an Oscar.) But their next big Broadway successes were *Carousel* and *South Pacific.*

Carousel opened at the Majestic on April 19, 1945, right across from the St. James, which was still playing *Oklahoma!* In this adaptation, Rodgers and Hammerstein had a different problem than in their earlier work. The new musical was based on *Liliom,* with a carnival setting and Hungarian background. The original drama had been revived in the 1930s and again in 1940, starring Ingrid Bergman and Burgess Meredith on Broadway. Now the Theatre Guild wanted it adapted for a musical, but there was a problem with playwright Ferenc Molnar. The author wanted nothing to do with changing his work in such a way; however, he was persuaded to see *Oklahoma!*, and that changed his mind—providing Rodgers and Hammerstein would do the adapting and not change the spirit of the play.

Rodgers and Hammerstein themselves weren't so sure about the setting, or the plot for that matter. So, they suggested taking the plot out of Hungary and putting it into New England. Once that was approved, they kept the original spirit of the play but made many other changes. In the original, Liliom is a bully at a carousel who has an affair with Julie, who becomes pregnant. He attempts a robbery to get money for the child and kills himself rather than get caught. When he returns to earth years later, he tries to give his now fifteen-year-old daughter a star, which she refuses. Liliom goes back to purgatory.

In the adaptation, once again with choreography by Agnes de Mille, Liliom becomes the more sympathetic Billy Bigelow and, in this case, he marries Julie. He kills himself to avoid capture and comes back fifteen years later. He sees his daughter graduate and sings "You'll Never Walk Alone." Then he returns to heaven. The sweeter ending delighted Broadway audiences for more than 899 performances. But the real success of the musical was undoubtedly the score, which, besides Billy's song, included "What's the Use of Wond'rin'" and "When the Children Are Asleep." The musical was also successful in the film version, which starred Gordon MacRae as Billy and Shirley Jones as Julie.

And then came *South Pacific* in 1949. It was based on two short stories by James Michener in his Pulitzer Prize–winning book *Tales of the South Pacific*. It also gave the Pulitzer Prize for Drama (1950) to Rodgers and Hammerstein, with cowriter Joshua Logan, and the show closely beat out *Kiss Me, Kate* as the best musical of the year. In addition, it picked up ten Tony Awards. The story takes place in the South Pacific during World War II and deals with a romance between Navy Ensign Nellie Forbush, from Little Rock, Arkansas, and a middle-aged French planter named Emile de Becque. The secondary romance involves young Lieutenant Cable and his attraction to Liat, daughter of Polynesian Bloody Mary.

The musical had two main attractions. One was the two leads. Mary Martin got her Broadway start in Cole Porter's *Leave It to Me* but went to Hollywood to star in ten films for Paramount. She returned to Broadway for *South Pacific* and took the show to London as well. Martin would later win Tonys for *Peter Pan* (1954) and *The Sound of Music* (1959). Ezio Pinza was on his second career when he starred in *South Pacific*. Born in Rome, Italy, he sang at La Scala opera house in Milan and at the New York Metropolitan

Opera over a long career. After retirement from the Met in 1948, he went on to new fame as Emile de Becque.

The other main attraction was the score, which audiences loved. The songs are perfect for the plot, including "Some Enchanted Evening," "Bali Ha'i," "Happy Talk," "I'm in Love with a Wonderful Guy," "Younger Than Springtime," and a showstopper by the group of sailors, seabees, and marines called "Bloody Mary." Another great pleaser was Martin's rendition of "I'm Gonna Wash That Man Right Outa My Hair." More than the song itself, audiences became intrigued with what the nightly washing was doing to Martin's scalp. It made wonderful newspaper copy. Martin had her hair cut very short for the role and also wore brightly colored turbans when she was off stage.

One song that caused political turmoil was Cable's rendition of "Carefully Taught," which sings about the ways in which people learn prejudice and how they are taught from their parents which people to hate. Hammerstein admitted the song was a protest against racial prejudice. Georgia legislators introduced a bill condemning the lyrics as un-American, but the song survived, and so did the show, including a highly successful revival at the Vivian Beaumont Theatre in 2008.

THE 1950s

Broadway ruled in the 1950s, even though the number of theatre houses continued to decline. People were preoccupied with war in Korea, or trouble with Cuba, or the assassinations of John F. Kennedy and Martin Luther King Jr., but there was still time for a show tune. In fact, the 1950s formed the heart of the Golden Age of American musical theatre, with Rodgers and Hammerstein at the forefront. Show after show won rave reviews, and many are still revived today. In fact, the decade produced an astounding number of hit shows, including *Call Me Madam* and *Guys and Dolls* in 1950, *The King and I* in 1951, *Can-Can* and *Kismet* in 1953, *The Pajama Game* in 1954, *Damn Yankees* in 1955, the wondrous *My Fair Lady* in 1956, *West Side Story* in 1957, *Flower Drum Song* in 1958, *Gypsy* and *The Sound of Music* in 1959, and many others. It was an inspired time for musical comedy.

Guys and Dolls might best be described in two words: "New Yorky." Some critics called it the best of all American musical comedies. It was based on a story by Damon Runyon, a longtime newspaperman and portrayer of the Broadway scene. His characters included such favorites as Harry the Horse,

Angie the Ox, and Nicely Nicely Johnson. The musical concerns two love affairs: a fourteen-year engagement between gambler Nathan Detroit and Miss Adelaide, a nightclub singer, and the romance between even bigger gambler Skye Masterson and Miss Sarah Brown of the Save a Soul Mission. Such tunes as "Luck Be a Lady," "If I Were a Bell," "A Bushel and a Peck," and "Sit Down You're Rockin' the Boat" delighted audiences and critics alike.

Successful as it was, *Guys and Dolls* faced a serious contender for the best on Broadway. Rodgers and Hammerstein's *The King and I* opened at the St. James on March 29, 1951, exactly eight years after *Oklahoma!* in the same theatre. It was based on Margaret Landon's *Anna and the King of Siam*, which was the story of governess Anna Leonowens who goes to Siam to teach King Mongkut's children in the early 1860s. It starred Gertrude Lawrence as Anna and Yul Brynner, who was fairly unknown at the time, as the king. The story concerns the two main characters as they match strong wills against each other.

Some critics found this musical the most spectacular of all works by Rodgers and Hammerstein, and audiences seemed to agree. It certainly was a huge production. Supposedly, sets and costumes filled six carloads, but it was the score that audiences found so enchanting, the way in which the tunes carried the plot. Early in the show, Anna and her son arrive in Siam and are visibly frightened by the sight of apparently unfriendly natives. So, Anna sings "I Whistle a Happy Tune." That was to be followed by such marvelous songs as "I Have Dreamed," "We Kiss in a Shadow," "Hello, Young Lovers," "Getting to Know You," and the wonderful scene between Anna and the King with "Shall We Dance?"

As the king, Yul Brynner, a former circus acrobat, surprised everyone with his powerful performance. He *was* the king of Siam, and his shaved head—shaved for the play—became his trademark. Brynner returned for a revival in 1985, knowing he was dying of cancer. He received a special Tony for his portrayal of the king, a role he played 4,524 times.

In 1954, producers Frederick Brisson, Robert Griffith, and Harold Prince had a hit on their hands with *The Pajama Game*, which ran for more than 1,000 performances. Feeling that if it worked once it could work again, they assembled the same production staff and once again adapted a popular book for the stage. In this case, it was *The Year the Yankees Lost the Pennant*, by Douglass Wallop. The result was a 1,019-performance hit called *Damn Yankees*. It seemed to promise a bright future, especially for the music and lyrics team of Richard Adler and Jerry Ross. Tragically, Ross died a few months after the musical opened of a chronic bronchial disease. He was twenty-nine years old.

The plot involves middle-aged Joe Boyd, a long-suffering fan of the Washington Senators baseball team. He sells his soul to Mr. Applegate, who is really the Devil. In return, he becomes slugger Joe Hardy. He leaves his wife Meg and helps the Senators move up in the standings. But Joe misses his wife, so Applegate Devil sends out temptress Lola, but Joe does not fall for her; however, false information is released about Joe and he is forced to court. Lola realizes he truly loves Meg and gets him to the Senators' final game on time. Joe hits a home run, and the Senators win the pennant. Applegate promises to make Joe young again and get a World Series victory, but Joe wants to be with Meg and refuses the deal.

The lead role of Lola had to be a dancer, said the producers. After Mitzi Gaynor turned the role down, the offer went to Gwen Verdon, who had sung just one song in *Can-Can*. It was a wise choice. In fact, she was so good that she caused what were really the only two criticisms of the show. Lola was so seductive that it seemed impossible anyone could resist her, certainly not a starstruck jock like Joe. In addition, whenever Lola walked off the stage, audience interest seemed to flicker. No wonder the hit song of the show was Lola's "Whatever Lola Wants, Lola Gets." The other two lead parts were played by Stephen Douglass as Joe Hardy and Ray Walston as Mr. Applegate.

Damn Yankees was revived on Broadway in 1994 and ran for 718 performances. Bebe Neuwirth was Lola, and Jerry Lewis took over the part of Mr. Applegate in 1995; however, the 1994 revival contained many revisions, so most consider the first true revival to be produced by the City Center Encores in July 2008. The movie production came out in 1958, with most of the original cast back in their roles, with the exception of the part of Joe Hardy, played by Tab Hunter.

The following year in this splendid decade of the musical theatre on Broadway appeared what some consider the finest of all American musical comedies. *My Fair Lady* opened on March 15, 1956, at the Mark Hellinger and ran for 2,717 performances (a record at the time). It has been called the perfect musical.

The show is based on George Bernard Shaw's *Pygmalion*, which had a long history of stage success before Alan Jay Lerner and Frederick Loewe adapted it. The story concerns Eliza Doolittle, a Cockney flower girl whose speech is overheard by gentleman Henry Higgins, who laments, "Why Can't the English Learn to Speak?." He tells his companion, Colonel Pickering, that in six months he could have her speaking like a lady. The very next day, Eliza arrives at his doorstep. She heard his boast and wants him to make good on it. What follows is Eliza's wondrous but painstaking transformation. Just as all is despair, she "gets it" in one of the most marvelous of showstoppers, "The Rain in Spain," in which Eliza, Henry, and the Colonel romp around the room in joy at her pronunciation. From there, Higgins takes her to the Ascot Racecourse, where Freddy Eynsford-Hill falls for her. The final test is the Embassy Ball, where Eliza fools them all into believing she was "born Hungarian."

But now Eliza feels used by Higgins, so she leaves his home. He awakens to find that he is lost without her; however, when he goes to find her, Eliza says she does not need him anymore. Higgins returns home to discover that, "I've Grown Accustomed to Her Face." When he hears a Cockney accent again, he sees that Eliza has returned. Will they get together? As the musical ends, Higgins says only, "Eliza, where the devil are my slippers?" In addition to the melodies noted above, the splendid score includes "Wouldn't It Be Loverly?" "I Could Have Danced All Night," "On the Street Where You Live," and "Get Me to the Church on Time."

Lerner and Loewe had first tried to adapt *Pygmalion* in the 1930s at producer Gabriel Pascal's request, but there were problems. Was there really a love story between Eliza and Higgins, which is essential in most all musicals? And what about a secondary romance, which is also usually the case? So, they gave up and abandoned the project for two years. When they went back to it, Broadway had changed, and the objections they first saw didn't seem important.

Next came the problem of casting. Noël Coward was first choice for Henry Higgins. He turned it down, and the role went to Rex Harrison, which proved a marvelous decision. The role of Eliza was more difficult. Mary Martin was offered the part and turned it down. After some fifty young women were auditioned, the part went to a relative unknown. She was Julie Andrews, whose only Broadway role had been in an English import, *The Boy Friend*. It proved to be another wise choice. Getting someone to direct was easy. Moss Hart heard just two songs and said yes.

Before Broadway, the production held a tryout at the Shubert Theatre in New Haven, Connecticut, but on opening night, Rex Harrison locked his dressing room door and declared he was not going on. The apparent stage fright declined about an hour before curtain call, and the performance was a triumph.

My Fair Lady broke records on Broadway, in London, and probably all over the world. It has been revived on Broadway three times, in 1976, 1981, and 1993. In 2007, the New York Philharmonic staged a full-costume concert rendition. When it had reached the 2,717th performance of its initial run, *My Fair Lady* became the longest-running musical comedy and the third-longest presentation of a drama in the history of New York theatre. Broadway had truly become accustomed to its face.

Interestingly, when the musical was adapted for film, Jack Warner of Warner Bros. insisted that the part of Eliza go to Audrey Hepburn because she was a box office star. Reportedly, Elizabeth Taylor had wanted the role as well. Rex Harrison was once again Henry Higgins. Both Andrews and Hepburn denied that there was any problem between them over the casting, but some saw vindication for Andrews when she won an Oscar for *Mary Poppins*. On that same night, Harrison won his Oscar for *My Fair Lady*, which was presented to him by Hepburn. A diplomat, Harrison thanked both Elizas for his award.

The magic of *My Fair Lady* might not have been matched, but the rest of the decade held some splendid moments as well. In 1957, a musical adaptation of Shakespeare's *Romeo and Juliet* opened at the Winter Garden. It is called *West Side Story*. It is still frequently produced today in regional theatres, schools, and opera companies. Directed and choreographed by Jerome Robbins, with music by Leonard Bernstein and lyrics by Stephen Sondheim in his Broadway debut, the production would win a Tony for choreography and a nomination for Best Musical, losing out to *The Music Man*.

The American Jets and Puerto Rican Sharks are rival teenage gangs in the city. At a neighborhood dance, Tony, former member of the Jets, and Maria, newly arrived from Puerto Rico, fall in love. They plan to marry, but first Maria asks Tony to stop a rumble between the gangs. He agrees and, in the fight, Shark leader Bernardo stabs Jet leader Riff, and Tony, in a rage, kills Bernardo. Finally, Tony is killed by another gang member, and all members of both gangs gather over his body, suggesting the feud may now come to an end.

Audiences loved this show, and they still do, but in at least two ways, it was far different from the usual Broadway musical. For one thing, the ending is not a happy one, even with a vague hope of peace between the gangs. For another, the songs were without humor, except for two that can hardly be called sunny. When the Shark girls sing "America," they are contrasting—frequently on the dark side—the differences between life in the United States and Puerto Rico. In "Gee, Officer Krupke," the American Jets carry on about delinquency.

Sunny or not, Bernstein's score is so appealing. In fact, since its opening, many critics have called this musical his most distinguished contribution to Broadway. The songs well express the passion and hates of the characters. There is "Somewhere," "I Feel Pretty," "One Hand, One Heart," and the beautifully expressed feelings between Tony and Maria in "Tonight."

West Side Story was revived in 1964 by the New York City Center Light Opera Company for a limited engagement and at Lincoln Center in 1968.

The Broadway revival opened at the Minskoff in 1980 for 333 performances, directed by Jerome Robbins. His Broadway production in 1989 featured several dances from the original show. Besides national and world touring companies, *West Side Story* enjoyed a run of 1,039 performances in London's West End.

The decade was nearing an end, but there was still much to entertain theatre buffs. In 1958, Rodgers and Hammerstein were back with *Flower Drum Song*, featuring for the first time in Broadway history a mostly Asian cast. The two had already shown interest in the Far East with *South Pacific* and *The King and I*. This time a high school friend of Hammerstein's got him interested in the novel, telling of cross-cultural conflict in the early 1950s.

Shy Mei Li and her father are illegal immigrants in San Francisco. She is to marry Sammy Fong, a nightclub owner, but hip Sammy is interested in showgirl Linda Low. He sends Mei Li to Master Wang's home, hoping to interest his shy son, Wang Ta. Master Wang is happy, but how can the arranged marriage be cancelled? Ta falls for Linda, until he meets Mei Li. After many complications, the Three Family Association decides that Sammy and Mei Li must marry, even though they don't want to, but at the wedding, the bride confesses she is an illegal alien. The marriage contract is off, and Sammy and Linda and Ta and Mei Li are now free to marry.

Miyoshi Umeki, Keye Luke, and Pat Suzuki led the Asian cast, with Juanita Hall, an African American of *South Pacific* fame, and Larry Blyden, as the non-Asians. The show ran for 600 performances and won six Tony nominations. Much of the praise went to the sweet and gentle score, which included "You Are Beautiful," "A Hundred Million Miracles," "I Am Going to Like It Here," "Don't Marry Me," "Love Look Away," and "The Other Generation."

The Broadway revival opened in 2002 for 169 performances. In it, Mei Li is more than a mail order bride but has escaped the communist regime at home. It enjoyed a run of 464 performances in London's West End in 1960.

Fittingly for the major decade of the Golden Age, the last year ended with two outstanding hits: *Gypsy* and *The Sound of Music*. Based on the memoirs of famed striptease artist Gypsy Rose Lee, *Gypsy* centers not on her but on her mother, Rose, the ultimate stage mom, played by Ethel Merman in perhaps her crowning role.

During the Great Depression, Rose plays the vaudeville circuit, pushing her children, Louise (based on Gypsy Rose Lee) and talented Baby June (based on Lee's sister, actress June Havoc). Rose persuades former agent Herbie to be their manager. As the girls grow up, June gets tired of the circuit and leaves. Rose is now determined to make Louise a star, but her second-rate act ends up in burlesque. In disgust at Rose's ambition, Herbie leaves, and Louise no longer needs her mother. The two argue, but at the end there is a hint of a reconciliation.

The original production ran for 702 performances and received eight Tony nominations. It was revived on Broadway in 1974, 1989, 2003, and 2008. It enjoyed 300 performances in London's West End. Rosalind Russell (who could not sing) played Rose in the 1962 film production, and Bette Midler took the role in the television movie in 1993.

The last big show of the 1950s belonged to Rodgers and Hammerstein. It was their final work together (Hammerstein died a few months after the opening) and contained probably more hit tunes than any of their other works. *The Sound of Music* opened at the Lunt-Fontane on November 16, 1959.

Based on the memoirs of the Trapp Family singers (with a few changes) and set in Austria just before World War II, the musical opens in an abbey where postulant Maria (Mary Martin) is being sent by the Mother Abbess as governess to the seven children of widower Captain Georg von Trapp (Theodore Bikel). The Abbess hopes that during those few months Maria will consider whether she is cut out to be a nun.

Maria disapproves of the militaristic way in which the children are being raised, and she teaches them to sing ("Do-Re-Me"). In time, the oldest child, Liesl, secretly begins to meet young Rolf. Baroness Elsa Schraeder arrives, presumably to marry the captain. Maria returns to the Abbey to take her vows, but the Abbess feels she is running away from her feelings for von Trapp and tells her to return.

Finally, Maria and von Trapp realize their love for one another and they marry. A telegram arrives for the captain to join the German navy. The von Trapp family asks for a last chance to sing together on stage. They sing "So Long, Farewell" and leave the stage in groups. When the Nazis search for them, they are missing. Rolf discovers them at the Abbey, but because of Lisel, he does not report them. The von Trapps flee over the mountains to safety.

The original production shared the Tony Award for Best Musical with *Fiorello!* and won Best Actress for Mary Martin, among other awards. The original cast album sold three million copies. The London production ran for 2,385 shows and was revived there in 1981 and 2006. It was revived on Broadway in 1998 and ran for fifteen months.

THE 1960s

The Golden Age was nearing its end in the 1960s, but the shows produced during those first few years of the decade were an impressive offering of musical comedies that resulted in an amazing number of performances. There was *Bye Bye Birdie* (607 shows), *Camelot* (873), *How to Succeed in*

Business without Really Trying (1,417), *Oliver!* (774), *Hello, Dolly!* (2,844), *Funny Girl* (1,348), and *Fiddler on the Roof* (3,242), among others.

Bye Bye Birdie opened on April 14, 1960, with a cast that included Dick Van Dyke, Chita Rivera, and Paul Lynde. Inspired by pop singer Elvis Presley, who got his draft notice for the army in 1957, this is the story of rock star Conrad Birdie, who gets drafted. This upsets agent Albert Peterson and his sweetheart, Rosie Alvarez, since they are about to lose money with Birdie gone. They devise a publicity stunt to have Birdie record one more song before he leaves. He is to give one last kiss to a lucky girl from his fan club, but she falls in love with him. Mayhem follows, Conrad lands in jail, Albert gets him out so he can report to the army, and Albert and Rosie leave for Pumpkin Falls, Iowa, where he will be an English teacher.

It won four Tonys in all, including Best Musical and Best Featured Actor. One of the songs, "Put on a Happy Face," became a popular hit and has been used in many television commercials. The successful musical became a film in 1963, with Dick Van Dyke again in the role of Albert, and it was adapted for television in 1995, with Jason Alexander in the lead.

Lerner and Loewe's *Camelot* opened at the Majestic on December 3, 1960, with Richard Burton, Julie Andrews, Robert Goulet, and Roddy McDowall in the cast. Although reviews of the opening were mixed, the production was stimulated by Ed Sullivan on his television show *The Toast of the Town* and by its association with the John F. Kennedy administration; Kennedy had been a classmate of Loewe's at Harvard.

The plot concerns King Arthur (Burton) and his marriage to Guenevere (Andrews), which is threatened when she and Lancelot (Goulet) fall in love. The two are torn by their loyalty to the king and their love for each other, but after Lancelot and Guenevere leave for France, Arthur must wage war against him. Before the final battle, Arthur comes face to face with them both and forgives them. Lancelot and Guenevere go their separate ways. Despite the mixed reviews, *Camelot* won four Tonys, including Best Actor and Best Actress. Goulet had a hit recording with "If Ever I Would Leave You."

Another big Tony winner (seven) that also won the Pulitzer Prize for Drama was *How to Succeed in Business without Really Trying*, which opened on October 14, 1961. Robert Morse starred as J. Pierrepont Finch, a window washer who thinks that all he needs to know to succeed is contained in the book he is reading. In startling fashion, he rises in the World Wide Wicket Company and in the end becomes chairman of the board with an eye on running for U.S. president.

The audiences loved it, and Morse won the Tony for Best Actor. The London production opened in 1963, and it was revived on Broadway in 1995. The 1967 film also starred Morse in the lead role.

The next big hit of the 1960s was *Oliver!*, which opened at the Imperial on January 6, 1963. It was the first musical adaptation of a Charles Dickens work to make a hit on Broadway. The London production had opened in 1960 and ran for 2,618 performances. It was revived in London in 1994 and 2009. A North American tour in 2003 ran for two years.

The plot centers on young Oliver and his life in the workhouse, which becomes unbearable when he dares to ask for more food from the heartless Mr. Bumble. Oliver goes from bad to worse as he gets mixed up with the criminal Fagin, who teaches young boys how to pick pockets. All ends well when wealthy Mr. Brownlow realizes that Oliver is actually his grandson, and Fagin decides it's time to straighten out his life.

A great hit of the 1960s starred the irrepressible Carol Channing as the irrepressible Dolly Levi in *Hello, Dolly!* It opened to rave reviews on January 16, 1964, at the St. James. Channing was actually the third choice for the role. It was originally intended for Ethel Merman, but she turned it down, as did Mary Martin, although both later played the part. As it turned out, Channing then had the chance to create what is her most memorable role on Broadway.

The story is based on Thornton Wilder's *The Merchant of Yonkers*, which was a flop in 1938. Wilder expanded the role of Dolly and revised it into *The Matchmaker* in 1955. It concerns the world's biggest meddler, Dolly Levi, and her attempts to bring romance to several couples. While she is doing so, she causes mayhem everywhere, but in the end she gets grumpy and wealthy Horace Vandergelder for herself.

The original production, directed and choreographed by Gower Champion, became the longest-running Broadway musical at the time, surpassing *My Fair Lady*. It won ten Tonys, including Best Musical and Best Actress for Channing and Best Choreography for Champion. The record of ten Tonys went unchallenged until *The Producers* won twelve in 2001. Louis Armstrong had a hit record with "Hello, Dolly" in 1964. At age sixty-two, he was the oldest person ever to reach number one on the pop chart. The red satin gown Channing wore in the production is now at the National Museum of American History, part of the Smithsonian in Washington, D.C. The 1969 film version, with Barbra Streisand in the lead, was nominated for seven Oscars and won three.

Hello, Dolly! has been revived three times on Broadway, in 1975 (an all-black production with Pearl Bailey) and in 1978 and 1995 (both with Channing). Mary Martin starred in the London production in 1965 and in a U.S. tour that same year.

Streisand was back on Broadway for a magnificent performance as Fanny Brice in *Funny Girl*, which opened on March 26, 1964, at the Winter

Garden. It was nominated for eight Tonys but failed to win because of tough competition from *Hello, Dolly!* The musical was produced by Ray Stark, who was Brice's son-in-law.

The plot revolves around Brice, film star and comedienne, and her stormy relationship with gambler and husband Nicky Arnstein, played by Sydney Chaplin. Set in the New York City area around World War I, it looks back on Brice's life as she awaits the return of her husband from prison. When he does return, the two decide to go their separate ways.

The songs were a great triumph for Streisand, including "I'm the Greatest Star," "His Love Makes Me Beautiful," "Don't Rain on My Parade," "Sadie, Sadie," and "Who Are You Now?" She also starred in the film version in 1968 opposite Omar Sharif and shared the Oscar for Best Actress with Katharine Hepburn (for her role in *The Lion in Winter*). It was the top-grossing movie of the year.

The last great production of the Golden Age held the record for almost ten years as the longest-running Broadway musical. It is *Fiddler on the Roof* with Zero Mostel, based on tales by Sholem Aleichem and set in Tsarist Russia in 1905. Mostel plays Tevye the milkman, who tries to keep religious traditions and see that his five daughters get married. His three oldest are very strong willed, and each one's choice of a husband moves further away from the old ways. In the end, the Russians force Tevye, his wife, and two daughters from their village, and they head to America for a new life.

After Mostel left the show, Herschel Bernardi, Theodore Bikel, and then Leonard Nimoy took the role, but the show was such a success and continues to enjoy such popularity that it no longer matters who is cast in the part of Tevye the milkman. The show and the music are enough. *Fiddler on the Roof* was nominated for ten Tonys and won nine. It was revived on Broadway in 1976, 1981, 1990, and 2004. It ran in London in 1983, 1994, and 2007, as well tours in Britain in 2003 and 2008 and the United States in 2009. The film version (1971), with Chaim Topol as Tevye, won three Oscars. *Fiddler on the Roof* tops the list of great Broadway success stories.

The Golden Age of American Musical Theatre ends with *On a Clear Day You Can See Forever*, to mark a changing Broadway. It opened on October 17, 1965. This was not the greatest or biggest or most-remembered hit of the period, although critics liked the score, and it starred Barbara Harris, which added up to a run of 280 performances. It concerns quirky Daisy Gamble (Harris), with low self-esteem and a smoking habit, for which she sees psychiatrist Mark Bruckner (John Cullum), who discovers she had a previous life as Melinda in eighteenth-century England. Things get complicated when Bruckner falls for Melinda. Daisy gets angry and goes to the airport, only to have her ESP tell her that the plane will crash. She now realizes her special powers and returns to Mark.

The musical received three Tony nominations, and the title song was recorded by Barbra Streisand, Robert Goulet, and Johnny Mathis. The London premiere opened in 2000. The 1970 film version starred Streisand and Yves Montand.

From *Oklahoma!* to *On a Clear Day You Can See Forever* covers a memorable and never-fading period in the American musical theatre. The talent was the best, the scores most melodic, the dances most foot-tapping. On any given night on Broadway, in one of the thirty-nine theatres and in any of the many revivals today, it was and is a time to listen and love, a time to stand up and cheer, and a time to tell each entire cast to go break a leg.

(3)

GOLDEN AGE TIMELINE

1943

March 31: *Oklahoma!*
October 7: *One Touch of Venus*
December 2: *Carmen Jones*

1944

January 13: *The Jackpot*
January 28: *Mexican Hayride*
April 8: *Follow the Girls*
April 20: *Allah Be Praised!*
May 18: *Dream with Music*
October: 5 *Bloomer Girl*
November 16: *Sadie Thompson*
December 28: *On the Town*

1945

April 19: *Carousel*
November 8: *The Girl from Nantucket*

November 10: *Are You with It?*
November 22: *The Day before Spring*
December 21: *Billion Dollar Baby*

1946

January 21: *Nellie Bly*
February 6: *Lute Song*
February 13: *The Duchess Misbehaves*
March 30: *St. Louis Woman*
May 16: *Annie Get Your Gun*
November 4: *Park Avenue*
December 22: *Beggar's Holiday*

1947

January 9: *Street Scene*
January 10: *Finian's Rainbow*
March 13: *Brigadoon*
April 3: *Barefoot Boy with Cheek*
June 2: *Louisiana Lady*
October 9: *High Button Shoes*
October 10: *Allegro*

1948

January 29: *Look, Ma, I'm Dancin'*
May 5: *Hold It!*
June 3: *Sleepy Hollow*
September 16: *Heaven on Earth*
September 20: *Magdalena*
October 7: *Love Life*
October 11: *Where's Charley?*
November 13: *As the Girls Go*
December 30: *Kiss Me Kate*

1949

April 7: *South Pacific*
July 15: *Miss Liberty*

October 30: *Lost in the Stars*
November 25: *Texas, L'il Darlin'*
December 8: *Gentlemen Prefer Blondes*

1950

January 6: *Happy as Larry*
March 23: *Great to be Alive*
October 12: *Call Me Madam*
November 10: *Guys and Dolls*
December 21: *Out of This World*

1951

March 29: *The King and I*
April 8: *By the Beautiful Sea*
April 18: *Make a Wish*
April 19: *A Tree Grows in Brooklyn*
May 14: *Flahooley*
June 13: *Courtin' Time*
June 21: *Seventeen*
November 1: *Top Banana*
November 12: *Paint Your Wagon*

1952

March 21: *Three Wishes for Jamie*
June 25: *Wish You Were Here*
October 14: *Buttrio Square*
October 27: *My Darlin' Aida*

1953

February 11: *Hazel Flagg*
February 18: *Maggie*
February 25: *Wonderful Town*
May 7: *Can-Can*
May 28: *Me and Juliet*
September 8: *Carnival in Flanders*
December 3: *Kismet*

1954

March 3: *The Girl in Pink Tights*
March 11: *The Golden Apple*
May 13: *The Pajama Game*
September 20: *The Boy Friend*
October 20: *Peter Pan*
November 4: *Fanny*
December 2: *Hit the Trail*
December 30: *House of Flowers*

1955

January 27: *Plain and Fancy*
February 24: *Silk Stockings*
April 18: *Ankles Aweigh*
May 5: *Damn Yankees*
May 16: *The Roar of the Greasepaint—The Smell of the Crowd*
May 26: *Seventh Heaven*
November 10: *The Vamp*
November 30: *Pipe Dream*

1956

March 15: *My Fair Lady*
March 22: *Mr. Wonderful*
May 3: *The Most Happy Fella*
June 13: *Shangri-La*
November 15: *L'il Abner*
November 29: *Bells Are Ringing*
December 6: *Happy Hunting*

1957

April 13: *Shinbone Alley*
May 14: *New Girl in Town*
September 26: *West Side Story*
October 17: *Copper and Brass*
October 31: *Jamaica*

November 6: *Rumple*
December 19: *The Music Man*

1958

January 23: *The Body Beautiful*
February 4: *Oh Captain!*
February 21: *Portofino*
April 3: *Say, Darling*
October 11: *Goldilocks*
December 1: *Flower Drum Song*
December 22: *Whoop-Up*

1959

February 5: *Redhead*
March 9: *Juno*
March 19: *First Impressions*
April 23: *Destry Rides Again*
May 11: *Once Upon a Mattress*
May 12: *The Nervous Set*
May 21: *Gypsy*
October 7: *Happy Town*
October 22: *Take Me Along*
November 16: *The Sound of Music*
November 23: *Fiorello!*
December 7: *Saratoga*

1960

February 10: *Beg, Borrow or Steal*
March 8: *Greenwillow*
April 14: *Bye Bye Birdie*
September 29: *Irma La Douce*
October 17: *Tenderloin*
November 3: *The Unsinkable Molly Brown*
December 3: *Camelot*
December 16: *Wildcat*
December 26: *Do Re Mi*

1961

January 16: *The Conquering Hero*
March 2: *13 Daughters*
April 3: *The Happiest Girl in the World*
April 13: *Carnival*
May 18: *Donnybrook!*
October 3: *Sail Away*
October 10: *Milk and Honey*
October 14: *How to Succeed in Business without Really Trying*
October 23: *Kwamina*
November 2: *Kean*
November 18: *The Gay Life*
December 27: *Subways Are for Sleeping*

1962

January 27: *A Family Affair*
March 15: *No Strings*
March 19: *All American*
March 22: *I Can Get It for You Wholesale*
May 8: *A Funny Thing Happened on the Way to the Forum*
May 19: *Bravo Giovanni*
October 3: *Stop the World—I Want to Get Off*
October 12: *Let It Ride*
October 20: *Mr. President*
November 10: *Nowhere to Go But Up*
November 17: *Little Me*

1963

January 6: *Oliver!*
March 18: *Tovarich*
April 15: *Sophie*
April 19: *Hot Spot*
April 23: *She Loves Me*
May 16: *The Beast in Me*
October 3: *Here's Love*
October 17: *Jennie*

October 24: *110 in the Shade*
December 8: *The Girl Who Came to Supper*

1964

January 16: *Hello, Dolly!*
February 16: *Foxy*
February 27: *What Makes Sammy Run?*
March 26: *Funny Girl*
April 4: *Anyone Can Whistle*
April 7: *High Spirits*
April 17: *Café Crown*
May 26: *Fade Out—Fade In*
September 22: *Fiddler on the Roof*
September 30: *Oh! What a Lovely War*
October 20: *Golden Boy*
October 27: *Ben Franklin in Paris*
November 10: *Something More!*
November 23: *Bajour*
December 15: *I Had a Ball*

1965

February 6: *Kelly*
February 16: *Baker Street*
March 18: *Do I Hear a Waltz?*
April 25: *Half a Sixpence*
May 11: *Flora, the Red Menace*
October 4: *Pickwick*
October 10: *Drat! The Cat!*
October 17: *On a Clear Day You Can See Forever*

4

THE GOLDEN AGE MUSICALS
OF BROADWAY

Note: Entries marked with an ° are designated as flops, indicating a run of fewer than 161 (1–160) performances.

°**ALL AMERICAN** (March 19, 1962; Winter Garden Theatre; 80 performances). *Director:* Joshua Logan; *Composer:* Charles Strouse; *Lyricist:* Lee Adams; *Librettist:* Mel Brooks; *Choreographer:* Danny Daniels. Ray Bolger, as university professor Fodorski, led the cast in a show that applied engineering principles to football strategies and featured muscular men stripped to the waist. Critics found the songs unmemorable, and the production was not helped by a city newspaper strike, which cut off most advertising.

    Tony nominations: Best Actor in a Musical (Bolger), Best Direction of a Musical

°**ALLAH BE PRAISED!** (April 20, 1944; Adelphi Theatre; 20 performances). *Directors:* Robert H. Gordon and Jack Small; *Composers:* Don Walker and Baldwin Bergersen; *Lyricist/Librettist:* George Marion Jr.; *Choreographer:* Jack Cole. This is a confusing tale about a search for a missing American, played by Edward Roecker, in the postwar harems of Sultanbad. When he is finally discovered, it turns out that he is the sultan.

ALLEGRO (October 10, 1947; Majestic Theatre; 315 performances)
    Production credits: *Producer:* Theatre Guild; *Director/Choreographer:* Agnes de Mille; *Composer:* Richard Rodgers; *Lyricist/Librettist:* Oscar Hammerstein II

Original cast: Marjorie Taylor (Annamary Dickey), Dr. Joseph Taylor (William Ching), Joe Jr. (John Battles), Jennie Brinker (Roberta Jonay), Emily West (Lisa Kirk), Charlie Townsend (John Conte)

Synopsis: In 1905, Marjorie and Joe have a son, Joe Jr. His father wants him to become a doctor, but Grandma says the child will decide. Joe Jr. grows into a shy lad who falls in love with Jenny. When he finishes college and does become a doctor, he goes back to their small town and they marry. But it is the Depression and times are hard. At Jenny's urging, they move to Chicago, where Joe builds a successful practice; however, his wife begins to cheat on him. When Joe finally realizes that, he moves back to his small town.

Songs: "Joseph Taylor Jr."; "I Know It Can Happen Again"; "One Foot, Other Foot"; "Children's Ballet"; "The Winters Go By"; "A Fellow Needs a Girl"; "Freshman Dance"; "It's a Darn Nice Campus"; "She Is Never Far Away"; "So Far"; "Money Isn't Everything"; "Yatata, Yatata, Yatata"; "The Gentleman Is a Dope"; "Allegro"; "Come Home"

Comments: This Broadway Musical collaboration (after *Oklahoma!* [1943] and *Carousel* [1945]) by Richard Rodgers and Oscar Hammerstein was the first time that Hammerstein did not adapt from an older work.

ANKLES AWEIGH (April 18, 1955; Mark Hellinger Theatre; 172 performances)

Production credits: *Producers:* Howard Hoyt, Reginald Hammerstein, and Fred F. Finklehoffe; *Director:* Fred F. Finklehoffe; *Composer:* Sammy Fain; *Lyricist:* Dan Shapiro; *Librettists:* Guy Bolton and Eddie Davis; *Choreographer:* Tony Charmoli

Original cast: Tommy (Bill Costin), Elsey (Betty Kean), Wynne (Jane Kean), Dinky (Lew Parker), Spud (Gabriel Dell), Lt. Bill Kelley (Mark Dawson), Captain Zimmerman (Mark Allen), Admiral Pottles (Will Hussung), Chipolata (Thelma Carpenter), Joe Mancinni (Mike Kellin), Tony (Herb Fields), Lucia (Betty George), The Duchess (Karen Shepard)

Synopsis: In what critics called a typical 1950s musical, Wynne, a Hollywood starlet, violates a clause in her contract while filming a movie in Sicily and weds a navy flier. He is Bill Kelley, whose ship is on maneuvers in the Mediterranean Sea. With the help of her sister, Elsey, and the groom's service buddies, Dinky and Spud, the bride dons the guise of a sailor and stows away on his ship. Their honeymoon in many exotic Mediterranean settings is constantly interrupted by demands from her studio in addition to those from some serious top navy brass. The young marrieds find themselves in the middle of a spy ring, led by Kelley's former girlfriend from Morocco. What with a chorus line, old-fashioned tap dancing routines, and comedians, the lovers are never alone. But in the end, Bill is cleared of all crimes and becomes a hero.

Songs: "Italy"; "Old-Fashioned Mothers"; "Skip the Build-Up"; "Nothing at All"; "Walk Like a Sailor"; "Headin' for the Bottom"; "Nothing Can Replace a Man"; "Here's to Dear Old Us"; "His and Hers"; "La Festa"; "Ready Cash"; "Kiss Me and Kill Me with Love"; "Honeymoon"; "The Villain Always Gets It"; "The Code"; "Eleven O'Clock Song"

Comments: Sonny Tufts was the original lead in the show, but he left while the production was still on the road. The musical returned somewhat to vaudeville-style entertainment; critic Walter Kerr in the *Tribune* did not think it worked.

ANNIE GET YOUR GUN (May 16, 1946; Imperial Theatre; 1,147 performances)

Production credits: *Producers:* Richard Rodgers and Oscar Hammerstein II; *Director:* Joshua Logan; *Composer/Lyricist:* Irving Berlin; *Librettists:* Herbert Fields and Dorothy Fields; *Choreographer:* Helen Tamiris

Original cast: Annie Oakley (Ethel Merman), Frank Butler (Ray Middleton), Colonel William F. Cody (William O'Neal), Charlie Davenport (Marty May), Trainman (John Garth III), Foster Wilson (Art Barnett), Dolly Tate (Lea Penman), Winnie Tate (Betty Ann Nyman), Tommy Keeler (Kenny Bowers), Minnie Oakley (Nancy Jean Rabb), Jessie Oakley (Camilla De Witt), Nellie Oakley (Marlene Cameron), Little Jake Oakley (Clifford Sales), Waiter (Leon Bibb), Porter (Clyde Turner), Chief Sitting Bull (Harry Bellaver)

Synopsis: Based loosely on the real life cowgirl, the show features Annie Oakley, a poor country girl who happens to be very accurate with a gun. When Buffalo Bill's Wild West show gets to Cincinnati, Ohio, star and womanizer Frank Butler challenges anyone to a shooting match. Annie wins, and her talent lands her in the show. She immediately falls for Frank, but Frank wants a dainty girl, which Annie is not, and he and Annie can agree on very little; however as time passes, Frank becomes interested in Annie. But when the show plays in Minneapolis, Annie does a surprise trick, which angers Frank, and he leaves to join a competing show. Both competing shows go broke, and Frank and Annie meet again at a reception and decide to make up and marry, but when Annie shows Frank all the sharpshooting medals she has won, he becomes angry again; however, they agree to one last shooting match between the two sharpshooters. Annie is advised by Sitting Bull to lose. Reluctantly, she loses the match to win the man, and they merge the shows.

Songs: "Doin' What Comes Natur'ly"; "The Girl That I Marry"; "You Can't Get a Man with a Gun"; "There's No Business Like Show Business"; "They Say It's Wonderful"; "I Got Lost in His Arms"; "I Got the Sun in the Morning"; "Anything You Can Do"

Comments: The producers originally chose Jerome Kern to write the score, but when he died, Irving Berlin was called in and produced what is generally regarded as his greatest work. As for Ethel Merman, if she had not been before, she became the leading musical comedy star of her generation in this production. Merman had been playing this type of role in musicals of the 1930s, tough and big-hearted more than glamorous, but this time, the role was just perfect for her voice and her talents. The road company starred Mary Martin. Judy Garland was originally supposed to play the role in the movie, but Betty Hutton became Annie in the 1950 movie version, with Howard Keel as her rival. The show won a Tony in 1999 for Best Revival.

°*ANYONE CAN WHISTLE* (April 4, 1964; Majestic Theatre; 9 performances). *Director:* Arthur Laurents; *Composer/Lyricist:* Stephen Sondheim; *Librettist:* Arthur Laurents; *Choreographer:* Herbert Ross. Angela Lansbury, Lee Remick, and Harry Guardino starred in a show about a corrupt mayoress (Lansbury) and the efforts to save a bankrupt town by advertising a miracle—water flowing from a rock. Critics thought Sondheim's music was fresh and original but not the show.
Tony nomination: Best Choreography

ARE YOU WITH IT? (November 10, 1945; New Century Theatre; 164 performances)
Production credits: *Producers:* Richard Kollmar and James W. Gardiner; *Director:* Edward Reveaux; *Composer:* Harry Revel; *Lyricist:* Arnold B. Horwitt; *Librettists:* Sam Perrin and George Balzer; *Choreographer:* Jack Donohue; *Original source:* George Malcolm Smith's novel *Slightly Imperfect*
Original cast: Wilbur Hawkins (Johnny Downs), Marge Keller (Jane Dulo), Bunny La Fleur (Dolores Gray), Goldie (Lew Parker), Cleo (June Richmond), Vivian Reilly (Joan Roberts), Sally Swivelhips (Diane Adrian), Mr. Bixby (Sydney Boyd), Cicero (Bunny Briggs), Snake Charmer's Daughter (Jane Deering), Carter (Lew Eckels), Office Boy (Hal Hunter), Balloon Seller (Mildred Jocelyn), Strong Man (William Lundy), Policeman (Duke McHale), Georgetta (Buster Shaver), George (George Shaver), Olive (Olive Shaver), Mr. Mapleton (Johnny Stearns), Loren (Loren Welch)
Synopsis: The setting is Hartford, Connecticut, where Goldie, a carnival barker, persuades Wilbur to join the troop. He has been fired from his job at the insurance company because he missed a decimal point. Literal and serious-minded, Wilbur does not seem to be the carnival type, although he does try to fit in, even though he looks out of place when he

orders a glass of milk at Joe's Bar Room. But it is there that he meets Vivian and falls in love.

Songs: "Five More Minutes in Bed"; "Nutmeg Insruance"; "When a Good Man Takes to Drink"; "Poor Little Me"; "Are You with It?"; "Send Us Back to the Kitchen"; "Here I Go Again"; "This Is My Beloved"; "Slightly Slightly"; "Just Beyond the Rainbow"; "In Our Cozy Little Cottage of Tomorrow"

AS THE GIRLS GO (November 13, 1948; Winter Garden Theatre; 414 performances)

Production credits: *Producer:* Michael Todd; *Director:* Howard Bay; *Composer:* Jimmy McHugh; *Lyricist:* Harold Adamson; *Librettist:* William Roos; *Choreographer:* Hermes Pan

Original cast: Waldo Wellington (Bobby Clark), Lucille Thompson Wellington (Irene Rich), Kenny Wellington (Bill Callahan), Mickey Wellington (Betty Lou Barto), Tommy Wellington (Donny Harris), Guard and Secret Service Man (John Shehan), Kathy Robinson (Betty Jane Watson), Barber (Hobart Cavanaugh), Guard and Ross Miller (Jack Russell), White House Visitor (John Brophy), Miss Swenson (Cavada Humphrey), Butler (Curt Stafford), Floyd Robinson (Douglas Luther), Diane (Mildred Hughes), Photographers (Kenneth Spaulding and William Reedy), Daphne (Dorothea Pinto), Blinky Joe (Dick Danna), Darlene (Rosemary Williamson), Secret Service Man (George Morris), Secret Service Women (June Kirby and Truly Barbara), Secretary (Ruth Thomas), President of Potomac College (Douglas Luther), Premier Danseuse (Katharine Lee)

Synopsis: The year is 1953, and the first woman has been elected president of the United States. She is now guarded by Secret Service women, and her husband is known as the First Gentlemen. With little to do, he mainly spends his time in the company of the beautiful girls who guard his wife. In his spare time, the First Gentlemen both helps and hinders his son Kenny's romance with Kathy Robinson.

Songs: "As the Girls Go"; "Nobody's Heart but Mine"; "Brighten Up and Be a Little Sunbeam"; "Rock, Rock, Rock"; "It's More Fun Than a Picnic"; "American Cannes"; "You Say the Nicest Things, Baby"; "I've Got the President's Ear"; "Holiday in the Country"; "There's No Getting Away from You"; "Lucky in the Rain"; "Father's Day"; "It Takes a Woman to Get a Man"

Tony Award: Best Conductor and Musical Director (Max Meth)

Comments: As a sign of things to come, the top ticket theatre price jumped to $7.20, unheard-of when Broadway tickets averaged about $4.00. The show, which cost $300,000 to produce, was hurt by an American Society of Composers, Authors, and Publishers (ASCAP) strike.

BAJOUR (November 23, 1964; Shubert Theatre; 311 performances)

Production credits: *Producers:* Edward Padula, Carol Masterson, Harris Masterson, and Norman Twain; *Director:* Lawrence Kasha; *Composer/Lyricist:* Walter Marks; *Librettist:* Ernest Kinoy; *Choreographer:* Peter Gennaro

Original cast: Johnny Dembo (Herschel Bernardi), Lt. Lou MacNiall (Robert Burr), Helen Kirsten (Mae Questel), Steve (Gus Trikonis), Emily Kirsten (Nancy Dussault), Anyanka (Chita Rivera), King of Newark (Herbert Edelman)

Synopsis: In this production set in present-day New York, Johnny Dembo and his gypsy family are studied by anthropologist Emily Kirsten, who reports their movements to Lt. Lou MacNial, her cousin. Dembo wants to marry his son Steven to Anyanka, the daughter of a gypsy king in Newark, New Jersey, but for the marriage to go ahead, Anyanka must pull off a swindle (a bajour in the gypsy language), which she does with the help of an unsuspecting Emily.

Songs: "Move Over, New York"; "Where Is the Tribe for Me?"; "The Haggie"; "Love-Line"; "Words, Words, Words"; "Mean"; "Bajour"; "Must It Be Love?"; "Soon"; "I Can"; "Living Simply"; "Honest Man"; "Guarantees"; "Love Is a Chance"; "The Sew-Up"; "Move Over, America"

Tony nominations: Best Actress in a Musical (Dussault), Best Choreography (Gennaro)

Comments: With a weak plot and not outstanding score, the show depended on Chita Rivera, who kept it on the boards for the season.

BAKER STREET (February 16, 1965; Broadway Theatre; 311 performances)

Production credits: *Producer:* Alexander H. Cohen; *Director:* Harold Prince; *Composer/Lyricists:* Marian Grudeff and Raymond Jessel; *Librettist:* Jerome Coopersmith; *Choreographer:* Lee Beeker Theodore

Original cast: Professor Moriarty (Martin Gabel), Irene Adler (Inga Swenson), Sherlock Holmes (Fritz Weaver), Mrs. Hudson (Paddy Edwards), Wiggins (Teddy Green), Killers (Avin Harum, Tommy Tune, and Christopher Walken), Captain Gregg (Patrick Horgan), Inspector Lestrade (Daniel Keyes), Perkins (George Lee), Duckbellows (Bert Michaels), Murillo (Jay Norman), Nipper (Sal Pernice), Dr. Watson (Peter Sallis), Macipper (Mark Jude Sheil), Daisy (Virginia Vestoff), Baxter (Martin Wolfson)

Synopsis: The musical is loosely based on the Sherlock Holmes stories by Arthur Conan Doyle, set in London in 1897, the Diamond Jubilee in the reign of Queen Victoria. The celebration is depicted by an elaborate royal possession of Bil Baird's marionettes. In this version, Irene Adler becomes an associate of Holmes rather than an opponent, which opens up the opportunity for romance between the two.

Songs: "It's So Simple"; "I'm in London Again"; "Leave It to Us, Gov"; "Letters"; "Cold, Clear World"; "Finding Words for Spring"; "What a Night This Is Going to Be"; "I Shall Miss You"; "Roof Space"; "A Married Man"; "I'd Do It Again"; "Pursuit"; "Jewelry"

Tony Award: Best Scenic Design of a Musical (Motley). **Tony nominations:** Best Actress in a Musical (Swenson), Best Author (Coopersmith), Best Costume Design of a Musical (Motley)

Comments: Dancer Tommy Tune made his Broadway debut in this production. Before opening night, producer Cohen established a dress code for the audience—jackets and ties for men, dresses for women—but quickly vetoed it when the mixed reviews came in. The top ticket theatre prices were now $9.90.

°*BAREFOOT BOY WITH CHEEK* (April 3, 1947; Martin Beck Theatre; 106 performances). *Producer/Director:* George Abbott; *Composer:* Sidney Lippman; *Lyricist:* Sylvia Dee; *Librettist:* Max Shulman; *Choreographer:* Richard Barstow. In another Abbott musical frolic, Nancy Walker played the lead as a woman who tries to convert the University of Minnesota to her "pink" views. She also tries to win the heart of Asa Hearthrug, but loses him to Clothilde Pfefferkorn. Critics said Walker's clowning kept the show running as long as it did.

°*THE BEAST IN ME* (May 14, 1963; Plymouth Theatre; 4 performances). *Director:* John Lehne; *Composer:* Don Elliot; *Lyricist/Librettist:* James Costigan; *Librettist:* W. S. Gilbert; *Choreographer:* John Butler; *Original source:* Based on the book *Fables for Our Times* by James Thurber. This musical could not be saved, even with the talents of Kaye Ballard. Audiences did not warm to almost all characters in the sketches and songs being portrayed as animals.

°*BEG, BORROW, OR STEAL* (February 10, 1960; Martin Beck Theatre; 5 performances). *Director:* David Doyle; *Composer:* Leon Pober; *Lyricist/Librettist:* Bud Freeman; *Choreographer:* Peter Hamilton. Beatniks Betty Garrett and Eddie Bracken played sister and brother who ran a health food store in a run-down section of a huge U.S. city in the 1950s. They meet with friends at the Pit. The focus of attention is the sister's agony over choosing between another beatnik or a square type of guy.

°*BEGGAR'S HOLIDAY* (December 6, 1946; Broadway Theatre; 111 performances). *Director:* Nicholas Ray; *Composer:* Duke Ellington; *Lyricist/Librettist:* John Latouche; *Choreographer:* Valerie Bettis. Duke

Ellington's music was lost in this production with Alfred Drake playing an American gangster type. An updated version of John Gay's *The Beggar's Opera*, it included an interracial relationship that resulted in pickets outside the theatre each night, which might have shortened the run.

BELLS ARE RINGING (November 29, 1956; Shubert Theatre; 925 performances)

Production credits: *Director:* Jerome Robbins; *Composer:* Jule Styne; *Lyricists/Librettists:* Betty Comden and Adolph Green; *Choreographers:* Jerome Robbins and Bob Fosse

Original cast: Ella Peterson (Judy Holliday), Jeff Moss (Sydney Chaplin), Blake Barton (Frank Aletter), Inspector Barnes (Dort Clark), Olga (Norma Doggett), Charles Bessemer, Another Anchor, Singer, and Nightclub (Frank Green), Telephone Man (Eddie Heim), Larry Hastings (George S. Irving), Sandor (Eddie Lawrence), Mrs. Mallet (Jeannine Masterson), Maitre D'Hotel (David McDaniel), Ludwig Smiley (Frank Milton), Man from Corvello Mob (John Perkins), Carol (Ellen Ray), Michelle (Michelle Reiner), Paul Arnold (Steve Roland), Madame Grimaldi (Donna Sanders), Sue (Jean Stapleton), Waiter (Ed Thompson), Dr. Kitchell (Bernie West), Francis (Jack Weston), Gwynne (Pat Wilkes), Police Officer (Gordon Woodburn)

Synopsis: Ella Peterson works for a telephone-answering service but can't seem to stop meddling in her customers' lives. Aspiring playwright Jeff Moss gets special attention, and they fall in love, although they have never met and she pretends to be a motherly old lady. Unbeknownst to Ella, she also takes orders for what is actually a betting ring. In come the police and out goes romance, but in the end the two are reunited.

Songs: "Bells Are Ringing"; "Better Than a Dream"; "Do It Yourself"; "Drop That Name"; "Hello, Mazurka"; "Hello, Hello There!"; "I Met a Girl"; "I'm Goin' Back"; "Is It a Crime?"; "It's a Perfect Relationship"; "It's a Simple Little System"; "Just in Time"; "Long Before I Knew You"; "The Midas Touch"; "Mu-Cha-Cha"; "The Party's Over"; "Salzburg"; "Santa's Lullaby"; "You've Got to Do It"

Tony Awards: Best Actress in a Musical (Holliday), Best Featured Actor in a Musical (Chaplin). **Tony nominations:** Best Musical, Best Choreography (Robbins/Fosse)

Comments: The main reason for the show's success was the charm and talent of Judy Holliday in her first star billing role on Broadway.

BEN FRANKLIN IN PARIS (October 27, 1964; Lunt-Fontanne Theatre; 216 performances)

Production credits: *Producers:* George W. George and Frank Granat; *Director/Choreographer:* Michael Kidd; *Composer:* Mark Sandrich Jr.; *Lyricist/Librettist:* Sidney Michaels

Original cast: Captain Wickes (Sam Greene), Benjamin Franklin (Robert Preston), Temple Franklin (Franklin Kiser), Benjamin Franklin Bache (Jerry Schaefer), Footman (Anthony Falco), Louis XVI (Oliver Clark), Vergennes (Art Bartow), Turgot (Clifford Fearl), Madame La Comtesse Diane de Vobrillac (Ulla Sallert), British Grenadier (Roger Le Page), David Lord Stormont (Byron Webster), Pierre Caron de Beaumarchais (Bob Kaliban), Jacques Finque (John Taliaferro), Pedro Count de Aranda (Jack Fletcher), Bookseller and Abbe de Morellet (Herb Mazzini), Janine Nicolet (Susan Watson), Spanish Aide-de-Camp (Kip Andrews), Spanish Solider (Art Matthews), Spanish Ambassador's Daughter (Suzanne France), Yvonne (Lauren Jones)

Synopsis: Ben Franklin arrives in Paris with his two grandsons to win over the king to the side of the colonies in their war against England. Franklin reunites with an old love, the Countess Diane de Vobrillac, and asks her to help persuade the king, but she needs proof that the colonies will triumph. He gets her to ride in a hot air balloon with him and also gets her to agree to help if he can find another country to contribute to the colonies' war effort. She agrees, Franklin gets Spain involved, and in the end the king greets him as the first ambassador from the new United States of America.

Songs: "We Sail the Seas"; "I Invented Myself"; "Too Charming"; "What Became of Old Temple"; "Half the Battle"; "A Balloon Is Ascending"; "To Be Alone with You"; "You're in Paris"; "How Laughable It Is"; "Hic Haec Hoc"; "God Bless the Human Elbow"; "When I Dance with the Person I Love"; "Diane Is"; "Look for Small Pleasures"; "I Love the Ladies"

Tony nomination: Best Author (Sidney Michaels)

Comments: Critics called the score mediocre and the book trite, but Robert Preston kept it running. The highlight of the evening was Ben Franklin landing on stage in a balloon.

BILLION DOLLAR BABY (December 21, 1945; Alvin Theatre; 219 performances)

Production credits: *Producers:* Paul Feigay and Oliver Smith; *Director:* George Abbott; *Composer:* Morton Gould; *Lyricists/Librettists:* Betty Comden and Adolph Green; *Choreographer:* Jerome Robbins

Original cast: Cigarette Girl and Singer (Jeri Archer), Dapper Welch (David Burns), M. M. Montague (Robert Chisholm), J. C. Creasy (Horace Cooper), Champ Watson (Danny Daniels), Pa Jones (William David), Jerry Bonanza (Don De Leo), Neighbor (Douglas Deane), Watchman (Robert Edwin), Miss Texas (Althea Elder), Neighbor (Helen Gallagher), Reporter

(Alan Gilbert), Georgia Motley (Mitzi Green), Neighbor (Maria Harriton), Art Leffenbush (Eddie Hodge), Maribelle Jones (Joan McCracken), Rocky (James Mitchell), Ma Jones (Emily Ross), Master of Ceremonies (Richard Sanford)

Synopsis: The show is set on Staten Island, New York, and in Atlantic City, New Jersey, in the late 1920s. Marabelle Jones, an ambitious young woman, ditches her nice-guy boyfriend for a gangster on the run. She is looking for wealth in the Prohibition Era. Her rise to fame includes a gaudy gangster funeral and finally a wealthy tycoon type—all this before the Stock Market crash of 1929.

Songs: "Million Dollar Smile"; "Who's Gonna Be the Winner"; "Dreams Come True"; "Charleston"; "Broadway Blossom"; "Speaking of Pals"; "There I'd Be"; "One-Track Mind"; "Bad Timing"; "The Marathoners"; "A Lovely Girl"; "Havin' a Time"; "The Marathon Dance Faithless"; "I'm Sure of Your Love"; "A Life with Rocky"; "The Wedding"

Comments: Reviewers felt that the show ran as long as it did, despite a mediocre score, because it faced no real competition for several months.

BLOOMER GIRL (October 5, 1944; Shubert Theatre; 567 performances)
Production credits: *Producers:* Nat Goldstone and John C. Wilson; *Directors:* E. Y. Harburg and William Schorr; *Composer:* Harold Arlen; *Lyricist:* E. Y. Harburg; *Librettists:* Sid Herzig and Fred Saidy; *Choreographer:* Agnes de Mille

Original cast: Evelina Applegate (Celeste Holm), Hetty (Arlene Anderson), Paula (Lee Barrie), Herman Brasher (William Bender), Horatio (Matt Briggs), Jeff Calhoun (David Brooks), Hamilton Calhoun (Blaine Cordner), Gus (John Call), Augustus (Hubert Dilworth), Dolly Bloomer (Margaret Douglass), Delia (Nancy Douglass), Hiram Crump (Dan Gallagher), Julia (Toni Hart), Governor Newton (Butler Hixon), Sheriff Quimby (Charles Howard), Alexander (Richard Huey), Prudence (Eleanor Jones), Lydia (Claudia Jordan), Joshua Dingle (Robert Lyon), Phoebe (Carol MacFarlane), Ebenezer Mimms (Joe E. Marks), Daisy (Joan McCracken), Octavia (Pamela Randell), Serena (Mabel Taliaferro), Wilfred Thrush (Vaughn Trinnier), Pompey (Dooley Wilson)

Synopsis: Based on the struggles of Dolly Bloomer for civil rights, the show takes place in Civil War days, where Evelina Applegate has a mind of her own in Cicero Falls, New York. She refuses to marry her father's choice and instead backs her aunt's campaign to replace the hoopskirt, which her father manufactures, with the more comfortable bloomer. In addition, she decides to marry a southern slaveholder.

Songs: "When the Boys Come Home"; "Evelina"; "Welcome Hinges"; "Farmer's Daughter"; "It Was Good Enough for Grandma"; "Eagle and

Me"; "Right as the Rain"; "T'Morra', T'Morra'"; "Rakish Young Man with the Wiskuhs"; "Sunday in Cicero Falls"; "I Got a Song"; "Satin Gown and Silver Shoe"; "Liza Crossing the Ice"; "Never Was Born"; "Man for Sale"

Comments: "Evelina" became one of the most popular tunes of the 1940s.

°**THE BODY BEAUTIFUL** (January 23, 1958; Broadway Theatre; 60 performances). *Director:* George Schaefer; *Composer:* Jerry Bock; *Lyricist:* Sheldon Harnick; *Librettists:* Joseph Stein and Will Glickman; *Choreographer:* Herbert Ross. A rich and handsome Dartmouth graduate (Steve Forrest) decides that he will box his way to fame and glory. The problem is that his girlfriend hates boxing. Singer Barbara McNair made her Broadway debut in this show.

THE BOY FRIEND (September 30, 1954; Royale Theatre; 485 performances)

Production credits: *Producers:* Cy Feuer and Ernest Martin; *Director:* Vida Hope; *Composer/Lyricist/Librettist:* Sandy Wilson; *Choreographer:* John Heawood

Original cast: Hortense (Paulette Girard), Nancy (Millicent Martin), Maisie (Ann Wakefield), Fay and Lolita (Stella Claire), Dulcie (Dilys Lay), Polly (Julie Andrews), Marcel and Pepe (Joe Milan), Alphonse (Buddy Schwab), Pierre (Jerry Newby), Madame Dubonnet (Ruth Altman), Bobby Van Husen (Bob Scheerer), Percival Browne (Eric Berry), Phillipe (Jimmy Alex), Monica (Berkley Marsh), Lord Brockhurst (Geoffrey Hibbert), Lady Brockhurst (Moyna MacGill), Susanne (Lyn Connorty), Gendarme (Douglas Deane), Waiter (Lyn Robert)

Synopsis: A reminder of the Jazz Age, the musical is set on the French Riviera in the 1920s. Polly arrives at the school for young ladies and tells everyone about her supposed boyfriend who will soon arrive from Paris. Polly's widowed father arrives instead and is attracted to the headmistress, once an old flame of his. Polly ends up as the only one without a boyfriend and a partner for the dress ball. Tony delivers her costume, and they are attracted to each other. They meet later at the ball, where Tony is at first mistaken for a thief. But it ends happily when Polly's father and the headmistress are to be married and Polly and Tony find love.

Songs: "Perfect Young Ladies"; "The Boy Friend"; "Won't You Charleston with Me?"; "Fancy Forgetting"; "I Could Be Happy with You"; "Sur La Plage"; "A Room in Bloomsbury"; "You Don't Want to Play with Me Blues"; "Safety in Numbers"; "It's Never Too Late to Fall in Love"; "Poor Little Pierrette"

Comments: The delight of the show was the arrival of Julie Andrews on Broadway.

°*BRAVO GIOVANNI* (May 19, 1962; Broadhurst Theatre; 76 performances). *Director:* Stanley Prager; *Composer:* Milton Schafer; *Lyricist:* Ronny Graham; *Librettist:* A. J. Russell; *Choreographer:* Carol Haney. Opera singer Cesare Siepi and Michelle Lee starred in a tale about the problems of a small, family-style trattoria in Rome. An upscale restaurant opens next door, and a friend suggests that the owner make a tunnel from his basement to steal food from the new restaurant's dumbwaiter.

Tony nominations: Best Composer and Lyricist, Best Choreography, Best Conductor and Musical Director

BRIGADOON (March 13, 1947; Ziegfeld Theatre; 581 performances)

Production credits: *Producer:* Cheryl Crawford; *Director:* Robert Lewis; *Composer:* Frederick Loewe; *Lyricist/Librettist:* Alan Jay Lerner; *Choreographer:* Agnes de Mille

Original cast: Stuart Dalrymple (Delbert Anderson), Fiona MacLaren (Marian Bell), Jean MacLaren (Virgina Bosler), Meg Brockie (Pamela Britton), Tommy Albright (David Brooks), Jane Ashton (Frances Charles), Andrew MacLaren (Edward Cullen), Maggie Anderson (Lidija Franklin), Mr. Lundle (William Hansen), Kate MacQueen (Margaret Hunter), Jeff Douglas (George Keane), Fishmonger (Bunty Kelley), Harry Veaton (James Mitchell), MacGregor (Earl Redding), Angus McGuffie (Walter Scheff), Archie Beaton (Elliot Sullivan), Charlie Dalrymple (Lee Sullivan), Sandy Dean (Jeffrey Warren)

Synopsis: Tommy and Jeff, two Americans lost in a Scottish wood, come upon a quaint village where the people are celebrating the upcoming marriage of Jean and Charlie. Tommy and Jean's sister Fiona are attracted to each other, as are Jeff and Meg, but Tommy is troubled because he feels the village is so odd, such as the fact that the villagers don't know about telephones. Fiona takes him to the schoolmaster, who tells Tommy that the village of Brigadoon is under a spell. It will return for only one day every 100 years. Learning this, the Americans flee, but Tommy's love is so strong that he returns to Scotland. The village reappears just long enough to take him in.

Songs: "Once in the Highlands"; "Brigadoon"; "Down on MacConnachy Square"; "Waitin' for My Dearie"; "I'll Go Home with Bonnie Jean"; "The Heather on the Hill"; "The Love of My Life"; "Jeannie's Packing Up"; "Come to Me, Bend to Me"; "Almost Like Being in Love"; "The Chase"; "There But for You Go I"; "My Mother's Weddin' Day"; "From This Day On"

Tony Award: Best Choreography (de Mille)

Comments: Al Jolson popularized "Come to Me, Bend to Me" on his radio shows. "Almost Like Being in Love" became an instant hit. The score was also the highlight of the highly successful movie version in 1954 with Gene Kelly, Van Johnson, and Cyd Charisse, and directed by Vincente Minnelli.

°*BUTTRIO SQUARE* (October 14, 1952; 59th Street Theatre; 7 performances). *Director/Choreographer:* Eugene Loring; *Composer:* Arthur Jones and Fred Stamer; *Lyricist:* Gen Genovese; *Librettists:* Billy Gilbert and Gen Genovese; *Choreographer:* Eugene Loring. Billy Gilbert headed a show about U.S. soldiers in an Italian village where fraternizing is forbidden. Critics called it tedious and trite, with too much strenuous dancing. The audience agreed, and the show closed in less than one week.

BY THE BEAUTIFUL SEA (April 8, 1954; Majestic Theatre; 270 performances)

Production credits: *Producers:* Robert Fryer and Lawrence Carr; *Director:* Marshall Jamison; *Composer:* Arthur Schwartz; *Lyricist:* Dorothy Fields; *Librettists:* Herbert Fields and Dorothy Fields; *Choreographer:* Helen Tamiris

Original cast: Cora Belmont (Mary Harmon), Molly Belmont (Cindy Robbins), Lillian Belmont (Gloria Smith), Ruby Monk (Mae Barnes), Mrs. Koch (Edith True Case), Carl Gibson (Cameron Prud'homme), Lottie Gibson (Shirley Booth), Half-Note (Robert Jennings), Diabolo (Thomas Gleason), Baby Betsy Busch (Carol Leigh), Mickey Powers (Richard France), Dennis Emery (Wilbur Evans), Flora Busch (Anne Francine), Willie Slater (Ray Dooley), Sidney (Eddie Roll), Mr. Curtis (Paul Reed), Burt Mayer (Larry Laurence), Viola (Gaby Monet)

Synopsis: In 1907, vaudevillian Lottie returns to the family boardinghouse on Coney Island after another tour. One of the boarders is actor Dennis Emery, with whom she falls in love. But there are problems. Dennis needs $1,000 to get his show working again, so Lottie decides to help him out by raising the money, even if that includes jumping out of a hot air balloon. To complicate her problems, Dennis's ex-wife shows up at the boardinghouse with his seventeen-year-old daughter. Already unhappy about the divorce, the daughter has no intention of sharing her father with Lottie.

Songs: "Mona from Arizona"; "The Sea Song"; "Old Enough to Love"; "Coney Island Boat"; "Alone Too Long"; "Happy Habit"; "Good Time Charlie"; "I'd Rather Wake Up by Myself"; "Hooray for George the Third"; "More Love Than Your Love"; "Lottie Gibson Specialty"; "Throw the Anchor Away"

Comments: The presence of Shirley Booth on stage was mainly the reason for the run.

BYE BYE BIRDIE (April 14, 1960; Martin Beck Theatre; 607 performances)

Production credits: *Producers:* Edward Padula, in association with L. Slade Brown; *Director/Choreographer:* Gower Champion; *Composer:* Charles Strouse; *Lyricist:* Lee Adams; *Librettist:* Michael Stewart

Original cast: Albert Peterson (Dick Van Dyke), Rose Grant (Chita Rivera), Ursula Merkle (Barbara Doherty), Kim MacAfee (Susan Watson), Mrs. MacAfee (Marijane Maricle), Mr. MacAfee (Paul Lynde), Mae Peterson (Kay Medford), Conrad Birdie (Dick Gautier), Mayor (Allen Knowles), Mayor's Wife (Amelia Haas), Hugo Peabody (Michael J. Pollard), Randolph MacAfee (Johnny Borden), Mrs. Merkle (Pat McEnnis)

Synopsis: Singing star Conrad Birdie is about to be drafted. That means Albert Peterson, his agent, will lose his commissions and will not be able to marry Rose Grant. Rose comes up with a plan to write a hit song so they can have the royalties while Birdie is away. Mayhem develops when they choose Kim as the girl Birdie will sing to in her hometown of Sweet Apple because she falls for him. But all ends well when Kim goes back to her boyfriend. Albert and Rose are happy, and Birdie is headed for the army.

Songs: "An English Teacher"; "The Telephone Hour"; "How Lovely to be a Woman"; "We Love You, Conrad!"; "Put on a Happy Face"; "Normal American Boy"; "One Boy"; "Honestly Sincere"; "Hymn for a Sunday Evening"; "What Did I Ever See in Him?"; "A Lot of Livin' to Do"; "Baby, Talk to Me"; "Shriners' Ballet"; "Spanish Rose"; "Rosie"

Tony Awards: Best Musical, Best Featured Actor in a Musical (Van Dyke), Best Choreography, Best Direction of a Musical. **Tony nominations:** Best Featured Actor in a Musical (Gautier), Best Featured Actress in a Musical (Rivera), Best Scenic Design (Robert Randolph), Best Conductor and Musical Director (Elliott Lawrence)

Comments: This show was Gower Champion's first direction on Broadway.

°CAFÉ CROWN (April 17, 1964; Martin Beck Theatre; 3 performances). *Director:* Jerome Eskow; *Composer:* Albert Hague; *Lyricist:* Marty Brill; *Librettist:* Hy Kraft; *Choreographer:* Ronald Field. The musical is set in and around the Café Crown on Second Avenue and 12th Street in New York City in the early 1930s, where the cafe's busboy (Sam Levene) dreams of a future in the theatre.

CALL ME MADAM (October 12, 1950; Imperial Theatre; 644 performances)

Production credits: *Producer:* Leland Hayward; *Director:* George Abbott; *Composer/Lyricist:* Irving Berlin; *Librettists:* Howard Lindsay and Russel Crouse; *Choreographer:* Jerome Robbins

Original cast: Mrs. Sally Adams (Ethel Merman), Secretary of State (Jeffrey Lumb), Supreme Court Justice and Grand Duke Otto (Owen Coll), Congressman Wilkins (Pat Harrington), Henry Gibson (William David), Kenneth Gibson (Russell Nype), Senator Gallagher (Ralph Chambers), Secretary to Mrs. Adams (Jeanne Bal), Butler (William Hail), Senator Brockbank (Jay Velie), Cosmo Constantine (Paul Lukas), Pemberton Maxwell (Alan Hewitt), Clerk (Stowe Phelps), Hugo Tantinnin (E. A. Krumschmidt), Sebastian Sebastian (Henry Lascoe), Princess Maria (Galina Talva), Court Chamberlain (William David), Maid (Lily Paget), Grand Duchess Sophie (Lilia Skala)

Synopsis: Mrs. Sally Adams is totally without diplomatic skills, but that does not stop her from becoming the new ambassador to Lichtenburg. She gets the job due to her one area of expertise—she is a dazzling society hostess. But when Sally arrives to take over duties in Lichtenburg, she immediately falls for Cosmo, the prime minister, while her assistant, Kenneth, becomes enchanted with Princess Maria; however, opposing factors doom both love affairs, and life becomes unbearable for all. In the end, the lovers win out in both cases.

Songs: "Mrs. Sally Adams"; "The Hostess with the Mostest on the Ball"; "Washington Square Dance"; "Lichtenburg"; "Can You Use Any Money Today?"; "Marrying for Love"; "The Ocarina"; "It's a Lovely Day Today"; "The Best Thing for You Would Be Me"; "Something to Dance About"; "Once a Time Today"; "They Like Ike"; "You're Just in Love"

Tony Awards: Best Actress in a Musical (Merman), Best Featured Actor in a Musical (Nype), Best Original Score (Berlin), Best Stage Technician (Pete Feller)

Comments: Reviewers called Ethel Merman a "blowsy delight." This was Irving Berlin's last Broadway success, honoring the famous hostess of Washington, D.C., Pearl Mesta, who was appointed ambassador to Luxembourg by President Harry S Truman. Elaine Stritch was Merman's standby. The 1953 movie version featured Merman, along with Donald O'Connor, Vera-Ellen, George Sanders, and Walter Slezak.

CAMELOT (December 3, 1960; Majestic Theatre; 873 performances)

Production credits: *Producers:* Alan Jay Lerner, Frederick Loewe, and Moss Hart; *Director:* Moss Hart; *Composer:* Frederick Loewe; *Lyricist/ Librettist:* Alan Jay Lerner; *Choreographer:* Hanya Holm; *Original source:* Based on the novel *The Once and Future King* by T. H. White

Original cast: Sir Dinadan (John Cullum), Sir Lionel (Bruce Yarnell), Sir Gwilliam (Jack Dabdoub), Merlyn (David Hurst), Arthur (Richard Burton), Guenevere (Julie Andrews), Nimue (Marjorie Smith), Pages (Leland Mayforth and Peter De Vise), Lancelot Du Lac (Robert Goulet),

Dap (Michael Clarke-Laurence), King Pellinore (Robert Coote), Clarius (Richard Kuch), Lady Anne (Christina Gillespie), Lady Sybil (Leesa Troy), Sir Sagramore (James Gannon), Herald (John Starkweather), Sir Castor of Cornwall (Frank Bouley), Lady Catherine (Virginia Allen), Mordred (Roddy McDowall), Morgan Le Fey (M'el Dowd), Sir Ozanna (Michael Kermoyan), Scottish Knight (Paul Huddleston), Tom (Robin Stewart)

Synopsis: In this love triangle, Arthur and Guenevere are nervous about their forthcoming marriage, and once they are married, Lancelot falls in love with her. He goes away but returns to court her secretly. Mordred discovers the two and exposes the romance. When the lovers flee to France, Arthur follows and confronts them just before he is going into battle.

Songs: "I Wonder What the King Is Doing Tonight?"; "The Simple Joys of Maidenhood"; "Camelot"; "The Lusty Month of May"; "Then You May Take Me to the Fair"; "How to Handle a Woman"; "Before I Gaze at You Again"; "If Ever I Would Leave You"; "The Seven Deadly Virtues"; "The Persuasion"; "Fie on Goodness!"; "I Loved You Once in Silence"; "Guenevere"

Tony Awards: Best Actor in a Musical (Burton), Best Scenic Design, Best Costume Design, Best Conductor and Musical Director. **Tony nomination:** Best Actress in a Musical (Andrews)

Comments: Director Moss Hart suffered a heart attack before the show opened. The costs of production had risen to more than $500,000 even before it got to Broadway. The musical opened to mixed reviews despite the attraction of Alan Jay Lerner and Frederick Loewe, Julie Andrews, and Richard Burton. Some critics thought the production suffered because it was too often compared to *My Fair Lady*.

CAN-CAN (May 7, 1953; Shubert Theatre; 892 performances)

Production credits: *Producers:* Cy Feurer and Ernest Martin; *Director/ Librettist:* Abe Burrows; *Composer/Lyricist:* Cole Porter; *Choreographer:* Michael Kidd

Original cast: Bailiff (David Collyer), Registrar and Doctor (Michael Cavallaro), Judge Paul Barriere (C. K. Alexander), Court President (David Thomas), Judge Aristide Forestier (Peter Cookson), Claudine (Gwen Verdon), Gabrielle (Mary Anne Cohan), Marie (Beverly Purvin), Celestine (Jean Kraemer), Hilaire Jussac (Erik Rhodes), Boris Adzinidzinadze (Hans Conried), Hercule (Robert Penn), Theophile (Phil Leeds), Etienne (Richard Purdy), Waiter (Clarence Hoffman), La Mome Pistache (Lilo), Second Waiter and Prosecutor (Ferdinand Hilt), Café Waiter (Jon Silo), Café Customer (Joe Cusanelli), Jailer (Deedee Wood), Model (Pat Turner), Mimi (Dania Krupska), Policeman and Second (Arthur Rubin)

Synopsis: Two stories take place in this production: In one, a judge, Aristide Forestier, investigates outrageous dancing at a café in Montmartre and falls in love with the café's owner, La Mome Pistache. After that, he helps to get the dance, the can-can, legalized. In the other story, Claudine, one of the café dancers, has two suitors, Boris and Hilaire, who end up fighting a duel on a rooftop.

Songs: "Maidens Typical of France"; "Never Give Anything Away"; "C'Est Magnifique"; "Quadrille"; "Come Along with Me"; "Live and Let Live"; "I Am in Love"; "If You Loved Me Truly"; "Montmartre"; "Never, Never Be an Artist"; "It's All Right with Me"; "Every Man Is a Stupid Man"; "The Apaches"; "I Love Paris"; "Can-Can"

Tony Awards: Best Featured Actress in a Musical (Verdon), Best Choreographer (Kidd)

Comments: Cole Porter's score was at first coolly received but eventually became a main reason for the long run. The other reason was Gwen Verdon, whose dancing was spectacular. After her opening night performance of an Apache number, the audience would not let the show continue until she came out for an extra bow.

CARMEN JONES (December 2, 1943; Broadway Theatre; 502 performances)

Production credits: *Producer:* Billy Rose; *Director:* Charles Friedman; *Composer:* Georges Bizet; *Lyricist/Librettist:* Oscar Hammerstein II; *Choreographer:* Eugene Loring; *Original source:* Based on Meilhac and Halevy's adaptation of *Carmen*

Original cast: Carmen (Muriel Smith and Muriel Rahn, alternating), Joe (Luther Saxon and Napoleon Reed, alternating), Cindy Lou (Carlotta Franzell and Elton J. Warren, alternating), Husky Miller (Glen Bryant), Frankie (June Hawkins), Remo the Drummer (Cosy Cole). Nearly all the original cast was new to the theatre.

Synopsis: With an all-black cast, the story of the volatile Carmen is modernized. Carmen Jones, a parachute maker, is interested in Joe, an air force man, who in turn is in love with sweet Cindy Lou, but Carmen charms and seduces him. However, while waiting for Joe to be released from military prison, she gets involved with boxer Husky Miller. Carmen gives in to the luxurious life he can offer her and abandons Joe. When Joe returns to try to convince her to come back to him, she spurns him and he kills her.

Songs: "Lift 'Em Up and Put 'Em Down"; "Dat's Love"; "You Talk Just Like My Maw"; "Dere's a Cafe on de Corner"; "Beat Out Dat Rhythm on a Drum"; "Stan' Up and Fight"; "Whizzin' Away along de Track"; "Dis Flower"; "De Cards Don't Lie"; "My Joe"; "Dat's Our Man"

Comments: Because the original story, although modernized, and score were retained, the lead singers had to alternate because the roles were so strenuous. The 1954 film version starred Dorothy Dandridge in the lead role. She became the first African American actress nominated for an Oscar.

CARNIVAL (April 13, 1961; Imperial Theatre; 719 performances)
   Production credits: *Producer:* David Merrick; *Director/Choreographer:* Gower Champion; *Composer/Lyricist:* Bob Merrill; *Librettist:* Michael Stewart; *Original source:* Based on material by Helen Deutsch
   Original cast: Jacquot (Pierre Olaf), Mr. Schlegel (Henry Lascoe), Roustabouts (George Marcy, Tony Gomez, Johnny Nola, and Buff Shurr), Cyclist (Bob Murray), Miguelito (George Marcy), Dog Trainer (Paul Sydell), Wardrobe Mistress (Carvel Carter), Harem Girls (Nicole Barth, Iva March, and Beti Seay), Bear Girl (Jennifer Billingsley), Princess Olga (Luba Lisa), Band (C. B. Bernard and Peter Lombard), Stilt Walker (Dean Crane), Jugglers (Martin Brothers), clowns (Bob Dixon and Harry Lee Rogers), Strongman (Pat Tolson), Gladys Zuwicki (Mary Ann Niles), Gloria Zuwicki (Christine Bartel), Gypsy (Christine Bartel), Marco the Magnificent (James Mitchell), Incomparable Rosalie (Kaye Ballard), Greta Schlegel (June Meshonek), Lili (Anna Maria Alberghetti), Paul Berthalet (Jerry Orbach), Aerialist (Dean Crane), Dr. Glass (Igors Gavon)
   Synopsis: Based on the film *Lili* but with a new score, this is the story of an orphan who is taken in by the folk at a small carnival in Europe. Lili fails at several jobs with the run-down troupe; however, she becomes the center of a rivalry between Marco the Magnificent, the troupe's magician, and Paul Berthalet, a puppeteer with an injured leg. Marco seems to be winning her affections, but Paul communicates through his charming puppets. Lili finally joins the puppet act, and in the end she dramatically rejects the beguiling Marco and exits with Paul, the one who is true.
   Songs: "Direct from Vienna"; "A Very Nice Man"; "Fairyland"; "I've Got to Find a Reason"; "Mira"; "Sword, Rose, and Cape"; "Humming"; "Yes, My Heart"; "Everybody Likes You"; "Magic, Magic"; "Tanz Mit Mir"; "Carnival Ballet"; "Yum Ticky"; "The Rich"; "Beautiful Candy"; "Her Face"; "Grand Imperial Cirque de Paris"; "I Hate Him"; "Always, Always You"; "She's My Love"
   Tony Awards: Best Actress in a Musical (Alberghetti), Best Scenic Design of a Musical (Will Steven Armstrong). **Tony nominations:** Best Musical, Best Author of a Musical, Best Featured Actor in a Musical (Olaf), Best Direction of a Musical, Best Producer of a Musical
   Comments: The two stars of the show were Anna Maria Alberghetti and Gower Champion's choreography.

°*CARNIVAL IN FLANDERS* (September 8, 1953; New Century Theatre; 6 performances). *Director:* Preston Sturges; *Composer:* Jimmy Van Heusen; *Lyricist:* Johnny Burke; *Librettist:* Preston Sturges; *Choreographer:* Helen Tamiris. Based on a 1934 French comedy and set in seventeenth-century Flanders, starring John Raitt and Dolores Gray, the show concerns a Spanish duke and his entourage descending upon a small community. In the shortest-lived Tony-honored performance ever, Gray won the Tony for Best Actress in a Musical.

CAROUSEL (April 19, 1945; Majestic Theatre; 890 performances)

Production credits: *Producer:* Theatre Guild; *Director:* Rouben Mamoulian; *Composer:* Richard Rodgers; *Lyricist/Librettist:* Oscar Hammerstein II; *Choreographer:* Agnes de Mille; *Original source:* Based on Ferenc Molnar's play *Lilion*, adapted by Benjamin F. Glazer

Original cast: Carrie Pipperidge (Margot Moser), Julie Jordan (Iva Withers), Mrs. Mullin (Jean Casto), Billy Bigelow (John Raitt), Nettie Fowler (Christine Johnson), Louise (Bambi Linn), Jigger Craigin (Murvyn Vye), Enoch Snow (Eric Mattson), Carrie (Jean Darling)

Synopsis: In the late 1800s, rowdy carnival barker Billy Bigelow wants to meet the lovely Julie Jordan but proves to be unexpectedly shy. He vows to change for the better, and they are married in June; however, when they are expecting a child, Billy and his evil friend Jigger stage a holdup to get money. Billy kills himself rather than be caught. He is allowed to return to earth and redeem himself and see his now grown daughter, Louise. When she refuses to accept a star he has stolen, he is angry and slaps her. For that, he returns to purgatory, but he knows she and Julie have a good life without him.

Songs: "You're a Queer One, Julie Jordan"; "When I Marry Mister Snow"; "If I Loved You"; "June Is Bustin' Out All Over"; "When the Children Are Asleep"; "Blow High, Blow Low"; "This Was a Real Nice Clambake"; "Geraniums in the Winder"; "What's the Use of Wond'rin"; "You'll Never Walk Alone"; "The Highest Judge of All"

Comments: This production was said to be the most ambitious and successful score ever written by Richard Rodgers. Instead of an overture, the show opened with a dance-pantomine set to the marvelous "Carousel Waltz," originally written for Paul Whiteman's jazz band but never performed by him. In this most musical musical, "If I Loved You," sung by Billy, runs nearly ten minutes. The 1956 movie version starred Gordon MacRae and Shirley Jones.

°*THE CONQUERING HERO* (January 16, 1961; ANTA Theatre; 8 performances). *Director:* Albert Marre; *Composer:* Moose Charlap; *Lyricist:* Norman Gimbel; *Librettist:* Larry Gelbart; *Choreographer:* Todd Bolender.

The timeliness of a man mistaken as a World War II hero (Tom Poston) was lost on 1961 audiences. There was much trouble in this production before opening night, including the fact that Bob Fosse was replaced as both director and choreographer.

°*COPPER AND BRASS* (October 17, 1957; Martin Beck Theatre; 36 performances). *Director:* Marc Daniels; *Composer:* David Baker; *Lyricist:* David Craig; *Librettists:* Ellen Violet and David Craig; *Choreographer:* Anna Sokolow. Nancy Walker was unable to bring to life this musical story of Katey O'Shea, a somewhat scatterbrained policewoman in New York City who constantly gets everything mixed up. Critics felt that one of Walker's first-act numbers correctly caught the tenor of the show; it was entitled "I Need All the Help I Can Get."

°*COURTIN' TIME* (June 14, 1951; National Theatre; 37 performances). *Director:* Alfred Drake; *Composers:* Don Walker and Jack Lawrence; *Lyricists:* Jack Lawrence and Don Walker; *Librettist:* William Roos; *Choreographer:* George Balanchine. Eden Phillpotts's play *The Farmer's Wife*, originally about a young farming couple in rural Nebraska, is set to music with a Maine 1898 setting. Trouble plagued the production; Lloyd Nolan was replaced by director Alfred Drake, who was later replaced by Joe E. Brown.

DAMN YANKEES (May 5, 1955; 46th Street Theatre; 1,019 performances)
   Production credits: *Producers:* Frederick Brisson, Robert E. Griffith, and Harold S. Prince, in association with Albert B. Taylor; *Director:* George Abbott; *Composers/Lyricists:* Richard Adler and Jerry Ross; *Librettists:* George Abbott and Douglas Wallop; *Choreographer:* Bob Fosse; *Original source:* Adapted from Wallop's book *The Year the Yankees Lost the Pennant*
   Original cast: Meg (Shannon Bolin), Joe Boyd (Robert Shafer), Applegate (Ray Walston), Sister (Jean Stapleton), Joe Hardy (Stephen Douglass), Henry (Al Lanti), Sohovik (Eddie Phillips), Smokey (Nathaniel Frey), Vernon (Albert Linville),Van Buren (Russ Brown), Rocky (Jimmie Komack), Gloria (Rae Allen), Lynch (Del Horstmann), Welch (Richard Bishop), Lola (Gwen Verdon), Miss Weston (Janie Janvier)
   Synopsis: This is a new approach to the Faustian legend about selling one's soul to the devil. Applegate (the devil) appears to Joe Boyd to accept his soul in exchange for making the Washington Senators champions of the baseball world. Suddenly, average Joe is athlete Joe Hardy. A winning streak follows, but Joe misses his wife. His wife, however, does not recognize him as a young man. Thinking that Joe might not go through with the plan to sell his soul, Applegate sends Lola to Joe as a warning. Instead, Joe goes home to his wife and watches the Senators lose again.

Songs: "Six Months Out of Every Year"; "Goodbye, Old Girl"; "Heart"; "Shoeless Joe from Hannibal, Mo"; "A Man Doesn't Know"; "A Little Brains"; "Whatever Lola Wants"; "Who's Got the Pain?"; "The Game"; "Near to You"; "Those Were the Good Old Days"; "Two Lost Souls"

Tony Awards: Best Musical, Best Actor in a Musical (Walston), Best Actress in a Musical (Verdon), Best Featured Actor in a Musical (Brown), Best Choreography (Fosse), Best Conductor and Musical Director (Hal Hastings), Best Stage Technician (Harry Green). **Tony nominations:** Best Actor in a Musical (Douglass), Best Featured Actress in a Musical (Allen)

Comments: Jerry Ross died shortly after the opening, and Richard Adler left the Broadway scene for years. During tryouts, Gwen Verdon as Lola did not appear until well into the first act. It was soon noted that whenever she was on, audience interest visibly increased; therefore, by the time the show hit Broadway, Lola appeared on stage much earlier in the production.

THE DAY BEFORE SPRING (November 22, 1945; National Theatre; 167 performances)

Production credits: *Producer:* John C. Wilson; *Director:* Edward Padula; *Composer:* Frederick Loewe; *Lyricist/Librettist:* Alan Jay Lerner; *Choreographer:* Anthony Tudor

Original cast: Lucille (Bette Anderson), Peter Townsend (John Archer), May Tompkins (Lucille Benson), Voltaire (Paul Best), Harry Scott (Robert Field), Leonore (Lucille Floetman), Plato (Ralph Glover), Susan (Ariouine Goodjohn), Gerald Barker (Tom Helmore), Alex Maitland (Bill Johnson), Freud (Hermann Leopoldi), Marjorie (Estelle Loring), Katherine Townsend (Irene Manning), Eddie Warren (Dwight Marfield), Christopher Randolph (Patricia Marshall), Joe McDonald (Don Mayo), Anne (Betty Jean Smythe)

Synopsis: Katherine and Peter Townsend go back to Harrison University for their tenth reunion, where Katherine is reunited with Alex Maitland, with whom she almost eloped ten years before. Stirred by a novel that he has written about her, Katherine decides to leave her husband and run away with Maitland again. This time, as before, the car breaks down. In the end, all is forgiven—at least partly.

Songs: "The Day Before Spring"; "God's Green World"; "You Haven't Changed at All"; "My Love Is a Married Man"; "Friends to the End"; "A Jug of Wine"; "I Love You This Morning"; "Where's My Wife?"; "This Is My Holiday"

Comments: Alan Jay Lerner and Frederick Loewe were reunited in this production. The cast and music were good, but the story—which included a ballet for each of the main characters—proved to be tedious on stage. The show was revived by the York Theatre Company in New York City in 2007 and included material missing from the production since it closed in 1946.

DESTRY RIDES AGAIN (April 23, 1959; Imperial Theatre; 473 performances)

Production credits: *Producers:* David Merrick, in association with Max Brown; *Director/Choreographer:* Michael Kidd; *Composer/Lyricist:* Howard Rome; *Librettist:* Leonard Gershe

Original cast: Bartender and Bailey (Ray Mason), Frenchy (Dolores Gray), Wash (Jack Prince), Sheriff Keogh (Oran Osburn), Kent's Gang (Marc Breaux, Swen Swenson, and George Reeder), Mayor Slade (Don McHenry), Claggett (Don Crabtree), Kent (Scott Brady), Chloe (Libi Staiger), Rose Lovejoy (Elizabeth Watts), Jack Tyndall (Nolan Van Way), Destry (Andy Griffith), Stage Driver (Chad Block), Ming Li (Reiko Sato), Mrs. Claggett (May Muth), Clara (Rosetta LeNoire), Dimples (Sharon Shore)

Synopsis: Adapted from a 1939 Marlene Dietrich and James Stewart film, the musical is set in the Wild West at the turn of the century. Destry is hired to stop a murderous gang that is terrorizing the town, but he is actually a shy sort against violence. Kent is the leader of the gang, and he unsuccessfully tries to get his girlfriend, Frenchy, to seduce Destry. In a gun battle that he is forced to enter, Destry must resort to violence. Frenchy helps save his life. With the gang gone, peace returns to the town, and Destry and Frenchy realize that they are in love.

Songs: "Bottleneck"; "Ladies"; "Hoop-de-Dingle"; "Tomorrow Morning"; "Ballad of the Gun"; "I Know Your Kind"; "I Hate Him"; "Paradise Alley"; "Anyone Would Love You"; "Once Knew a Fella"; "Every Once in a While"; "Fair Warning"; "Are you Ready, Gyp Watson?"; "Not Guilty"; "Only Time Will Tell"; "Respectability"; "That Ring on the Finger"; "I Say Hello"

Tony Award: Best Choreography. **Tony nominations:** Best Direction of a Musical (Kidd), Best Actor in a Musical (Griffith), Best Actress in a Musical (Gray)

Comments: Although it ran more than a year, the show was a financial failure; however, reviewers praised Kidd's choreography, especially the number where the dancers fill the air with slashing bullwhips.

DO I HEAR A WALTZ? (March 18, 1965; 46th Street Theatre; 220 performances)

Production credits: *Producer:* Richard Rodgers; *Director:* John Dexter; *Composer:* Richard Rodgers; *Lyricist:* Steven Sondheim; *Librettist:* Arthur

Laurents; *Choreographer:* Herbert Ross; *Original source:* Based on Arthur Laurents's play *The Time of the Cuckoo*

Original cast: Leona Samish (Elizabeth Allen), Mauro (Christopher Votos), Signora Fioria (Carol Bruce), Eddie Yaeger (Stuart Damon), Mrs. McIllhenny (Julienne Marie), Mr. McIllhenny (Jack Manning), Giovanna (Fleury D'Antonakis), Vito (James Dybas), Renato di Rossi (Sergio Franchi), Man on Bridge (Steve Jacobs), Mrs. Victoria Haslam (Helon Blount)

Synopsis: Lonely and alone in Venice, Leona Samish has convinced herself that she will hear a waltz in the air when the right man comes along. Then she meets romantic shopowner Renato and is enchanted when he gives her a necklace, but enchantment turns to sorrow when she later learns he is married. To make matters worse, she discovers that he has not paid for the necklace, which she is now obligated to do. And there is one more final blow, when Leona discovers that the romantic-appearing Renato is not only a liar, but he has also been given a commission on the sale of the necklace.

Songs: "Someone Woke Up"; "This Week Americans"; "What Do We Do? We Fly!"; "Someone Like You"; "Bargaining"; "Here We Are Again"; "Thinking"; "No Understand"; "Take the Moment"; "Moon in My Window"; "We're Gonna Be All Right"; "Do I Hear a Waltz?"; "Stay"; "Perfectly Lovely Couple"; "Thank You So Much"

Tony nominations: Best Actress in a Musical (Allen), Best Composer and Lyricist, Best Scenic Design (Beni Montresor)

Comments: This was the shortest run of a Richard Rodgers musical during the era, due mainly to a competent but not outstanding score and the absence of a big star.

°*DONNYBROOK!* (May 18, 1961; 46th Street Theatre; 68 performances). *Director/Choreographer:* Jack Cole; *Composer/Lyricist:* Johnny Burke; *Librettist:* Robert E. McEnroe; *Original source:* Based on the film *The Quiet Man* (1952). Art Lund and Joan Fagan played the roles created by John Wayne and Maureen O'Hara in this story of a prizefighter who killed a man in the ring in the United States and returns to Ireland with a vow never to fight again. But he woos a tempestuous lass who wants a man who will stand up and fight for her.

DO RE MI (December 26, 1960; St. James Theatre; 400 performances)

Production credits: *Producer:* David Merrick; *Director:* Garson Kanin; *Composer:* Jule Styne; *Lyricists:* Betty Comden and Adolph Green; *Librettist:* Garson Kanin; *Choreographers:* Marc Breaux and Dee Dee Wood

Original cast: Hubert Cram (Phil Silvers), Kay Cram (Nancy Walker), Fatso O'Rear (George Mathews), John Henry Wheeler (John Reardon),

Brains Berman (David Burns), Tilda Mullen (Nancy Dussault), Skin Demopoulos (George Givot), Moe Shtarker (Al Lewis)

Synopsis: Hubert and Kay Cram live the high life anytime one of his hairbrain schemes pays off, but this time they feel they have really run into success. Hubert decides to get into the jukebox business, even though such a move means he will have to associate with the mob. Although the scheme pays off and they are soon very wealthy, Kay begins to long for the good old days. Finally, Hubert is forced out of the jukebox business, and things return to normal, until his next big idea.

Songs: "Adventure"; "All of My Life"; "All You Need Is a Quarter"; "Ambition"; "Asking for You"; "Cry Like the Wind"; "Fireworks"; "He's a V.I.P."; "I Know about Love"; "It's Legitimate"; "The Juke Box Hop"; "The Late, Late Show"; "Make Someone Happy"; "Success"; "Take a Job"; "V.I.P."; "Waiting, Waiting"; "What's New at the Zoo?"; "Who Is Mister Big?"

Tony nominations: Best Musical, Best Actor in a Musical (Silvers), Best Actress in a Musical (Walker), Best Featured Actress in a Musical (Dussault), Best Direction of a Musical (Kanin)

Comments: This was another show with a good run that ended in the loss column. The strength of the production rested with its two star comics.

°DRAT! THE CAT! (October 10, 1965; Martin Beck Theatre; 8 performances). *Director/Choreographer:* Joe Layton; *Composer:* Milton Schafer; *Lyricist/Librettist:* Ira Levin. The story revolves around a love affair between a policeman and a heiress in 1890s New York society, where a cat burglar is plundering the rich. Patrolman Bob Purefoy vows to uphold the law as he guards the social event of the season; however, he falls in love with the daughter of the rich couple who is throwing the party, and she vows to help him catch the burglar.

Tony nomination: Best Scenic Design

°DREAM WITH MUSIC (May 18, 1944; Majestic Theatre; 28 performances). *Director:* Richard Kollmar; *Composer:* Clay Warnick; *Lyricist/Librettist:* Edward Eager; *Choreographer:* George Ballanchine. Another Arabian Nights theme, this concerns a soap-opera author (Vera Zorina) with settings in her apartment, in a palace in Baghdad, on a magic carpet in the clouds, China, and in the palace of Aladdin, who is played by Ronald Graham.

°THE DUCHESS MISBEHAVES (February 13, 1946; Adelphi Theatre; 5 performances). *Director:* Martin Manulis; *Composer:* Frank Black; *Lyricist/Librettist:* Gladys Shelley; *Choreographer:* George Tapps. Jackie Gleason

thought so little of the show that he left during tryouts. It was the only Broadway musical for Shelley, who was a favorite of New York nightclub singers.

FADE OUT—FADE IN (May 26, 1964; Mark Hellinger Theatre; 271 performances)

Production credits: *Producers:* Lester Osterman and Jule Styne; *Director:* George Abbott; *Composer:* Jule Styne; *Lyricists/Librettists:* Betty Comden and Adolph Green; *Choreographer:* Ernest Flatt

Original cast: Bryon Prong (Jack Cassidy), Woman (Diana Eden), Man and Rex (Darrell J. Askey), Helga Sixtrees (Judy Cassmore), Pops (Frank Tweddell), Rosco (Bob Neukum), Billy Vespers (Glenn Kezer), Lyman and Frank Governor (John Dorrin), Hope Springfield (Carol Burnett), Chauffeur (William Louther), First Girl (Wendy Taylor), Ralph Governor (Mitchell Jason), Rudolph Governor (Dick Patterson), George Governor (Howard Kahl), Harold Governor (Gene Varrone), Arnold Governor (Stephen Elmore), Myra May Melrose (Virginia Payne), Seamstress (Diane Arnold), Miss Mallory (Jo Tract), Custer Corkley (Dan Resin), Approval (Smaxie), Photographer (Sean Allan), Max Welch (Richard Frisch), Lou Williams (Tiger Haynes), Dora Dailey (Aileen Poe), Lionel Z. Governor (Lou Jacobi), Dr. Anton Traurig (Reuben Singer), Gloria Curie (Tina Louise), Madame Barrymore (Penny Egelston)

Synopsis: In the 1930s, Hope Springfield, a chorus girl, is accidentally given a starring part in a motion picture. When the mistake is discovered, the film is put on the shelf; however, Rudolf Governor, who is the nephew of the studio head, sees the film and arranges a preview. Unexpectedly, the movie is successful. Now, Hope becomes a star, and she and Rudolf become a team.

Songs: "The Thirties"; "It's Good to Be Back Home"; "Fear"; "Call Me Savage"; "The Usher from the Mezzanine"; "I'm with You"; "My Fortune Is My Face"; "Lila Tremaine"; "Go Home Train"; "Close Harmony"; "You Mustn't Be Discouraged"; "The Dangerous Age"; "L. Z. in Quest of His Youth"; "The Fiddler and the Fighter"; "Fade Out—Fade In"

Tony nomination: Best Featured Actor in a Musical (Cassidy)

Comments: Carol Burnett suffered from neck and back problems during the run, so the show had to close for a three-month period since no one else could be found to replace her.

*****A FAMILY AFFAIR** (January 27, 1962; Billy Rose Theatre; 84 performances). *Director:* Harold Prince; *Composer:* John Kander; *Lyricists:* James Goldman and John Kander; *Librettists:* James Golden and William Golden; *Choreographer:* John Butler. Rita Gardner and Larry Kert starred as a young couple living in Chicago. Their chaotic marriage plans set off World War III among their extended family. The musical ends with what some critics referred to as the looniest wedding of the year.

FANNY (November 4, 1954; Majestic Theatre; 888 performances)

Production credits: *Producers:* David Merrick and Joshua Logan; *Director:* Joshua Logan; *Composer/Lyricist:* Harold Rome; *Librettists:* S. N. Behrman and Joshua Logan; *Choreographer:* Helen Tamiris; *Original source:* Based on the trilogy of Marcel Pagnoli

Original cast: The Admiral (Gerald Price), First Sailor (Tom Gleason), Sailor (Herb Banke), Marius (Steve Wiland), Sailmaker (Jack Washburn), Honorine (Edna Preston), Fanny (Florence Henderson), Claudette and Claudine (Tani Seitz and Dran Seitz), Charles (Wally Strauss), Nanette (Norma Doggett), Mimi (Carolyn Maye), Marie (Ellen Matthews), Michellette (Jane House), Panisse (Walter Slezak), Escartifigue (Alan Carney), M. Brun (Don McHenry), Cesar (Ezio Pinza), Nun (Ruth Schumacher), Cesario (Lloyd Reese)

Synopsis: Marius dreams of going off to sea, but his father, Cesar, who owns a waterfront café in Marseilles, wants him to marry Fanny. Instead, Marius defies his father and leaves behind a pregnant and still-unwed Fanny. She marries Panisse, a kindly old sailmaker. When Marius returns and looks for Fanny, Cesar steps in to prevent a rekindling of the romance to spare the feelings of Panisse. Marius leaves once more and returns several years later. When the boy born to Fanny reaches his twelfth birthday, Panisse, who is about to die, tells Fanny to wed Marius so that the boy will have a father.

Songs: "Octopus Song"; "Restless Heart"; "Never Too Late for Love"; "Cold Cream Jar Song"; "Does He Know?"; "Welcome Home"; "I Like You"; "I Have to Tell You"; "Fanny"; "The Sailing"; "Oysters, Cockles, and Mussels"; "Panisse and Son"; "Birthday Song"; "To My Wife"; "The Thought of You"; "Love Is a Very Light Thing"; "Other Hands, Other Hearts"; "Be Kind to Your Parents"

Tony Award: Best Actor in a Musical (Slezak)

Comments: Reviewers called this one of Slezak's best roles.

FIDDLER ON THE ROOF (September 22, 1964; Imperial Theatre; 3,242 performances)

Production credits: *Producer:* Harold Prince; *Director/Choreographer:* Jerome Robbins; *Composer:* Jerry Bock; *Lyricist:* Sheldon Harnick; *Original source:* Based on a book by Joseph Stein adapted from Sholom Aleicheim's stories

Original cast: Tevye (Zero Mostel), Golde (Maria Karnilova), Tzeitel (Joanna Merlin), Hodel (Julia Migenes), Chava (Tanya Everett), Shprintze (Marilyn Rogers), Bielke (Linda Ross), Yente (Beatrice Arthur), Motel (Austin Pendleton), Perchik (Bert Convy), Lazar (Michael Granger), Mordcha (Zvee Scooler), Rabbi (Gluck Sandor), Mendel (Leonard Frey), Avram (Paul Lipson), Nachum (Maurice Edwards), Grandma Tzeitel (Sue Babel), Constable (Joseph Sullivan), Fyedka (Joe Ponazecki), Shandel (Helen Verbit)

Synopsis: It is 1905 in a poor Jewish community in a Russian village. Dairyman Tevye has five daughters, and he and his wife have asked the village matchmaker to find a husband for the eldest. When Lazar asks for Tzeitel's hand, the problem seems to be solved, except that Tzeitel does not want him. She loves Motel, the tailor. Tevye decides not to object, but the wedding is postponed because of a pogrom. Then the second daughter, Hodel, falls in love with a radical, Perchik. He is shipped to Siberia, and Hodel follows him. Unhappiest of all for Tevye, his third daughter decides to marry a Christian. This time he opposes the marriage, so Chava and Fyedka elope. When Tevye learns that the Jews must leave his village for the United States, he joins the exodus.

Songs: "Tradition"; "Matchmaker, Matchmaker"; "If I Were a Rich Man"; "Sabbath Prayer"; "To Life"; "Miracle of Miracles"; "The Tailor"; "Motel Kamzoil"; "Sunrise, Sunset"; "Now I Have Everything"; "Do You Love Me?"; "I Just Heard"; "Far from the Home I Love"; "Anatevka"

Tony Awards: Best Musical, Best Actor in a Musical (Mostel), Best Featured Actress in a Musical (Karnilova), Best Composer and Lyricist (Bock and Harnick), Best Author (Stein), Best Direction of a Musical, Best Producer of a Musical, Best Choreography, Best Costume Design (Patricia Zipprodt). **Tony nomination:** Best Scenic Design (Boris Aronson).

Comments: This was the season's biggest hit, and it is often called the last great masterwork of the era. The show closed on July 2, 1972, the longest run of the Golden Age.

FINIAN'S RAINBOW (January 10, 1947; 46th Street Theatre; 725 performances)

Production credits: *Producers:* Lee Sabinson and William R. Katzell; *Director:* Bretaigne Windust; *Composer:* Burton Lane; *Lyricist:* E. Y. Harburg; *Librettists:* E. Y. Harburg and Fred Saidy; *Choreographer:* Michael Kidd

Original cast: Finian McLonergan (Albert Sharpe), Sharon McLonergan (Ella Logan), Og (David Wayne), Senator Billboard Rawkins (Robert Pitkin), Woody Mahoney (Donald Richards)

Synopsis: Finian McLonergan, who says he is from Glocca Morra, has stolen a crock of gold from the leprechauns and comes to the United States to the town of Rainbow Valley. He and his daughter, Sharon, intend to plant the gold at Fort Knox in the mistaken belief that it will grow and multiply. At Rainbow Valley, Woody Mahoney falls for Sharon, as does the leprechaun Og, who tries to stir up trouble until he realizes his love for her is hopeless. Woody discovers the same thing, and Finian and Sharon are free to wander once more.

Songs: "This Time of the Year"; "How Are Things in Glocca Morra?"; "If This Isn't Love"; "Look to the Rainbow"; "Old Devil Moon"; "Something Sort of Grandish"; "Necessity"; "When the Idle Poor Become the Idle Rich"; "The Begat"; "When I'm Not Near the Girl I Love"; "That Great Come and Get It Day"

Tony Awards: Best Featured Actor in a Musical (Wayne; this was the first time this award was given), Best Choreography (Kidd), Best Conductor and Musical Director (Milton Rosenstock)

Comments: The critics loved everything about this musical, praising the score, with some saying it was the best musical of the season. It has been revived three times on Broadway, in 1955, 1960, and 1967. The 1968 film version starred Fred Astaire and Petula Clark.

FIORELLO! (November 23, 1959; Broadhurst Theatre; 795 performances)

Production credits: *Producers:* Robert E. Griffith and Harold S. Prince; *Director:* George Abbott; *Composer:* Jerry Bock; *Lyricist:* Sheldon Harnick; *Librettists:* Jerome Weidman and George Abbott; *Choreographer:* Peter Gennaro

Original cast: Announcer and Second Player (Del Horstmann); Fiorello (Tom Bosley), Neil (Bob Holiday), Morris (Nathaniel Frey), Mrs. Pomerantz (HelenVerbit), Mr. Lopez and Politician (H. F. Green), Mr. Zappatella (David Collyer), Dora (Pat Stanley), Marie (Patricia Wilson), Ben (Howard Da Silva), Ed Peterson and Frantic (Stanley Simmonds), Third Player and Commissioner (Michael Quinn), Fourth Player (Ron Husmann), Fifth Player and Tough Man (David London), Sixth Player (Julian Patrick), Seedy Man, Fourth Heckler, and Judge Carter (Joseph Toner), First Heckler (Bob Bernard), Second Heckler, Frankie Scarpini, and Second Man (Michael Scrittorale), Third Heckler (Jim Maher), Nina (Pat Turner), Floyd (Mark Dawson), Sophie (Lynn Ross), Thea (Ellen Hanley), Secretary and Florence (Mara Landi), Senator (Frederic Downs), Mitzi (Eileen Rogers), First Man (Scott Hunter)

Synopsis: The show, which took the Pulitzer Prize for Drama, features highlights in the career of Mayor Fiorello LaGuardia and opens with him reading comics to children over the radio during a newspaper strike in New York City. With warmth and humor, it tells the story of his rise to power as mayor of New York City in a time when the political machine known as Tammany Hall ruled the town with vice and corruption.

Songs: "On the Side of the Angels"; "Politics and Poker"; "Unfair"; "Marie's Law"; "The Name's LaGuardia"; "The Bum Won"; "I Love a Cop"; "Till Tomorrow"; "Home Again"; "When Did I Fall in Love"; "Gentleman Jimmy"; "Little Tin Box"; "The Very Next Man"

Tony Awards: Best Musical (tie with *The Sound of Music*), Best Featured Actor in a Musical (Bosley), Best Direction of a Musical. **Tony nominations:** Best Featured Actor in a Musical (Da Silva), Best Scenic Design (William and Jean Eckart), Best Choreography, Best Conductor and Musical Director (Hal Hastings)

°*FIRST IMPRESSIONS* (March 19, 1959; Alvin Theatre; 108 performances). *Director/Librettist:* Abe Burrows; *Composers/Lyricists:* Robert Goldman, Glenn Paxton, and George Weiss, with James Mitchell; *Choreographer:* Jonathan Lucas; *Original source:* Based on Jane Austin's book *Pride and Prejudice* in musical form. The story centers on the Bennett family in England in 1813. Mrs. Bennett's primary aim in life is to see that her daughters—all five of them—get married. She is pleased when the wealthy Fitzwilliam Darcy arrives in nearby Netherfield Hall, but an instant dislike springs up between daughter Elizabeth and Darcy.

°*FLAHOOLEY* (May 14, 1951; Broadhurst Theatre; 50 performances). *Director/Lyricist:* E. Y. Harburg; *Composer:* Sammy Fain; *Librettists:* E. Y. Harburg and Fred Saidy; *Choreographer:* Helen Tamiris. Barbara Cook headed the cast of a show, which also included Yma Sumac, which deals with sales from a laughing doll. The score sung by Cook and Jerome Courtland was pleasing, but reviewers were critical.

°*FLORA, THE RED MENACE* (May 11, 1965; Alvin Theatre; 87 performances). *Director:* George Abbott; *Composer:* John Kander; *Lyricist:* Fred Ebb; *Librettists:* George Abbott and Robert Russell; *Choreographer:* David Baker. Liza Minnelli was in the title role about a girl whose boyfriend persuades her to join the Communist party, even though it compromises her job. In the end, she must sacrifice one or the other for true happiness. Minnelli won the Tony for Best Actress in a Musical that year at age nineteen, the youngest to win until Frankie Michaels took the award (as featured actor in *Mame*) in 1966 at age eleven.

Tony Award: Best Actress in a Musical (Minelli)

FLOWER DRUM SONG (December 1, 1958; St. James Theatre; 600 performances)

Production credits: *Producers:* Richard Rodgers and Oscar Hammerstein II, in association with Joseph Fields; *Director:* Gene Kelly; *Composer:* Richard Rodgers; *Lyricist:* Oscar Hammerstein II; *Librettists:* Oscar Hammerstein II and Joseph Fields; *Choreographer:* Carol Haney; *Original source:* Based on the novel by C. Y. Lee

Original cast: Madam Liang (Juanita Hall), Liu Ma (Rose Quong), Wang San (Patrick Adiarte), Wang Ta (Ed Kenny), Wang Chi Yang (Keye Luke), Sammy Fong (Larry Blyden), Dr. Li (Conrad Yama), Mei Li (Miyoshi Umeki), Linda Low (Pat Suzuki), Mr. Lung (Harry Shaw Lowe), Helen Chao (Arabella Hong), Professor Cheng (Peter Chan), Frankie Wing (Jack Soo), Night Club Singer (Anita Ellis), Dr. Lu Fong (Chao Li), Madam Fong (Eileen Nakamura)

Synopsis: In the ways of their ancestors, Sammy is under contract to marry Mei Li; however, he is actually in love with Linda Low, a nightclub hostess. Sammy tries to arrange a marriage for Mei Li with Wang Ta, who Sammy thinks also likes Linda, but Wang Ta begins to cool toward Linda and is attracted to Mei Li, which causes the Three Family Association to declare that Sammy and Mei Li must marry right away. With no other choice, the wedding takes place, but it is Linda who is under the veil, and now Mei Li and Wang Ta are free to marry.

Songs: "You Are Beautiful"; "A Hundred Million Miracles"; "I Enjoy Being a Girl"; "I Am Going to Like It Here"; "Like a God"; "Chop Suey"; "Don't Marry Me"; "Grant Avenue"; "Love Look Away"; "Fan Tan Fannie"; "Gliding through My Memoree"; "The Other Generation"; "Sunday"

Tony Awards: Best Conductor and Musical Director (Salvatore Dell'Isola). **Tony nominations:** Best Musical, Best Actor in a Musical (Blyden), Best Actress in a Musical (Umeki), Best Costume Design, Best Choreography

Comments: The cast was excellent and the score humorous and sentimental. Although not considered a major work for Richard Rodgers and Oscar Hammerstein, the production nonetheless pleased audiences for two seasons.

FOLLOW THE GIRLS (April 8, 1944; New Century Theatre; 882 performances)

Production credits: *Producers:* David Wolper, in association with Albert Dorde; *Directors:* Harry Delmar and Fred Thompson; *Composers/Lyricists:* Phil Charig, Dan Shapiro, and Milton Pascal; *Librettists:* Guy Bolton, Fred Thompson, and Eddie Davis; *Choreographer:* Catherine Littlefield

Original cast: Bubbles La Marr (Gertrude Niesen), Goofy Gale (Jackie Gleason), Spud Doolittle (Tim Herbert), Sailor Val and Felix Charrel (Val Valentinoff), Dinky Riley (Buster West), Anna Viskinova (Irina Baranova), Petty Officer Banner (Lee Davis), Phyllis Brent (Toni Gilman), Peggy Baker (Dorothy Keller), Seaman Pennywhistle and Archie Smith (Frank Kreig), Captain Hawkins (Walter Long), Bob Monroe (Frank Parker), Officer Flanagan (George Spaulding), Catherine Pepburn (Geraldine Strock), Yokel Sailor (Bill Tabbert), Dan Daley (Robert Tower)

Synopsis: The thin story line concerns a striptease queen who becomes the star attraction at a servicemen's club in Great Neck, Long Island, New York, during World War II. As a contribution to the war effort, burlesque Bubbles La Marr takes over the servicemen's canteen, but her boyfriend, Goofy Gale, is 4-F, so he steals a Wave's uniform to gain entrance to the club.

Songs: "At the Spotlight Canteen"; "Where You Are"; "You Don't Dance"; "Strip Flips Hip"; "Thanks for Lousy Evening"; "You're Perf"; "Twelve O'Clock and All Is Well"; "Out for No Good"; "Follow the Girls"; "John Paul Jones"; "I Wanna Get Married"; "Today Will Be Yesterday Tomorrow"; "A Tree That Grows in Brooklyn"

Comments: This was one of the last Golden Age "rowdy" musicals that much resembled burlesque.

°**FOXY** (February 16, 1964; Ziegfeld Theatre; 72 performances). *Director:* Robert Lewis; *Composer:* Robert Emmett Dolan; *Lyricist:* Johnny Mercer; *Librettists:* Ian Hunter and Ring Lardner Jr.; *Choreographer:* Jack Cole. Best known for his movie portrayal of the Lion in *The Wizard of Oz*, Bert Lahr had the title role in this musical set in the days of the Klondike gold rush. It was his last Broadway appearance before his death. Despite poor reviews and a mediocre score, Lahr won the Tony for Best Actor in a Musical.

Tony Award: Best Actor in a Musical (Lahr). **Tony nomination:** Best Featured Actress in a Musical (Julienne Marie)

FUNNY GIRL (March 26, 1964; Winter Garden Theatre; 1,348 performances)

Production credits: *Producer:* Ray Stark; *Director:* Garson Kanin; *Composer:* Jule Styne; *Lyricist:* Bob Merrill; *Librettist:* Isobel Lennart; *Choreographer:* Carol Haney; *Original source:* Based on Isobel Lennart's original story

Original cast: Fanny Brice (Barbra Streisand), John (Robert Howard), Emma (Royce Wallace), Mrs. Brice (Kay Medford), Mrs. Strakosh (Jean Stapleton), Mrs. Meeker (Lydia S. Fredericks), Mrs. O'Malley (Joyce

O'Neil), Tom Keeney (Joseph Macaulay), Eddie Ryan (Danny Meehan), Heckie (Victor R. Helou), Snub Taylor and Ben (Buzz Miller), Trombone Smitty (Blair Hammond), Five Finger Finney (Alan E. Weeks), Bubbles (Shellie Farrell), Polly (Joan Lowe), Maud (Ellen Halpin), Nick Arnstein (Sydney Chaplin), Florenz Ziefeld Jr. (Roger De Koven), Mimsey (Sharon Vaughn), Ziegfeld Tenor and Adoph (John Lankston), Mrs. Nadler (Rose Randolf), Paul (Larry Fuller), Kathy (Joan Cory), Vera (Lainie Kazan), Jennie (Diane Coupe), Mr. Renaldi (Marc Jordan), Mike Halsey (Robert Howard)

Synopsis: The Funny Girl of the show was the real life Fanny Brice, a comedienne and Broadway and film star who hid her shyness and imperfections behind a display of bravado and gags. The musical is set in and around New York City following World War I. It traces the rise of the talented performer from her beginnings on the burlesque stage to stardom in the Ziegfeld Follies. It also traces her romance and finally her troubled marriage to entrepreneur and gambler Nicky Arnstein, who is sent to prison for embezzlement. At the end of the show, Arnstein is released from prison, and they decide to separate.

Songs: "If A Girl Isn't Pretty"; "I'm the Greatest Star"; "Cornet Man"; "Who Taught Her Everything?"; "His Love Makes Me Beautiful"; "I want to Be Seen with You Tonight"; "Henry Street"; "People"; "You Are Woman"; "Don't Rain on My Parade"; "Sadie, Sadie"; "Find Yourself a Man"; "Rat-Tat-Tat-Tat"; "Who Are You Now?"; "The Music That Makes Me Dance"

Tony nominations: Best Musical, Best Actor in a Musical (Chaplin), Best Actress in a Musical (Streisand), Best Featured Actor in a Musical (Meehan), Best Featured Actress in a Musical (Medford), Best Composer and Lyricist, Best Choreography (Haney), Best Producer (Stark).

Comments: With this show, Barbra Streisand became a star, reaching a lofty pinnacle she never left. At the opening, orchestra seats were $8.80, but her drawing power was such that all seats were raised to $9.60 not long afterward. Streisand took the show to London for fourteen weeks and also starred in the acclaimed movie version in 1968 with Omar Sharif. She sang many Fanny Brice songs on her television program, but the biggest song hit of *Funny Girl*—"People"—belonged not to Brice, but to Streisand.

A FUNNY THING HAPPENED ON THE WAY TO THE FORUM
(May 8, 1962; Alvin Theatre; 966 performances)

Production credits: *Producer:* Harold Prince; *Director:* George Abbott; *Composer/Lyricist:* Stephen Sondheim; *Librettists:* Burt Shevelove and Larry Gelbart; *Choreographer:* Jack Cole; *Original source:* Based on the plays of Plautus

Original cast: Prologus and Pseudolus (Zero Mostel), Proteans (Eddie Phillips, George Reeder, and David Evans), Senex (David Burns), Domina (Ruth Kobart), Hero (Brian Davies), Hysterium (Jack Giford), Lycus (John Carradine), Tintinabula (Roberta Keith), Panacea (Lucienne Breidou), Germinae (Liza James and Judy Alexander), Vibrata (Myrna White), Gymnasia (Gloria Kristy), Philia (Preshy Marker), Erronius (Raymond Walburn), Miles Gloriosus (Ronald Holgate)

Synopsis: A mixture of burlesque and comedy, the story centers on Pseudolus, the slave of Hero, who bids for his freedom by obtaining the courtesan Philia for his master; however, Miles Gloriosus has already bought Philia from Lycus, and Hero's father, Senex, has other plans for her. So Pseudolus spreads the word that Philia has died of the plague, and a mock funeral follows. When Miles finds out he is Philia's brother, he gives her to Hero, who gives Pseudolus his freedom.

Songs: "Comedy Tonight"; "Love, I Hear"; "Free"; "The House of Marcus Lycus"; "Lovely"; "Pretty Little Picture"; "Everybody Ought to Have a Maid"; "I'm Calm"; "Impossible"; "Bring Me My Bride"; "That Dirty Old Man"; "That'll Show Him"

Tony Awards: Best Musical, Best Actor in a Musical (Mostel), Best Featured Actor in a Musical (Burns), Best Author of a Musical (Shevelove and Gelbart), Best Direction of a Musical, Best Producer of a Musical. **Tony nominations:** Best Featured Actor in a Musical (Gilford), Best Featured Actress in a Musical (Kobart)

°*THE GAY LIFE* (November 18, 1961; Shubert Theatre; 113 performances). *Director:* Gerald Freedman; *Composers/Lyricists:* Arthur Schwartz and Howard Dietz; *Librettists:* Fay Kanin and Michael Kanin; *Choreographer:* Herbert Ross. Set in Vienna in 1904, this is the story of a bachelor and man about town (Walter Chiari), who, on the day of his marriage to Liesl (Barbara Cook), is discovered to have a woman in his bedroom. When Liesl finds out, the marriage is off—for a time.

Tony Awards: Best Costume Design. **Tony nominations:** Best Featured Actress in a Musical (Elizabeth Allen), Best Scenic Design (Oliver Smith), Best Conductor and Musical Director (Herbert Greene)

GENTLEMEN PREFER BLONDES (December 8, 1949; Ziegfeld Theatre; 740 performances)

Production credits: *Producers:* Herman Levin and Oliver Smith; *Director:* John C. Wilson; *Composer:* Jule Styne; *Lyricist:* Leo Robin; *Librettists:* Joseph Fields and Anita Loos; *Choreographer:* Agnes de Mille; *Original source:* Based on the novel by Anita Loos

Original cast: Dorothy Shaw (Yvonne Adair), Steward (Jerry Craig), Lorelei Lee (Carol Channing), Gus Esmond (Jack McCauley), Frank (Robert Cooper), George (Eddie Weston), Sunbathers (Pat Donahue and Marjorie Winters), Lady Phyllis Beekman (Rita Shaw), Sir Francis Beekman (Rex Evans), Mrs. Ella Spofford (Alice Pearce), Deck Stewards (Bob Buckhart and Jay Harnick), Henry Spofford (Eric Brotherson), Olympic (Kurt Stafford), Josephus Cage (George S. Irving), Deck Walkers (Fran Kegan and Junior Standish), Bill (Peter Birch), Gloria Stark (Anita Alvarez), Pierre (Bob Neukum), Taxi Driver and Head Waiter (Kazimir Kokic), Leon (Peter Holmes), Robert Lemanteur (Mort Marshall), Louis Lemanteur (Howard Morris), Flower Girl (Nicole France), Maitre d'Hotel (Crandall Diehl), Zizi (Judy Sinclair), Fifi (Hope Zee), Coles and Atkins (Charles Coles and Cholly Atkins), Tenor (William Krach), Policeman (William Diehl), Mr. Esmond Sr. (Irving Mitchell)

Synopsis: Lorelei Lee is a little girl from Little Rock, Arkansas, and she is about to head for Europe on a ship. Lorelei does not hide the fact that her mission in life is to get money—anyway she can. At the moment, all her expenses for the trip are paid by a button manufacturer named Gus. He finances the trip to Europe not only for Lorelei but also for her best friend, Dorothy. Once in England, Lorelei dates a dashing young Englishman. When she learns that he is richer than her button manufacturer, she makes plans to dump Gus and then discovers that Dorothy has already moved in.

Songs: "It's High Time"; "Bye, Bye Baby"; "A Little Girl from Little Rock"; "I Love What I'm Doing"; "Just a Kiss Apart"; "The Practice Scherzo"; "It's Delightful Down in Chile"; "Sunshine"; "I'm a Tingle, I'm a Glow"; "House on Rittenhouse Square"; "You Say You Care"; "Mamie Is Mimi"; "Coquette"; "Diamonds Are a Girl's Best Friend"; "Gentlemen Prefer Blondes"; "Homesick Blues"; "Keeping Cool with Coolidge"; "Button Up with Esmond"

Comments: Carol Channing made such an impression in this role that it made her an instant star. A little more than a year after the show opened, Channing's name appeared in lights above the title. On May 13, 1952, she gave her 1000th performance in the role. The highly successful 1953 movie starred Jane Russell and Marilyn Monroe as Dorothy and Lorelei. Through the years, the musical has been revised in its original version and also revised as *Lorelei*.

°*THE GIRL FROM NANTUCKET* (November 8, 1945; Adelphi Theatre; 12 performances). *Directors:* Henry Adrian and Edward Clarke Lilley; *Composer:* Jacques Belasco; *Lyricist:* Kay Twomey; *Librettists:* Paul Stamford, Harold Sherman, and Hy Cooper; *Choreographer:* Val Raset. Set in

New York City and Nantucket, Massachusetts, this is a tale about a house painter who, in a mix-up, is assigned the job of painting a museum mural. In one reviewer's opinion, "It lacks everything."

°*THE GIRL IN PINK TIGHTS* (March 5, 1954; Mark Hellinger Theatre; 115 performances). *Director:* Shepard Traube; *Composer:* Sigmund Romberg; *Lyricist:* Leo Robin; *Librettist:* Jerome Chodorov; *Choreographer:* Agnes de Mille. The music of operetta composer Sigmund Romberg (who died in 1951) highlights this tale about the opening of a French ballet company at the end of the Civil War. The show introduced ballerina Jeanmaire in her stage debut.

°*THE GIRL WHO CAME TO SUPPER* (December 8, 1963; Broadway Theatre; 112 performances). *Director/Choreographer:* Joe Layton; *Composer/Lyricist:* Noël Coward; *Librettist:* Harry Kurnitz. Neither Noël Coward's music nor the presence of José Ferrer and Florence Henderson could bring to life this musical version of *The Sleeping Prince*. In addition, the show was not helped by opening so soon after John F. Kennedy's assassination.

Tony Award: Best Featured Actress in a Musical (Tessie O'Shea). **Tony nominations:** Best Author, Musical (Coward), Best Author, Musical (Kurnitz), Best Costume Design (Irene Sharaff)

THE GOLDEN APPLE (April 20, 1954; Alvin Theatre; 173 performances)

Production credits: *Producers:* Alfred De Liagre Jr. and Roger L. Stevens; *Director:* Norman Lloyd; *Composer:* Jerome Moross; *Lyricist/Librettist:* John Latouche; *Choreographer:* Hanya Holm

Original cast: Helen (Kaye Ballard), Lovey Mars (Bibi Osterwald), Mrs. Juniper (Charlotte Rae), Miss Minerva Oliver (Portia Nelson), Mother Hare (Martha Larrimore), Penelope (Virginia Copeland), Menelaus (Dean Michener), Ulysses (Gary Gordon), Theron (Stephen Couglass), Mayor Juniper (Jerry Stiller), Paris (Jonathan Lucas), Hector Charybdis (Jack Whiting)

Synopsis: This is an adaptation of Homer's epic poems of the Trojan War, reset in the American northwest. Traveling salesman Paris drops in on the little town of Angel's Roost, Washington, in a hot air balloon. The sheriff's wife, Helen, who is much younger than her husband and a woman of easy virtue, promptly falls for him. The two run off to Rhododendron, with Ulysses, a veteran of the Spanish-American War, and the other townsfolk in close pursuit. Ulysses and Paris end up in a boxing match. Ulysses returns home where ever-faithful, loyal, and long-suffering Penelope waits.

Songs: "Nothing Ever Happens in Angel's Roost"; "Mother Hare's Séance"; "My Love Is on the Way"; "The Heroes Come Home"; "It Was a

Glad Adventure"; "Come Along, Boys"; "It's the Going Home Together"; "Mother Hare's Prophecy"; "Helen Is Always Willing"; "The Church Social"; "Introducin' Mr. Paris"; "The Judgment of Paris"; "Lazy Afternoon"; "The Departure for Rhododendron"; "My Picture in the Papers"; "The Taking of Rhododendron"; "Hector's Song"; "Windflowers"; "Store-Bought Suit"; "Calypso"; "Scylla and Charybdis"; "Goona-Goona"; "Doomed, Doomed, Doomed"; "Circe, Circe"; "Ulysses' Soliloquy"; "The Sewing Bee"; "The Tirade"

Comments: The show actually opened on March 11, 1954, at the Phoenix Theatre, and got such rave reviews that it was hurriedly transferred uptown. but the uptown crowds did not come and, although it cost only $75,000 to produce, it was taken off the boards at a loss. No one was ever sure why; critics suspect one of the reasons was that uptown audiences did not like the fact that the show had no dialogue.

GOLDEN BOY (October 20, 1964; Majestic Theatre; 569 performances)
   Production credits: *Producer:* Hillard Elkins; *Director:* Arthur Penn, *Composer:* Charles Strouse; *Lyricist:* Lee Adams; *Librettists:* Clifford Odets and William Gibson; *Choreographer:* Donald McKayle; *Original source:* Based on the play by Clifford Odets
   Original cast: Tom Moody (Kenneth Tobey), Roxy Gottlieb (Ted Beniades), Tokio (Charles Welch), Joe Wellington (Sammy Davis Jr.), Lorna Moon (Paula Wayne), Mr.Wellington (Roy Glenn), Anna (Jeannette DuBois), Ronnie (Johnny Brown), Frank (Louis Gossett), Terry (Terrin Miles), Hoodlum (Buck Heller), Eddie Satin (Billy Daniels), Benny (Benny Payne), Al (Albert Popwell), Lola (Lola Falana), Lopez (Jaime Rogers), Mabel (Mabel Robinson), Les (Lester Wilson), Drake (Don Crabtree), Fight Announcer (Maxwell Glanville), Reporter (Bob Daley), Driscoll (Ralph Vucci)
   Synopsis: Joe is a young black man who wants to get rich quick. His way to wealth is boxing, despite his father's objections. His white manager feels that Joe would be a better fighter if he put his heart into it, so he asks Lorna, the manager's girlfriend, to persuade Joe to fight harder. Joe and Lorna fall in love. In a major fight, Joe knocks out Lopez and later learns the boxer is dead. That knowledge, coupled with the realization that Lorna is his manager's girl, drives Joe to his Ferrari and his death.
   Songs: "Workout"; "Night Song"; "Everything's Great"; "Gimme Some"; "Stick Around"; "Don't Forget 127th Street"; "Lorna's Here"; "The Road Tour"; "This Is the Life"; "Golden Boy"; "While the City Sleeps"; "Colorful"; "I Want to Be with You"; "Can't You See It?"; "No More"; "The Fight"
   Tony nominations: Best Musical, Best Actor in a Musical (Davis), Best Choreography, Best Producer of a Musical

Comments: The choreography included a boxing match, but the score was judged lackluster, and the show ran as long as it did mainly because of Sammy Davis Jr. The 1939 movie, with the lead character a white boxer, presented Willian Holden in his starring debut and also starred Lee J. Cobb and Barbara Stanwyck.

GOLDILOCKS (October 11, 1958; Lunt-Fontanne Theatre; 161 performances)

Production credits: *Producer:* Producers Theatre; *Director:* Walter Kerr; *Composer:* Leroy Anderson; *Lyricists:* Joan Ford, Walter Kerr, and Jean Kerr; *Librettists:* Walter Kerr and Jean Kerr; *Choreographer:* Agnes de Mille

Original cast: Maggie Harris (Elaine Stritch), George Randolph Brown (Russell Nype), Max Grady (Don Ameche), Lois Lee (Pat Stanley), Pete (Nathaniel Frey), Andy (Richard Armbruster), J. C. (Martin Wolfson), Bessie (Margaret Hamilton), Chauffeur (Samye Van)

Synopsis: This is a love letter to the silent movies that Walter Kerr remembered as a child. In the movie colony of 1913 Fort Lee, New Jersey, there are many clashes between silent star actress Maggie Harris and vain movie producer Max Grady. Their rocky relationship becomes more complicated with the appearance of the beautiful Lois Lee, who decides that she wants Max for herself. But Maggie is intent on making one more picture under the title of Goldilocks, and this time the sardonic actress and cocky movie director find the way to true romance.

Songs: "Lazy Moon"; "Give the Little Lady"; "Save a Kiss"; "No One'll Ever Love You"; "If I Can't Take It with Me"; "Who's Been Sitting in My Chair?"; "There Never Was a Woman"; "The Pussy Foot"; "Tom Cat"; "Brunette"; "Blondo"; "Lady in Waiting"; "The Beast in You"; "Shall I Take My Heart and Go?"; "Bad Companions"; "I Can't Be in Love"; "I Never Know When"; "Two Years in the Making"; "Heart of Stone"

Tony Awards: Best Featured Actor in a Musical (Nype), Best Featured Actress in a Musical (Stanley). **Tony nominations:** Best Choreography, Best Costume Design (Castillo), Best Conductor and Musical Director (Lehman Engel)

°GREAT TO BE ALIVE (March 23, 1950; Winter Garden Theatre; 52 performances). *Director:* Mary Hunter; *Composers:* Abraham Ellstein and Robert Russell Bennett; *Lyricist:* Walter Bullock; *Librettists:* Walter Bullock and Sylvia Regan; *Choreographer:* Helen Tamiris. Originally titled *What a Day!*, the show is set in an old Pennsylvania mansion and starred Vivienne Segal and Stuart Erwin in a tale about those who live happily among ghosts.

°*GREENWILLOW* (March 8, 1960; Alvin Theatre; 95 performances). *Director:* George Roy Hill; *Composer/Lyricist:* Frank Loesser; *Librettists:* Lesser Samuel and Frank Loesser; *Choreographer:* Joe Layton. In the magical rural American town of Greenwillow, it is the fate of the eldest male in the Briggs family—in this case Gideon (Anthony Perkins)—to leave his home to wander, even if that means breaking the heart of his sweetheart. But this time, with the help of a newcomer to Greenwillow, the Reverend Birdsong, Gideon is able to stay in the place he loves with the woman he loves.

Tony nominations: Best Featured Actress in a Musical (Pert Kelton), Best Choreography, Best Scenic Design, Musical (Peter Larkin), Best Costume Design (Alvin Colt), Best Conductor and Musical Director (Abba Bogin), Best Stage Technician (James Orr)

GUYS AND DOLLS (November 24, 1950; 46th Street Theatre; 1,194 performances)

Production credits: *Producers:* Cy Feuer and Ernest Martin; *Director:* George S. Kaufman; *Composer/Lyricist:* Frank Loesser; *Librettists:* Jo Swerling and Abe Burrows; *Choreographer:* Michael Kidd; *Original source:* Based on Damon Runyon stories and characters

Original cast: Sky Masterson (Robert Alda), Miss Adelaide (Vivian Blaine), Nathan Detroit (Sam Levene), Sarah Brown (Isabel Bigley), Arvide Abernathy (Pat Rooney Sr.), Nicely-Nicely Johnson (Stubby Kaye), Benny Southstreet (Johnny Silver), Big Jule (B. S. Pully), The Horse (Tom Pedi)

Synopsis: The musical revolves around two love stories and the colorful Damon Runyon characters. Nathan Detroit and Miss Adelaide have been engaged for fourteen years. The date gets no closer because Nathan always has another floating crap game to attend. Sky Masterson, also a gambler, makes a bet with Nathan that he can date Sarah from the Mission. They fall in love, but she is infuriated when she learns about the bet. In the crap game in an underground sewer, Sky wins and all the losers have to attend a Mission meeting. In the end, he marries Sarah, and Nathan and Adelaide are to be married at the Mission.

Songs: "Runyonland"; "Fugue for Tinhorns"; "Follow the Fold"; "The Oldest Established"; "I'll Know"; "A Bushel and a Peck"; "Adelaide's Lament"; "Guys and Dolls"; "If I Were a Bell"; "My Time of Day"; "I've Never Been in Love Before"; "Take Back Your Mink"; "More I Cannot Wish You"; "Luck Be a Lady"; "Sue Me"; "Sit Down, You're Rockin' the Boat"; "Marry the Man Today"

Tony Awards: Best Musical, Best Actor in a Musical (Alda), Best Featured Actress in a Musical (Bigley), Best Director, Best Choreography

Comments: Most of the reviewers gave raves to the production. Marlon Brando, Jean Simmons, Frank Sinatra, Vivian Blaine, and Stubby Kaye headlined the 1955 hit movie, which added some songs to the score, such as "Woman in Love." "If I Were a Bell" made the hit parade in 1950.

GYPSY (May 21, 1959; Broadway Theatre; 702 performances)

Production credits: *Producers:* David Merrick and Leland Hayward; *Director/Choreographer:* Jerome Robbins; *Composer:* Jule Styne; *Lyricist:* Stephen Sondheim; *Librettist:* Arthur Laurents; *Original source:* Based on the memoirs of Gypsy Rose Lee

Original cast: Uncle Jocko and Mr. Goldstone (Mort Marshall), Baby Louise (Karen Moore), Baby June (Jane Mayo), Louise (Sandra Church), June (Lane Bradbury), Herbie (Jack Klugman), Rose Lee (Ethel Merman), Tulsa (Paul Wallace), Yonkers (David Winters), Agnes (Marilyn Cooper), Miss Cratchitt (Peg Murray), Dolores (Marilyn D'Honau), Phil (Joe Silver)

Synopsis: This is the story of Gypsy Rose Lee's rise to the top in burlesque, although the central figure is her mother, Rose, the ultimate stage mother. Rose, with children Baby June and Louise, searches for fame and fortune. June and Louise grow up on stage. June eventually elopes, which infuriates Rose after all she has worked for. Then she turns to Louise, who is at first reluctant but at last becomes a star.

Songs: "May We Entertain You"; "Some People"; "Small World"; "Baby June and Her Newsboys"; "Mr. Goldstone"; "You'll Never Get Away from Me"; "Dainty June and Her Farmboys"; "If Momma Was Married"; "All I Need Is the Girl"; "Everything's Coming Up Roses"; "Madame Rose's Toreadorables"; "Together, Wherever We Go"; "You Gotta Get a Gimmick"; "Let Me Entertain You"; "Rose's Turn"

Tony nominations: Best Musical, Best Actress in a Musical (Merman), Best Featured Actor in a Musical (Klugman), Best Featured Actress in a Musical (Church), Best Direction of a Musical (Robbins), Best Conductor (Milton Rosenstock), Best Scenic Design (Jo Mielziner), Best Costume Design (Raoul Penne Du Bois)

Comments: Most reviewers praised the show (although it won no Tonys), but all were adamant that this was Ethel Merman's finest hour on Broadway. The film (1962), starring Rosalind Russell and Natalie Wood, was generally praised, but it lacked the electricity of Merman. A television adaptation in 1993 starred Bette Midler, for which she won the Golden Globe Award for Best Actress that year.

HALF A SIXPENCE (April 25, 1965; Broadhurst Theatre; 512 performances)

Production credits: *Producers:* Allen-Hodgden, Stevens Productions, and Harold Fielding; *Director:* Gene Saks; *Composer/Lyricist:* David

Heneker; *Librettist:* Beverly Cross; *Choreographer:* Onna White; *Original source:* Based on H. G. Wells's book *Kipps*

Original cast: Arthur Kipps (Tommy Steele), Sid Pornick (Will Mackenzie), Ann Pornick (Polly James), Helen Walsingham (Carrie Nye), Buggins (Norman Allen), Walsingham (John Cleese), Pearce (Grover Dale), Carshot (William Larsen), Flo (Michele Hardy), Emma (Reby Howells), Kate (Louise Quick), Victoria (Sally Lee), Mr.Shalford (Mercer McLeod)

Synopsis: Half a sixpence is the small gift that Arthur Kipps, an apprentice, gives to sweetheart Ann, a maid, but when he goes to school at night, he falls in love with the teacher, Helen. After learning that he has come into a large inheritance, he asks Helen to marry him, but he changes his mind when he discovers how snobbish she is. Arthur marries Ann, but she does not care for the way that wealth has changed him; however, Arthur is cheated out of his money by Helen's brother, so he and Ann open a small shop and are happy.

Songs: "All in the Cause of Economy"; "Half a Sixpence"; "Money to Burn"; "A Proper Gentleman"; "She's Too Far Above Me"; "If the Rain's Got to Fall"; "The Old Military Canal"; "Long Ago"; "Flash Bang Wallop"; "I Know What I Am"; "The Party's On the House"

Tony nominations: Best Musical, Best Composer and Lyricist, Best Actor in a Musical (Steele), Best Featured Actor in a Musical (James Grout), Best Featured Actress in a Musical (Nye), Best Direction of a Musical, Best Choreography, Best Producer of a Musical, Best Author, Musical

Comments: Originally produced in London, the show delighted Broadway audiences, especially with Tommy Steele in the star role. But after he left the cast, audience interest dropped, and it closed on July 16, 1966, losing about one-third of its original $300,000 investment.

°*THE HAPPIEST GIRL IN THE WORLD* (April 3, 1961; Martin Beck Theatre; 96 performances). *Director:* Cyril Ritchard; *Composer:* Jacques Offenbach; *Lyricist:* E. Y. Harburg; *Librettists:* Fred Saidy and Henry Mayers; *Choreographer:* Dania Krupska. Cyril Ritchard directed and starred as the chief of state of Athens in this musical based on an ancient Greek comedy. Critics gave it glowing reviews, but audiences were generally lukewarm.

Tony nomination: Best Choreography

°*HAPPY AS LARRY* (January 6, 1950; Coronet Theatre; 3 performances). *Director:* Burgess Meredith; *Composer:* Mischa Portnoff; *Lyricist:* Donagh MacDonagh; *Librettist:* Donagh MacDonagh; *Choreographer:* Anna Sokolow. This short-lived musical fantasy is set anytime, anywhere, featuring

Burgess Meredith. He played the role of Larry, an Irish tailor who goes back to his grandfather's time. A weak score and plot hastened its demise.

HAPPY HUNTING (December 6, 1956; Majestic Theatre; 412 performances)

Production credits: *Producer:* Joe Mielziner; *Director:* Abe Burrows; *Composer:* Harold Karr; *Lyricisit:* Matt Dubey; *Librettists:* Howard Lindsay and Russel Crouse; *Choreographers:* Alex Romero and Bob Herget

Original cast: Sanford Stewart Jr. (Gordon Polk), Mrs. Sanford Stewart Sr. (Olive Templeton), Joseph (Mitchell M. Gregg), Beth Livingstone (Virginia Gibson), Jack Adams (Seth Riggs), Harry Watson (Gene Wesson), Charlie (Delbert Anderson), Liz Livingstone (Ethel Merman), Lord Foley (Mary Finney), Police Sergeant (Marvin Zeller), Arturo (Leon Belasco), Duke of Granada (Fernando Lamas), Count Carlos (Renato Cibella), Waiter (Don Weismuller), Ship's Officer and Mr. T. (John Leslie), Barman (Warren J. Brown), Mrs. B. (Florence Dunlap), Mrs. D. (Madeline Clive), Mrs. L. (Kelly Stevens), Terrence (Jim Hutchison), Tom (Eugene Louis), Daisy (Moe), Mr. M. (Jay Velie), Albert (George Martin), Margaret (Mara Landi)

Synopsis: Liz Livingstone, a rich, widowed Philadelphia hostess with a heart of gold, experiences what she regards as a snub when she is not invited to the Grace Kelly–Prince Rainier wedding in Monaco. So, she decides to arrange an even grander marriage for her daughter, Beth. She soon discovers the impressively titled Duke of Granada, but then she falls for him herself. In the meantime, Beth only has eyes for Sanford Stewart, the society lawyer. Liz eventually finds love, even though it turns out that the Duke is quite possibly penniless.

Songs: "Postage Stamp-Principality"; "Don't Tell Me"; "It's Good to Be Here"; "Mutual Admiration Society"; "For Love or Money"; "Bikini Dance"; "It's Like a Beautiful Woman"; "Wedding-of-the-Year Blues"; "Mr. Livingstone"; "If'n"; "This Is What I Call Love"; "A New-Fangled Tango"; "She's Just Another Girl"; "The Game of Love"; "Happy Hunting"; "I'm a Funny Dame"; "This Much I Know"; "Just Another Guy"; "Anyone Who's Who"

Tony nominations: Best Actor in a Musical (Lamas), Best Actress in a Musical (Merman), Best Featured Actress in a Musical (Gibson), Best Costume Design

Comments: This was one of Ethel Merman's rare failures, mostly because she had no "belting" tunes.

°HAPPY TOWN (October 7, 1959; 54th Street Theatre; 5 performances). *Director:* Alan A. Buckhantz; *Composer:* Gordon Duffy; *Lyricist:* Harry M.

Haldane; *Librettist:* Max Hampton; *Choreographer:* Lee Scott. Set in various locales in Back-A-Heap, Texas, this musical tells the tale of the townspeople who are upset because this is one Texas town without a millionaire. Despite poor reviews and only five performances, choreographer Lee Scott was nominated for a Tony.

Tony nomination: Best Choreography

HAZEL FLAGG (February 11, 1953; Mark Hellinger Theatre; 190 performances)

Production credits: *Producers:* Jule Styne, in association with Anthony B. Farrell; *Director:* David Alexander; *Composer:* Jule Styne; *Lyricist:* Bob Hilliard; *Librettist:* Ben Hecht; *Choreographer:* Robert Alton; *Original source:* Based on a story by James Street and the film *Nothing Sacred*

Original cast: Editor (Dean Campbell), Oleander (Jonathan Harris), Laura Carew (Benay Venuta), Wallace Cook (John Howard), Mr. Billings (Lawrence Weber), Mr. Jenkins (Robert Lenn), Hazel Flagg (Helen Gallagher), Dr. Downer (Thomas Mitchell), Man on the Street (George Reeder), Bellboy (Jerry Craig), Maximilian Lavian (John Pelletti), Miss Winterbottom (Betsy Holland), Tenth Avenue Merchant (Ross Martin), Mayor of New York (Jack Whiting), Whitey (Sheree North), Willie (John Brascia), Dr. Egelhofer (Ross Martin), Policeman (Eric Schepard)

Synopsis: Hazel Flagg is a country girl from Vermont. A New York magazine gets word that she is near death from radium poisoning. The magazine sponsors her trip to the big city, where she promptly falls in love with the worldly Wallace Cook. As it turns out, Hazel is not going to die after all, but the country girl is now in love with New York, and the romance continues.

Songs: "A Little More Heart"; "The World Is Beautiful Today"; "I'm Glad I'm Leaving"; "Hello, Hazel"; "Make the People Cry"; "Every Street's a Boulevard in Old New York"; "How Do You Speak to an Angel?"; "I Feel Like I'm Gonna Live Forever"; "You're Gonna Dance with Me, Willie"; "Who Is the Bravest?"; "Laura De Maupassant"

Tony Awards: Best Actor in a Musical (Mitchell), Best Costume Design (Miles White)

Comments: Dancer Sheree North got her first Broadway notice in a lively number that had little to do with the plot. At 190 performances, the show was a financial loss.

°HEAVEN ON EARTH (September 16, 1948; New Century Theatre; 12 performances). *Director:* John Murray Anderson; *Composer:* Jay Gorney; *Lyricist:* Barry Trivers; *Librettist:* Barry Trivers; *Choreographer:* Nick

Castle. Critics called this a rather dismal affair about a New York taxi driver who, with the help of a pixie, aids a poor couple who live in a tree. The only highlight was the sets by Raoul Pene Du Bois, including Central Park recreated on stage.

HELLO, DOLLY! (January 16, 1964; St. James Theatre; 2,844 performances)

Production credits: *Producer:* David Merrick; *Director/Choreographer:* Gower Champion; *Composer/Lyricist:* Jerry Herman; *Librettist:* Michael Stewart; *Original source:* Based on Thornton Wilder's play *The Matchmaker*

Original cast: Mrs. Dolly Gallagher Levi (Carol Channing), Ernestina (Mary Jo Catlett), Ambrose Kemper (Igors Gavon), Horse (Jan LaPrade and Bonnie Mathis), Horace Vandergelder (David Burns), Cronelius Hackl (Charles Nelson Reilly), Barnaby Tucker (Jerry Dodge), Irene Molly (Eileen Brennan), Minnie Fay (Sondra Lee), Mrs. Rose (Amelia Haas), Rudolph (David Hartman), Judge (Gordon Connell), Court Clerk (Ken Ayers)

Synopsis: The setting is New York City and environs in the 1890s, and the musical centers around Dolly Levi, who is into everything and everyone's business, as she is fond of saying, "I meddle." At the moment, she is mostly concerned with finding a suitable wife for wealthy Horace Vandergelder. Actually, Dolly is secretly scheming to get him for herself. Between the distractions of Dolly's communications with her deceased husband Ephraim and her plans to get Horace's daughter a husband, she leads everyone on a merry chase. Finally, Horace decides there is no use resisting, and they plan to marry.

Songs: "I Put My Hand In"; "It Takes a Woman"; "Put on Your Sunday Clothes"; "Ribbons Down My Back"; "Motherhood"; "Dancing"; "Before the Parade Passes By"; "Elegance"; "The Waiters' Gallop"; "Hello, Dolly!"; "Come and Be My Butterfly"; "It Only Takes a Moment"; "So Long Dearie"

Tony Awards: Best Musical, Best Actress (Channing), Best Composer/Lyricist (Herman), Best Librettist (Stewart), Best Choreographer and Director (Champion), Best Producer (Merrick), Best Scenic Design (Oliver Smith), Best Costume Design (Freddy Wittop), Best Conductor (Shepard Coleman)

Comments: The cast was superb and the title song the most musical to come out of Broadway in many a season. It got a boost from Louis Armstrong's great recording. Reviewers called this role the best of Carol Channing's career. Strangely enough, the highly successful show ran into trouble during the try-out period. David Merrick was originally displeased with the musical numbers, and there was a good deal of fast rewriting.

HERE'S LOVE (October 3, 1963; Shubert Theatre; 338 performances)

Production credits: *Producer/Director:* Stuart Ostrow; *Composer/Lyricist/Librettist:* Meredith Willson; *Choreographer:* Michael Kidd; *Original source:* Based on the film *Miracle on 34th Street*

Original cast: Mr. Kris Kringle (Laurence Naismith), Fred Gaily (Craig Stevens), Susan Walker (Valerie Lee), Marvin Shellhammer (Fred Gwynne), Doris Walker (Janis Paige), R. H. Macy (Paul Reed), Harry Finfer (Sal Lombardo), Mrs. Finfer and Girl Scout Leader (Mara Landi), Hendrika (Kathy Cody), Hendrika's New Mother (Suzanne France), Miss Crookshank (Reby Howells), Mr. Psawyer (David Doyle), Governor (Darrell Sandeen), Mayor and Mailman (Hal Norman), Mr. Gimbel and Murphy (William Griffis), Policeman (Bob McClure), Clara (Mary Louise), Judge Martin Group (Cliff Hall), District Attorney Thomas Mara (Larry Douglas), Tammany O'Halloran (Arthur Rubin), Nurse (Leesa Troy), Bailiff (Del Horstman), Thomas Mara Jr. (Dewey Golkin)

Synopsis: Macy's hires the real Kris Kringle because its regular Santa Claus is drunk. Kris is so honest that no one can believe him, and the government takes him to court. In the meantime, young Susan Walker manages to find a husband, Fred Gaily, for her divorced mother and a new father for herself. In the end, the true spirit of Christmas prevails.

Songs: "Arm in Arm"; "You Don't Know"; "The Plastic Alligator"; "The Bugle"; "Here's Love"; "My Wish"; "Pine Cones and Holly Berries"; "Look, Little Girl"; "Expect Things to Happen"; "Love Come Take Me Again"; "She Hadda Go Back"; "That Man Over There"; "My State"; "Nothing in Common"

Comments: This was Meredith Willson's third musical on Broadway. Most reviewers felt the show was appealing but forgettable.

HIGH BUTTON SHOES (October 9, 1947; New Century Theatre; 727 performances)

Production credits: *Producers:* Monte Proser and Joseph Kipness; *Director:* George Abbott; *Composers/Lyricists:* Jule Styne and Sammy Cahn; *Librettists:* George Abbott and Stephen Longstreet; *Choreographer:* Jerome Robbins

Original cast: Harrison Floy (Phil Silvers), Mr. Pontdue (Joey Faye), Uncle Willie (Donald Saddler), Henry Longstreet (Jack McCauley), Stevie Longstreet (Johnny Stewart), Fran (Loris Lee), Sara Longstreet (Nanette Fabray), Nancy (Helen Gallagher), Hubert Ogglethorpe (Mark Dawson), Shirley Simpkins (Carole Coleman), Elmer Simpkins (Nathaniel Frey), Elmer Simpkins Jr. (Donald Harris), Coach (Tom Glennon), Mr. Anderson (William David), Boy at the Picnic (Arthur Partington), Playmate (Sondra Lee), Popular Girl (Jacqueline Dodge), Betting Man (George Spelvin), Another Betting Man (Howard Lenters)

Synopsis: Harrison Floy is a small-time con man who returns to his small-town New Jersey home, where his neighbors think he has become a tycoon. After he starts selling real estate to them and they discover the land is a swamp, he leaves town for Atlantic City, taking Sara's sister, Fran, with him. They both return, Fran to her old boyfriend and Floy to make amends. He bets on the Princeton-Rutgers football game to get cash, even trying to get Rutgers to throw the game. When Rutgers wins, Floy gets out of town again.

Songs: "He Tried to Make a Dollar"; "Can't You Just See Yourself in Love with Me?"; "There's Nothing Like a Model T"; "Next to Texas, I Love You"; "Security"; "Bird Watcher's Song"; "Get Away for a Day in the Country"; "A Summer Incident"; "Papa, Won't You Dance with Me?"; "On a Sunday by the Sea"; "You're My Girl"; "I Still Get Jealous"; "You're My Boy"; "Nobody Ever Died for Dear Old Rutgers"; "Castle Walk"

Tony Award: Best Choreographer (Robbins)

Comments: Although a successful musical, this was Jule Styne's and Sammy Cahn's last collaboration for almost a decade. Nanette Fabray and Jack McCauley stopped the show with their musical numbers, but the highlight of the evening was the Mack Sennett Ballet staged by Jerome Robbins in which the Keystone Cops, among others, chase Floy and end in a jumbled heap of bodies with a flag-waving cop on top. Sennett won a lawsuit for using his name as well as the Keystone Cops in the ballet scene without permission.

HIGH SPIRITS (April 7, 1964; Alvin Theatre; 376 performances)

Production credits: *Producers:* Lester Osterman, Robert Fletcher, and Richard Horner; *Director:* Noël Coward; *Composers/Lyricists/Librettists:* Hugh Martin and Timothy Gray; *Choreographer:* Danny Daniels; *Original source:* Based on Noël Coward's *Blithe Spirit*

Original cast: Charles Condomine (Edward Woodward), Edith (Carol Arthur), Ruth Condomine (Louise Troy), Mrs. Bradman (Margaret Hall), Dr. Bradman (Lawrence Keith), Madame Arcati (Beatrice Lillie), Elvira (Tammy Grimes), Bob (Robert Lenn), Beth (Beth Howland), Rupert (Gene Castle)

Synopsis: Writer Charles Condomine hosts a séance conducted by Madame Arcati so he can learn her tricks for his next novel. He assumes she is a fake, but instead she goes into a trance and manages to bring back his first wife, Elvira, even though he is the only one who can see her. This greatly upsets his second marriage to Ruth, who thinks this is all a joke, until Elvira moves into the Condomine household and plans to kill Charles so he can join her. She accidentally kills Ruth instead. Now both female apparitions drive Charles crazy.

Songs: "Was She Prettier Than I?"; "The Bicycle Song"; "You'd Better Love Me"; "Where Is the Man I Married?"; "The Sandwich Man"; "Go into Your Trance"; "Forever and a Day"; "Something Tells Me"; "I Know Your Heart"; "Faster Than Sound"; "If I Gave You"; "Talking to You"; "Home Sweet Heaven"; "Something Is Coming to Tea"; "The Exorcism"; "What in the World Did You Want?"

Tony nominations: Best Musical, Best Actress in a Musical (Lillie), Best Featured Actress in a Musical (Troy), Best Composer and Lyricist, Best Choreography (Daniels), Best Direction of a Musical (Coward), Best Author, Best Conductor (Fred Werner)

Comments: This was Beatrice Lillie's last Broadway show. When she could not get along with director Noël Coward, Gower Champion took over. Lillie treated her audiences to such elegant madnesses as taking a series of curtain calls early in the second act. Although the show had a respectable run, it failed financially.

°*HIT THE TRAIL* (December 2, 1954; Mark Hellinger Theatre; 4 performances). *Directors:* Charles W. Christenberry Jr. and Byrie Carr; *Composer:* Frederico Valerio; *Lyricist:* Elizabeth Miele; *Librettist:* Frank O'Neill; *Choreographer:* Gene Baylies. A primadonna hits Virginia City, Nevada, during the late nineteenth century.

°*HOLD IT!* (May 5, 1948; National Theatre; 46 performances). *Director:* Robert E. Perry; *Composer:* Gerald Marks; *Lyricist:* Samuel M. Lerner; *Librettists:* Matt Brooks and Art Arthur; *Choreographer:* Michael Kidd. The production is set in and around Lincoln University and centers on the tale of a boy dressed as a girl who wins a Hollywood beauty contest. Most critics thought it unprofessional, and so did the audiences, who mainly stayed away.

°*HOT SPOT* (April 19, 1963; Majestic Theatre; 43 performances). *Director:* Morton DaCosta; *Composer:* Mary Rodgers; *Lyricist:* Martin Charnin; *Librettists:* Jack Weinstock and Willie Gilbert; *Choreographer:* Onna White. Inspired by the furor caused when a Peace Corps volunteer described conditions in Nigeria in 1961, fictional volunteer Sally Hopwinder concocts a plan to get aid for the pretend country of D'hum. In a Broadway record, opening night was postponed four times. Even Judy Holliday, in her final stage performance, could not save this musical.

HOUSE OF FLOWERS (December 30, 1954; Alvin Theatre; 165 performances)

Production credits: *Producer:* Saint Subber; *Director:* Peter Brook; *Composer:* Harold Arlen; *Lyricists:* Truman Capote and Harold Arlen; *Librettist:* Truman Capote; *Choreographer:* Geoffrey Holder

Original cast: Madame Fleur (Pearl Bailey), Alvin (Alvin Ailey), Mother (Miriam Burton), Ottillie, alias Violet (Diahann Carroll), Townspersons (Joseph Comacho and Hubert Dilworth), Carmen (Carmen De Lavallade), Monsier Jamison (Dino DiLuca), Madame Tango (Juanita Hall), Mamselle Honolulu (Mary Mon Toy), Gladiola (Ada Moore), Pansy (Enid Mosier), Chief of Police (Don Redman), Mamselle Ibo-Lele (Pearl Reynolds), Royal (Rawn Spearman), Mamselle Cigarette (Glory Van Scott), Captain Jones (Ray Walston)

Synopsis: On a West Indies island, there is trouble between the brothel run by Madame Tango and the one run by Madame Fleur. All the girls are named for flowers. When mumps breaks out, Madame Fleur wants to sell Ottillie, whose professional name is Violet, to a merchant, but she wants to marry Royal. So Madame Fleur has Royal kidnapped, but he escapes in time to stop the marriage.

Songs: "Waitin'"; "One Man Ain't Quite Enough"; "A Sleepin' Bee"; "Bamboo Cage"; "House of Flowers"; "Two Ladies in the Shade"; "What Is a Friend For?"; "Mardi Gras"; "I Never Has Seen Snow"; "I'm Gonna Leave Off Wearing My Shoes"; "Has I Let You Down?"; "Slide, Boy, Slide"; "Don't Like Goodbyes"; "Turtle Song"

Tony Award: Best Scenic Design (Oliver Messel)

Comments: Some reviewers were surprised the show opened at all since rumors spread that the backstage fighting during tryouts was vicious. This was Diahann Carroll's Broadway debut. Barbra Streisand featured "A Sleepin' Bee" in her first Grammy-winning album.

HOW TO SUCCEED IN BUSINESS WITHOUT REALLY TRYING
(October 14, 1961; 46th Street Theatre; 1,417 performances)

Production credits: *Producers:* Cy Feuer and Ernest Martin, in association with Frank Productions; *Director:* Abe Burrows; *Composer/Lyricist:* Frank Loesser; *Librettists:* Abe Burrows, Jack Weinstock, and Willie Gilbert; *Choreographer:* Hugh Lambert; *Original source:* Based on the book by Shepherd Mead

Original cast: J. Pierpont Finch (Robert Morse), Gatch and Toynbee (Ray Mason), Jenkins (Robert Kaliban), Tackaberry (David Collyer), Peterson (Casper Roos), J. B. Biggley (Rudy Vallee), Rosemary (Bonnie Scott), Bratt (Paul Reed), Smitty (Claudette Sutherland), Frump (Charles Nelson Reilly), Miss Jones (Ruth Kobart), Mr. Twimble and Womper (Sammy Smith), Hedy (Virginia Martin), Scrubwomen (Mara Landi and Silver

Saundors), Miss Krumholtz (Mara Landi), Ovington (Lanier Davis), Policeman (Bob Murdock)

Synopsis: Satirizing the "rags-to-riches" story by Horatio Alger, this
show both lampoons and cheers the corporate way. Ambitious J. Pierpont
Finch is a window washer who buys a book on how to succeed in business
and consults it whenever necessary, which is quite often. In an amazingly
short period of time, he gets the attention of the company boss, gets the
girl, and goes from a nobody to chairman of the board.

Songs: "How To"; "Happy to Keep His Dinner Warm"; "Coffee Break";
"The Company Way"; "A Secretary Is Not a Toy"; "Been a Long Day";
"Grand Old Ivy"; "Paris Original"; "Rosemary"; "Finaletto"; "Cinderella,
Darling"; "Love from a Heart of Gold"; "I Believe in You"; "The Yo Ho
Ho"; "Brotherhood of Man"

Tony Awards: Best Musical, Best Actor in a Musical (Morse), Best
Featured Actor in a Musical (Reilly), Best Author of a Musical, Best Direc-
tion of a Musical, Best Producer of a Musical, Best Conductor and Musical
Director (Elliot Lawrence). **Tony nominations:** Best Composer.

Comments: Even after Robert Morse and Rudy Vallee left the show, it
continued as a hit with numerous replacements. The 1967 movie version
featured Morse and Vallee and was the film debut for Michele Lee.

I CAN GET IT FOR YOU WHOLESALE (March 22, 1962; Shubert
Theatre; 300 performances)

Production credits: *Producer:* David Merrick; *Director:* Arthur Laurents; *Composer/Lyricist:* Howard Rome; *Librettist:* Jerome Weidman;
Choreographer: Herbert Ross; *Original source:* Based on Howard Rome's
novel

Original cast: Miss Marmelstein (Barbra Streisand), Maurice Pulver-
macher (Jack Kruschen), Meyer Bushkin (Ken Le Roy), Harry Bogen
(Elliot Gould), Tootsie Maltz (James Hickman), Ruthie Rivkin (Marilyn
Cooper), Mrs. Bogen (Lillian Roth), Martha Mills (Sheree North), Mario
(William Reilly), Mitzi (Barbara Monte), Eddie (Edward Verso), Blanche
Bushkin (Bambi Linn), Teddy Asch (Harold Lang), Buggo (Kelly Brown),
Miss Springer (Pat Turner), Velma (Francine Bond), Lenny (William
Sumner), Norman (Stanley Simmonds), Manette (Luba Lisa), Gail
(Wilma Curley), Rosaline (Marion Fels), Noodle (Jack Murrary), Sam
(Don Grilley), Moxie (Ed Collins), Sheldon Bushkin (Steve Curry), Edith
(Margaret Gathright)

Synopsis: In the 1930s world of the New York City garment district,
pushy Harry Bogen gets rid of his partners as he shoves his way to the
top. His mother and girlfriend, Ruthie, try to warn him that what he is
doing is unethical, but he ignores them. He even ditches Ruthie for a

flamboyant nightclub performer. In the end, Harry's double dealings end in bankruptcy, and the only ones left to console him are his mother and Ruthie.

Songs: "Well Man"; "The Way Things Are"; "When Gemini Meets Capricorn"; "Momma, Momma"; "The Sound of Money"; "Family Way"; "Too Soon"; "Who Knows?"; "Have I Told You Lately?"; "Ballad of the Garment Trade"; "A Gift Today"; "Miss Marmelstein"; "A Funny Thing Happened"; "What's in It for Me?"; "What Are They Doing to Us Now?"; "Eat a Little Something"

Tony nomination: Best Featured Actress in a Musical (Streisand)

Comments: At age nineteen, future superstar Barbra Streisand made her debut on Broadway and took the show's only Tony nomination.

I HAD A BALL (December 15, 1964; Martin Beck Theatre; 199 performances)

Production credits: *Producer:* Joseph Kipness; *Director:* Lloyd Richards; *Composers/Lyricists:* Jack Lawrence and Stan Freeman; *Librettist:* Jerome Chodorov; *Choreographer:* Onna White

Original cast: Garside (Buddy Hackett), Stan the Shpieler (Richard Kiley), Ma Maloney (Rosetta LeNoire), Addie (Luba Lisa), Morocco (Morocco), Jeannie (Karen Morrow), Gimlet (Al Nesor), Brooks (Steve Roland), Officer Millhauser (Ted Thurston), Joe the Muzzler (Jack Wakefield), George Osaka (Conrad Yama), Lifeguard (Marty Allen), Jimmy (Nathaniel Jones)

Synopsis: The setting is in and around Coney Island, New York, where Garside decides to turn matchmaker, although he doesn't prove very good at it. He tries to make a couple out of Brooks and Jeannie, a loan shark and a ferris wheel operator, as well as pitchman Stan and hustler Addie. Brooks and Jeannie discover that they actually might work out, but the others are not so sure.

Songs: "Garside the Great"; "Coney Island, U.S.A."; "The Other Half of Me"; "Addie's at It Again"; "I've Got Everything I Want"; "Dr. Freud"; "Think Beautiful"; "Faith"; "Can It Be Possible?"; "Neighborhood"; "The Affluent Society"; "Almost"; "Fickle Finger of Fate"; "You Deserve Me"; "Lament"; "Be a Phony"; "Tunnel of Love Chase"

Tony nomination: Best Featured Actress in a Musical (Lisa)

IRMA LA DOUCE (September 29, 1960; Plymouth Theatre; 524 performances)

Production credits: *Producers:* David Merrick, in association with Donald Albery and H. M. Tennent Ltd., by arrangement with Henry Hall; *Director:* Peter Brook; *Composer:* Marguerite Monnot; *Lyricist:* Julian More

(English); *Librettists:* Julian More, David Heneker, and Monty Norman; *Choreographer:* Onna White; *Original source:* Adapted from the original French book

Original cast: Bob-Le-Hotu (Clive Revill), Irma-La-Douce (Elizabeth Seal), Client (Eddie Gasper), Jojo-Les-Yeux-Sales (Zack Matalon), Roberto-Les-Diams (Aric Lavie), Persil-Le-Noir (Osborne Smith), Frangipane (Stuart Damon), Polyte-Le-Mou (Fred Gwynne), Police Inspector (George S. Irving), Nestor-Le-Fripe (Keith Michell), M. Bougne and Second Warder (George Del Monte), Counsel for the Prosecution and Third Warder (Rico Froehlich), Counsel for the Defense and Tax Inspector (Rudy Tronto), Usher, First Warder, and Priest (Elliott Gould), Honest Man (Joe Rocco), Court Gendarme (Byron Mitchell)

Synopsis: This is the story of a bad girl with a good heart. Irma is a prostitute in the red-light district who is supporting her law student boyfriend, Nestor. Nestor becomes jealous of Irma's occupation, so he poses as Monsieur Oscar, who pays Irma 10,000 francs for her services, but she gives the money to Nestor, so the same money goes back and forth. When Irma falls for Oscar, Nestor decides it is time to get rid of him. He gets arrested but escapes and returns to Irma as they are about to have a child.

Songs: "Valse Milieu"; "Sons of France"; "The Bridge of Caulaincourt"; "Our Language of Love"; "She's Got the Lot"; "Dis-Donc"; "Le Grisbi Is le Root of le Evil in Man"; "Wreck of a Mec"; "That's a Crime"; "From a Prison Cell"; "Irma-la–Douce"; "There Is Only One Paris for That"; "The Freedom of the Seas"; "But"; "Christmas Child"

Tony nominations: Best Musical, Best Featured Actor in a Musical (Revill), Best Direction of a Musical, Best Costume Design (Musical), Best Choreography, Best Conductor and Musical Director (Stanley Lebowsky)

Comments: There was some audience and critic objection to the story line but not so much that it spoiled a run of more than 500 performances.

°*THE JACKPOT* (January 13, 1944; Alvin Theatre; 69 performances). *Director:* Roy Hargrave; *Composer:* Vernon Duke; *Lyricist:* Howard Dietz; *Librettists:* Guy Bolton, Sidney Sheldon, and Ken Roberts; *Choreographers:* Lauretta Jefferson and Charles Weidman. This is an old-fashioned musical about Sally Madison (Nanette Fabray), who becomes first prize in a bond rally. It also starred Wendell Cory, Allan Jones, Jerry Lester, and Betty Garrett.

JAMAICA (October 31, 1957; Imperial Theatre; 555 performances)
Production credits: *Producer:* David Merrick; *Director:* Robert Lewis; *Composer:* Harold Arlen; *Lyricist:* E. Y. Harburg; *Librettists:* E. Y. Harburg and Fred Saidy; *Choreographer:* Jack Cole

Original cast: Koli (Richardo Montalban), Quico (Augustine Rios), Savannah (Lena Horne), Grandma Obeah (Adelaide Hall), Giner (Josephine Premice), Snodgrass (Roy Thompson), Hucklebuck (Hugh Dilworth), The Governor (Erik Rhodes), Cicero (Ossie Davis), Lancaster (James E. Wall), First Ships Officer (Tony Martinez), Second Ships Officer (Michael Wright), Joe Nashua (Joe Adams)

Synopsis: Koli is a poor fisherman on the tropical paradise island of Jamaica. He is in love with Savannah, but she dreams only of living in New York City. Joe Nashua comes to Jamaica on a pearl-diving vacation. Savannah decides that Joe may be her ticket north, but before she can leave, a hurricane hits the island, during which Savannah's brother is nearly killed. His life is saved by Koli, which makes Savannah change her mind and stay in Jamaica. She does get her wish to visit New York, however, in a dream ballet sequence.

Songs: "Savannah"; "Little Biscuit"; "Cocoanut Sweet"; "Pity the Sunset"; "Yankee Dollar"; "What Good Does It Do?"; "Monkey in the Mango Tree"; "Take It Slow, Joe"; "Ain't It the Truth"; "Leave the Atom Alone"; "For Every Fish"; "I Don't Think I'll End It All Today"; "Napoleon"

Tony nominations: Best Musical, Best Actor in a Musical (Montalban), Best Actress in a Musical (Horne), Best Featured Actor in a Musical (Davis), Best Featured Actress in a Musical (Premice), Best Scenic Design (Oliver Smith), Best Costume Design (Miles White)

Comments: This was David Merrick's second hit and Lena Horne's first appearance in a starring Broadway role. It was an average musical with an average plot, but the audiences flocked to see Horne.

°*JENNIE* (October 17, 1963; Majestic Theatre; 82 performances). *Director:* Vincent J. Donehue; *Composers/Lyricists:* Howard Dietz and Arthur Schwartz; *Librettist:* Howard Dietz; *Choreographer:* Matt Mattox. Based on the life of actress Laurette Taylor, this is a musical about a gymnastics teacher in a small town. Mary Martin supposedly turned down the leads in *Hello, Dolly!* and *Funny Girl* for this one. She is the reason it ran as long as it did.

°*JUNO* (March 9, 1959; Winter Garden Theatre; 16 performances). *Director:* José Ferrer; *Composer/Lyricist:* Marc Blitzstein; *Librettist:* Joseph Stein; *Choreographer:* Agnes de Mille. Juno, played by Shirley Booth, is the hardworking matriarch of an Irish family in Dublin in the early 1920s. Based loosely on Sean O'Casey's *Juno and the Peacock*, critics felt it too dark for a musical. José Ferrer was the third director, replacing Tony Richardson and then Vincent J. Donehue. Revivals of the musical have been attempted a few times with little success.

°*KEAN* (November 2, 1961; Broadway Theatre; 92 performances). *Director/ Choreographer:* Jack Cole; *Composers/Lyricists:* Robert Wright and George Forrest; *Librettist:* Peter Stone. Set in London in the early nineteenth century, Alfred Drake starred as Edmund Kean, a man who wants to be appreciated for more than being a fine actor. Drake originally turned down the role when it was presented as a drama in London. Critics found the musical version inadequate.

Tony nominations: Best Actor in a Musical (Drake), Best Conductor and Musical Director (Pembroke Davenport)

°*KELLY* (February 6, 1965; Broadhurst Theatre; 1 performance). *Director/ Choreographer:* Herbert Ross; *Composer:* Moose Charlap; *Lyricist/Librettist:* Eddie Lawrence. The dread of everyone involved in show business; the musical closed on opening night. Set in New York City in the 1880s with a large cast, the story revolves around the first man who was said to have jumped from the Brooklyn Bridge.

THE KING AND I (March 29, 1951; St. James Theatre; 1,246 performances)

Production credits: *Producers:* Richard Rodgers and Oscar Hammerstein II; *Director:* John Van Druten; *Composer:* Richard Rodgers; *Lyricist/ Librettist:* Oscar Hammerstein II; *Choreographer:* Jerome Robbins; *Original source:* Adapted from the novel *Anna and the King of Siam* by Margaret Landon

Original cast: Captain Orton (Charles Francis), Louis Leonowens (Sandy Kennedy), Anna Leonowens (Gertrude Lawrence), The Interpreter (Leonard Graves), The Kralahome (John Juliano), The King (Yul Brynner), Phra Alack (Len Mence), Tuptim (Doretta Morrow), Lady Thiang (Dorothy Sarnoff), Prince Chulalongkorn (Jackie Collins), Prince Ying Yaowalak (Baayork Lee), Lun Tha (Larry Douglas), Sir Edward Ramsay (Robin Craven)

Synopsis: English widow Anna Leonowens and her young son arrive in Siam in 1862 to tutor the king's children. They are ushered into a kingdom ruled by a man that most people consider to be a barbarian who insists on his own ways and will listen to no one else. Anna is there to instruct the young royalty, which she does, at the same time maintaining her own traditions and values. In time, the king begrudgingly comes to respect Anna, and she begins to see beyond his arrogance. The two eventually begin to understand and care for one another.

Songs: "I Whistle a Happy Tune"; "My Lord and Master"; "Hello, Young Lovers!"; "A Puzzlement"; "The Royal Bangkok Academy"; "Getting to Know You"; "We Kiss in a Shadow"; "Shall I Tell You What I Think of You?"; "Something Wonderful"; "Western People Funny"; "I Have Dreamed"; "Shall We Dance?"

Tony Awards: Best Musical, Best Actress in a Musical (Lawrence), Best Featured Actor in a Musical (Brynner), Best Scenic Design (Jo Mielziner), Best Costume Design (Irene Sharaff)

Comments: "The boys have done it again [meaning Rodgers and Hammerstein]," said John Chapman of the *Journal-American*. Yul Brynner was not first choice for the role of the king but got it over Rex Harrison, Noël Coward, and Alfred Drake. Brynner went on to play the role more than 4,600 times on stage and television and also starred in the movie. This was the first musical by Richard Rodgers and Oscar Hammerstein based on a true story. The 1956 movie version starred Deborah Kerr as Anna (Gertrude Lawrence died in 1952). Brynner won an Oscar for Best Actor, and the movie took five Academy Awards in all.

KISMET (December 3, 1953; Ziegfeld Theatre; 583 performances)

Production credits: *Producer:* Charles Lederer; *Director:* Albert Marre; *Composer:* Aleksandr Borodin; *Lyricists:* Robert Wright and George Forrest; *Librettists:* Charles Lederer and Luther Davis; *Choreographer:* Jack Cole

Original cast: Doorman and Akbar (Jack Dodds), Omar (Francis Compton), Hajj (Alfred Drake), Marsinah (Doretta Morrow), Taman (Ted Thurston), Hassan-Ben (Clifford Fearl), Jawan (Truman Gaige), Chief Policeman (Kirby Smith), Second Policeman (Bruce MacKay), Wazir of Police (Henry Calvin), Lalume (Joan Diener), Caliph (Richard Kiley), Princess Zubbediya (Florence Lessing), Ayah to Zubbediya (Lucy Andonian), Princess Samaris (Beatrice Kraft), Ayah to Samaris (Thelma Dare), Prosecutor (Earle MacVeigh), Widow Yussef (Erica Twiford)

Synopsis: Hajj is the king of beggars, a master magician and poet who becomes involved in a series of adventures. His daughter steals the wares of a fruit merchant and is pursued by him, but Hajj rescues her. Soon she is seen by the young Caliph, who falls in love with her, but she is abducted and placed in a harem by the Wazir. Once again, Hajj comes to the rescue. Through some wizardry, he saves his daughter, and the Caliph announces that she will become his commoner bride.

Songs: "Rhymes Have I"; "Fate"; "Not Since Nineveh"; "Baubles, Bangles, and Beads"; "Stranger in Paradise"; "He's in Love!"; "Gesticulate"; "Night of My Nights"; "Was I Wazir?"; "Rahadlakum"; "And This Is My Beloved"; "The Olive Tree"

Tony Awards: Best Musical, Best Actor in a Musical (Drake), Musical Conductor (Louis Adrian)

Comments: In the 1944 movie version, Marlene Dietrich danced one number with her body and famous legs painted gold. The film was remade in 1955 with Howard Keel and Ann Blyth.

KISS ME, KATE (December 30, 1948; New Century Theatre; 1,077 performances)

Production credits: *Producers:* Saint Subber and Lemuel Ayers; *Director:* John C. Wilson; *Composer/Lyricist:* Cole Porter; *Librettists:* Sam Spewack and Bella Spewack; *Choreographer:* Hanya Holm; *Original source:* Based on Shakespeare's play *The Taming of the Shrew*

Original cast: Fred Graham/Petruchio (Alfred Drake), Harry Trevor/Baptista (Thomas Hoier), Lois Lane/Bianca (Lisa Kirk), Ralph (Don Mayo), Lilli Vanessi/Katharine (Patricia Morison), Hattie (Annabelle Hill), Paul (Lorenzo Fuller), Bill Calhoun/Lucentio (Harold Lang), First Man (Harry Clark), Second Man (Jack Diamond), Stage Doorman (Dan Brennan), Harrison Howell (Denis Green), Gremio (Edwin Clay), Hortensio (Charles Wood), Haberdasher (John Castello)

Synopsis: Fred and Lilli have been divorced for one year when they open in a musical version of *The Taming of the Shrew*. On opening night, Lilli gets a bouquet of flowers, which she mistakenly believes are sent to her from Fred, and she realizes she still loves him. But before the curtain goes up, she discovers that the flowers were meant to be delivered to Lois. Opening night on stage now becomes a battlefield; however, by evening's end, the two discover that they still really do love each other.

Songs: "Another Op'nin', Another Show"; "Why Can't You Behave?"; "Wunderbar"; "So in Love"; "We Open in Venice"; "I've Come to Wive It Wealthily in Padua"; "I Hate Men"; "Were Thine That Special Face"; "I Sing of Love"; "Kiss Me, Kate"; "Too Darn Hot"; "Where Is the Life That Late I Led?"; "Always True to You (in My Fashion)"; "Bianca"; "Brush Up Your Shakespeare"; "I Am Ashamed That Women Are So Simple"

Tony Awards: Best Musical, Best Composer and Lyricist (Porter), Best Author of a Musical, Best Producer of a Musical, Best Costume Design (Lemuel Ayers)

Comments: A Viennese journalist wrote, "Kiss me, Kate—again, again, and again," and most critics agreed. This was a personal triumph and comeback for Cole Porter, who had been suffering from the effects of an accident since 1937. It was his only musical to record more than 1,000 performances on Broadway. The highly successful 1953 movie starred Howard Keel, Kathryn Grayson, Ann Miller, and Keenan Wynn and featured Bob Fosse.

°*KWAMINA* (October 23, 1961; 54th Street Theatre; 32 performances). *Director:* Robert Lewis; *Composer/Lyricist:* Richard Adler; *Librettist:* Robert Alan Aurther: *Choreographer:* Agnes de Mille. The title role was played by Terry Carter as a white woman suffering great complications because she falls in love with a black man in a West African country. Despite the short run, Adler got a Tony nomination for Best Original Score.

Tony nominations: Best Composer, Best Choreography, Best Costume Design (Motley)

°*LET IT RIDE* (October 12, 1961; Eugene O'Neill Theatre; 68 performances). *Director:* Stanley Praeger; *Composers/Lyricists:* Jay Livingston and Ray Evens; *Librettist:* Abram S. Ginnes; *Choreographer:* Onna White. George Gobel, Sam Levene, and Barbara Nichols briefly starred in a musical version of George Abbott's 1935 farce *Three Men on a Horse*. Eddie Cantor had tried it with little success in 1941 in *Banjo Eyes*.

L'IL ABNER (November 15, 1956; St. James Theatre; 693 performances)

Production credits: *Producers:* Norman Panama, Melvin Frank, and Michael Kidd; *Director/Choreographer:* Michael Kidd; *Composer:* Gene de Paul; *Lyricist:* Johnny Mercer; *Librettists:* Norman Panama and Melvin Frank; *Original source:* Based on characters created by Al Capp

Original cast: Lonesome Polecat (Anthony Mordente), Hairless Joe (Chad Block), Romeo Scragg and Dr. Schleifitz (Marc Breaux), Clem Scragg (James Hurst), Alf Scragg (Anthony Saverino), Moonbeam Mc-Swine (Carmen Alvarez), Marryin' Sam (Stubby Kay), Earthquake McGoon (Bern Hoffman), Daisy Mae (Edith Adams), Pappy Yokum (Joe E. Marks), Mammy Yokum (Charlotte Rae), L'il Abner (Peter Palmer), Mayor Dowgmeat (Oran Osburn), Senator Jack S. Phogbound (Ted Thurston), Dr. Rasmussen T. Finsdale (Stanley Simmonds), Government Man (Richard Maitland), Available Jones (William Lanteau), Stupefyin' Jones (Julie Newmar), Colonel and Dr. Smithborn (George Reeder), President, State Department Man, and Colonel (Lanier Davis), General Bullmoose (Howard St. John), Appassionata Von Climax (Tina Louise), Evil Eye Fleagle (Al Nesor), Dr. Krogmeyer (Ralph Linn), Butler (James J. Jefferies)

Synopsis: Dogpatch is in its usual state of excitement as Sadie Hawkins Day nears, and as usual, Daisy Mae is all set to get L'il Abner at the annual festivities. But this time, she has an added problem. She is both helped and hindered by the various characters in Dogpatch. As if they didn't have enough to worry about, their attention is now focused on the federal government. It seems that government leaders are thinking of conducting atomic bomb tests in Dogpatch.

Songs: "If I Had My Druthers"; "Jubilation T. Cornpone"; "Rag Offen the Bush"; "Namely You"; "Unnecessary Time"; "What's Good for General Bullmoose"; "The Country's in the Very Best Hands"; "Oh Happy Day";

"I'm Past My Prime"; "Love in a Home"; "Progress is the Route of All Evil"; "Society Party"; "Put 'Em Back"; "The Matrimonial Stomp"

Tony Awards: Best Actress in a Musical (Adams), Best Choreography (Kidd). **Tony nominations:** Best Costume Design (Alvin Colt)

Comments: Critics were generally divided; some said the plot was a jumble, but most liked the score. Critics and audiences alike applauded Michael Kidd's direction and choreography.

LITTLE ME (November 17, 1962; Lunt-Fontanne Theatre; 257 performances)

Production credits: *Producers:* Cy Feuer and Ernest Martin; *Directors:* Cy Feuer and Bob Fosse; *Composer:* Cy Coleman; *Lyricist:* Carolyn Leigh; *Librettist:* Neil Simon; *Choreographer:* Bob Fosse; *Original source:* Based on the novel by Patrick Dennis

Original cast: Butler (John Anania), Patrick Dennis (Peter Turgeon), Miss Poitrine and Today (Nancy Andrews), Momma (Adnia Rice), Belle and Baby (Virginia Martin), George Musgrove as a boy (John Sharpe), Brucey (James Senn), Ramona (Else Olufsen), Noble Eggleston, Mr. Pinchley, Val du Val, Fred Poitrine, Otto Schnitzler, Prince Cherney, Noble, Junior (Sid Caesar), Mrs. Eggleston (Nancy Cushman), Bentley (Harris Hawkins), Miss Kepplewhite (Gretchen Cryer), Nurse (Margery Beddow), Kleeg (Burt Bier), Newsboy (Michael Smuin), Bernie Buchsbaum (Joey Faye), Bonnie Buchsbaum (Mort Marshall), Defense Lawyer (Mickey Deems), George Musgrove (Swen Swenson), Preacher (Ken Ayers), German Officer, Production Assistant, and Yulnick (Mickey Deems), General (Michael Quinn), Courier (Eddie Gasper), Red Cross Nurse (Sandra Stahl), Steward (David Gold), Secretary (Marcia Gilford), Victor (Marc Jordan)

Synopsis: In this vehicle for Sid Caesar, he played eighty-year-old and very wealthy Mr. Pinchley, along with six other characters. The musical tells the story of Belle Poitrine (Virgina Martin), who was born on the wrong side of the tracks in Venezuela, Illinois, and never forgot it. Through a series of adventures, she ends up with Mr. Pinchley, but when he dies, she goes to trial for his murder. What follows are a number of romances for the ambitious Belle.

Songs: "The Truth"; "The Other Side of the Tracks"; "Birthday Party"; "I Love You"; "Deep Down Inside"; "Be a Performer!"; "Dimples"; "Boom-Boom"; "I've Got Your Number"; "Real Live Girl"; "Poor Little Hollywood Star"; "Little Me"; "The Prince's Farewell"; "Here's to Us"

Tony Award: Best Choreography. **Tony nominations:** Best Musical, Best Actor in a Musical (Caesar), Best Featured Actor in a Musical (Swenson), Best Featured Actress in a Musical (Martin), Best Author of a Musical, Best Composer and Lyricist, Best Costume Design (Robert Fletcher), Best Direction of a Musical, Best Producer of a Musical

LOOK, MA, I'M DANCIN'! (January 29, 1948; Adelphi Theatre; 188 performances)

Production credits: *Producer:* George Abbott; *Directors/Choreographers:* George Abbott and Jerome Robbins; *Composer/Lyricist:* Hugh Martin; *Librettists:* Jerome Lawrence and Robert E. Lee; *Original source:* Conceived by Jerome Robbins

Original cast: Wotan (Don Liberto), Larry (Loren Welch), Dusty Lee (Alice Pearce), Ann Bruce (Janet Reed), Snow White (Virginia Gorski), Eddie Winkler (Harold Lang), Tommy (Tommy Rall), F. Plancek (Robert H. Harris), Tanya Drinskaya (Katharine Sergava), Lily Malloy (Nancy Walker), Mr. Gleeb (James Lane), Mr. Ferbish (Eddie Hodge), Tanya's Partner (Raul Celada), Bell Boy (Dean Campbell), Stage Manager (Dan Sattler), Suzy (Sandra Deel)

Synopsis: An heiress to a beer fortune is also an aspiring ballerina, but since she can't get recognition anywhere else, she subsidizes a second-rate dance troupe. They travel cross-country with many unexpected and comical adventures. Then, to the surprise of them all, a ballet that the heiress choreographs is a big hit, but that is her one glory, for after that, the company collapses.

Songs: "Gotta Dance"; "I'm the First Girl"; "I'm Not So Bright"; "I'm Tired of Texas"; "Tiny Room"; "The Little Boy Blues"; "Jazz"; "The New Look"; "If You'll Be Mine"; "Pajama Dance"; "Shauny O'Shay"; "The Two of Us"

LOST IN THE STARS (October 30, 1949; Music Box Theatre; 281 performances)

Production credits: *Producers:* Maxwell Anderson, Elmer Rice, Robert E. Sherwood, Kurt Weill, and John F. Wharton; *Director:* Rouben Mamoulian; *Composer:* Kurt Weill; *Lyricist/Librettist:* Maxwell Anderson; *Choreographer:* Kevin R. Hauge; *Original source:* Based on Alan Paton's novel *Cry, the Beloved Country*

Original cast: Leader (Frank Roane), Answerer (Joseph James), Nita (Elayne Richards), Grace Kumalo (Gertrude Jeannette), Stephen Kumalo (Todd Duncan), Young Man (La Verne French), Young Woman (Mabel Hart), James Jarvis (Leslie Banks), Edward Jarvis (Judson Rees), Arthur Jarvis (John Morley), John Kumalo (Warren Coleman), Paulus (Charles McRae), William (Joseph James), Jared (William C. Smith), Alex (Herbert Coleman), Forman (Jerome Shaw), Mrs. M'kize (Georgette Harvey), Hlabeni (William Marshall), Eland (Charles Grunwell), Linda (Sheila Guyse),

Johannes Pafuri (Roy Allen), Mathew Kumalo (Van Prince), Absalom
Kumalo (Julian Mayfield), Rose (Gloria Smith), Irina (Inez Mathews),
Policeman (Robert Burn), White Woman (Biruta Ramoska), White Man
(Mark Kramer), Guyard (Jerome Shaw), Burton (John W. Stanley), Judge
(Guy Spaull), Villager (Robert McFerrin)

Synopsis: A black South African preacher and his wife go to Johan-
nesburg because they have not heard from their son, Absalom, in some
time. The son has been living with his pregnant girlfriend, Irina. Absolom
is accused of murdering a white man, not just any white man, but one who
advocated giving freedom to black South Africans. He confesses and the
preacher visits his son and Irina and agrees to marry them in prison. The
preacher also attempts to talk to the father of the murder victim. Absalom
is sentenced to death by hanging.

Songs: "The Hills of Ixopo"; "Thousands of Miles"; "Train to Johannes-
burg"; "The Search"; "The Little Grey House"; "Who'll Buy?"; "Trouble
Man"; "Murder in Parkwold"; "Fear!"; "Lost in the Stars"; "The Wild Justice"; "O Tixo, Tixo, Help Me!"; "Stay Well"; "Cry, the Beloved Country";
"Big Mole"; "A Bird of Passage"; "Four O'Clock"

Comments: A Greeklike chorus gave a static quality to the show. The
lovely title song was written years earlier. This was Weill's last new work on
Broadway; he died during the run.

°*LOUISIANA LADY* (June 2, 1947; New Century Theatre; 4 performances). *Director:* Edgar MacGregor; *Composers/Lyricists:* Monte Carlo
and Alma M. Sanders; *Librettists:* Issac Green Jr. and Eugene Berton;
Choreographer: Felicia Sorel. The husband and wife team of Monte Carlo
and Alma M. Sanders were back on Broadway after seventeen years with
a musical about a bordello in New Orleans. They did not try again. Sanders is credited with being the first woman to compose a full musical score,
although her works never achieved any lasting fame.

LOVE LIFE (October 7, 1948; 46th Street Theatre; 252 performances)
Production credits: *Producer:* Cheryl Crawford; *Director:* Elia Kazan;
Composer: Kurt Weill; *Lyricist/Librettist:* Alan Jay Lerner; *Choreographer:*
Michael Kidd

Original cast: Magician (Jay Marshall), Susan (Nanette Fabray), Sam
(Ray Middleton), Mary Joe (Holly Harris), Tim (Evans Thornton), George
Hamilton Beacon (David Thomas), Jonathan Anderson (Gene Tobin),
Charlie (Victor Clarke), Will (Mark Kramer), Ben (Lenn Dale), Child (Vin-
cent Gugleotti), Elizabeth Cooper (Cheryl Archer), Johnny Cooper (Johnny
Stewart)

Synopsis: Regarded as one of the first "concept musicals," this is a story of family values in America. The Cooper family never ages, but they progress through different eras, and the musical shows how their relationship changes and weakens as stress grows in the home. Interspersed are different kinds of vaudeville numbers such as a trapeze act and vocal ensembles. At the end, the Coopers are trying to save their marriage, and they feel stronger because they finally understand all the pressures that face them.

Songs: "Who Is Samuel Cooper?"; "My Name Is Samuel Cooper"; "Here I'll Stay"; "Progress"; "I Remember It Well"; "Green-Up Time"; "Economics"; "Mother's Getting Nervous"; "My Kind of Night"; "Women's Club Blues"; "Love Song"; "I'm Your Man"; "Ho, Bill O!"; "Is It Him or Is It Me"; "This Is the Life"; "Minstrel Parade"; "Madame Zuzu"; "Taking No Chances"; "Mr. Right"

Tony Award: Best Actress, Musical (Fabray)

°*LUTE SONG* (February 6, 1946; Plymouth Theatre; 142 performances). *Director:* John Houseman; *Composer:* Raymond Scott; *Lyricist:* Bernard Hanighen; *Librettists:* Sidney Howard and Will Irwin; *Choreographer:* Yeichi Nimura. Mary Martin appeared in an offbeat love story based on a fourteenth-century Chinese play. It was called too esoteric for general theatre audiences. This was the only Broadway appearance of Nancy Davis, who later married Ronald Reagan.

°*MAGDALENA* (September 20, 1948; Ziegfeld Theatre; 88 performances). *Director:* Jules Dassin; *Composer:* Heitor Villa-Lobos; *Lyricists:* Robert Wright and George Forrest; *Librettists:* Frederick Hazlitt Brennan and Homer Curran; *Choreographer:* Jack Cole. A colorful score by the Brazilian composer highlights the show, but audiences largely ignored the story of a devout woman (Dorothy Sarnoff) trying to convert her fiancé (John Raitt) to Christianity. When the show opened after successful runs in Los Angeles and San Francisco, it was the most expensive production ever staged on Broadway.

°*MAGGIE* (February 18, 1953; National Theatre; 5 performances). *Director:* Michael Gordon; *Composer/Lyricist:* William Roy; *Librettist:* Hugh Thomas; *Choreographer:* June Graham. Critics and audiences largely ignored this musical retelling of James Barrie's *What Every Woman Knows*. It featured Betty Paul and Keith Andes in the story of an ambitious woman who guides her husband into a successful political career without his being aware of how he is being maneuvered.

°*MAKE A WISH* (April 18, 1951; Winter Garden Theatre; 103 performances). *Director:* John C. Wilson; *Composer/Lyricist:* Hugh Martin; *Librettists:* Preston Sturges and Abe Burrows; *Choreographer:* Gower Champion. The action takes place on the Left Bank of Paris. Nanette Fabray starred as a French orphan whose fascination with Paris causes her to break away from a guided tour of the city. She sings and dances and falls in love with the city and a man.

ME AND JULIET (May 28, 1953; Majestic Theatre; 358 performances)
   Production credits: *Producers:* Richard Rodgers and Oscar Hammerstein II; *Director:* George Abbott; *Composer:* Richard Rodgers; *Lyricist/Librettist:* Oscar Hammerstein II; *Choreographer:* Robert Alton
   Original cast: George (Randy Hall), Sidney (Edwin Philips), Jeanie (Isabel Bigley), Herbie (Jackie Kelk), Chris (Barbara Carroll), Milton (Herb Wasserman), Stu (Joe Shulman), Michael (Michael King), Bob (Mark Dawson), Larry (Bill Hayes), Mac (Ray Walston), Monica (Patty Ann Jackson), Ruby (Joe Lautner), Charlie (Arthur Maxwell), Dario (Geroge S. Irving), Lily (Helena Soctt), Jim (Bob Fortier), Susie (Svetlana McLee), Voice of Mr. Harrison (Henry Hamilton), Voice of Miss Davenport (Deborah Remsen), Hilda (Norma Thornton), Marcia (Thelma Tadlock), Betty (Joan McCracken), Buzz (Buzz Miller), Ralph (Ralph Linn), Miss Oxford (Gwen Harmon), Sadie (Francine Bond), Mildred (Lorraine Havercroft), Theatre Patron (Barbara Lee Smith), Theatre Patron (Susan Lowell)
   Synopsis: In this show within a show; the focus is on various people all involved with a stage musical. Two stories run at once. Chorus girl Jeanie is involved with assistant stage manager Larry, but his rival and Jeanie's ex-boyfriend Bob will go to any lengths to get her back. In the other plot, dancer Betty loves stage manager Mac, who doesn't want to get involved with people in his own show. The solution is that Mac changes shows.
   Songs: "A Very Special Day"; "That's the Way It Happens"; "Marriage Type Love"; "Keep It Gay"; "The Big Black Giant"; "No Other Love"; "It's Me"; "Intermission Talk"; "It Feels Good"; "We Deserve Each Other"; "I'm Your Girl"
   Comments: The production by Richard Rodgers and Oscar Hammerstein ran mostly on the strength of their names but ended in the red. It is generally considered their least successful collaboration.

MEXICAN HAYRIDE (January 28, 1944; Winter Garden Theatre; 479 performances)
   Production credits: *Producer:* Mike Todd; *Director:* Charles Barton; *Composer/Lyricist:* Cole Porter; *Librettists:* Herbert Fields and Dorothy Fields; *Choreographer:* Paul Haakon

Original cast: Joe Bascom (Bobby Clark), Lottery Girl (Eva Reyes), Woman Vendor (Claire Anderson), Chief of Police (Richard Bengali), Tillie Leeds (Lois Bolton), Billy (Bill Callahan), Mrs. Augustus Adamson (Jean Cleveland), Miguel Correres (Sergio DeKarlo), Ms. Lupescu (Dorothy Durkee), Lydia (Toddle), David Winthrop (Wilbur Evans), Lombo Campos (George Givot), Carol (Arthur Gondra), Paul (Paul Haakon), Montana (June Havoc), Mr. Augustus Adamson (William A. Lee), Senor Martinez (David Leonard), Dagmar Marshak (Luba Malina), Eadie Johnsn (Edith Meiser), Lolita Cantine (Corinna Mura), Jose (Raul Reyes), Augustus Jr. (Eric Roberts), Mrs. Molly Wincor (Jeanne Shelby), Lottery Boy (Hank Wolf)

Synopsis: Joe Bascom, a fugitive from the United States, catches the bull's ear thrown by Montana, an American female bullfighter in Mexico. For that, he becomes a guest of the Mexican government, and as such he sets up an illegal lottery with the help of his new friend Lombo. American David Winthrop sets out to get the two, even though he believes that Montana, whom he loves, is in love with Joe. The two crooks are finally caught, and David and Montana make plans to marry.

Songs: "Sing to Me Guitar"; "I Love You"; "There Must Be Someone for Me"; "Carlotta"; "Girls"; "What a Crazy Way to Spend Sunday"; "Abracadabra"; "Count Your Blessings"; "I Get a Kick Out of You"; "What Is This Thing?"; "Katie Went to Haiti"; "Why Shouldn't I?"; "Let's Do It"; "My Heart Belongs to Daddy"

Comments: A good but not great Cole Porter score plus a lavish setting gave the production a fine sendoff.

MILK AND HONEY (October 10, 1961; Martin Beck Theatre; 543 performances)

Production credits: *Producer:* Gerard Oestreicher; *Director:* Albert Marre; *Composer/Lyricist:* Jerry Herman; *Librettist:* Don Appell; *Choreographer:* Donald Saddler

Original cast: Ruth (Mimi Benzell), Clara Weiss (Molly Picon), Phil (Robert Weede), Adi (Juki Arkin), Mrs. Segal (Diane Goldberg), Mrs. Perlman (Thelma Pelish), David (Tommy Rall), Barbara (Lanna Saunders), The Guide (Ellen Berse), Porter (Burt Bier), Shepherd Boy (Johnny Borden), Mrs. Kessler (Ceil Delli), Mrs. Breslin (Rose Lischner), Cantor (David London), Zipporah (Ellen Madison), Mrs. Weinstein (Addi Negri), Mrs. Strauss (Dorothy Richardson), Mr. Horowitz (Reuben Singer), Man of the Moshav (Art Tookoyan)

Synopsis: Phil is an American Jew visiting Israel, where his daughter and son-in-law now live. He is an unhappy man who is separated from his wife, but during his stay he meets an American woman named Ruth, to whom he is attracted; however, when Phil tells her about his wife in the United States, she flees to Tel Aviv. When she returns and sees him again, this time Phil is not so sure about the relationship. So, Ruth returns to the United States to wait and see.

Songs: "Shepherd's Song"; "Shalom"; "Independence Day Hora"; "Like a Young Man"; "I Will Follow You"; "Hymn to Hymie"; "Milk and Honey"; "There's No Reason in the World"; "Chin Up, Ladies"; "That Was Yesterday"; "Let's Not Waste a Moment"; "The Wedding"; "As Simple as That"

Tony nominations: Best Musical, Best Actress in a Musical (Picon), Best Composer (Herman), Best Costume Design (Miles White), Best Producer

Comments: Nobody is happy in this musical except Molly Picon, who plays a "yenta" gone to Israel to find a husband. Although it ran about a year and a half, it was never out of the red.

MISS LIBERTY (July 15, 1949; Imperial Theatre; 308 performances)

Production credits: *Producers:* Irving Berlin, Robert E. Sherwood, and Moss Hart; *Director:* Moss Hart; *Composer/Lyricist:* Irving Berlin; *Librettist:* Robert E. Sherwood; *Choreographer:* Jerome Robbins

Original cast: Maisie Doll (Mary McCarty), Herald Reader (Rowan Tudor), James Gordon Bennett (Charles Dingle), Horace Miller (Eddie Albert), Police Captain, Policeman, and Immigration Officer (Evans Thornton), Mayor and Richard K. Fox (Donald McCelland), French Ambassador (Emile Renan), Carthwright (Sid Lawson), Joseph Pulitzer (Phillip Bourneuf), Barthodi (Herbert Berghof), Monique Dupont (Allyn McLerie), Boy, Lamplighter, and Dandy (Tommy Rall), Girl and Ruby (Maria Karnilova), Strong Man (Kazimir Kokic), Countess (Ethel Griffies), Lover and Minister (Ed Chappel), His Girl and Actress (Helene Whitney), Gendarme (Robert Penn), Lamplighter (Johnny V. R.Thompson), Model and Socialite (Marilyn Frechette), Admiral and Policeman (Robert Patterson), Mother (Elizabeth Watts), Maid (Gloria Patrice), Sailor (Eddie Phillips), His Girl (Dolores Goodman), Judge (Erick Christen), Boy (William Calhoun)

Synopsis: The show is built around the presentation of the Statue of Liberty to the American people by the people of France. Two rival newspapers are trying to find the model who posed for Miss Liberty. A bungling newspaper photographer (Horace) ends up taking pictures of the crate the statue came in instead of the statue itself, and he is fired. Newspaper woman Maisie convinces him to go to Paris, where he wrongly identifies the woman who modeled for the statue and is attracted to her. They both return to New York, where the mistake is finally straightened out, but now Maisie is left out in the cold.

Songs: "Extra, Extra"; "What Do I Have to Do to Get My Picture Took?"; "The Most Expensive Statue in the World"; "A Little Fish in a Big

Pond"; "Let's Take an Old Fashioned Walk"; "Homework"; "Paris Wakes Up and Smiles"; "Only for Americans"; "Just One Way to Say I Love You"; "Miss Liberty"; "The Train"; "You Can Have Him"; "The Policeman's Ball"; "Me and My Bundle"; "Falling Out of Love Can Be Fun"

Tony Award: Stage Technician (Joe Lynn)

Comments: Audiences didn't find the songs memorable, and the *New York Times* called it "without sparkle or originality." A $400,000 advance sale kept it alive for the run.

THE MOST HAPPY FELLA (May 3, 1956; Imperial Theatre; 676 performances)

Production credits: *Producers:* Kermit Bloomgarden and Lynn Loesser; *Director:* Joseph Anthony; *Composer/Lyricist/Librettist:* Frank Loesser; *Choreographer:* Dania Krupska; *Original source:* Based on Sidney Howard's play *They Knew What They Wanted*

Original cast: Cashier and Postman (Lee Cass), Cleo (Susan Johnson), Rosabella (Jo Sullivan), Tony (Robert Weede), Marie (Mona Paulee), Max (Louis Polacek), Herman (Shorty Long), Clem (Alan Gilbert), Jake and Ciccio (John Henson), Al (Roy Lazarus), Joe (Art Lund), Giuseppe (Arthur Rubin), Pasquale (Ricco Froehlich), Country Girl (Meri Miller), City Boy (John Sharpe), Doctor (Keith Kaldenberg), Priest (Russell Goodwin), Tessie (Zena Bethune), Gussie (Christopher Snell), Brakeman (Norris Greer), Busdriver (Ralph Farnworth)

Synopsis: Older vintner Tony sees a young lady, Rosabella, in a San Francisco restaurant and writes to her. When she asks for a photograph, he sends a picture of Joe, one of his handsome hired hands. Rosabella goes to the ranch and learns that Tony has been injured. She remains and the two marry; however, she and Joe have an affair and she becomes pregnant. When Tony learns of the child, he wants to kill Joe, but he knows he will be lonely. Rosabella feels the same way, and they agree to stay together.

Songs: "Ooh! My Feet!"; "Somebody, Somewhere"; "Standing on the Corner"; "I Know How It Is"; "The Most Happy Fella"; "A Long Time Ago"; "Joey, Joey, Joey"; "Rosabella"; "Abbondanza"; "Benvenuta"; "Aren't You Glad?"; "Don't Cry"; "Fresno Beauties"; "Love and Kindness"; "Happy to Be"; "Big D"; "How Beautiful the Days"; "Warm All Over"

Tony nominations: Best Musical, Best Actor in a Musical (Weede), Best Featured Actress in a Musical (Sullivan), Best Direction, Best Choreography, Conductor and Musical Director (Herbert Greene)

MR. PRESIDENT (October 20, 1962; St. James Theatre; 256 performances)

Production credits: *Producer:* Leland Hayward; *Director:* Joshua Logan; *Composer/Lyricist:* Irving Berlin; *Librettists:* Howard Lindsay and Russel Crouse; *Choreographer:* Peter Gennaro

Original cast: President Stephen Decatur Henderson (Robert Ryan), Nell Henderson (Nanette Fabray), Leslie Henderson (Anita Gillette), Larry Henderson (Jerry Strickler), Youssein Davair (Jack Washburn), Tippy Taylor (Charlotte Fairchild), Pat Gregory (Jack Haskell), Charley Wayne (Stanley Grover), Princess Kyra (Wisa D'Orso), Russian Soldier (Jack Mette), Colonel Wilson (Van Stevens), Mrs. Lotta Pendleton (Marian Haraldson), George Perkins (Beau Tilden), Mr. Thomas (Carl Nicholas), Deborah Chakronin (Baayork Lee), Arthur Blanchard and Commentator (Jack McMinn), Radio Operator (Anthony Falco), Abou (Carlos Bas), Commentator, Dancer, and Tahitian (Louis Kosman), Workman (Dan Siretta), Miss Barnes (Lispet Nelson), Deacon (Carl Nicholas), Sergeant Stone (Beau Tilden), Chester Kincaid (John Cecil Holm), Betty Chandler (Carol Lee Jensen), Spieler (Jack Rains), Governor Harmon Bardahl (David Brooks)

Synopsis: It is the White House in the 1960s, home to President Stephen Decatur Henderson and family. The president is en route to Russia when he finds out that his meeting there has been cancelled, but he insists on landing in Moscow anyway. The resulting mix-up and humiliation cost him reelection, and although his wife is happy to be home, he is not. When he is offered a Senate seat, there are conditions attached, so he turns it down, but in the end, love of country causes him to reconsider.

Songs: "Let's Go Back to the Waltz"; "In Our Hide-Away"; "The First Lady"; "Meat and Potatoes"; "I've Got to Be Around"; "The Secret Service"; "It Gets Lonely in the White House"; "Is He the Only Man in the World?"; "They Love Me"; "Pigtails and Freckles"; "Don't Be Afraid of Romance"; "Laugh It Up"; "Empty Pockets Filled with Love"; "Glad to Be Home"; "You Need a Hobby"; "The Washington Twist"; "The Only Dance I Know"; "I'm Gonna Get Him"; "This Is a Great Country"

Tony Award: Best Stage Technician (Solly Pernick). **Tony nominations:** Best Actress in a Musical (Fabray), Best Conductor and Musical Director (Jay Blacton)

Comments: This was Irving Berlin's last musical. None of the songs captured the public's fancy, and *Variety* called it a flop.

MR. WONDERFUL (March 22, 1956; Broadway Theatre; 383 performances)

Production credits: *Producers:* Jule Style and George Gilbert, in association with Lester Osterman Jr.; *Director:* Jack Donahue; *Composers/Lyricists:* Jerry Bock, Larry Holofcener, and George Weiss; *Librettists:* Joseph Stein and Will Glickman; *Choreographers:* Ted Royal and Morton L. Stevens

Original cast: Unemployed Actress (Ann Buckles), Hal (Hal Loman), Song Plugger (Richard Curry), Soprano (Rina Falcone), Rita Romano (Chita Rivera), Audition Annie (Pat Wilkes), Johnnie (John Pelletti), Singer (Karen Shepard), Sister (Dorothy D'Honau), Talent Scout (T. J. Halligan), Fred Campbell (Jack Carter), Counterman (Herb Fields), Mr. Foster
Original cast: Koli (Richardo Montalban), Quico (Augustine Rios), Savannah (Lena Horne), Grandma Obeah (Adelaide Hall), Giner (Josephine Premice), Snodgrass (Roy Thompson), Hucklebuck (Hugh Dilworth), The Governor (Erik Rhodes), Cicero (Ossie Davis), Lancaster (James E. Wall), First Ships Officer (Tony Martinez), Second Ships Officer (Michael Wright), Joe Nashua (Joe Adams)
Synopsis: Koli is a poor fisherman on the tropical paradise island of Jamaica. He is in love with Savannah, but she dreams only of living in New York City. Joe Nashua comes to Jamaica on a pearl-diving vacation. Savannah decides that Joe may be her ticket north, but before she can leave, a hurricane hits the island, during which Savannah's brother is nearly killed. His life is saved by Koli, which makes Savannah change her mind and stay in Jamaica. She does get her wish to visit New York, however, in a dream ballet sequence.

°°°(Malcom Lee Beggs), Uncle (Will Mastin), Dad (Sammy Davis Sr.), Charlie Welch (Sammy Davis Jr.), Ethel Pearson (Olga James), Stage Manager (Bob Kole), Script Girl (Ginny Perlowin), Cigarette Girl (Jerri Gray), Little Girl (Marilyn Cooper), Sophie's Boy (Ronnie Lee)
Synopsis: Black small-time performer Charlie Welch is persuaded by fiancé Ethel and white friend Fred to open his act at the Palm Club in Miami Beach. He is highly successful, and the second act shows off the real-time act of Sammy Davis Jr., his father, and uncle. The entire musical serves as a vehicle to introduce the talents of Davis and closely follows his night club acts at the time.
Songs: "1617 Broadway"; "Without You, I'm Nothing"; "Jacques D'Iraq"; "Ethel, Baby"; "Mr. Wonderful"; "Charlie Welch"; "Talk to Him"; "Too Close for Comfort"; "Rita's Audition"; "The Audition"; "There"; "Miami"; "I've Been Too Busy"
Tony nomination: Best Actor in a Musical (Davis Jr.)
Comments: Although the show was staged as a vehicle to introduce Sammy Davis Jr. to Broadway, "Mr. Wonderful," the hit number of the production, was sung by Olga James.

THE MUSIC MAN (December 19, 1957; Majestic Theatre; 1,375 performances)
Production credits: *Producers:* Kermit Bloomgarden, with Herbert Green, in association with Frank Productions, Inc.; *Director:* Morton

DaCosta; *Composer/Lyricist:* Meredith Willson; *Librettists:* Meredith Wilson and Franklin Lacey; *Choreographer:* Onna White; *Original source:* Based on a story by Meredith Willson and Franklin Lacey

Original cast: Charlie Cowell (Paul Reed), Conductor (Carl Nicholas), Harold Hill (Robert Preston), Mayor Shinn (David Burns), Marcellus Washburn (Iggie Wolfington), Tommy Djilas (Danny Carroll), Marian Paroo (Barbara Cook), Mrs. Paroo (Pert Kelton), Amaryllis (Marilyn Siegel), Winthrop Paroo (Eddie Hodges), Eulalie Mackecknie Shinn (Helen Raymond), Zaneeta Shinn (Dusty Worrall), Gracie Shinn (Barbara Travis), Alma Hix (Adnia Rice), Maud Dunlop (Elaine Swann), Ethel Toffelmier (Peggy Mondo), Mrs. Squires (Martha Flynn), Constable Locke (Carl Nicholas)

Synopsis: Harold Hill is the ultimate con man. He arrives in River City, Iowa, to sell band instruments. His plan is to talk the good people into giving him money for the instruments, then get out of town before the goods actually arrive. It has worked before, but this time, in this place, Marian the librarian is on to him. She is about to expose him, but instead she forces Harold to stay in River City and teach music to the children when the ordered instruments arrive. Since the music man cannot read music, the resulting concert is horrendous. In the meantime, Harold falls in love with Marian.

Songs: "Rock Island"; "Iowa Stubborn"; "Trouble"; "Piano Lesson"; "Goodnight, My Someone"; "Seventy-Six Trombones"; "Sincere"; "The Sadder-But-Wiser Girl"; "Pickalittle"; "Goodnight Ladies"; "Marion the Librarian"; "My White Knight"; "Wells Fargo Wagon"; "It's You"; "Shipoopi"; "Lida Rose"; "Will I Ever Tell You?"; "Gary, Indiana"; "Till There Was You"

Tony Awards: Best Musical, Best Actor in a Musical (Preston), Best Featured Actor in a Musical (Burns), Best Featured Actress in a Musical (Cook), Conductor and Musical Director (Herbert Greene), Stage Technician (Sammy Knapp, 1959). **Tony nominations:** Best Featured Actor in a Musical (Wolfington), Best Director, Best Choreography, Best Stage Technician (Sammy Knapp, 1958)

°*MY DARLIN' AIDA* (October 27, 1952; Winter Garden Theatre; 89 performances). *Director/Lyricist:* Charles Friedman; *Composer:* Giuseppe Verdi; *Librettist:* Charles Friedman; *Choreographer:* Hanya Holm. Giuseppe Verdi's opera of the romantic love triangle is reset in the Confederacy in the first year of the Civil War. Matinee and evening performances had different principal actors because of the difficult score. The principal Aida was Elaine Malbin.

MY FAIR LADY (March 15, 1956; Mark Hellinger Theatre; 2,717 performances)

Production credits: *Producer:* Herman Leven; *Director:* Moss Hart; *Composer:* Frederick Loewe; *Lyricist/Librettist:* Alan Jay Lerner; *Choreographer:* Hanya Holm; *Original source:* Based on George Bernard Shaw's play *Pygmalion*

Original cast: Mrs. Eynsford Hill (Viola Roache), Eliza Doolittle (Julie Andrews), Freddy Eynsford-Hill (Michael King), Colonel Pickering (Robert Coote), Henry Higgins (Rex Harrison), Alfred P. Doolittle (Stanley Holloway), Mrs. Pearce (Philippa Bevans), Mrs. Hopkins and Lady Boxington (Olive Reeves-Smith), Mrs. Higgins (Cathleen Nesbitt), Lord Boxington (Gordon Dilworth), Constable (Barton Mumaw), Flower Girl (Cathy Conklin), Zoltan Karpathy (Christopher Hewett), Queen of Transylvania (Maribel Hammer), Ambassador (Rod McClennan), Bartender (Paul Brown), Mrs. Higgins's Maid (Judith Williams)

Synopsis: Faithfully adapted, the show centers on the efforts of an English gentleman (Higgins) to turn a scruffy Cockney flower seller (Doolittle) into a lady. When Higgins hears the speech of the raucous Doolittle in the marketplace, he casually tells his friend Pickering that with a little time, he could make a lady of her. The girl overhears him and arrives on his doorstep to take him up on his boast. It is a long, hard, amusing struggle, but in the end, Eliza Doolittle fools even the highest of English society and captures the heart—although with great reluctance—of the stuffy Henry Higgins.

Songs: "Why Can't the English?"; "Wouldn't It Be Loverly?"; "With a Little Bit of Luck"; "I'm an Ordinary Man"; "Just You Wait"; "The Rain in Spain"; "I Could Have Danced All Night"; "On the Street Where You Live"; "The Embassy Waltz"; "You Did It"; "Show Me"; "Get Me to the Church on Time"; "A Hymn to Him"; "Without You"; "I've Grown Accustomed to Her Face"

Tony Awards: Best Musical, Best Actor in a Musical (Harrison), Best Direction, Best Scenic Design (Oliver Smith), Best Costume Design (Cecil Beaton), Conductor and Musical Director (Franz Allers). **Tony nominations:** Best Actress in a Musical (Andrews), Best Featured Actor in a Musical (Coote), Best Featured Actor in a Musical (Holloway), Best Choreography

Comments: The *New York Times* said that the energy expended for the show might equal that for splitting the atom, "which many consider a good deal less spectacular." Many also consider *My Fair Lady* to be the finest of all American musicals of the Golden Age, a triumph for performers, writers, and the director.

°*NELLIE BLY* (January 21, 1946; Adelphi Theatre; 16 performances). *Director:* Edgar J. MacGregor; *Composer:* James Van Heusen; *Lyricist:*

Johnny Burke; *Librettist:* Joseph Quillan; *Choreographers:* Edward Caton and Lee Sherman. Bly (Joy Hodges) is a lady reporter who in 1889 gets the job of beating Phileas Fogg's eighty-day trip around the world. Critics said the musical caught none of Nellie's speed or her story's excitement.

°*THE NERVOUS SET* (May 12, 1959; Henry Miller Theatre; 31 performances). *Director:* Theodore J. Flicker; *Composer/Choreographer:* Tommy Wolf; *Lyricist:* Fran Landesman; *Librettists:* Jay Landesman and Theodore J. Flicker. Contemporary New York City and Fairfield, Connecticut, are the backgrounds against which the ups and downs of a marriage are spelled out. The brief run starred Larry Hagman, Richard Hayes, and Toni Seitz.

NEW GIRL IN TOWN (May 14, 1957; 46th Street Theatre; 431 performances)

Production credits: *Producers:* Frederick Brisson, Robert E. Griffith, and Harold S. Prince; *Director:* George Abbott; *Composer/Lyricist:* Bob Merrill; *Librettist:* George Abbott; *Choreographer:* Bob Fosse; *Original source:* Based on Eugene O'Neill's play *Anna Christie*

Original cast: Lily (Lulu Bates), Moll (Pat Ferrier), Katie (Dorothy Dushock), Alderman (Michael Quinn), Chris (Cameron Prud'homme), Johnson (Jeff Killion), Seaman (H. F. Green), Marthy (Thelma Ritter), Oscar (Del Anderson), Pete (Eddie Phillips), Mrs. Dowling (Ann Williams), Smith (Stokley Gray), Mrs. Smith (Dorothy Stinnette), Bartender (Mark Dawson), Ivy (Rita Noble), Rose (Ginny Perlowin), Little Girl (Claiborne Cary), Anna (Gwen Verdon), Flo (Drusilla Davis), Pearl (Mara Landi), Mat (George Wallace), Reporter (Herb Fields), Masher (John Aristides), Svenson (Ray Mason), Waiter (Rudy Adamo), Dowling (Ripple Lewis), Krimp (John Ford), Henry (Edgar Daniels)

Synopsis: Aging seaman Chris does not know that his daughter Anna, who is staying with him while recovering from tuberculosis, was a former streetwalker in turn-of-the-century New York City. Anna is welcomed in town and falls in love with sailor Mat, but she hides the relationship from her father. Marthy, Chris's common-law wife, drunkenly reveals her past, and Mat leaves on the next ship. Anna tries to build a new life as a farmer on Staten Island. Mat eventually returns to port, and Chris tries to keep the lovers apart, but the two reunite and realize they are truly in love.

Songs: "Roll Yer Socks Up"; "Anna Lilla"; "Sunshine Girl"; "On the Farm"; "Flings"; "It's Good to Be Alive"; "Look at 'Er"; "Yer My Friend, Aintcha?"; "Did You Close Your Eyes?"; "There Ain't No Flies on Me"; "Ven I Valse"; "If That Was Love"; "Chess and Checkers"

Tony Awards: Best Actress in a Musical (shared by Ritter and Verdon). **Tony nominations:** Best Musical, Best Featured Actor in a Musical (Prud'homme), Best Choreography

Comments: Critics said it was mostly the lack of competition that kept the show running for more than a year.

NO STRINGS (March 15, 1962; 45th Street Theatre; 580 performances)

Production credits: *Producers:* Richard Rodgers, in association with Samuel Taylor; *Director/Choreographer:* Joe Layton; *Composer/Lyricist:* Richard Rodgers; *Librettist:* Samuel Taylor

Original cast: Barbara Woodruff (Diahann Carroll), David Jordan (Richard Kiley), Jeanette Valmy (Noelle Adam), Luc Delbert (Alvin Epstein), Mollie Plummer (Polly Rowles), Mike Robinson (Don Chastain), Louis dePourtal (Mitchell Gregg), Comfort O'Connell (Bernice Massi), Gabrielle Bertin (Ann Hodges), Marcello Agnolotti (Paul Cambeilh)

Synopsis: This unhappy romance is set mainly in Paris and Monte Carlo. American writer David Jordan has come to France after winning the Pulitzer Prize. In Paris, he meets black model Barbara Woodruff and they fall in love, but there is trouble when David learns that she has an older admirer, although they finally make up. Before long, however, David feels he must go back home to write again. Barbara believes that he thinks their romance would be frowned upon in the United States, so the lovers part.

Songs: "The Sweetest Sounds"; "How Sad"; "Loads of Love"; "The Man Who Has Everything"; "Be My Host"; "La La La"; "You Don't Tell Me"; "Love Makes the World Go"; "Nobody Told Me"; "Look No Further"; "Maine"; "An Orthodox Fool"; "Eager Beaver"; "No Strings"

Tony Awards: Best Actress in a Musical (Carroll), Best Composer, Best Choreography. **Tony nominations:** Best Musical, Best Actor in a Musical (Kiley), Best Direction of a Musical, Best Scenic Design (David Hays), Best Costume Design (Donald Brooks), Best Conductor and Musical Director (Peter Matz)

Comments: Although his lyrics received much praise, after this show Richard Rodgers left the job of lyricist to others.

°*NOWHERE TO GO BUT UP* (November 10, 1962; Winter Garden Theatre; 9 performances). *Director:* Sidney Lumet; *Composer:* Sol Berkowitz; *Lyricist/Librettist:* James Lipton; *Choreographer:* Ronald Field. Tom Bosley, Martin Balsam, and Bert Convy appeared in this musical about flamboyant prohibition agents in a big city somewhere in the United States. It was also the stage debut of Dorothy Loudon, who would go on to a long, highly acclaimed career in musical comedy, but she was unable to save this one.

OH CAPTAIN! (February 4, 1958, Alvin Theatre; 192 performances)

Production credits: *Producers:* Howard Merrill and Theatre Corporation of America; *Director:* José Ferrer; *Composers/Lyricists:* Jay Livingston and Ray Evans; *Librettists:* Al Morgan and José Ferrer; *Choreographer:* James Starbuck; *Original source:* Based on the Alec Guinness film *The Captain's Paradise*

Original cast: Captain Henry St. James (Tony Randall), Mrs. Maud St. James (Jacquelyn McKeever), Enrico Manzoni (Edward Platt), Clerk (Jack Eddleman), Lisa (Alexandra Danilova), Bobo (Abbe Lane), Guide (Stanley Carlson), Spaniard (Paul Valentine), Mae (Susan Johnson)

Synopsis: The priggish Captain Henry St. James has a wife, Maud, at home in London and a foreign mistress, Bobo, in Paris as he sails the English Channel. The run with his ship gives him a weekend in London, five days at sea, a weekend in Paris, and then back again. Wife Maud feels that she would like to leave home once in a while for some fun, but the captain disagrees. When Maud wins first prize in a recipe contest, which is a weekend in Paris, she surprises the captain. After some wild adventures, both women finally realize they have been duped, and both leave the captain to live their own lives.

Songs: "A Very Proper Town"; "Life Does a Man a Favor"; "A Very Proper Week"; "Captain Henry St. James"; "Three Paradise"; "Surprise"; "Hey Madame"; "Femininity"; "It's Never Quite the Same"; "We're Not Children"; "Give It All You Got"; "Love Is Hell"; "Keep It Simple"; "The Morning Music of Montmartre"; "You Don't Know Him"; "I've Been There and I'm Back"; "You're So Right for Me"; "All the Time"

Tony nominations: Best Musical, Best Actor in a Musical (Randall), Best Featured Actress in a Musical (Johnson), Best Featured Actress in a Musical (McKeever), Best Scenic Design (Jo Mielziner), Best Costume Design (Miles White)

Comments: This production was an uninspired adaptation that ended in a financial loss.

°OH, WHAT A LOVELY WAR! (September 30, 1964; Broadhurst Theatre; 125 performances). *Director:* Joan Littlewood; *Composer/Lyricist:* Various; *Librettist:* Various; *Choreographer:* Bob Stevenson. Generals flounder around in this antiwar production with music and lyrics that Cole Porter had composed years earlier. The tragedy of World War I, set in music-hall terms, concentrates on a family whose five sons are killed. In the final scene, the family has a picnic in a graveyard.

Tony Award: Best Featured Actor in a Musical (Victor Spinetti). **Tony nominations:** Best Musical, Best Featured Actress in a Musical (Barbara Windsor), Best Direction of a Musical

OKLAHOMA! (March 31, 1943; St. James Theatre; 2,212 performances)

Production credits: *Producer:* Theatre Guild; *Director:* Rouben Mamoulian; *Composer:* Richard Rodgers; *Lyricist/Librettist:* Oscar Hammerstein II, *Choreographer:* Agnes de Mille; *Original source:* Based on the play *Green Grow the Lilacs* by Lynn Riggs

Original cast: Aunt Eller (Betty Garde), Curly McLain (Alfred Drake), Laurey Williams (Joan Roberts), Will Parker (Lee Dixon), Jud Fry (Howard Da Silva), Ado Annie Carnes (Celeste Holm), Ali Hakim (Joseph Buloff), Gertie Cummings (Jane Cummings), Andrew Carnes (Ralph Riggs)

Synopsis: Set in the Oklahoma territory around 1907, this is a story of farmers and cowhands and especially of a spunky girl (Laurey) who runs her aunt's farm and is courted by two very different young men, a brash cowboy named Curly and a rather somber farmhand named Jud. As the territory heads toward statehood, Laurey decides on the man of her dreams, who turns out to be Curly. In the final scene, they are married, and just as the folks are throwing a shivaree for the newlyweds, Jud shows up, he and Curly fight, and Jud is killed by his own knife. Curly is acquitted, and Oklahoma has just become a state.

Songs: "Oh, What a Beautiful Mornin'"; "The Surrey with the Fringe on Top"; "Kansas City"; "I Cain't Say No"; "Many a New Day"; "It's a Scandal!, It's an Outrage!"; "People Will Say"; "Pore Jud"; "Lonely Room"; "Out of My Dreams"; "The Farmer and the Cowman"; "All 'Er Nothin'"; "Oklahoma!"

Comments: This musical, which won the Pulitzer Prize for Drama in 1944, is regarded by many and this book as the beginning of the Golden Age of American musical comedy. It was the first to have a plot, score, and dances all as necessary ingredients to the story line. It was the first show choreographed by Agnes de Mille and the first of nine collaborations by Richard Rodgers and Oscar Hammerstein II. For fifteen years it held the record as the longest-running musical (later surpassed by *My Fair Lady*), with 2,212 performances. Before the opening, not one hit Broadway show had run for more than 500 performances.

OLIVER! (January 6, 1963; Imperial Theatre; 774 performances)

Production credits: *Producers:* David Merrick and Donald Albery; *Director:* Peter Coe; *Composer/Lyricist/Librettist:* Lionel Bart; *Choreographer:* Malcolm Clare; *Original source:* Adapted from Charles Dickens's novel *Oliver Twist*

Original cast: Oliver Twist (Paul O'Keefe), Mr. Bumble (Willoughby Goddard), Mrs. Corney (Helena Carroll), Old Sally (Ruth Mannard), Mr. Sowerberry (Robin Ramsay), Mrs. Sowerberry (Ruth Maynard), Charlotte (Cherry Davis), Noah Claypole (Terry Lomax), Fagin (Clive Revill), Artful

Dodger (David Jones), Nancy (Georgia Brown), Bet (Alice Playten), Bill Sikes (Danny Sewell), Mr. Brownlow (Geoffrey Lumb), Dr. Grimwig (John Call), Mrs. Bedwin (Dortha Duckworth)

Synopsis: This musical tells the story of Oliver, a foundling born in the workhouse in nineteenth-century London, who commits the unspeakable crime of asking for more gruel. Oliver runs away but gets into a gang of thieves headed by Fagin. He is forced to take part in a burglary and is wounded. Oliver is nursed back to health, his true heritage is eventually disclosed, the gang members are caught, and he is adopted by wealthy Mr. Brownlow.

Songs: "Food, Glorious Food"; "Oliver!"; "I Shall Scream"; "Boy for Sale"; "That's Your Funeral"; "Where Is Love?"; "Consider Yourself"; "You've Got to Pick a Pocket or Two"; "It's a Fine Life"; "I'd Do Anything"; "Be Back Soon"; "Omm-Pah-Pah"; "My Name"; "As Long as He Needs Me"; "Who Will Buy?"; "Reviewing the Situation"

Tony Awards: Best Composer and Lyricist, Best Scenic Design (Sean Kenny), Best Conductor and Musical Director (Donald Pippin). **Tony nominations:** Best Musical, Best Actor in a Musical (Revill), Best Actress in a Musical (Brown), Best Featured Actor in a Musical (Jones), Best Author of a Musical, Best Direction of a Musical, Best Producer of a Musical

Comments: *Oliver!* opened during a New York newspaper strike; however, radio and television kept the public informed. The entire show won rave reviews. During the long run on Broadway, the part of Oliver was played by several young actors who kept growing out of the role.

ON A CLEAR DAY YOU CAN SEE FOREVER (October 17, 1965; Mark Hellinger Theatre; 280 performances)

Production credits: *Producers:* Alan Jay Lerner, in association with Rogo Productions; *Director:* Robert Lewis; *Composer:* Burton Lane; *Lyricist/Librettist:* Alan Jay Lerner; *Choreographer:* Herbert Ross

Original cast: Dr. Mark Bruckern (John Cullum), Daisy Gamble and Melinda (Barbara Harris), Warren Smith (William Daniels), Edward Moncrief (Clifford David), Themistocles Kriakos (Titos Vandis), Evans Bolagard (Hamilton Camp), Mrs. Welles (Blanche Collins), Samuel Welles (Gordon Dilworth), Flora (Carol Flemming), Blackamoor (Bernard Johnson), Dr. Conrad Bruckner (Michael Lewis), Dr. Paul Bruckner (Gerry Matthews), Muriel Bunson (Barbara Monte), Mrs. Hatch (Evelyn Page), James Preston (William Reilly), Dolly Wainwhistle (Hanne Marie Reiner), Prudence Cumming (Barbara Remington), T.A.A. Official (David Thomas), Sir Hubert Insdale (Byron Webster)

Synopsis: Daisy Gamble is hypnotized by Dr. Mark Bruckner in his class so that he can cure her smoking habit because her boyfriend, Warren, doesn't like it, but Dr. Brucker finds that Daisy has ESP, and under hypnosis, she remembers life in an earlier century as Melinda. In fact, Daisy remembers that Melinda went to America on the ship *Trelawney*. Dr. Brucker loses his job because of his infatuation with Daisy. She has a plane ticket to California, but when she hears that the name of the plane is Trelawney, she remembers that Melinda dies in a shipwreck. She and Mark get together to try to figure out this mystery.

Songs: "Hurry! It's Lovely Up Here!"; "Ring Out the Bells"; "Tosy and Cosh"; "On a Clear Day You Can See Forever"; "On the S.S. Bernard Cohn"; "Don't Tamper with My Sister"; "She Wasn't You/He Isn't You"; "Melinda"; "When I'm Being Born Again"; "What Did I Have That I Don't Have?"; "Wait 'Til We're Sixty–Five"; "Come Back to Me"

Tony nominations: Best Actor in a Musical (Cullum), Best Actress in a Musical (Harris), Best Composer and Lyricist

Comments: For this book, this production marks the end of the Golden Age of American musical comedy. Alan Jay Lerner and Richard Rodgers started to collaborate on this production but could not get along because of different work habits, so Burton Lane was brought in. The original title was *I Picked a Daisy*. Linda Lavin later replaced Barbara Harris in the top role. Barbra Streisand starred in the movie version (1970) directed by Vincente Minnelli.

ON THE TOWN (December 28, 1944; Adelphi Theatre; 462 performances)

Production credits: *Producer:* Arthur R. Freed; *Director:* George Abbott; *Composer:* Leonard Bernstein; *Lyricists/Librettists:* Betty Comden and Adolph Green; *Choreographer:* Jerome Robbins; *Original source:* Based on the 1944 Jerome Robbins ballet *Fancy Free*

Original cast: Gaby (John Battles), Ozzie (Adolph Green), Chip (Chris Alexander), Miss Turnstiles (Sono Osato), Hildy (Nancy Walker), Claire DeLoone (Phyllis Newman)

Synopsis: On a twenty-four-hour leave in New York City, three sailors look for adventure. Gaby falls in love with a picture of Miss Turnstiles, and the three friends race around the city trying to find her. In the chase, two of them find romance with a cab driver and an anthropology student. Gaby eventually does find Miss Turnstiles, but then the sailors must leave for war and a very uncertain future.

Songs: "I Feel Like I'm Not Out of Bed Yet"; "New York, New York"; "Gaby's Comin'"; "Come Up to My Place"; "So Long, Baby"; "I Wish I Was Dead"; "Diana Dream"; "Senorita Dolores, Dolores"; "Ya Got Me"; "I Understand"; "Carried Away"; "Lonely Town"; "Lucky to Be Me"; "I Can Cook Too"; "Some Other Time"

Comments: Leonard Bernstein was new on the Broadway scene with this production. The show was revived twice (1971 and 1998), with neither being successful. The movie version (1949) starred Gene Kelly, Frank Sinatra, Ann Miller, and Vera-Ellen.

ONCE UPON A MATTRESS (May 11, 1959; Phoenix Theatre; 460 performances)

Production credits: *Producers:* T. Edward Hambleton, Norris Houghton, and William and Jean Eckart; *Director:* George Abbott; *Composer:* Mary Rodgers; *Lyricist:* Marshall Barer; *Librettists:* Jay Thompson, Dean Fuller, and Marshall Barer; *Choreographer:* Joe Layton; *Original source:* Adapted from the tale by Hans Christian Andersen

Original cast: Minstrel (Harry Snow), Prince (Jim Maher), Princess (Chris Krner), Queen and Lady Beatrice (Gloria Stevens), Wizard (Robert Weil), Princess Number Twelve (Mary Stanton), Lady Rowena (Dorothy Aull), Lady Merrill (Patsi King), Prince Dauntless (Joe Bova), The Queen (Jane White), Lady Lucille (Luce Ennis), Lady Larken (Anne Jones), Sir Studley (Jerry Newby), Jester (Matt Mattox), Sir Harry (Dan Resin), Princess Winnifred (Carol Burnett), Sir Harold (David Neuman), Sir Luce (Tom Mixon), Lady Mabelle (Chris Karner), Nightingale of Samarkand (Ginny Perlowan), Lady Dorothy (Dorothy D'Honau), Sir Christopher (Christopher Edwards), Lord Howard (Howard Parker), Lady Dora (Dorothy Frank), Sir Daniel (Casper Roos), Sir Steven (Jim Stevenson), Lord Patrick (George Blackwell)

Synopsis: In this adaptation, the princess and the pea tale comes alive on Broadway. A law in the kingdom says that no one can marry until the Prince Dauntless the Drag marries, but each time a possible princess appears, she fails a test set up by the queen. Sir Harry, who wants to marry his pregnant Lady Larken right away, vows to find a suitable mate for the prince. He returns with Princess Winnifred the Woebegone, an unrefined lass from the marshland. The queen puts her to the sleeping-on-a-pea test, which—with a little help—Winnifred passes.

Songs: "Many Moons Ago"; "An Opening for a Princess"; "In a Little While"; "Shy"; "The Minstrel, The Jester, and I"; "Sensitivity"; "Swamps of Home"; "Normandy"; "Spanish Panic"; "Song of Love"; "Quiet"; "Happily Ever After"; "Man to Man Talk"; "Very Soft Shoes"; "Yesterday I Loved You"; "Lullaby"

Tony nominations: Best Musical, Best Actress in a Musical (Burnett)

Comments: This was Carol Burnett's Broadway debut. Even so, critics were baffled as to why the show ran so long, although audiences loved it.

110 IN THE SHADE (October 24, 1963; Broadhurst Theatre; 330 performances)

Production credits: *Producer:* David Merrick; *Director:* Joseph Anthony; *Composer:* Harvey Schmidt; *Lyricist:* Tom Jones; *Librettist:* Richard Nash; *Choreographer:* Agnes de Mille; *Original source:* Based on the play *The Rainmaker* by Richard Nash

Original cast: Toby (George Church), File (Stephen Douglass), H.C. Curry (Will Geer), Noah Curry (Steve Roland), Jimmie Curry (Scooter Teague), Lizzie Curry (Inga Swenson), Snookie (Lesley Warren), Mrs. Jensen (Diane Deering), Phil Mackey (Seth Riggs), Tommy (Christopher Votos), Belinda (Renee Dudley), Geshy Toops (Don Crabtree), Gil Demby (Jerry Dodge), Olive Barrow (Leslie Franzos), Hanah (Dori Davis), Wally Skacks III and Townperson (Loren Hightower), Maurine Toops (Evelyn Taylor), Bo Dollivon (Vernon Lusby), Mr. Curtis (Robert Shepard), Bill Starbuck (Robert Horton), Wally Skacks (Carl Nicholas)

Synopsis: Bill Starbuck appears at the Curry farm in the middle of a drought and promises to produce rain for $100. Lizzie Curry warns her father and brothers that Starbuck is a fraud, but she falls in love with him despite the attention of Sheriff File. To everyone's amazement, including Starbuck, it rains on time. Starbuck leaves town, and Lizzie and the sheriff get together.

Songs: "Another Hot Day"; "Lizzie's Coming Home"; "Love, Don't Turn Away"; "Poker Polka"; "Hungry Men"; "The Rain Song"; "You're Not Foolin' Me"; "Raunchy"; "A Man and a Woman"; "Old Maid"; "Everything Beautiful Happens at Night"; "Melisande"; "Simple Little Things"; "Little Red Hat"; "Is It Really Me?" "Wonderful Music"

Tony nominations: Best Composer and Lyricist, Best Actress in a Musical (Swenson), Best Featured Actor in a Musical (Geer), Best Direction (Musical)

ONE TOUCH OF VENUS (October 7, 1943; Imperial Theatre; 567 performances)

Production credits: *Producer:* Cheryl Crawford; *Director:* Elia Kazan; *Composer:* Kurt Weill; *Lyricist:* Ogden Nash; *Librettists:* S. J. Perelman and Ogden Nash; *Choreographer:* Agnes de Mille

Original cast: Whitelaw Savory (John Boles), Venus (Mary Martin), Rodney Hatch (Kenny Baker), Gloria Kramer (Ruth Bond), Store Manager and Anatolian (Sam Bonnell), Sam (Zachary A. Charles), Stanley (Harry Clark), Mrs. Moats (Florence Dunlap), Police Lieutenant (Bert Freed), Taxi Black (Teddy Hart), Rose (Jane Hoffman), Molly Grant (Paula Lawrence), Mrs. Kramer (Helen Raymond), Dr. Rook (Johnny Stearns), Zkuvelti (Harold J. Stone), Bus Starter (Lou Wills Jr.)

Synopsis: Art expert Savory finds a statue of Venus, which comes to life when his barber, Rodney, puts a ring on the statue's finger. Venus falls in love with the unwilling barber, who is engaged, until she realizes that she will have to live in Ozone Heights. She goes back to Olympus, leaving the barber forlorn until a woman appears who not only looks just like the statue but also loves Ozone Heights.

Songs: "New Art Is True Art"; "One Touch of Venus"; "How Much I Love You"; "I'm a Stranger Here Myself"; "West Wind"; "Way Out West in Jersey"; "That's How I Am Sick of Love"; "Foolish Heart"; "The Trouble with Women"; "That's Him"; "Speak Low"

Comments: This was Mary Martin's starring debut on Broadway. The movie version (1948) featured Ava Gardner and Robert Walker but eliminated most of the score.

°**OUT OF THIS WORLD** (December 21, 1950; New Century Theatre; 157 performances). *Director:* Agnes de Mille; *Composer/Lyricist:* Cole Porter; *Librettists:* Dwight Taylor and Reginald Lawrence; *Choreographer:* Hanya Holm. A lovely Cole Porter score brought Charlotte Greenwood out of retirement as the goddess Juno, who is roaming the earth searching for her cheating husband Jupiter, but it was not enough to save this musical, stranded far uptown at the New Century Theatre.

PAINT YOUR WAGON (November 12, 1951; Shubert Theatre; 289 performances)

Production credits: *Producer:* Cheryl Crawford; *Director:* Daniel Mann; *Composer:* Frederick Loewe; *Lyricist/Librettist:* Alan Jay Lerner; *Choreographer:* Agnes de Mille

Original cast: Ben Rumson (James Barton), Julio Valveras (Tony Bavaar), Pete Billings (James Mitchell), Jennifer Rumson (Olga San Juan), Edgar Crocker (Richard Aherne), Salem Trumbull (Ralph Bunker), Suzanne Duval (Mary Burr), Lee Zen (Stephen Cheng), Yvonne Sorel (Gemze de Lappe), Reuben Sloane and Raymond Janney (Gordon Dilworth), Carmelita (Lorraine Havercroft), Elizabeth Woodling (Marijane Maricle), Wait (Bert Matthews), Cherry (Kay Medford), Jake Whippany (Robert Penn), Mike Mooney (John Randolph), Sandy Twist (Jared Reed), Dutchie (Jack Sheehan), Sarah Woodling (Jan Sherwood), Steve Bullnack (Rufus Smith), Elsie (Gisella Svetlik), Rocky (James Tarbutton), Dr. Newcomb (David Thomas)

Synopsis: Jennifer falls in love with Julio, a miner who has come to town after gold is found on her father's (Ben's) land, but Ben wants better things for his daughter and sends her to school in the East. When the gold runs out and the town is deserted once more, Ben thinks of leaving but dies before he can do so. Jennifer returns, and she and Julio plan to bring the town back to life as a farming community.

Songs: "I'm on the Way"; "Rumson"; "What's Goin' on Here?"; "I Talk to the Trees"; "They Call the Wind Maria"; "I Still See Elisa"; "How Can I Wait?"; "In Between"; "Whoop-Ti-Ay!"; "Carino Mio"; "There's a Coach Comin' In"; "Hand Me Down That Can O'Beans"; "Another Autumn"; "All for Him"; "(I Was Born Under a) Wand'rin' Star"

Comments: Even though *Paint Your Wagon* had a relatively long run, it lost money. The movie version (1969) featured Lee Marvin, Clint Eastwood, and Jean Seberg.

THE PAJAMA GAME (May 13, 1954; St. James Theatre; 1,063 performances)

Production credits: *Producers:* Frederick Brisson, Robert E. Griffith, and Harold S. Prince; *Directors:* George Abbott and Jerome Robbins; *Composers/Lyricists:* Richard Adler and Jerry Ross; *Librettists:* George Abbott and Richard Bissell; *Choreographer:* Bob Fosse; *Original source:* based on Richard Bissell's novel *7½ Cents.*

Original cast: Hines (Eddie Foy Jr.), Prez (Stanley Prager), Joe (Gordon Woodburn), Hasler (Ralph Dunn), Gladys (Carol Haney), Sid Sorokin (John Raitt), Mabel (Reta Shaw), Charlie (Ralph Chambers), Babe Williams (Janis Paige), Mae (Thelma Pelish), Brenda (Marion Coley), Poopsie (Rae Allen)

Synopsis: Babe Williams, leader of the grievance committee at the Sleep-Tite Pajama Factory, wants a raise for the girls because production manager Hines wants them to speed up their work. Superintendent Sid Sorokin refuses the seven-and-a-half-cent increase, but he is sweet on Babe. After a work slowdown, he threatens to fire the whole crew, although only Babe gets the axe. But Hines loves Babe, so he decides to try to get her and the others a raise by inviting the company bookkeeper, Gladys, out for a drink. She gets drunk, and he gets the key to the books, which show that the company owners are up to some dirty dealings. The girls get their raise.

Songs: "The Pajama Game"; "Racing with the Clock"; "A New town Is a Blue Town"; "I'm Not at All in Love"; "I'll Never Be Jealous Again"; "Hey There"; "Her Is"; "Sleep-Tite"; "Once a Year Day"; "Small Talk"; "There Once Was a Man"; "Steam Heat"; "Think of the Time I Save"; "Hernando's Hideaway"; "7½ Cents"

Tony Awards: Best Musical, Best Featured Actress in a Musical (Haney) Best Choreography (Fosse)

Comments: This production put Bob Fosse and dancer Carol Haney in the public eye.

°*PARK AVENUE* (November 4, 1946; Shubert Theatre; 72 performances). *Director:* David Fuller; *Composer:* Arthur Schwartz; *Lyricist:* Ira Gershwin;

Librettists: George S. Kaufman and Nunnally Johnson; *Choreographer:* Helen Tamiris. Reviewers called the entire production, which revolves around a wealthy sophisticate on Park Avenue who is making plans to wed a simple Southerner, without humor, and audiences tended to agree.

°*PETER PAN* (October 20, 1954, Winter Garden Theatre; 152 performances)

Production credits: *Producer:* Richard Halliday; *Director/Choreographer:* Jerome Robbins; *Composer:* Mark Charlap; *Lyricist:* Carolyn Leigh; *Librettists:* Milt Banta and others; *Original source:* Based on the book by James M. Barrie

Original cast: Wendy and Jane (Kathy Nolan), John (Robert Harrington), Liza (Heller Halliday), Michael (Joseph Stafford), Nana (Norman Shelly), Mrs. Darling (Margalo Gillmore), Mr. Darling and Smee (Cyril Ritchard), Peter Pan (Mary Martin), Lion (Richard Wyatt), Kangaroo (Don Lurio), Ostrich (Joan Tewkesbury), Slightly (David Bean), Tootles (Ian Tucker), Curly (Stanley Stenner), Nibs (Paris Theodore), Captain Hook (Darryl Duran), Crocodile (Joe E. Marks), Tiger Lily (Sondra Lee), Starkey (Robert Vanselow), Noodler (Frank Lindsay), Mullins (James White), Cecco (William Burke), Jules (Chester Fisher), Wendy Grown-Up (Sallie Brophy)

Synopsis: The musical follows James M. Barrie's story of Peter Pan, the boy who never grew up. He comes to visit the Darling children, Wendy and John, with a fairy called Tinker Bell and tells them of his island called Neverland. Peter Pan not only promises to take the children there, but he also vows to teach them to fly. He does this by sprinkling them with fairy dust and telling them to think lovely thoughts. Soon the children are flying just like Peter, and they fly though the night to Neverland. (Peter Pan and the Darling children actually fly out over the audience.)

Songs: "Tender Shepherd"; "I've Got to Crow"; "Neverland"; "I'm Flying"; "Pirate Song"; "A Princely Scheme"; "Indians!"; "Wendy"; "Neverland Waltz"; "I Won't Grow Up"; "Mysterious Lady"; "Ugg-a-Wugg"; "The Pow-Wow Polka"; "Distant Melody"; "To the Ship"; "Hook's Waltz"; "The Battle"

Tony Awards: Best Actress in a Musical (Martin), Best Featured Actor in a Musical (Ritchard), Stage Technician (Richard Rodda)

Comments: At 152 performances, the show could technically be called a flop; however, it closed not because of bad reviews (they were mixed), but because a contract had been signed earlier to present the show on television at a certain date.

°*PICKWICK* (October 4, 1965; 46th Street Theatre; 56 performances). *Director:* Peter Coe; *Composer:* Cyril Omadel; *Lyricist:* Leslie Bricusse;

Librettist: Wolf Mankowitz; *Choreographer:* Gillian Lynne; *Original source:* Adapted from material by Charles Dickens. Mr. Pickwick is chairman of the Pickwick Club, a scholarly group in seventeenth-century London. The musical was intended to follow the success of *Oliver!*, which it did not.

Tony nominations: Best Actor in a Musical (Harry Secombe), Best Featured Actor in a Musical (Roy Castle), Best Featured Actress in a Musical (Charlotte Rae)

PIPE DREAM (November 30, 1955; Shubert Theatre; 246 performances)

Production credits: *Producers:* Richard Rodgers and Oscar Hammerstein II; *Director:* Harold Clurman; *Composer:* Richard Rodgers; *Lyricist/ Librettist:* Oscar Hammerstein II; *Choreographer:* Boris Runanin; *Original source:* Based on John Steinbeck's novel *Sweet Thursday*

Original cast: Doc (William Johnson), Hazel (Mike Kellin), Millicent Henderson (Jayne Heller), Beulah (Mildred Slavin), Mac (G. D.Wallace), Suzy (Judy Tyler), Fauna (Helen Traubel), Jim Blaikey (Rufus Smith), Ray Busch (John Call), George Herman (Guy Raymond), Bill (Steve Roland), Marjorie (Louise Troy), Cho Cho Sen (Pat Creighton), Sonny Boy (Joseph Leon), Harriet (Patricia Wilson), Hilda (Ruth Kobart), Fred (Marvin Krauter), Slick (Gene Kevin), Slim (Don Weissmuller), Bubbles (Marsha Reynolds), Sonya (Annabelle Gold), Kitty (Jenny Workman), Johnny Carriagra (Scotty Engel), Pedro (Rudolfo Cornejo), Dr. Ormondy (Calvin Thomas)

Synopsis: This short-lived musical is set in Cannery Row, Monterey, California. After penniless Suzy is arrested for stealing food, she is taken in by brothel owner Fauna. Suzy soon falls for marine biologist Doc, who is also extremely poor. Doc has befriended a number of men in the neighborhood, so they decide to stage a fake lottery for him. This seems like a fine idea until Doc and Suzy have an argument. Suzy declares that she will not see Doc again unless he needs her. To solve the problem, the men break Doc's arm. Now Doc needs her, so Suzy must take care of him.

Songs: "All Kinds of People"; "The Tide Pool"; "Everybody's Got a Home but Me"; "A Lopsided Bus"; "Bums' Opera"; "The Man I Used to Be"; "Sweet Thursday"; "Suzy Is a Good Thing"; "All at Once You Love Her"; "The Happiest House on the Block"; "The Party That We're Gonna Have Tomorrow Night"; "Thinkin'"; "How Long?"; "The Next Time It Happens"

Tony Award: Best Costume Design (Alvin Colt). **Tony nominations:** Best Musical, Best Actor in a Musical (Johnson), Best Featured Actor in a Musical (Kellin), Best Featured Actress in a Musical (Tyler), Best Choreography, Best Scenic Design (Jo Mielziner), Best Director, Conductor and Musical Director

Comments: Although it ran through the season, the musical stayed in the red and was a financial flop.

PLAIN AND FANCY (January 27, 1955; Mark Hellinger Theatre; 461 performances)

Production credits: *Producers:* Richard Kollmar and James W. Gardiner, in association with Yvette Schumer; *Director:* Franz Allers; *Composer:* Albert Hague; *Lyricist:* Arnold B. Horwitt; *Librettists:* Joseph Stein and Will Glickman; *Choreographer:* Helen Tamiris

Original cast: Ruth Winters (Shirl Conway), Dan King (Richard Derr), Papa Yoder (Stefan Schnabel), Katie Yoder (Gloria Marlowe), Isaac Miller (Sammy Smith), Hilda Miller (Barbara Cook), Ezra Reber (Douglas Fletcher Rodgers), Peter Reber (David Daniels), Rachel (Ethel May Cody), Samuel Zook (Daniel Nagrin), Levi Stolzfuss (William Weslow), Jacob Yoder (Will Able), Samuel Lapp (Christ Robinson), Abner Zook (Edgar Thompson)

Synopsis: New Yorkers Ruth and Dan go to Amish country to sell a farm. Papa Yoder is interested. His daughter Katie is told to marry Ezra, but before the wedding her true love, Peter, returns; however, since Peter left the Amish community, he is shunned. The Yoder's farm burns down, and Peter decides to leave so as not to cause any more friction. Ezra gets drunk, and Peter helps minimize the disgrace. After that, Papa Yoder thinks again about Peter as a son-in-law, and Ruth and Dan decide to marry.

Songs: "You Can't Miss It"; "It Wonders Me"; "Plenty of Pennsylvania"; "Young and Foolish"; "Why Not Katie?"; "It's a Helluva Way to Run a Love Affair"; "This Is All Very New to Me"; "Plain We Live"; "The Shunning"; "How Do You Raise a Barn?"; "Follow Your Heart"; "City Mouse, Country Mouse"; "I'll Show Him!"; "Take Your Time and Take Your Pick"

Comments: "Young and Foolish" became one of the year's most popular tunes.

°*PORTOFINO* (February 21, 1958; Adelphi Theatre, 3 performances). *Director:* Karl Genus; *Composers:* Louis Bellson and Will Irwin; *Lyricists:* Richard Ney and Sheldon Harnick; *Librettist:* Richard Ney; *Choreographers:* Charles Weidman and Ray Harrison. The show, which centers on American tourists in the lovely resort town of Portofino, Italy, was totally rejected by the critics. In fact, reviewers called it a "legendary flop."

REDHEAD (February 5, 1959; 46th Street Theatre; 452 performances)
Production credits: *Producers:* Robert Fryer and Lawrence Carr; *Director/Choreographer:* Bob Fosse; *Composer:* Albert Hague; *Lyricist:*

Dorothy Fields; *Librettists:* Herbert Fields, Dorothy Fields, Sidney Sheldon, and David Shaw

Original cast: Ruth LaRue, Tilly, and Dancer (Pat Ferrier), Maude Simpson (Cynthia Latham), Sarah Simpson (Doris Rich), May (Joy Nichols), Essie Whimple (Gwen Verdon), Inspector White (Ralph Sumpter), Howard Cavanaugh (William LeMassena), George Poppett (Leonard Stone), Tom Baxter (Richard Kiley), Alfy (Lee Krieger), Sir Charles Willingham (Patrick Horgan), Tenor (Bob Dixon), Inez (Bette Graham), Jailer (Buzz Miller)

Synopsis: In this first musical directed by Bob Fosse and set in London in the 1880s around the time of Jack the Ripper, a killer of actresses is on the loose. The partner of Tom Baxter, part of a strong man act, has been murdered. Tom meets Essie Whimple, who works in the Simpson Sisters' Waxworks. She is apparently being stalked by the same killer. Suspicion centers on Sir Charles Willingham, but the murderer turns out to be George Poppett, an entertainer who disguised himself as Willingham. Poppett goes to jail, and Essie and Tom find love.

Songs: "The Simpson Sisters"; "The Right Finger of My Left Hand"; "Just for Once"; "Merely Marvelous"; "The Uncle Sam Rag"; "Erbie Fitch's Twitch"; "She's Not Enough Woman for Me"; "Behave Yourself"; "Look Who's in Love"; "My Girl Is Just Enough Woman for Me"; "Essie's Vision"; "Two Faces in the Dark"; "I'm Back in Circulation"; "We Loves Ya, Jimey"; "Pick-Pocket Tango"; "I'll Try"

Tony Awards: Best Musical, Best Actor in a Musical (Kiley), Best Actress in a Musical (Verdon), Best Choreography (Fosse), Best Costume Design of a Musical (Rouben Ter-Arutunian). **Tony nominations:** Best Featured Actor in a Musical (Stone), Best Conductor and Musical Director (Jay Blackton)

Comments: The show ran as long as it did on the strength of Gwen Verdon's performance and Bob Fosse's dance routines. It was Richard Kiley's route to stardom.

THE ROAR OF THE GREASEPAINT—THE SMELL OF THE CROWD (May 16, 1955; Shubert Theatre; 232 performances)

Production credits: *Producer:* David Merrick, in association with Bernard Delfront; *Director:* Anthony Newley; *Composers/Lyricists/Librettists:* Leslie Bricusse and Anthony Newley; *Choreographer:* Gillian Lynne

Original cast: Cocky (Anthony Newley), The Girl (Joyce Jillson), The Negro (Gilbert Price), Sir (Cyril Ritchard), The Kid (Sally Smith), The Bully (Murray Tannebaum)

Synopsis: This production is an allegory between the haves, personified by Sir, and the have nots, led by Cocky. The single set represents the world.

Sir is forever changing the rules of the game of life, so young Cocky always gets the short end of the stick. Anthony Newley hoped to match the success of *Stop the World—I Want to Get Off* but it missed by a mile.

Songs: "The Beautiful Land"; "A Wonderful Day Like Today"; "It Isn't Enough"; "Things to Remember"; "With All Due Respect"; "This Dream"; "Where Would You Be without Me?"; "My First Love Song"; "Look at That Face"; "The Joker"; "Who Can I Turn To (When Nobody Needs Me)?"; "That's What It Is to Be Young"; "What a Man!"; "Feeling Good"; "My Way"

Tony nominations: Best Actor in a Musical (Ritchard), Best Direction of a Musical, Best Producer of a Musical (Merrick), Best Composer and Lyricist, Best Scenic Design (Sean Kenny), Best Costume Design (Freddy Whittop)

Comments: The songs from the show, especially "Who Can I Turn To (When Nobody Needs Me)?," became popular after it closed. The production was scheduled for London after New York, but since the Broadway showing was less than expected, it did not go on.

°*RUMPLE* (November 6, 1957; Alvin Theatre; 45 performances). *Director:* Jack Donahue; *Composer:* Ernest G. W. Schweikert; *Lyricist:* Frank Reardon; *Librettist:* Irving Phillips; *Choreographer:* Bob Hamilton. Rumple is a cartoon character who is about to lose his life because his creator has lost his inspiration and can no longer create him. *Time* magazine said the show had only one asset: Eddie Foy, the master of the soft shoe. Critics said the songs were untuneful and the lyrics "ruggedly mediocre."

Tony nomination: Best Actor in a Musical (Eddie Foy Jr.)

°*SADIE THOMPSON* (November 16, 1944; Alvin Theatre; 60 performances). *Director:* Rouben Mamoulian; *Composer:* Vernon Duke; *Lyricist:* Howard Dietz; *Librettists:* Howard Dietz and Rouben Mamoulian; *Choreographer:* Edward Caton. The show was originally planned around Ethel Merman, who refused the role because her husband was not the lyricist. June Havoc was called in to play the sharp-tongued lady of the streets. Reviewers felt the staging outclassed the cast; actual rain drenched the stage.

SAIL AWAY (October 3, 1961; Broadhurst Theatre; 167 performances)

Production credits: *Producers:* Bonard Productions, in association with Charles Russell; *Director/Composer/Lyricist/Librettist:* Noël Coward; *Choreographer:* Joe Layton

Original cast: Joe and Ali (Charles Braswell), Shuttleworth (Keith Prentice), Rawlings (James Pritchett), Sir Gerard Nutfield (C. Stafford Dickens), Lady Nutfield (Margaret Mower), Barnaby Slade (Grover Dale),

Elmer Candijack (Henry Lawrence), Maimie Candijack (Betty Jane Watson), Glen Candijack (Alan Helms), Shirley Candijack (Patti Mariano), Mr. Sweeney (Jon Richards), Mr. Sweeney (Paula Bauersmith), Elinor Spencer-Bollard (Alice Pearce), Nancy Foyle (Patricia Harty), Alvin Lush (Paul O'Keefe), Mrs. Lush (Evelyn Russell), John Van Mier (James Hurst), Mrs. Van Mier (Margalo Gillmore), Mimi Paragon (Elaine Stritch), Carrington (David Evans), American Express Man (Richard Woods)

Synopsis: All the action takes place in various parts of the Cunard steamship *Coronia*. Everything, including love triangles, personal problems, and all sorts of disagreements among the passengers, revolves around the overworked Mimi Paragon, cruise director, as they sail through the Mediterranean Sea.

Songs: "Come to Me"; "Sail Away"; "Where Shall I Find Him?"; "Beatnik Love Affair"; "Later Than Spring"; "The Passenger's Always Right"; "Useful Phrases"; "Go Slow, Johnny"; "The Little Ones' ABC"; "You're a Long, Long Way from America"; "Something Very Strange"; "Don't Turn Away from Love"; "When You Want Me"; "Why Do the Wrong People Travel?"

Tony nominations: Best Actress in a Musical (Stritch), Best Producer of a Musical

Comments: Even with Elaine Stritch in the lead, the show had a short run.

°*SARATOGA* (December 7, 1959; Winter Garden Theatre; 90 performances). *Director/Librettist:* Morton DaCosta; *Composer:* Harold Arlen; *Lyricist:* Johnny Mercer; *Choreographer:* Ralph Beaumont. The hope was a long run for this show to follow the success of Edna Ferber's *Show Boat* and based on her novel *Saratoga Trunk*. It starred Carol Lawrence and Howard Keel in this story of an illegitimate Creole woman who seeks revenge on a New Orleans family because they exiled her mother after she was made pregnant by their son. Audiences did not warm to the production.

Tony Award: Best Costume Design, Musical (Cecil Beaton). **Tony nomination:** Best Scenic Design, Musical (Beaton)

SAY, DARLING (April 3, 1958, ANTA Theatre; 332 performances)

Production credits: *Producers:* Jule Styne and Lester Osterman; *Director:* Abe Burrows; *Composers:* Jule Styne; *Lyricists:* Betty Comden and Adolph Green ; *Librettists:* Abe Burrows, Marion Bissell, and Richard Bissell; *Choreographer:* Matt Mattox; *Original source:* Based on the novel by Richard Bissell

Original cast: Mr. Schneider (Gordon B. Clarke), Frankie Jordan (Constance Ford), Jack Jordan (David Wayne), Photographer and Waiter (Jack Naughton), Pilot Roy Peters (Jack Manning), Ted Snow (Robert Morse),

June (Eileen Letchworth), Schatzie Harris (Horace McMahon), Richard Hackett (Jerome Cowan), Irene Lovelle (Vivian Blaine), Charlie Williams (Robert Downing), Maurice (Colin Romoff), Arlene McKee (Wana Allison), Jennifer Stevenson and Tatiana (Jean Mattox), Earl Jorgeson (Elliott Gould), Cheryl Merrill (Virgina Martin), Sammy Miles (Steve Condos), Boris Reshevsky (Matt Mattox), Morty Krebs (Walter Klavun), Joyce (Kelly Leigh)

Synopsis: This show concerns the trials and tribulations of a novelist who is brought to New York City to turn his novel into a musical. It was based on Bissell's novel about turning *7½ Cents* into *The Pajama Game*, including the tough director and the has-been star.

Songs: "Try to Love Me"; "It's Doom"; "The Husking Bee"; "It's the Second Time You Meet That Matters"; "Chief of Love"; "Say, Darling"; "The Carnival Song"; "Dance Only with Me"; "Something's Always Happening on the River"

Tony nomination: Best Featured Actor in a Play (Morse)

Comments: Robert Morse stole the show in a remarkably funny performance.

SEVENTEEN (June 21, 1951; Broadhurst Theatre; 160 performances)

Production credits: *Producers:* Milton Berle, Sammy Lambert, and Bernie Foyer; *Director:* Richard Whorf; *Composer:* Walter Kent; *Lyricist:* Kim Gannon; *Librettist:* Sally Benson; *Choreographer:* Dania Krupska; *Original source:* Based on the book by Booth Tarkington

Original cast: Genesis (Maurice Ellis), Johnnie Watson (John Sharpe), Willie Baxter (Kenneth Nelson), Jane Baxter (Betty Jane Seagle), Bert (Greg O'Brien), Charlie (Jim Moore), Dave (Bill Reilly), Joe Bullitt (Dick Kallman), Lete (Richard France), Darrell (Darrell Notara), Don (Bob Bakanic), Lola Pratt (Ann Crowley), Mrs. Baxter (Doris Dalton), May Parcher (Ellen McCown), Emmie (Helen Wood), Ida (Carol Cole), Madge (Bonnie Brae), Sue (Elizabeth Pacetti), Jenny (Sherry McCutcheon), Nan (Joan Bowman), Mr. Baxter (Frank Albertson), Mr. Parcher (King Calder), Mrs. Parcher (Penny Bancroft), George Crooper (Harrison Muller), Mr. Genesis (Alonzo Bosan), Porter (Joseph James)

Synopsis: This musical is set in Indianapolis in 1907, where Willie Baxter is going through all the pangs of puppy love. His heart yearns for Lola Pratt, who has come to visit her aunt, who is the Baxter's neighbor, for the summer. Lola constantly talks baby talk, and Willie is convinced he has found true love, much to the annoyance of family and friends. At summer's end, Lola goes home, Willie is forlorn, and his family is relieved.

Songs: "Weatherbee's Drug Store"; "This Was Just Another Day"; "Things Are Gonna Hum This Summer"; "How Do You Do, Miss Pratt?";

"Summertime Is Summertime"; "Reciprocity"; "Ode to Lola"; "OO-OOO-OOO, What You Do to Me"; "The Hosier Way"; "I Could Get Married Today"; "After All, It's Spring"; "If We Only Could Stop the Old Town Clock"

Comments: This was the second adaptation of Booth Tarkington's novel, and some reviewers thought it too "old timey" for Broadway in the 1950s.

°*SEVENTH HEAVEN* (May 26, 1955; ANTA Theatre; 44 performances). *Director:* John C. Wilson; *Composer:* Victor Young; *Lyricist:* Stella Unger; *Librettists:* Victor Wolfson and Stella Unger; *Choreographer:* Peter Gennaro. This musical version of Janet Gaynor's and Charles Farrell's silent film classic featured Ricardo Montalban, Chita Rivera, and Gloria DeHaven. The tale of two lovers separated by war and then reunited after much misery succeeded as a play in 1922 (with Helen Menken and George Gaul), but it proved too sentimental for 1950s Broadway musical viewers.

°*SHANGRI-LA* (June 13, 1956; Winter Garden Theatre; 21 performances). *Director:* Albert Marre; *Composer:* Harry Warren; *Lyricists/Librettists:* James Hiton, Jerome Lawrence, and Robert E. Lee; *Choreographer:* Donald Saddler. James Hilton's novel *Lost Horizon* about four kidnapped victims who are taken to the secret lamasery of Shangri-La is set to music. But even with the talents of Jack Cassidy, Carol Lawrence, and Alice Ghostley, the production lasted less than three weeks.

Tony nomination: Best Costume Design (Irene Sharaff)

SHE LOVES ME (April 23, 1963; Eugene O'Neill Theatre; 302 performances)

Production credits: *Producer:* Harold Prince, in association with Lawrence N. Kasha and Philip C. McKenna; *Director:* Harold Prince; *Composer:* Jerry Bock; *Lyricist:* Sheldon Harnick; *Librettist:* Joe Masteroff; *Choreographer:* Carol Haney; *Original source:* Based on a play by Miklós László

Original cast: Arpad (Ralph Williams), Mr. Sipos (Nathaniel Frey), Miss Ritter (Barbara Baxley), Steven Kodaly (Jack Cassidy), Georg Nowack (Daniel Massey), Mr. Maraczek (Ludwig Donath), Window Shoppers (Jety Herlick and Judy West), First Customer (Marion Brash), Second Customer (Peg Murray), Third Customer (Trude Adams), Amalia Balash (Barbara Cook), Fourth Customer and Magda (Judy West), Fifth Customer and Nurse (Jety Herlick), Sixth Customer and Stefanie (Vicki Mansfield), Mr. Keller (Gino Conforti), Waiter (Wood Romoff), Busboy (Al De Sio), Viktor (Pepe De Chazza), Ferencz (Bob Bishop), A Couple (Peg Murray and Joe Ross), Paul (Les Martin)

Synopsis: In the early 1930s, Amalia Balash looks for work in a Budapest music shop. She is reluctantly hired after she picks up a music box and sells it to the first customer. The other employees are ladies' man Steven Kodaly and shy Georg Nowack. Unbeknownst to Amalia and Georg, they have been secretly writing to people who turn out to be each other. The rest of the plot involves the tangled events until the two realize their writing partners and fall in love.

Songs: "Good Morning, Good Day"; "Sounds While Selling"; "Thank You, Madam"; "Days Gone By"; "No More Candy"; "Three Letters"; "Tonight at Eight"; "I Don't Know His Name"; "Perspective"; "Goodbye, Georg"; "Will He Like Me?"; "Ilona"; "I Resolve"; "A Romantic Atmosphere"; "Tango Tragique"; "Dear Friend"; "Try Me"; "Where's My Shoe?"; "Ice Cream"; "She Loves Me"; "A Trip to the Library"; "Grand Knowing You"; "Twelve Days to Christmas"

Tony Award: Best Featured Actor in a Musical (Cassidy). **Tony nominations:** Best Musical, Best Author (Musical), Best Direction (Musical), Best Producer (Musical)

Comments: The story line became three highly successful films: *The Shop around the Corner* (1940), with Margaret Sullavan and James Stewart; *In the Good Old Summertime* (1949), with Judy Garland and Van Johnson; and *You've Got Mail* (1998), with Meg Ryan and Tom Hanks.

°**SHINBONE ALLEY** (April 13, 1957; Broadway Theatre; 49 performances). *Director:* Norman Lloyd (who asked that his name be removed from the credits); *Composer:* George Kleinsinger; *Lyricist:* Joe Darion; *Librettists:* Joe Darion and Mel Brooks; *Choreographers:* Joe Alexander and Rod Alexander. One of the first Broadway shows to feature a fully integrated cast, this "Archie and Mehitabel" story had Eartha Kitt as Mehitabel and Eddie Bracken as Archie.

Tony nomination: Best Costume Design (Motley).

SILK STOCKINGS (February 24, 1955; Imperial Theatre; 478 performances)

Production credits: *Producers:* Cy Feuer and Ernest Martin; *Director:* Cy Feuer; *Composer/Lyricist:* Cole Porter; *Librettist:* George S. Kaufman; *Choreographer:* Eugene Loring

Original cast: Peter Ilyitch Boroff (Philip Sterling), Ivanov (Henry Lascoe), Brankov (Leon Belasco), Bibinski (David Opatoshu), Steve Canfield (Don Ameche), Vera (Julie Newmar), Comissar Markovitch (George Tobias), Ninotchka (Hildegarde Neff), Janice Dayton (Gretchen Wyler), Pierre Bouchard (Marcel Hillaire)

Synopsis: This musical was patterned after the 1939 comedy *Ninotchka*, in which Greta Garbo plays a cold Russian agent who goes to Paris and falls in love with a gay blade. In the musical version, theatrical agent Steve Canfield entices Russian composer Peter Boroff to stay in the West; however, the communists want him back and send trustworthy Ninotchka to dissuade him. But Ninotchka is so enchanted with Paris that a Russian delegation has to bring her back. For a happy ending, she is followed by Steve, and they both return to the West.

Songs: "Too Bad"; "Paris Loves Lovers"; "Stereophonic Sound"; "It's a Chemical Reaction, That's All"; "All of You"; "Satin and Silk"; "Without Love"; "Hail, Bibinski"; "As on Through the Seasons We Sail"; "Josephine"; "Siberia"; "Silk Stockings"; "The Red Blues"

Comments: Although it never reached the popularity of his other musicals, Cole Porter's score was the main reason for the show's run.

°**SLEEPY HOLLOW** (June 3, 1948; St. James Theatre; 12 performances). *Directors:* John O'Shaughnessy and Marc Connelly; *Composer:* George Lessner; *Lyricists/Librettists:* Russell Maloney and Miriam Battista; *Choreographer:* Anna Sokolow. Ichabod Crane and the legend of Sleepy Hollow are depicted in 1795 by the Tappan Zee on the east bank of the Hudson River. The show ran a little more than one week at the St. James, where *Oklahoma!* had run for six years.

Tony Award: Best Scenic Design (Jo Mielziner)

°**SOMETHING MORE!** (November 10, 1964; Eugene O'Neill Theatre; 15 performances). *Director:* Jule Styne; *Composer:* Sammy Fain; *Lyricists:* Marilyn Bergman and Alan Bergman; *Librettist:* Nate Monaster; *Choreographer:* Bob Herget. Barbara Cook was the star in this short-lived production about a novelist and his family, including Arthur Hill, who leave Mineola, New York, for Portofino, Italy. Problems in rehearsals delayed the opening.

°**SOPHIE** (April 15, 1963; Winter Garden Theatre; 8 performances). *Director:* Jack Sydow; *Composer/Lyricist:* Steve Allen; *Librettist:* Phillip Pruneau; *Choreographer:* Donald Saddler. Producers had high hopes for this musical biography of famed star Sophie Tucker, who was known as the "red hot mama" (played by Libi Straiger); however, critics and audiences disagreed, and the production hardly lasted the week.

THE SOUND OF MUSIC (November 16, 1959; Lunt-Fontanne Theatre; 1,443 performances)

Production credits: *Producers:* Leland Hayward, Richard Halliday, Richard Rodgers, and Oscar Hammerstein II; *Director:* Vincent J. Donehue; *Composer:* Richard Rodgers; *Lyricist:* Oscar Hammerstein II; *Librettists:* Howard Lindsay and Russel Crouse; *Choreographer:* Joe

Layton; *Original source:* Based on Maria Augusta Trapps's *The Trapp Family Singers*

Original cast: Maria Rainer (Mary Martin), Sister Berthe (Elizabeth Howell), Sister Margaretta (Muriel O'Malley), Mother Abbess (Patricia Neway), Sister Sophia (Karen Shepard), Captain Georg von Trapp (Theodore Bikel), Franz (John Randolph), Frau Schmidt (Nan McFarland), Liesl (Lauri Peters), Friedrich (William Snowden), Louisa (Kathy Dunn), Kurt (Joseph Stewart), Brigitta (Marilyn Rogers), Marta (Mary Susan Locke), Gretl (Evanna Lien), Rolf Gruber (Brian Davies), Elsa Schraeder (Marion Marlowe), Max Detweiler (Luce Ennis), Herr Zeller (Stefan Gierasch), Baron Elberfeld (Kirby Smith), Postulant (Sue Yaeger), Admiral von Schreiber (Michael Gorrin)

Synopsis: The good sisters decide that Maria seems a bit unsettled for the convent life, so she is sent as governess to the seven children of a stern, widowed naval officer, Georg von Trapp. Maria soon falls in love with him, but after a visit to Vienna, Trapp comes home with a fiancé. However, he is delighted that Maria is teaching his children to sing. Hitler's Nazi government is now emerging in Germany, and Trapp and his fiancé disagree over what is happening to the country. When he is ordered to report for duty in Germany's service, he, the family, and Maria escape to Switzerland.

Songs: "The Sound of Music"; "Maria"; "My Favorite Things"; "Do-Re-Me"; "You Are Sixteen"; "The Lonely Goatherd"; "How Can Love Survive?"; "So Long, Farewell"; "Climb Every Mountain"; "No Way to Stop It"; "Ordinary Couple"; "Edelweiss"

Tony Awards: Best Musical (tied with *Fiorello!*), Best Actress in a Musical (Martin), Best Featured Actress in a Musical (Neway), Best Scenic Design (Oliver Smith), Best Conductor and Musical Director (Frederick Dvonch). **Tony nominations:** Best Featured Actor in a Musical (Bikel), Best Featured Actor in a Musical (Kasznar), Best Featured Actress in a Musical (Lauri Peters, along with the other child actors), Best Direction of a Musical

Comments: The end of one of Broadway's most successful partnerships came with the death of Oscar Hammerstein II shortly after the show opened. Some reviewers thought the production "too sweet," but all praised the outstanding performance of Mary Martin. It was turned into a movie in 1965 with Julie Andrews in the leading role and became the lead grossing musical film of the time, winning Oscars for Best Picture, Best Director, Best Score Adaptation, and Best Editing.

SOUTH PACIFIC (April 7, 1949; Majestic Theatre; 1,925 performances)

Production credits: *Producers:* Richard Rodgers and Oscar Hammerstein II, in association with Leland Hayward and Joshua Logan; *Director:* Joshua Logan; *Composer:* Richard Rodgers; *Lyricist:* Oscar Hammerstein

II; *Librettists:* Oscar Hammerstein II and Joshua Logan; *Choreographer:* Joshua Logan; *Original source:* Adapted from the Pulitzer Prize-winning book *Tales of the South Pacific* by James A. Michener

Original cast: Ngana (Barbara Luna and Bunny Warner), Jerome (Michael De Leon and Robvert Cortazal), Henry (Richard Silvera), Ensign Nellie Forbush (Mary Martin), Emile de Becque (Ezio Pinza), Bloody Mary (Juanita Hall), Bloody Mary's Assistant (Musa Williams), Abner (Archie Savage), Stewpot (Henry Slate), Luther Billis (Myron McCormick), Professor (Fred Sadoff), Lt. Joseph Cable (William Tabbert), Capt. George Brackett (Martin Wolfson), Cmdr. William Harbison (Harvey Sephens), Yeoman Herbert Quale (Alan Gilbert), Sgt. Kenneth Johnson (Thomas Gleason), Seabee Richard West (Dickinson Eastham), Seabee Morton Wise (Henry Michel), Seaman Tom O'Brien (William McGraw), Radio Operator Bob McCaffrey (Jack Fontan), Petty Officer Hamilton Steves (Jim Hawthorne), Staff Seagant Thomas Hassinger (Eugene Smith), Seaman James Hayes (Beau Tilden), Lt. Genevieve Marshall (Jacqueline Fisher), Ensign Dinah Murphy (Roslynd Lowe), Ensign Janet MacGregor (Sandra Deel), Ensign Cora MacRae (Bernice Saunders), Ensign Sue Yaeger (Pat Northrop), Ensign Lisa Minelli (Gloria Meli), Ensign Connie Walewska (Mardi Bayne), Ensign Pamela Witmore (Evelyn Colby), Ensign Bessie Noonan (Helena Schurgot), Liat (Betta St. John), Marcel (Richard Loo), Lt. Buzz Adams (Don Fellows)

Synopsis: On a South Pacific island during World War II, middle-aged planter Emile de Becque and young Navy lieutenant Nellie Forbush fall in love. So do a young marine officer, Lt. Joseph Cable, and a young native girl, the daughter of Bloody Mary. Old prejudices and fears crop up in both romances, but Emile and Nellie overcome their problems, and the young marine is killed on a mission. Winner of the Pulitzer Prize for Drama, it was only the second musical to be so honored (after *Of Thee I Sing*, 1932).

Songs: "Dites-Moi Pourquoi?"; "A Cockeyed Optimist"; "Twin Soliloquies"; "Some Enchanted Evening"; "Blood Mary Is the Girl I Love"; "There's Nothing Like a Dame"; "Bali Ha'i"; "I'm Gonna Wash That Man Right Outta My Hair"; "I'm in Love with a Wonderful Guy"; "Younger Than Springtime"; "Happy Talk"; "Honey Bun"; "You've Got to Be Carefully Taught"; "This Nearly Was Mine"

Tony Awards: Best Musical, Best Original Score, Best Libretto, Best Actor in a Musical (Pinza), Best Actress in a Musical (Martin), Best Featured Actor in a Musical (McCormick), Best Featured Actress in a Musical (Hall), Best Producer of a Musical, Best Director, Best Scenic Design (Jo Mielziner, 1949)

Comments: This musical is generally placed in the top five musicals of all time; especially cited for performances by Ezio Pinza and Mary Martin.

Oscar Hammerstein's lyrics that preach about racial prejudice (e.g., "You've Got to Be Carefully Taught") caused trouble for the show in the South, but the songs were sung for years by the general public. One of the most successful of modern musicals, critics generally regarded the movie version (1958) as a disappointment, with Rossano Brazzi and Mitzi Gaynor in the lead roles and directed by Joshua Logan. A highly successful stage revival had a long run at the Vivian Beaumont Theatre starting in 2008.

°*ST. LOUIS WOMAN* (March 30, 1946; Martin Beck Theatre; 113 performances). *Director:* Rouben Mamoulian; *Composer:* Harold Arlen; *Lyricist:* Johnny Mercer; *Librettists:* Arna Bontemps and Countee Cullen; *Choreographer:* Charles Walters. The show was originally written to headline Lena Horne; however, when some leading African Americans criticized the fact that the production centered on a black woman of so-called easy virtue in early twentieth-century St. Louis, Horne pulled out. She was replaced by Ruby Hill. In addition, the presence of Pearl Bailey helped to keep the show going as long as it did.

STOP THE WORLD—I WANT TO GET OFF (October 3, 1962; Shubert Theatre; 556 performances)

Production credits: *Producer:* David Merrick, in association with Bernard Delfont; *Director:* Anthony Newley; *Composers/Lyricists:* Leslie Bricusse and Anthony Newley; *Librettists:* Leslie Bricusse and Anthony Newley; *Choreographer:* John Broome

Original cast: Littlechap (Anthony Newley), Evie, Anya, Ilse, and Ginnie (Anna Quayle), Jane (Jennifer Baker), Susan (Susan Baker), Chorus Members (Rawley Bates, Bonnie Brody, Diana Corto, Jo Anne Leeds, Stephanie Winters, Mark Hunter, Paul Rufo, Sylvia Tysick, Karen Lynn Reed)

Synopsis: This is a musical allegory that tells the life story of everyman, called "Littlechap," in a setting resembling a circus tent. Littlechap goes from birth to death, much of the progress demonstrated with the use of symbolic gestures that mark his bouts with success and failure. Saddled with the responsibilities of a family, his dissatisfaction grows, leading him into the arms of other women. In the twilight of his life, he realizes that he needs only what he has always had—the love of his wife.

Songs: "The A.B.C. Song"; "I Want to be Rich"; "Typically English"; "A Special Announcement"; "Lumbered"; "Welcome to Sludgepool"; "Gonna Build a Mountain"; "Glorious Russian"; "Meilinki, Meilchick"; "Family Fugue"; "Nag! Nag! Nag!"; "All-American"; "Once in a Lifetime"; "Mumbo Jumbo"; "Welcome to Sunvale"; "Someone Nice Like You"; "What Kind of Fool Am I?"

Tony Award: Best Featured Actress in a Musical (Quayle). **Tony nominations:** Best Musical, Best Actor in a Musical (Newley), Best Author of a Musical, Best Composer and Lyricist

Comments: Both audiences and critics were divided on this one (most critics found it heavy handed), but "What Kind of Fool Am I?" became one of the most popular tunes of the year.

°*STREET SCENE* (January 9, 1947; Adelphi Theatre; 148 performances). *Director:* Charles Friedman; *Composer:* Kurt Weill; *Lyricist:* Langston Hughes; *Librettist:* Elmer Rice; *Choreographer:* Anna Sokolow. The Kurt Weill score based on the Elmer Rice 1929 hit concerns a star-crossed romance. It takes place on the East Side of New York in 1946, and tells of the mounting tensions among the irritable neighbors.

Tony Awards: Best Original Score, Best Costume Design (Lucinda Ballard)

SUBWAYS ARE FOR SLEEPING (December 27, 1961; St. James Theatre; 205 performances)

Production credits: *Producer:* David Merrick; *Director/Choreographer:* Michael Kidd; *Composer:* Jule Styne; *Lyricists/Librettists:* Betty Comden and Adolph Green; *Original source:* Based on the book by Edmund G. Love

Original cast: Myra Blake (Grayson Hall), Angela McKay (Carol Lawrence), Tom Bailey (Sydney Chaplin), Station Guard (Robert Howard), J. Edward Sykes, Social Worker, and Mr. Barney (Joe Hill), Jack, Max Hillman, and Museum Guard (Anthony Saverino), Gus Holt (Cy Young), Charlie Smith (Orson Bean), A Drunk (Jim Weiss), Martha Vail (Phyllis Newman), Mr. Pittman (Gordon Connell), Delivery Boy (Michael Bennett), Lancelot Zuckerman (Horase), Freddie (Bob Gorman), Mac and Photographer (John Sharpe), Models (Sari Clymas and Diane Ball), Zack Flint (Lawrence Pool), Lieutenant Pilsudski and Relief Doorman (Robert Howard), Mary Thompkins (Dean Taliaferro)

Synopsis: Two romances have a rough time in Manhattan. Tom Bailey is a neat-looking type who sleeps in the subway and attracts magazine writer Angela McKay. McKay interviews Martha Vail, a beauty contest winner who lost all her clothing and is about to lose her apartment. She is romanced by another ne'er-do-well, Charlie Smith. All's well in the end.

Songs: "Subways Are for Sleeping"; "Girls Like Me"; "Station Rush"; "I'm Just Taking My Time"; "Subway Directions"; "Ride Through the Night"; "I Was a Shoo-In"; "Who Knows What Might Have Been?"; "Swing Your Projects"; "Strange Duet"; "I Said It and I'm Glad"; "Be a Santa"; "Subway Incident"; "How Can You Describe a Face?"; "I Just Can't Wait"; "Comes Once in a Lifetime"; "What Is This Feeling in the Air?"

Tony Awards: Best Featured Actress in a Musical (Newman). **Tony nominations:** Best Featured Actor in a Musical (Bean), Best Choreography

Comments: So-so reviews are credited for the short run.

TAKE ME ALONG (October 22, 1959; Shubert Theatre; 448 performances)

Production credits: *Producer:* David Merrick; *Director:* Peter Glenville; *Composer/Lyricist:* Bob Merrill; *Librettists:* Joseph Stein and Robert Russell; *Choreographer:* Onna White; *Original source:* Based on Eugene O'Neill's play *Ah, Wilderness*

Original cast: Nat Miller (Walter Pidgeon), Mildred Miller (Zeme North), Richard Miller (Robert Morse), Arthur Miller (James Cresson), Tommy Miller (Luke Halpin), Essie Miller (Una Merkel), Lily Miller (Eileen Herlie), Muriel Macomber (Susan Luckey), Dave Macomber (Fred Miller), Sid Davis (Jackie Gleason), Wint (Peter Conlow), Bartender (Jack Collins), Belle (Arlen Golonka), The Drunk (Gene Varrone), Salesman (Bill McDonald), The Beardsley Dwarf (Charles Bolender), Salome (Rae McLean), Camille (Paula Lloyd)

Synopsis: Nat Miller is the town's newspaper editor in Centerville, Connecticut. His heavy drinking brother-in-law Sid is courting neighbor Lily, and his son Richard is stuck on Muriel Macomber. When his son's romance is broken off, Richard goes on a drinking binge, which sends the boy on a drunk that leads to a dream ballet. Richard sobers up and goes away to college, still swearing his eternal love to Muriel, and Sid promises Muriel that he will stop drinking if she will marry him.

Songs: "The Parade"; "Oh, Please"; "I Would Die"; "Sid, Ol' Kid"; "Staying Young"; "I Get Embarrassed"; "We're Home"; "Take Me Along"; "For Sweet Charity"; "Pleasant Beach House"; "That's How It Starts"; "Promise Me a Rose"; "Little Green Snake"; "Nine O'Clock"; "But Yours"

Tony Awards: Best Actor in a Musical (Gleason). **Tony nominations:** Best Musical, Best Actor in a Musical (Morse), Best Actor in a Musical (Pidgeon), Best Actress in a Musical (Herlie), Best Direction of a Musical, Best Choreography, Best Costume Design (Miles White), Best Conductor and Musical Director (Lehman Engel), Best Stage Technician (Al Alloy)

Comments: This was another long-running show that was a financial washout; however, it was Jackie Gleason's best Broadway role of his career.

TENDERLOIN (October 17, 1960; 46th Street Theatre; 216 performances)

Production credits: *Producers:* Robert E. Griffith and Harold S. Prince; *Director:* George Abbott; *Composer:* Jerry Bock; *Lyricist:* Sheldon

Harnick; *Librettists:* George Abbott and Jerome Weidman; *Choreographer:* Joe Layton; *Original source:* Based on the novel by Samuel Hopkins Adams

Original cast: Tommy (Ron Husmann), Nita (Eileen Rodgers), Lt. Schmidt (Ralph Dunn), Reverend Brock (Maurice Evans), Gertie (Lee Becker), Margie (Margery Gray), Dorothy (Dorothy Frank), Girl (Patsy Peterson), Young Man (Dargan Montgomery), Jessica (Irene Kane), Laura (Wynne Miller), Ellington (Gordon Cook), Joe (Rex Everhart), Purdy (Lanier Davis), Deacon (Roy Fant), Frye (Eddie Phillips), Rooney (Jordon Howard), Nellie (Marguerite Shaw), Becker (Michael Roberts), Callahan (Jack McCann), Maggie (Pat Turner), Liz (Christine Norden), Mrs. Barker (Elaine Rogers), Chairman (Joe Hill)

Synopsis: Reverend Brock wants to clean up the old Tenderloin red-light district around West 23rd Street in New York City. He runs into opposition at every point, especially from the corrupt politicians and police who are taking cuts from the earnings of the prostitutes who work there. Brock enlists the help of a reporter, Tommy, who has ties to a dishonest cop, Lt. Schmidt. They frame Brock, but the truth comes out when Tommy has a change of heart due to a girl named Laura. Next, Brock is on his way to clean up Detroit.

Songs: "Bless This Land"; "Little Old New York"; "Dr. Brock"; "Artificial Flowers"; "What's in It for You?"; "Reform"; "Tommy, Tommy"; "The Picture of Happiness"; "Dance"; "Dear Friend"; "The Army of the Just"; "How the Money Changes Hands"; "Good Clean Fun"; "My Miss Mary"; "My Gentle Young Johnny"; "The Trial"; "The Tenderloin Celebration"

Tony nominations: Best Actor in a Musical (Evans), Best Featured Actor (Husmann), Best Costume Design (Cecil Beaton)

Comments: With a run of about six months, the musical was still a commercial failure.

TEXAS, LI'L DARLIN' (November 25, 1949; Mark Hellinger Theatre; 293 performances)

Production credits: *Producers:* Studio Productions and Anthony Brady Farrell Productions; *Director:* Paul Crabtree; *Composer:* Robert Emmett Dolan; *Lyricist:* Johnny Mercer; *Librettists:* John Whedon and Sam Moore; *Choreographer:* Al White Jr.

Original cast: Harvey Small (Loring Smith), John Baxter Trumbull and Radio Announcer (Charles Bang), Parker Stuart Eliot and Engineer (Alden Aldrich), William Dean Benson Jr. (Edward Platt), Frothingham Fry (Ned Wertimer), Brewster Ames II (Fredd Wane), Three Coyotes (Eddie Smith, Bill Horan, and Joel McConky), Hominy Smith (Kenny Delmar), Dogie Smith (Betty Lou Keim), Amos Hall (Dante Di Paolo), Sherm (Cameron Andrews), Dwayne Fawcet (William Ambler), Branch

Pedley (Ray Long), Delia Pratt (Ronnie Hartmann), Red (Merrill Hilton), Jo An Woods and Cheerleader (Elyse Weber), Calico Munson (Dorothy Love), Rebecca Bass (Carol Lee), Sally Tucket (Ruth Ostrander), Sue Crockett (Doris Schmitt), Sara Boone (Arlene Ethane), Belle Cooper (Yvonne Tibor), Sam (Jared Reed), Dallas Smith (Mary Hatcher), Easy Jones (Danny Scholl), Melissa Tatum (Kate Murtah), Stan (Edmund Hall), Herb (Ralph Patterson), Jack Prow (Bob Bernard), Harry Stern (Joey Thomas), Drum Majorette (Jacqueline James), Football Player (Carl Conway), Guard (Ray Long)

Synopsis: Hominy Smith is a grassroots Texas politician who coasts along with an easy lifestyle and not much to worry about politically. All that changes when along comes danger in the form of a crusading veteran. With that as motivation, Smith now considers the possibility of moving up to the presidency.

Songs: "Whoop'in' and a-Hollerin'"; "Texas, L'l Darlin'"; "They Talk a Different Language"; "A Month of Sundays"; "Down in the Valley"; "Hootin' Owl Trail"; "The Big Movie Show in the Sky"; "Horseshoes Are Lucky"; "Love Me, Love My Dog"; "Take a Crank Letter"; "Politics"; "Ride 'em Cowboy"; "Square Dance"; "Affable Balding Me"; "Whichaway'd They Go?"; "It's Good to Be Alive"

Comments: At the time of the opening, Kenny Delmar was at the top of his popularity as Senator Claghorn on Fred Allen's radio show.

°*13 DAUGHTERS* (March 2, 1961; 54th Street Theatre; 28 performances). *Director:* Billy Matthews; *Composer/Lyricist/Librettist:* Eaton Magoon Jr.; *Choreographer:* Rod Alexander. Don Ameche starred in this musical set in Hawaii about Chun, who has thirteen daughters. According to family tradition, the oldest daughter must be the first to be married; however, Chun's oldest daughter is more interested in missionary work than in wedding bells, so the other girls resolve to remain unmarried.

°*THREE WISHES FOR JAMIE* (March 21, 1952; Mark Hellinger Theatre; 91 performances). *Director:* Abe Burrows; *Composer/ Lyricist:* Ralph Blane; *Librettists:* Charles O'Neal and Abe Burrows; *Choreographers:* Herbert Ross, Ted Cappy, and Eugene Loring. Troubles plagued this musical from the start, even though it starred John Raitt as a man granted three wishes by a fairy. New Yorkers found it embarrassingly sentimental.

Tony nominations: Best Scenic Design, Musical (George Jenkins), Best Conductor and Musical Director (Pembroke Davenport)

TOP BANANA (November 1, 1951; Winter Garden Theatre; 350 performances)

Production credits: *Producers:* Paula Sloane and Mike Stone; *Director:* Jack Donohue; *Composer/Lyricist:* Johnny Mercer; *Librettist:* Hy Kraft; *Choreographer:* Ron Feitcher

Original cast: Jerry Biffle (Phil Silvers), Jack Albertson (Vic Davis), Sales Girl (Florence Baum), Model (Marion Burke), Announcer (Dean Campbell), Russ Wiswell (Zachary A. Charles), Stagehand and Photogrpaher (Donald Covert), Bubble Girl (Sara Dillon), Cliff Lane (Lindy Doherty), Moe (Herbie Faye), Pinky (Joey Faye), Customer (Joan Fields), Danny (Ed Harley), TV Technician, Photographer, and Singer (Ken Harvey), Mr. Parker (Bradford Hatton), Juggler and Singer (Claude Heater), Script Girl (Eve Hebert), Miss Pillsbury, Customer, and Singer (Betsy Holland), Customer (B. J. Keating), Customer (Douglas Luther), Sally Peters (Judy Lynn), Betty Dillon (Rose Marie), Photogrpaher (Don McKay), Ted Morgan (Ted Morgan), Model and Magician's Assistant (Basha Regis), Tommy (Bob Scheerer), Customer (Laurel Shelby), Widow and Singer (Judy Sinclair), Sales Girl (Joy Skylar), Bubbles (Gloria Smith)

Synopsis: Jerry Biffle (supposedly modeled after Milton Berle) is the star of the Blendo Soap Program. He hires Sally Peters, one of the department store models, because he is told to get a love interest on his show. He falls in love with her, but she falls in love with Cliff Lane, the tenor of his television company, who sings to her over the phone. Uncharacteristically, Biffle helps her find romance with her true love.

Songs: "Man of the Year This Week"; "You're So Beatiful That—"; "Top Banana"; "Elevator Song"; "Only If You're in Love"; "My Home Is in My Shoes"; "I Fought Every Step of the Way"; "O.K. for TV"; "Slogan Song"; "Meet Miss Blendo"; "Sans Souci"; "That's for Sure"; "A Dog Is a Man's Best Friend"; "Word a Day"

Tony Award: Best Actor in a Musical (Silvers)

Comments: This was another show that ended in the red.

TOVARICH (March 18, 1963; Broadway Theatre; 264 performances)

Production credits: *Producers:* Abel Farbman and Sylvia Harris, in association with Joseph Harris; *Director:* Peter Glenville; *Composer:* Lee Pockriss; *Lyricist:* Anne Croswell; *Librettist:* David Shaw; *Choreographer:* Herbert Ross; *Original source:* Based on Jacques Deval's and Robert E. Sherwood's 1936–1937 hit play

Original cast: Gorotchenko (Alexander Scourby), Vassily (Paul Michael), Mikail (Jean-Pierre Aumont), Admiral Boris Soukhomine (Michael Kermoyan), Count Ivan Shamforoff (Gene Varrone), Baroness Roumel (Katia Geleznova), Marina (Rita Metzger), M. Chauffourier-Dubieff (Doc McHenry), Tatiana (Vivien Leigh), Natalia Mayovskaya (Louise Troy), Helen Davis (Margery Gray), George Davis (Byron Mitchell), Charles

Davis (George S. Irving), Grace Davis (Louise Kirtland), Louise (Maggie Task), Ballet Master (Tom Abbott), Nadia (Barbara Monte), Mme. Van Hemert (Pat Kelly), Mme. Van Steuben (Eleonore Treiber), Footman at the Davis Home (Harald Horn), Night Club Singer and General Boruvsky (Dale Malone), Kukla Katusha (Bettye Jenkins), Ivan (William Reilly), Sergei, Prince Ossipovsky, and Dancer (Larry Roquemore)

Synopsis: The prince and grand duchess manage to get out of Russia with four billion francs, but they are broke because the money actually belongs to the czar. So, they take jobs as a butler and maid in an American home. Soviet agents track them down and get the fortune, and the two decide to retain their positions with the American family.

Songs: "Nitchevo"; "I Go to Bed"; "You'll Make an Elegant Butler"; "Stuck with Each Other"; "Say You'll Stay"; "You Love Me"; "Introduction Tango"; "That Face"; "Wilkes-Barre, PA"; "No! No! No!"; "A Small Cartel"; "It Used to Be"; "Kukla Katusha"; "Make a Friend"; "The Only One"; "Uh-Oh!"; "Managed"; "I Know the Feeling"; "All for You"

Tony Award: Best Actress in a Musical (Leigh), Best Featured Actress in a Musical (Troy)

Comments: Most critics thought the work was uninspired, and the show was saved only by the presence of star Vivien Leigh.

A TREE GROWS IN BROOKLYN (April 19, 1951; Alvin Theatre; 270 performances)

Production credits: *Producer/Director:* George Abbott; *Composer:* Arthur Schwartz; *Lyricist:* Dorothy Fields; *Librettists:* Betty Smith and George Abbott; *Choreographer:* Herbert Ross; *Original source:* Based on Betty Smith's novel

Original cast: Willie (Billy Parsons), Allie (Joe Calvan), Hildy (Dody Heath), Della (Beverly Purvin), Petey (Lou Wills Jr.), Katie (Marcia Van Dyke), Aloysius (Jordan Bentley), Johnny Nolan (Johnny Johnston), Aunt Cissy (Shirley Booth), Harry (Nathaniel Frey), Max (Henry Sherwood), Mae (Isabelle Price), Moriarty (Roland Wood), Annie (Claudia Campbell), Girl in Mae's Place and Singer (Joan Kibrig), Old Clothes Man and Judge (Harland Dixon), Florence (Janet Parker), Edgie and Child (Donald Duerr), Francie (Nomi Mitty), Junior (Howard Martin), Swanswine (Albert Linville), Hick (Alan Gilbert), Salesman (Art Carroll), Maudie (Celine Flanagan)

Synopsis: The scene is Brooklyn, New York, around the turn of the twentieth century, and the story concerns star-crossed lovers Katie and Johnny Nolan. Johnny cannot keep a job or stay sober. Katie and Johnny's story is played out against a background of comic Aunt Cissy, who suffers through the tribulations of a bigamous marriage.

Songs: "Payday"; "Mine 'Til Monday"; "Make the Man Love Me"; "I'm Like a New Broom"; "Look Who's Dancing"; "Love Is the Reason"; "Mine Next Monday"; "If You Haven't Got a Sweetheart"; "I'll Buy You a Star"; "That's How It Goes"; "He Had Refinement"; "Growing Pains"; "Is That My Prince?"; "Halloween"; "Don't Be Afraid"

Comments: Shirley Booth stopped the show each night when she sang "He Had Refinement." Although the songs were lovely, some reviewers felt that the musical suffered because the movie verison (1945), starring Dorothy McGuire, Joan Blondell, and James Dean, had been so acclaimed.

THE UNSINKABLE MOLLY BROWN (November 3, 1960; Winter Garden Theatre; 532 performances)

Production credits: *Producers:* Theatre Guild and Dore Schary; *Director:* Dore Schary; *Composer/Lyricist:* Meredith Willson; *Librettist:* Richard Morris; *Choreographer:* Peter Gennaro

Original cast: Molly Tobin (Tammy Grimes), Michael Tobin (Sterling Clark), Aloysius Tobin, Wounded Sailor, and Dancer (Bill Starr), Patrick Tobin, Baron of Auld, and Dancer (Bob Daley), Father Flynn, Mr. Wadlington, Singer, and Dancer (Norman Fredericks), Shamus Tobin (Cameron Prud'homme), Brawling Miner and Dancer (Alex Stevens), Brawling Miner, Gitter, and Dancer (Joe Pronto), Charlie (Woody Hurst), Christmas Morgan (Joseph Sirola), Banjo (Billy Faier), Johnny "Leadville" Brown (Harve Presnell), Boy (Paul Floyd), Sheriff (Terry Violino), Mrs. McGlone (Edith Meiser), Monsignor Ryan (Jack Harrold), Roberts (Christopher Hewett), Professor Gardella, Maitre D', and Singer (Dale Malone), Germaine, Saloon Girl, and Dancer (Lynn Gay Lorino), Princess DeLong (Mony Dalmes), Prince DeLong (Mony Daimes), Countess Ethanotous and Singer (Wanda Saxon), Jenab-ashros, Male Passenger, and Singer (Marvin Goodis), Grand Duchess Marie Nicholaiovna and Singer (Patricia Kelly), Count Feranti, Young Waiter, and Singer (Michael Davis), Duchess of Burlingame and Dancer (Barbara Newman), Duke of Burlingame and Dancer (Ted Adkins), Malcolm Broderick and Singer (Barney Johnston), Mrs. Wadlington and Singer (Lynne Osborne), Mother and Singer (Nada Rowand), Singer (June Card)

Synopsis: Molly is sure she is going to be rich one day. Her dream seems to come true when she marries Johnny Brown, a miner who gives her $300,000 from a claim; however, she hides it in an oven and burns it by mistake. The couple moves to Denver, where Molly is snubbed, but they go on to Europe where she becomes the darling of society. They return to Denver, where Molly expects to flaunt herself, but her party is wrecked by Johnny's old mining buddies. So she returns to Europe, but decides to go back to Johnny, taking the *Titanic*. She is one of the survivors and a heroine.

Songs: "I Ain't Down Yet"; "Belly Up to the Bar, Boys"; "I've Already Started In"; "I'll Never Say No"; "My Own Brass Bed"; "The Denver Police"; "Beautiful, People, of Denver"; "Are You Sure?"; "Happy Birthday, Mrs. J. J. Brown"; "Bon Jour"; "If I Knew"; "Chick-a-Pen"; "Keep-a-Hoppin'"; "Leadville Johnny Brown"; "Up Where the People Are"; "Dolce Far Niente"

Tony Award: Best Featured Actress in a Musical (Grimes)

Comments: The reviews were mixed; one said that Molly "fails to float." Most audience reaction depended on how the theatregoers liked Tammy Grimes in the lead role.

°***THE VAMP*** (November 10, 1955; Winter Garden Theatre; 60 performances). *Director:* David Alexander; *Composer:* James Mundy; *Lyricist:* John Latouche; *Librettists:* John C. Touche and Sam Locke; *Choreographer:* Robert Alton. Audiences were unenthusiastic even with Carol Channing, well-known by then for *Gentlemen Prefer Blondes*, heading the cast. She was Flora Weems, a farm girl from the Bronx who goes on to fame in the early film studios of New York. Critics found nothing exciting about the story, music, or choreography.

Tony nominations: Best Actress in a Musical (Channing), Best Choreography, Conductor and Musical Director (Milton Rosenstock)

WEST SIDE STORY (September 26, 1957; Winter Garden Theatre; 732 performances)

Production credits: *Producers:* Robert E. Griffith and Harold S. Prince, by arrangement with Roger L. Stevens; *Director/Choreographer:* Jerome Robbins; *Composer:* Leonard Bernstein; *Lyricist:* Stephen Sondheim; *Librettist:* Arthur Laurents; *Original source:* Based on a conception of Jerome Robbins

Original cast: Riff (Mickey Calin), Tony (Larry Kert), Action (Eddie Roll), A-Rab (Tony Mordente), Baby John (David Winters), Snowboy (Grover Dale), Big Deal (Martin Charnin), Diesel (Hank Brunjes), Gee-Tar (Tommy Abbott), Mouth Piece (Frank Green), Tiger (Lowell Harris), Graziella (Wilma Curley), Velma (Carole D'Andrea), Minnie (Nanette Rosen), Clarice (Marilyn D'Honau), Pauline (Julie Oser), Anybodys (Lee Becker), Bernardo (Ken Le Roy), Maria (Carol Lawrence), Anita (Chita Rivera), Chino (Jamie Sanchez), Pepe (George Marcy), Indio (Noel Schwartz), Luis (Al De Sio), Anxious (Gene Gavin), Nibbles (Ronnie Lee), Juano (Jay Norman), Toro (Erne Castaldo), Moose (Jack Murray), Rosalia (Marilyn Cooper), Consuela (Reri Grist), Teresita (Carmen Gutierrez), Francisca (Elizabeth Taylor), Estella (Lynn Ross), Marguerita (Liane Plane), Doc

(Art Smith), Schrank (Arch Johnson), Krupke (William Bramley), Gladhand (John Harkins)

Synopsis: Two rival gangs, the American Jets and the Puerto Rican Sharks, vie for territory in New York City. Jet member Tony dreams of a life outside of the gangs. At a dance, he meets Maria, sister of the Shark leader Bernardo. They fall in love and plan a life together. But Bernardo is furious when he finds out. A rumble occurs between the two gangs, which Tony tries to stop, but when Bernardo stabs the Jet leader, Riff, Tony kills him. Tony goes to Maria to beg her forgiveness. Chino of the Sharks finds and kills Tony. Marie threatens to kill herself but cannot do it. At the end, both gangs gather around Tony's body to suggest that the feud may be over.

Songs: "Jet Song"; "Something's Coming"; "The Dance at the Gym"; "Maria"; "Tonight"; "America"; "Cool"; "One Hand, One Heart"; "I Feel Pretty"; "Somewhere"; "Gee, Officer Krupke"; "A Boy Like That"; "I Have a Love"; "Taunting"

Tony Award: Best Choreography, Best Scenic Design (Oliver Smith). **Tony nominations:** Best Musical, Best Featured Actress in a Musical (Lawrence), Best Costume Design (Irene Sharaff), Conductor and Musical Director (Max Goberman)

Comments: This is one of Broadway's best-loved musicals.

WHAT MAKES SAMMY RUN? (February 27, 1964; 54th Street Theatre; 540 performances)

Production credits: *Producer:* Joseph Cates; *Director:* Abe Burrows; *Composer/Lyricist:* Ervin Drake; *Librettists:* Budd Schulberg and Stuart Schulberg; *Choreographer:* Matt Mattox; *Original source:* Based on Budd Schulberg's novel

Original cast: Al Manhaim (Robert Alda), Sammy Glick (Steve Lawrence), O'Brien (Ralph Stantley), Osborn (John Dorrin), Bartender (George Blackwell), Julian Blumberg (George Coe), Rita Rio (Graciela Daniele), Tracy Clark (Richard France), Lucky Dugan (Edward McNally), Sheik Orsini (Barry Newman), Sidney Fineman (Arny Freeman), Kit Sargent (Sally Ann Howes), H. L. Harrington (Walter Klavun), Laurette Harrington (Bernice Massi), Seymour Glick (Mace Barrett)

Synopsis: Sammy Glick is a heel who has made good in the newspaper business by stealing someone else's material. He writes a movie script that gets him to Hollywood, where he is befriended by famous producer Sidney Fineman and loved by secretary Kit Sargent. But in his drive to the top, Sammy maneuvers Fineman out of his job, after which the producer commits suicide. Then, Sammy ditches Kit for Laurette, the daughter of the chairman of the board. They are married, and Sammy learns that his wife is more ruthless than he.

Songs: "A New Pair of Shoes"; "You Help Me"; "A Tender Spot"; "Lites —Camera—Platitude"; "My Hometown"; "Monsoon"; "I See Something"; "Maybe Some Other Time"; "You Can Trust Me"; "A Room without Windows"; "Kiss Me No Kisses"; "I Feel Humble"; "Something to Live For"; "Paint a Rainbow"; "You're No Good"; "The Friendliest Thing"; "Wedding of the Year"; "Some Days Everything Goes Wrong"

Tony nominations: Best Actor in a Musical (Lawrence), Best Conductor and Musical Director (Lehman Engel)

Comments: Steve Lawrence was a popular nightclub singer at the time the show opened. After five months, attendance began to drop off, as he missed twenty-four performances during a four-month period. The show closed more than $285,000 in the red.

WHERE'S CHARLEY? (October 11, 1948; St. James Theatre; 792 performances)

Production credits: *Producers:* Cy Feuer and Ernest H. Martin, with Gwen Rickard; *Director:* George Abbott; *Composer/Lyricist:* Frank Loesser; *Librettist:* George Abbott; *Choreographer:* George Balanchine; *Original source:* Based on Brandon Thomas's play *Charley's Aunt*

Original cast: Brassett (John Lynds), Jack Chesney (Byron Palmer), Charley Wykeham (Ray Bolger), Kitty Verdun (Doretta Morrow), Amy Spettigue (Allyn Ann McLerie), Wilkinson (Edgar Kent), Sir Francis Chesney (Paul England), Mr. Spettigue (Horace Cooper), Professor (Jack Friend), Donna Lucia D'Alvadorez (Jane Lawrence), Photographer (James Lane), Patricia (Marie Foster), Reggie (Douglas Deane)

Synopsis: Charley's aunt is a millionairess. She does not arrive at a luncheon that Charley and Jack had planned for their girlfriends; however, when Charley arrives at a student theatrical production decked out in women's clothes, he suddenly finds himself playing the role of his aunt. A mad romp follows as Jack's father is smitten and begins to woo the bogus aunt. All ends well when the masquerade is finally revealed. Charley and Jack get their girls, and Jack's father, Sir Francis Chesney, meets the real Charley's aunt.

Songs: "The Years Before Us"; "Better Get Out of Here"; "The New Ashmolean Marching Society and Students' Conservatory Band"; "My Darling, My Darling"; "Make a Miracle"; "Serenade with Asides"; "Lovelier Than Ever"; "The Woman in His Room"; "Pernambuco"; "Where's Charley?"; "Once in Love with Amy"; "The Gossips"

Tony Award: Best Actor in a Musical (Bolger)

Comments: What was intended as the hit song—"Once in Love with Amy"—did not become one until several weeks after the opening, when Ray Bolger began urging the audience to sing along. Bolger recreated his movie role (1952) in a production that was filmed in England.

°*WHOOP-UP* (December 22, 1958; Shubert Theatre; 56 performances). *Director:* Cy Feuer; *Composer:* Moose Charlap; *Lyricist:* Norman Gimbel; *Librettists:* Cy Feuer, Dan Cushman, and Ernest Martin; *Choreographer:* Onna White. Susan Johnson was bar owner Glenda in this short-lived tale of life on a modern-day (for the time) Native American reservation. A better-than-average score did not save the show.

Tony nominations: Best Featured Actress in a Musical (Julienne Marie), Best Choreography

WILDCAT (December 16, 1960; Alvin Theatre; 171 performances)

Production credits: *Producers:* Michael Kidd and N. Richard Nash; *Director/Choreographer:* Michael Kidd; *Composer:* Cy Coleman; *Lyricist:* Carolyn Leigh; *Librettist:* N. Richard Nash

Original cast: Jane Jackson (Paula Stewart), Wildcat Jackson (Lucille Ball), Sheriff Sam Gore (Howard Fischer), Barney and Singer (Ken Ayers), Luke and Dancer (Anthony Saverino), Countess Emily O'Brien (Edith King), Joe Dynamite (Keith Andes), Hank (Clifford David), Miguel (H. F. Green), Sookie (Don Tomkins), Matt (Charles Braswell), Corky (Bill Linton), Oney (Swen Swenson), Sandy (Ray Mason), Tattoo (Bill Walker), Postman (Bill Richards), Inez and Dancer (Marsha Wagner), Blonde (Wendy Nickerson)

Synopsis: Wildcat Jackson convinces the people of Centavo City that she has drilling rights there. Joe Dynamite becomes her foreman, but he gets discouraged when no oil is found. Just when the crew is ready to run out, Wildcat tosses some dynamite into the well and—lo and behold—a gusher. She gets the oil, and she gets Joe.

Songs: "Corduroy Road"; "The Day I Do"; "El Sombrero"; "Give a Little Whistle"; "Hey, Look Me Over"; "One Day We Dance"; "Tall Hope"; "Tippy Toes"; "Wildcat"; "What Takes My Fancy"; "You're a Liar"; "You've Come Home"

Comments: Most reviewers agreed that the only reason to see the show was Lucille Ball. The book was slight and the songs not particularly memorable.

WISH YOU WERE HERE (June 25, 1952; Imperial Theatre; 598 performances)

Production credits: *Producers:* Leland Hayward and Joshua Logan; *Director/Choreographer:* Joshua Logan; *Composer/Lyricist:* Harold Rome; *Librettists:* Arthur Kober and Joshua Logan; *Original source:* Based on Arthur Kober's play *Having a Wonderful Time*

Original cast: Teddy Stern (Patricia Marand), Chick Miller (Jack Cassidy), Fay Fromkin (Sheila Bond), Itchy Flexner (Sidney Armus), Pinky

Harris (Paul Valentine), Harry "Muscles" Green (John Perkins), Lou Kandel (Sammy Smith), Herman Fabricant (Harry Clark), Miriam (Nancy Franklin), New Girl (Florence Henderson), Acrobat (Steve Wiland), Girl Diver (Beverly Weston), Eccentric Diver (Joseph Thomas), Seymour's Girl Friend (Nancy Baker)

Synopsis: Life at a Jewish summer camp, complete with swimming pool on stage, focuses on the romance between Teddy Stern and Chick Miller. The social director, Itchy, causes some trouble when he, inadvertantly, gives Chick the idea that Teddy has spent the night with Pinky Harris. All is well in the end.

Songs: "Camp Karefree"; "There's Nothing Nicer Than People"; "Social Director"; "Shopping Around"; "Bright College Days"; "Mix and Mingle"; "Could Be"; "Tripping the Light Fantastic"; "Where Did the Night Go?"; "Certain Individuals"; "They Won't Know Me"; "Summer Afternoon"; "Don Jose"; "Everybody Loves Everybody"; "Wish You Were Here"; "Relax"; "Flattery"

Tony Awards: Best Featured Actress in a Musical (Bond), Stage Technician (Abe Kurnit)

Comments: The show was named for the standard greeting on most postcards of the time.

WONDERFUL TOWN (February 25, 1953; Winter Garden Theatre; 559 performances)

Production credits: *Producer:* Robert Fryer; *Director:* George Abbott; *Composer:* Leonard Bernstein; *Lyricists:* Betty Comden and Adolph Green; *Librettists:* Joseph Fields and Jerome Chodorov; *Choreographer:* Donald Saddler

Original cast: Tour Guide and Associate Editor (Warren Galjour), Greenwich Villager (Joe Layton), Appopolous (Henry Lascoe), Officer Lonigan (Walter Kelvin), Helen (Michele Burke), Wreck (Jordan Bentley), Violet and Greenwich Villager (Dody Goodman), Speedy Valenti (Ted Beniades), Eileen Sherwood (Edith Adams), Ruth Sherwood (Rosalind Russell), Strange Man, Italian Chef, and Policeman (Nathaniel Frey), Drunk, Shore Patrolman, Greenwich Villager, and Policeman (Lee Papell), Drunk, Italian Waiter, Greenwich Villager, and Policeman (Delbert Anderson), Robert Baker (George Gaynes), Associate Editor and Policeman (Albert Linville), Mrs. Wade (Isabella Hoopes), Frank Lippencott (Cris Alexander), Waiter (Delbert Anderson), Delivery Boy (Alvin Beam), Chick Clark (Dort Clark), First Cadet and Greenwich Villager (David Lober), Second Cadet and Greenwich Villager (Ray Dorian), Ruths's Escort, Greenwich Villager, and Policeman (Chris Robinson)

Synopsis: This musical is based on *My Sister Eileen*, featuring Ruth and sister Eileen who have come to the big city from Ohio. They find a small basement apartment and immediately think about going home. Ruth wants to be a writer and Eileen an actress. Ruth's editor, Robert Baker, tells her to go home. Through many a mishap, Ruth is about to get published, and Eileen gets an offer of a job in a nightclub.

Songs: "Christopher Street"; "Ohio"; "Conquering New York"; "One Hundred Easy Ways"; "What a Waste"; "A Little Bit in Love"; "Pass the Football"; "Conversation Piece"; "A Quiet Girl"; "Conga!"; "My Darlin' Eileen"; "Swing!"; "It's Love"; "Wrong Note Rag"

Tony Awards: Best Musical, Best Actress in a Musical (Russell), Best Choreographer, Best Scenic Design (Raoul Pène Du Bois), Conductor and Musical Director (Lehman Engel)

⑤

THE GOLDEN AGE STARS
OF BROADWAY

During the Golden Age of musical theatre in America, countless perform-ers appeared before the footlights. Some made a lasting impression in one performance; others span a lifetime. Musicals, as well as drama, often en-tice audiences by casting well-known actors in the leading roles. Although in modern times many Broadway actors also have a career in films or televi-sion, a number are still primarily stage actors who spend most of their time "on the boards." But the increase in film and television work has led to an easing of the once prominent attitude that stage actors—meaning perform-ers in the so-called legitimate theatre—are of higher quality than those in other acting forms.

Just about anyone involved in a Broadway show belongs to a union or professional/trade organization. Actors, singers, dancers, and members of the chorus belong to the Actors' Equity Association (AEA). Musicians are part of the American Federation of Musicians (AFM). Directors and choreographers are members of the Society of Stage Directors and Chore-ographers (SSD&C). Playwrights are in the Dramatists Guild; press agents and company managers are part of the Association of Theatrical Press Agents and Managers (ATPAM). Such personnel as stagehands, ushers, or hairdressers belong to locals of the International Alliance of Theatrical Stage Employees (IA). The only theatre group not unionized so far are the casting directors.

Along with memorable directors, composers, lyricists, and choreogra-phers, this section lists some of the brightest, most talented, and/or most remembered stars on Broadway during the twenty-two years of the Golden Age. Tony awards and nominations are listed primarily for Golden Age Broadway musical productions, though many post–Golden Age nominations and awards are also noted.

ACTORS, MALE

ROBERT ALDA (February 26, 1914–May 3, 1986; born Alphonso Giuseppe Giovanni Roberto D'Abruzzo, New York, NY). A singer and dancer in vaudeville, Alda portrayed George Gershwin in the film *Rhapsody in Blue* (1945) and starred on Broadway in *Guys and Dolls* (1950) and *What Makes Sammy Run?* (1964). He was the father of actor Alan Alda and twice appeared with his son on the hit TV show *M°A°S°H°*. *Tony Award:* Best Actor in a Musical, *Guys and Dolls*, 1951.

THEODORE BIKEL (May 2, 1924; born Theodor Meir Bikel, Vienna, Austria). Bikel came to the United States in 1954 and originated the role of Captain von Trapp in *The Sound of Music* (1959). He was nominated for an Academy Award for his role as the southern sheriff in *The Defiant Ones* (1958). *Tony nomination:* Best Featured Actor in a Musical, *The Sound of Music*, 1959.

LARRY BLYDEN (June 23, 1925–June 6, 1975; born Ivan Lawrence Blieden, Houston, TX). Probably best known for his television work, Blyden appeared on Broadway in a number of roles, including Ensign Pulver in *Mister Roberts* (1948) and Sammy Fong in *Flower Drum Song* (1958). He won the Tony for Best Featured Actor in a Musical for the revival of *A Funny Thing Happened on the Way to the Forum* in 1972 and received a nomination for Best Featured Actor in a Play in 1975 for *Absurd Person Singular*. He died in an auto accident in Morocco. *Tony nomination:* Best Actor in a Musical, *Flower Drum Song*, 1959.

RAY BOLGER (January 10, 1904–January 15, 1987; born Raymond Wallace Bulcao, Dorchester, MA). Bolger's signature work was the part of the Scarecrow in *The Wizard of Oz* (1939). He also had four Broadway shows to his credit: *On Your Toes* (1936) and *By Jupiter* (1942) before the Golden Age, and *All American* (1962) and *Where's Charley* (1948), in which he delighted audiences with "Once in Love with Amy." *Tony Award:* Best Actor in a Musical, *Where's Charley?*, 1949. *Tony nomination:* Best Actor in a Musical, *All American*, 1962

TOM BOSLEY (October 1, 1927–October 19, 2010; born Thomas Edward Bosley, Chicago, IL). Well known for his work in television, Bosley won a Tony for playing the title role in *Fiorello!* (1959). He also appeared in the Broadway production of *Beauty and the Beast* (1994) and the Broadway revival of *Cabaret* (2002). *Tony Award:* Best Featured Actor in a Musical, *Fiorello!*, 1960.

EDDIE BRACKEN (February 7, 1915–November 14, 2002; born Edward Vincent Bracken, Astoria, NY). A vaudeville performer at age nine, Bracken began his Broadway musical career in *Too Many Girls*. After a stint in Hollywood, he returned to the stage for two musicals, *Shinbone Alley* (1957) and *Hello, Dolly!* (1964), as well as *The Odd Couple* (1965) and *Sugar Babies* (1979).

DAVID BROOKS (October 24, 1917–March 31, 1999; born Portland, OR). Brooks made his Broadway debut in *Bloomer Girl* (1944) and appeared as Tommy in *Brigadoon* (1947). He was also featured in a number of Off-Broadway productions.

YUL BRYNNER (July 11, 1920–October 10, 1985; born Yuli Borisovich Brynner, Vladivostok, Russia). Noted for his deep baritone voice and shaved head, Brynner made his mark on both stage and screen (winning an Oscar) in the role of King Mongkut of Siam in *The King and I* (1951). He played the role 4,626 times during the span of his career. The shaved head, which he adopted for the role and kept afterward, became his trademark. *Tony Award:* Best Featured Actor in a Musical, *The King and I*, 1952

RICHARD BURTON (November 10, 1925–August 5, 1984; born Richard Walter Jenkins, Pontrhydyfen, Wales, UK). The twelfth of thirteen children who became the highest-paid actor in Hollywood, Burton made his professional acting career in Liverpool and London. He appeared in both London's West End productions and on Broadway. Married five times, he is probably best known for his two marriages to Elizabeth Taylor and his six nominations for a Best Actor Oscar. He appeared on Broadway in *Time Remembered* (1958); as King Arthur in *Camelot* (1960); in *Hamlet* (1964), which had the longest run of the play in Broadway history (136 shows); in *Equus* (1976); and in *Private Lives* (1983), with Taylor. A notoriously heavy drinker, Burton died of a cerebral hemorrhage at his home in Switzerland at the age of fifty-eight. *Tony Award:* Best Actor in a Musical, *Camelot*, 1961.

SID CAESAR (September 8, 1922; born Isaac Sidney Caesar, Yonkers, NY). A comedian, actor, and musician, Caesar sang the lead role on Broadway in *Little Me*. He is best known for his comedy routines with Imogene Coca. *Tony nomination:* Best Actor in a Musical, *Little Me*, 1963.

JOHN CARRADINE (February 5, 1906–November 27, 1988; born Richmond Reed Carradine, New York, NY). Carradine began his career as a Shakespearean dramatic actor but is best known for his film work, including ten John Ford productions, and his deep, resonant voice. On Broadway, he appeared in *The Duchess of Malfi* (1946), *The Madwoman of Chaillot* (1950), *A Funny Thing Happened on the Way to the Forum* (1962), and the one-night flop *Frankenstein* (1981).

JACK CASSIDY (March 5, 1927–December 12, 1976; born John Joseph Edward Cassidy, New York, NY). A Tony winner for *She Loves Me* (1964), Cassidy got his start in show business from a relative who was a contortionist in the circus. He was married to actress Shirley Jones. Cassidy died when his couch caught fire after he fell asleep with a lit cigarette. *Tony Award:* Best Supporting Actor in a Musical, *She Loves Me*, 1964.

SYDNEY CHAPLIN (March 30, 1926–March 3, 2009; born Beverly Hills, CA). Third son of the legendary Charlie Chaplin, Sydney began his acting career in Hollywood but achieved fame on Broadway. He opened in *Bells Are Ringing* (1956) with Judy Holliday. His second great triumph was in *Funny Girl* (1964), playing gambler Nick Arnstein opposite Barbra Streisand as Fanny Brice. In both cases, he had problems with his leading ladies, which led to other actors, notably Dean Martin and Omar Sharif, respectively, taking the parts when the musicals were transferred to film. *Tony Award:* Best Featured Actor in a Musical, *Bells Are Ringing*, 1957. *Tony nomination:* Best Actor in a Musical, *Funny Girl*, 1965.

BOBBY CLARK (June 16, 1888–February 12, 1960; born Robert Edwin Clark, Springfield, OH). Part of the comedy team of Clark & McCullough, after Paul McCullough's death, Clark appeared in two Michael Todd Broadway musicals, *Mexican Hayride* (1944) and *As the Girls Go* (1948), as well as in revues. His last Broadway credit was as Mr. Applegate in *Damn Yankees* (1955).

ROBERT COOTE (February 4, 1909–November 26, 1982; born London, UK). Coote arrived in Hollywood in the late 1930s and also served in the Canadian Air Force during World War II. He is forever remembered as Colonel Pickering, the sidekick of Henry Higgins, in *My Fair Lady* (1956), which is often referred to as the greatest musical of the Golden Age. He also played in the musical's 1976 revival. Coote died in his sleep at the New York Athletic Club at the age of seventy-three. *Tony nomination:* Best Featured Actor in a Musical, *My Fair Lady*, 1957.

HOWARD DA SILVA (May 4, 1909–February 16, 1986; born Howard Silverblatt, Cleveland, OH). Da Silva appeared in the first production of *The Cradle Will Rock* (1937) and costarred in the 1943 production of *Oklahoma!*, in which he played Jud Fry. He made several films but was blacklisted in Hollywood in the 1950s and returned to the stage. *Tony nomination:* Best Featured Actor in a Musical, *Fiorello!*, 1960.

OSSIE DAVIS (December 18, 1917–February 4, 2005; born Raiford Chatman Davis, Cogdell, GA). The county clerk thought his mother's pronunciation of his initials—R. C.—was "Ossie" and the name stuck. Davis and wife Ruby Dee were awarded the American National Medal of Arts in 1995. They were also honored at the Kennedy Center in 2004 for their lifetime contributions to the performing arts. *Tony nomination:* Best Featured Actor, *Jamaica*, 1958.

SAMMY DAVIS JR. (December 8, 1925–May 16, 1990; born Harlem, NY). Billed as the "greatest living entertainer in the world," Davis was the son of a vaudeville star. He could do it all—sing, dance, act, do stand-up, and play musical instruments. Davis starred on Broadway in *Golden Boy* (1964). A chain smoker, he died of lung cancer at the age of sixty-four. *Tony Award:* Best Actor in a Musical, *Golden Boy*, 1965.

ALFRED DRAKE (October 7, 1914–July 25, 1992; born Alfred Capurro, Bronx, NY). One of the musical theatre's most respected actors, Drake created the male leads in *Oklahoma!* (1943), *Kiss Me, Kate* (1949), and *Kismet* (1953). He did not, however, take those roles to Hollywood. He became the highest-paid leading man in Broadway history when he earned $5,000 weekly for *Kismet*. That distinction lasted until 1959, when Jackie Gleason demanded—and got—$5,050 a week to star in *Take Me Along*. Pleading a full schedule, Drake turned down the role of the king in *The King and I* (1951). The lead went to Yul Brynner. *Tony Awards:* Best Actor in a Musical, *Kismet*, 1954; *Tony nomination:* Best Actor in a Musical, *Kean*, 1962. Special Tony Award for Excellence in the Theatre, 1990.

MAURICE EVANS (June 3, 1901–March 12, 1989; born Maurice Herbert Evans, Rottingdean, UK). A British classical actor, Evans was considered one of the best interpreters of Shakespeare. He received a Tony for producing the Best Play of 1954, *The Teahouse of the August Moon*. *Tony nomination:* Best Actor in a Musical, *Tenderloin*, 1961.

JOSÉ FERRER (January 8, 1912–January 26, 1992; born José Vicente Ferrer de Otero y Cintron, Santurce, Puerto Rico). Actor, director, and producer, Ferrer made his Broadway debut in *A Slight Case of Murder* (1935) and won a Tony for the drama *Cyrano de Bergerac* (1946), a role for which he also won the Oscar in 1951. Ferrer also won a Tony in 1952 for directing three plays—*The Fourposter*, *Stalag 17*, and *The Shrike*—the latter earning him another Tony for Best Actor in a Play. He also appeared in the Noël Coward musical *The Girl Who Came to Supper* (1963). His final stage appearance was in the musical *Born Again* (1990). Ferrer was married to actress Uta Hagen (1938–1948) and singer Rosemary Clooney (1953–1961, 1964–1966). *Tony nomination:* Best Musical (Book), *Oh Captain*, 1958.

JACKIE GLEASON (February 26, 1916–June 24, 1987; born Herbert Walton Gleason Jr., Brooklyn, NY). Gleason was one of early television's biggest stars, noted for his brash humor. *The Jackie Gleason Show* (1952–1957, 1966–1970) became television's brightest hour in the 1950s. But his most popular character was blustery bus driver Ralph Kramden in *The Honeymooners* (1955–1956). Gleason also appeared in several Broadway productions, including *Follow the Girls* (1944); *Along Fifth Avenue* (1949); and *Take Me Along* (1959), for which he received the highest weekly salary (*see* Alfred Drake bio). *Tony Award:* Best Actor in a Musical, *Take Me Along*, 1960.

ELLIOT GOULD (August 29, 1938; born Elliott Goldstein, Brooklyn, NY). A prominent film actor of the 1970s, Gould was once on the cover of *Time* magazine. His Broadway musical credits include *Irma La Douce* (1960); *I Can Get It for You Wholesale* (1962), where he met Barbra Streisand, whom he later married; and *Drat! The Cat!* (1965).

ROBERT GOULET (November 26, 1933–October 30, 2007; born Robert Gerald Goulet, Lawrence, MA). Goulet made several television appearances before he met Alan Lerner and Frederick Loewe, who were looking for someone to play the role of Lancelot in *Camelot*. Goulet got the part and received favorable reviews when it opened in 1960, especially for the ballad "If Ever I Would Leave You." He also appeared on Broadway in *The Happy Time* (1968), for which he won a Best Actor Award, *Rose Marie* (1982), and a revival of *La Cage aux Folles* (2005). He toured in several musicals, including *Carousel*. Goulet died in Los Angeles while awaiting a lung transplant.

FRED GWYNNE (July 10, 1926–July 2, 1993; born Frederick Hubbard Gwynne, New York, NY). A talented character actor in many films, Gwynne is best known for his role as Herman Munster in television's *The Munsters*, (1964–1966). On Broadway he portrayed the pimp Polyte-Le-Mou in *Irma La Douce* (1960).

BUDDY HACKETT (August 31, 1924–June 30, 2003; born Leonard Hacker, Brooklyn, NY). Known mainly as a nightclub comic with a slightly off-color offering, Hackett appeared in many Hollywood films. His stage highlight during the Golden Age was in the musical *The Music Man* (1962), where he played Robert Preston's sidekick.

REX HARRISON (March 5, 1908–June 2, 1990; born Reginald Carey Harrison, Lancashire, UK). Harrison attained international fame when he portrayed the king in *Anna and the King of Siam* (1946), his first American film. In 1949, he won a Tony for Best Actor for *Anne of the Thousand Days*. But the defining role of his stage career was his portrayal of Professor Henry Higgins in *My Fair Lady* (1956), for which he received a Tony, as well as an Oscar for the film version. Two of Harrison's five wives were actresses Lilli Palmer and Kay Kendall. He was knighted in 1989. *Tony Award:* Best Actor in a Musical, *My Fair Lady*, 1957.

STUBBY KAYE (November 11, 1918–December 14, 1997; born Bernard Katzin, New York, NY). Kaye of the butterball frame kept his real name a secret throughout his career, which began after winning a radio contest in 1939. His big Broadway hit came in 1950, when he played Nicely-Nicely Johnson in *Guys and Dolls* and sang "Sit Down, You're Rockin' the Boat." He was also a winner as Marryin' Sam in *Li'l Abner* (1956). He played both roles in film as well.

RICHARD KILEY (March 31, 1922–March 5, 1999; born Richard Paul Kiley, Chicago, IL). Although Kiley is best known for his signature role in the post–Golden Age musical *Man of La Mancha* (1966), for which he won a Tony, he also appeared in *Redhead* (1959), for which he also won a Tony, and in *No Strings* (1962). *Tony Award:* Best Actor in a Musical, *Redhead*, 1959. *Tony nomination:* Best Actor in a Musical, *No Strings*, 1962.

BERT LAHR (August 13, 1895–December 4, 1967; born Irving Lahrheim, New York, NY). Lahr will forever be remembered as the Cowardly Lion in *The Wizard of Oz*, but he was no stranger to Broadway. He appeared in eighteen Broadway shows from 1927 through 1964, most notably in the musical *Foxy* (1964). *Tony Award:* Best Actor in a Musical, *Foxy*, 1964.

STEVE LAWRENCE (July 8, 1935; born Sidney Liebowitz, New York, NY). Lawrence and wife Eydie Gorme have been appearing regularly together since they were first seen on Steve Allen's *The Tonight Show* in the mid-1950s. Among his many musical awards, he was nominated for a Tony for *What Makes Sammy Run*, for which he also received a Drama Critics Circle Award. *Tony nomination:* Best Actor in a Musical, *What Makes Sammy Run?*, 1964.

PAUL LYNDE (June 13, 1926–January 10, 1982; born Paul Edward Lynde, Mount Vernon, OH). Best known for being a regular guest on the game show *Hollywood Squares*, he also made a hit on Broadway as the befuddled father in *Bye Bye Birdie* (1960).

RODDY MCDOWALL (September 17, 1928–October 3, 1998; born Roderick Andrew Anthony Jude McDowall, London, UK). One of the few child actors to continue successfully into adulthood, McDowall is best known for his film work, which included *How Green Was My Valley* (1941), *Lassie Come Home* (1943), *Cleopatra* (1963), and *The Poseidon Adventure* (1972). On stage, he appeared in ten productions, including *No Time for Sergeants* (1955), *Camelot* (1960), and *The Fighting Cock*, for which he won the Tony for Best Featured Actor (1960).

RAY MIDDLETON (February 8, 1907–April 10, 1984; born Raymond Earl Middleton Jr., Chicago, IL). The first actor to play Superman (at the 1939 World's Fair), Middleton spent most of his career on the Silver Screen; however, he costarred with Ethel Merman in the original production of *Annie Get Your Gun* (1946).

THOMAS MITCHELL (July 11, 1892–December 17, 1962; born Elizabeth, NJ). Actor, playwright, and screenwriter, Mitchell was nominated for an Oscar for his performance in *The Hurricane* (1937). He was the first person to win an Oscar (Best Supporting Actor in *Stagecoach*, 1939), an Emmy (Comedy Actor category, 1952), and a Tony. *Tony Award:* Best Actor in a Musical, *Hazel Flagg*, 1953.

ROBERT MORSE (May 18, 1931; born Newton, MA). Morse made his Broadway debut with the musical *On the Town* (1949) and appeared in *Say, Darling* (1958) and *Take Me Along* (1958) before his big hit as J. Pierrepont Finch in *How to Succeed in Business without Really Trying* (1961), for which he won a Tony and then another for the post–Golden Age production of *Tru*. *Tony Award:* Best Actor in a Musical, *How to Succeed in Business without Really Trying*, 1962. His composition of "What Kind of Fool Am

I," written with Leslie Bricusse for *Stop the World,* won the Grammy for Song of the Year in 1963. *Tony nomination:* Best Actor in a Musical, *Take Me Along,* 1960

ZERO MOSTEL (February 28, 1915–September 8, 1977; born Samuel Joel Mostel, Brooklyn, NY). Blacklisted by the house of Un-American Activities Committee in the 1950s, Mostel got his nickname from a press agent, who said of the then comedian, "Here's a guy who's starting from nothing." He first appeared on Broadway in 1942 in *Café Crown,* but he reached star status with his performances in *A Funny Thing Happened on the Way to the Forum* (1962) and as Tevye the milkman in *Fiddler on the Roof* (1964). *Tony Awards:* Best Actor in a Musical, *A Funny Thing Happened on the Way to the Forum,* 1963; Best Actor in a Musical, *Fiddler on the Roof,* 1965.

ANTHONY NEWLEY (September 24, 1931–April 14, 1999; born George Anthony Newley, London, UK). Newley had a successful career as a pop music vocalist and in films. His great successes on Broadway were writing and performing in *Stop the World—I Want to Get Off* (1962) and cowriting music and lyrics with Leslie Bricusse for *The Roar of the Greasepaint—The Smell of the Crowd* (1965). His composition of "What Kind of Fool Am I," written with Leslie Bricusse for *Stop the World,* won the Grammy for Song of the Year in 1963. *Tony nominations:* Best Musical, Best Actor in a Musical, Best Author of a Musical (Book), and Best Composer and Lyricist of a Musical, *Stop the World—I Want to Get Off,* 1963; Best Composer and Lyricist, *The Roar of the Greasepaint—The Smell of the Crowd,* 1965, Best Direction of a Musical, *The Roar of the Greasepaint—The Smell of the Crowd.*

JERRY ORBACH (October 20, 1935–December 28, 2004; born Jerome Bernard Orbach, Bronx, NY). Best known for his role as Detective Lennie Briscoe in the television series *Law and Order,* Orbach was also an accomplished Broadway and Off-Broadway actor. He first big role was El Gallo in the Off-Broadway, decades-long production of *The Fantasticks* (1960). He was the replacement for Rome Smith in *The Threepenny Opera* (1955) and appeared in *Carnival* (1961) and in a revival of *Guys and Dolls* (1965). He earned three Tony nominations, winning Best Actor in a Musical for *Promises, Promises* in 1969. He was a fixture in the Hell's Kitchen section of New York City, and a portion of 53rd Street near Eighth Avenue is renamed Jerry Orbach Way in his honor.

EZIO PINZA (May 18, 1892–May 9, 1957; born Rome, Italy). An outstanding opera singer during the first half of the twentieth century, Pinza is noted for his stage performance opposite Mary Martin in *South Pacific* (1949). His rendition of "Some Enchanted Evening" made him a matinee idol. He also appeared opposite Florence Henderson in *Fanny* (1954). *Tony Award:* Best Actor in a Musical, *South Pacific*, 1950.

ROBERT PRESTON (June 8, 1918–March 21, 1987; born Robert Preston Meservey, Newton Highlands, MA). Preston mesmerized Broadway audiences as Professor Harold Hill in *The Music Man* (1957), a feat made all the more remarkable because he had never appeared in a musical nor sung a song on stage until that time. He grew up in Los Angeles and got a contract to Paramount Studio, which dropped his last name. After World War II, he concentrated on theatre in New York City, until the part that immortalized him on Broadway. After *The Music Man*, he earned two more Best Actor Tony nominations for *I Do! I Do* (1967) and *Mack and Mabel* (1975), winning for the former. *Tony Award:* Best Actor in a Musical, *The Music Man*, 1958.

JOHN RAITT (January 29, 1917–February 20, 2005; born John Emmett Raitt, Santa Ana, CA). Raitt set the standard for the handsome, strong leading man of the Golden Age. His musicals include *Oklahoma!* (1943), *Carousel* (1945), *The Pajama Game* (1954), *Carnival in Flanders* (1953), *Three Wishes for Jamie* (1952), and *A Joyful Noise* (1966). Father of singer Bonnie Raitt, his only leading role in Hollywood was *The Pajama Game* (1957), with Doris Day. He toured with Mary Martin in *Annie Get Your Gun*, and they recreated the roles for television in 1957.

CYRIL RITCHARD (December 1, 1897–December 18, 1977; born Cyril Trimnell-Ritchard, Sydney, New South Wales, Australia). With a career that spanned six decades, Ritchard is probably best remembered as the prancing Captain Hook in *Peter Pan* (1954), a role he recreated in several film versions. In addition to his success in musicals, Ritchard was nominated twice in 1959 for Best actor and Best Director for *The Pleasure of His Company*. He also had a long film career and appeared at the Metropolitan Opera in New York City. *Tony Award:* Best Featured Actor in a Musical, *Peter Pan*, 1955. *Tony nomination:* Best Actor in a Musical, *The Roar of the Greasepaint—The Smell of the Crowd*, 1965

PHIL SILVERS (May 11, 1911–November 1, 1985; born Philip Silver, New York, NY). Multitalented Silvers was a comedian and film and stage actor. He also wrote the lyrics to "Nancy with the Laughing Face," for Frank Sinatra's oldest child. Silvers was seen on Broadway in *High Button Shoes* (1948), *Top Banana* (1951), and *Do Re Mi* (1960), as well as a 1971 revival of *A Funny Thing Happened on the Way to the Forum*, for which he won his second Tony. His eyeglasses were so much a trademark that he wore them even after he had cataract surgery and implants and no longer needed them. *Tony Award:* Best Actor in a Musical: *Top Banana*, 1952. *Tony nomination:* Best Actor in a Musical, *Do Re Mi*, 1961.

WALTER SLEZAK (May 3, 1902–April 21, 1983; born Vienna, Austria-Hungary [now Austria]). Known as a portly character film actor in the 1940s, Slezak starred on Broadway in *Fanny* (1954). In despair over illness, he committed suicide by shooting himself in his Flower Hill, New York, home. *Tony Award:* Best Actor in a Musical, *Fanny*, 1955.

RAY WALSTON (December 2, 1914–January 1, 2001; born Herman Walston, New Orleans, LA). Walston made his Broadway debut in a 1945 production of *Hamlet* but gained success as Satan in *Damn Yankees* (1955) opposite Gwen Verdon. Both Walston and Verdon won awards and reprised their roles in the film version. Best known for his television roles on *My Favorite Martian* and *Picket Fences*, the latter earned Walston consecutive Emmys for Best Supporting Actor in 1995 and 1996. *Tony Award:* Best Actor in a Musical, *Damn Yankees*, 1956.

DAVID WAYNE (January 30, 1914–February 9, 1995; born Wayne James McMeekan, Traverse City, MI). Famous for movie and television roles, Wayne was the first to receive a Tony Award for acting in 1947, the first year the Tonys were presented. He went on to win again for Best Actor in a Play for *The Teahouse of the August Moon* (1954) and was nominated for Best Actor in a Musical in 1968 for *The Happy Time*. *Tony Award:* Best Featured Actor in a Musical, *Finian's Rainbow*, 1947.

ACTORS, FEMALE

ANNA MARIA ALBERGHETTI (May 15, 1936; born Pesaro, Italy). A child prodigy who performed at Carnegie Hall in New York City at the age of thirteen, Alberghetti appeared in films as a teenager and was twice on the cover of *Life* magazine. She later appeared in *Carnival* (1961). Her sister Carla eventually replaced her on Broadway in the role. *Tony Award:* Best Actress in a Musical, *Carnival*, 1962.

ELIZABETH ALLEN (January 25, 1929–September 19, 2006; born Elizabeth Ellen Gillease, Fishkill, NY). A former fashion model for the Ford Modeling Agency, Allen was a member of the Helen Hayes Repertory Company and first starred on Broadway in *Romanoff and Juliet* (1957). She was also known as the "Away We Go" girl on *The Jackie Gleason Show*, introducing his variety skits each week. *Tony nominations:* Best Featured Actress in a Musical, *The Gay Life*, 1962; Best Actress in a Musical, *Do I Hear a Waltz?*, 1965.

JULIE ANDREWS (October 1, 1935; born Julia Elizabeth Wells, Walton-on-Thames, England). With a long career in films and on stage, Julie Andrews is best known for her portrayal of Eliza Doolittle opposite Rex Harrison in the great Broadway hit *My Fair Lady* (1956). In 1960, she starred as Queen Guinevere in *Camelot* opposite Richard Burton. Her work in films and on television has earned her many awards, including the Oscar for *Mary Poppins* in 1964. She received another nomination for Best Actress in a Musical for *Victoria/Victoria* (1996) adapted from the film, for which she received an Oscar nomination in 1983. She was made a dame commander of the British Empire in 2000 and was honored at the Kennedy Center in 2001 for her work in performing arts. *Tony nominations:* Best Actress in a Musical, *My Fair Lady*, 1957; Best Actress in a Musical, *Camelot*, 1961.

BEATRICE ARTHUR (May 13, 1922–April 25, 2009; born Bernice Frankel, New York, NY). Bea Arthur took the name of her first husband, Robert Alan Aurthur, and modified it for her stage name. She began her acting career in the 1940s in an Off-Broadway group at the Cherry Lane Theatre. She played Lucy Brown in the Off-Broadway premiere of *Threepenny Opera* (1954) and Yente the Matchmaker in the premiere of *Fiddler on the Roof* on Broadway (1964). In 1966 she received the Tony for Best Featured Actress in a Musical for *Mame*. She also appeared in Woody Allen's *The Floating Lightbulb* (1981). Arthur is best known for her television portrayals as outspoken liberal in the title character in *Maude* and Dorothy Zbornak in the highly successful sitcom *The Golden Girls*, earning Emmys for both shows. In 2002, she returned to Broadway with *Bea Arthur on Broadway: Just between Friends*.

KAYE BALLARD (November 20, 1925; born Catherine Gloria Balotta, Cleveland, OH). A comedienne and television star, Ballard appeared on Broadway in *The Golden Apple* (1954), *Carnival!* (1961), and the revival of *The Pirates of Penzance* (1981).

ISABEL BIGLEY (February 23, 1926–September 30, 2006; born Bronx, NY). Bigley made her Broadway debut in the chorus of *Oklahoma!* (1943). She starred in the London production opposite Howard Keel for three years. Bigley was also Sarah Brown in *Guys and Dolls* (1950), for which she won a Tony. *Tony Award:* Best Featured Actress in a Musical, *Guys and Dolls*, 1951.

VIVIAN BLAINE (November 21, 1921–December 9, 1995; born Vivian Stapleton, Newark, NJ). Blaine stopped the show each night as the original long-suffering Miss Adelaide in *Guys and Dolls* (1950), singing "Miss Adelaide's Lament." She played the same role in the film and as a command performance in London for Queen Elizabeth II. Besides many national tours, she also appeared on Broadway in *Hatful of Rain* (1955), *Say, Darling* (1958), *Zorba* (1968), and *Company* (1970). In 1952, she appeared on the best-dressed women of America list, along with actresses Ann Sheridan and Betty Furness.

CAROL BRUCE (November 15, 1919–October 9, 2007; born Shirley Levy, Great Neck, NY). A radio and television star as well as a singer, Bruce had a number of stage appearances before her hit as Annie Oakley in a revival of *Annie Get Your Gun* (1950). She also appeared as Signora Fiora in *Do I Hear a Waltz?* (1965).

CAROL BURNETT (April 26, 1933; born Carol Creighton Burnett, San Antonio, TX). Actress, comedian, dancer, singer, and writer, Burnett is best known for the award-winning *The Carol Burnett Show* (1967–1978). She appeared on Broadway in *Once upon a Mattress* (1959), *Fade Out—Fade In* (1964), *Moon over Buffalo* (1995), and *Putting It Together* (1999). *Tony nomination:* Best Actress in a Musical, *Once Upon a Mattress*, 1960.

CAROL CHANNING (January 31, 1921; born Carol Elaine Channing, Seattle, WA). Best known for her unforgettable roles as Lorelei Lee in *Gentlemen Prefer Blondes* (1949) and as Dolly Levi in *Hello, Dolly!* (1964), Channing made her stage debut in the chorus of *No for an Answer* (1941). Her fame was assured when she appeared in *Lend an Ear* (1948), with a voice that goes from baby squeaks to a baritone. She studied dance and drama at Bennington College before dropping out to head for New York. Noted for her popping eyes and bushy blonde hairdo, Channing is also a film and television star. *Tony Awards:* Best Actress in a Musical, *Hello, Dolly!*, 1964; Lifetime Achievement Award, 1995. *Tony nomination:* Best Actress in a Musical, *The Vamp*, 1956.

JEAN DARLING (August 23, 1922; born Dorothy Jean LeVake, Santa Monica, CA). A child actress and regular on the Our Gang series, Darling made her Broadway debut as Jean Darling in *Count Me In* (1942). But the height of her stage career was as Carrie Pipperidge in *Carousel* (1945), when she appeared in 850 consecutive performances. After retirement, she went to Ireland and has been writing mystery stories.

NANETTE FABRAY (October 27, 1920; born Ruby Bernadette Nanette Fabares, San Diego, CA). Legally deaf since the 1950s, Fabray appeared in such Broadway productions as *By Jupiter* (1942), *Bloomer Girl* (1944), *High Button Shoes* (1947), *Love Life* (1948), and *Mr. President* (1962) during the Golden Age. *Tony Award:* Best Actress in a Musical, *Love Life*, 1949. *Tony nomination:* Best Actress in a Musical, *Mr. President*, 1962.

DOLORES GRAY (June 7, 1924–June 26, 2002; born Chicago, IL). A stage and film actress, Gray appeared on Broadway in *Two on the Aisle* (1951), *Carnival in Flanders* (1953), *Destry Rides Again* (1959), *Sherry!* (1967), and *42nd Street* (1980). She holds a stage record unlikely to be broken for the shortest run in a play that merited a Tony; *Carnival in Flanders* had only six performances, but Gray won a Tony. *Tony Award:* Best Actress in a Musical, *Carnival in Flanders*, 1954. *Tony nomination:* Best Actress in a Musical, *Destry Rides Again*, 1960.

CHARLOTTE GREENWOOD (June 25, 1890–December 28, 1977; born Frances Charlotte Greenwood, Philadelphia, PA). A nightclub and high-kick dancer, Greenwood was the original choice for Aunt Eller in the stage version of *Oklahoma!*, but film commitments gave the part to Betty Garde. She eventually played the role in the 1955 film version. Greenwood originally had a large role in *Annie Get Your Gun*, but it was toned down considerably at the insistence of star Ethel Merman.

CAROL HANEY (December 24, 1924–May 10, 1964; born in New Bedford, MA). A dancer and choreographer, Haney owned her own dance school before she left high school. She got her start in films when she teamed with Bob Fosse and stopped the show in the movie *Kiss Me, Kate* (1953). Fosse brought Haney to Broadway to dance a minor role in *The Pajama Game* (1954). Producer George Abbott was so impressed with Haney that he enlarged her part, and that led to a Tony. *Tony Award:* Best Featured Actress in a Musical, *The Pajama Game*, 1954. *Tony nominations:* Best Choreography, *Flower Drum Song*, 1959; Best Choreography, *Bravo Giovanni*, 1963; Best Choreography, *Funny Girl*, posthumously, 1964.

FLORENCE HENDERSON (February 14, 1934; born Dale, IN). Henderson started her stage career in the touring productions of *Oklahoma!*

and *South Pacific* and made her Broadway debut in *Wish You Were Here* (1952). She later played in *The Girl Who Came to Supper* (1963). She is best known for her television work as Carol Brady on *The Brady Bunch*, which ran from 1969 until 1974.

JUDY HOLLIDAY (June 21, 1921–June 7, 1965; born Judith Tuvim [Jewish for "holiday"], New York, NY). Holliday's first job after high school was as an assistant switchboard operator at the Mercury Theatre, run by Orson Welles and John Houseman. She opened on Broadway in March 1945 in *Kiss Them for Me* and played the scatterbrained Billie Dawn in *Born Yesterday* (1946); she won an Oscar for the film version (1950). In 1956, she starred in *The Solid Gold Cadillac* and won raves as Ella Peterson in *Bells Are Ringing*. Holliday died of breast cancer at the age of forty-three. *Tony Award:* Best Actress in a Musical, *Bells Are Ringing*, 1957.

CELESTE HOLM (April 29, 1917; born New York, NY). After several mostly short-lived Broadway appearances, Holm was cast as Ado Annie in the smash *Oklahoma!* (1943) and got raves for her rendition of "I Cain't Say No." She followed that with *Bloomer Girl* (1944) and then signed a long-term film contract with 20th Century Fox. In 1948, she received a best Supporting Actress Oscar for *Gentleman's Agreement* and was nominated two more times in 1950 and 1951. She returned to Broadway for two musicals, *The Tender Trap* (1955) and *High Society* (1956). In 1977, she turned down the Broadway revival of *Oklahoma!* because she was wanted for the part of Aunt Eller, not Ado Annie.

LAINIE KAZAN (May 15, 1940; born Lanie Levine, Brooklyn, NY). Kazan's Broadway debut was in *The Happiest Girl in the World* (1961), followed by *Bravo Giovanni* (1961). She was Barbra Streisand's understudy in *Funny Girl* (1964), finally getting on stage eighteen months into the run when Streisand had a sore throat. In 1993 she received a nomination for Best Featured Actress in a Musical for *My Favorite Year*, recreating her role from the 1982 film.

LISA KIRK (February 25, 1925–November 11, 1990; born Elise Marie Kirk, Charleroi, PA). Kirk played Emily in the original cast of *Allegro* (1947) but is best known as Bianca in the hit show *Kiss Me, Kate* (1948). She also introduced Cole Porter's tunes "Why Can't You Behave?" and "Always True to You (in My Fashion)."

ABBE LANE (December 14, 1932; born Abigail Francine Lassman, Brooklyn, NY). Lane's greatest success was as a nightclub singer during the years she was married to bandleader Xavier Cugat (1952–1964). Besides television work, she starred on Broadway opposite Tony Randall in *Oh, Captain!* (1958).

ANGELA LANSBURY (October 16, 1925; born Angela Brigid Lansbury, Poplar, London, UK). One of the most well-loved ladies of the Broadway theatre, Lansbury began her stage career in the short-lived *Anyone Can Whistle* (1964) by Stephen Sondheim. Her big triumph came after the Golden Age with *Mame* (1966), which ran for 1,508 performances. She also starred in the first Broadway revival of *Gypsy* (1974) and was entrepreneur Mrs. Lovett in Sondheim's ballad opera *Sweeney Todd* (1979). It was that role, she told Robert Osborne on Turner Classic Movies, for which she would most like to be remembered. Lansbury returned to Broadway after twenty-five years to star in *Deuce* (2007) with Marian Seldes for a limited run of eighteen weeks. Despite her impressive Broadway career, she is probably best known for her portrayal of Jessica Fletcher in the long-running television mystery series *Murder, She Wrote* (1984–1996). She also holds the record for most Emmy nominations (twelve) for Best Actress without a single win; she has also never won an Oscar despite three nominations. She became a commander in the Order of the British Empire in 1994, won the National Medal of Arts in 1997, and was honored at the Kennedy Center in 2000 for her contribution to the performing arts. In 2009, Lansbury won her fifth Tony for *Blithe Spirit*. *Tony Awards:* Best Actress in a Musical, *Mame*, 1966; Best Actress in a Musical, *Dear World*, 1969; Best Actress in a Musical, *Gypsy*, 1975; Best Actress in a Musical, *Sweeney Todd*, 1979; Best Featured Actress in a Musical, *Blithe Spirit*, 2009. *Tony nominations:* Best Actress in a Play, *Deuce*, 2007; Best Featured Actress in a Musical, *A Little Night Music*, 2010

CAROL LAWRENCE (September 5, 1932; born Carol Maria Laraia, Melrose Park, IL). An actress, singer, and dancer, Lawrence created the role of Maria in *West Side Story* (1957). She also starred on Broadway in *Saratoga* (1959), *Subways Are for Sleeping* (1961), *I Do! I Do!* (1966), and *Kiss of the Spider Woman* (1993), besides her many television appearances. *Tony nomination:* Best Featured Actress in a Musical, *West Side Story*, 1958.

GERTRUDE LAWRENCE (July 4, 1898–September 6, 1952; born Gertrude Alexandria Dagmar Lawrence-Klasen, London, England). Lawrence's last and best-known role was as Anna Leonowens in the original Broadway production of *The King and I* (1951). She discovered she had cancer early in the stage run and died the following year. She was buried in the pink ball gown she wore for the role when she sang "Shall We Dance?" Her last request before her death was that the name of Yul Brynner, the leading man in the production, be upgraded to share top billing with whomever would play Anna in future performances. *Tony Award:* Best Actress in a Musical, *The King and I*, 1952.

MICHELE LEE (June 24, 1942; born Michele Lee Dusick, Los Angeles, CA). Lee launched her career with the Broadway revue *Vintage '60* (1960), followed by landing the lead as Rosemary in *How to Succeed in Business without Really Trying* (1961); she also starred in the 1967 film. Movie and television work followed, and Lee was nominated for a Tony for her work in the post–Golden Age musical *Seesaw* (1973).

VIVIEN LEIGH (November 5, 1913–July 7, 1967; born Vivian Mary Hartley, Darjeeling, India). Born to a British stockbroker and his wife, Leigh made her professional acting debut in London's West End in 1935 and then alternated between stage and film work. From 1940 to 1960, she was married to noted British actor Laurence Olivier, with whom she appeared in a number of productions. But she will always be remembered as the beautiful and defiant Scarlett O'Hara in *Gone with the Wind* (1939), for which she won the first of two Academy Awards. Her Broadway stage fame came as Tatiana in *Tovarich* (1963); the production was poor, but Leigh got the Tony. *Tony Award:* Best Actress in a Musical, *Tovarich*, 1963.

ELLA LOGAN (March 6, 1913–May 1, 1969; born Georgina Allan, Glasgow, Scotland). Logan made her debut in London's West End in 1930 and immigrated to the United States, where she sang in various clubs. She also appeared in several Broadway shows but is best known as Sharon McLonergan in *Finian's Rainbow* (1947), in which she sang the show's most famous song, "How Are Things in Glocca Morra?"

TINA LOUISE (February 11, 1934; born Tatiana Josivovna Chernova Blacker, New York, NY). A model, nightclub singer, and television star, Louise made it to Broadway for her successful role in *L'il Abner* (1956) as Apassionata Von Climax. Louise is best known for the role of Ginger on the series *Gilligan's Island* (1964–1967).

MARY MARTIN (December 1, 1913–November 3, 1990; born Mary Virginia Martin, Weatherford, TX). One of the great stars of the musical comedy stage, Martin began her career in 1938 when she sang "My Heart

Belongs to Daddy" in the Cole Porter musical *Leave It to Me!* Although she made ten films for Paramount in four years, the Broadway stage was truly her home. In her role in *Peter Pan* (1954), Martin, who was then in her forties, began flying around the stage suspended by cables. Her four Tony awards include special recognition in 1948 for the touring production of *Annie Get Your Gun*. *Tony Awards:* Best Actress in a Musical, *South Pacific*, 1950; Best Actress in a Musical, *Peter Pan*, 1955; Best Actress in a Musical, *The Sound of Music*, 1960. *Tony nomination:* Best Actress in a Musical, *I Do! I Do!*, 1967.

BARBARA MCNAIR (March 4, 1934–February 4, 2007; born Barbara Joan McNair, Chicago, IL). A popular vocalist and entertainer, McNair appeared on Broadway in *The Pajama Game* (1954); *The Body Beautiful* (1958); *No Strings* (1962), replacing the original star Diahann Carroll; and *Sophisticated Ladies* (1981).

KAY MEDFORD (September 14, 1914–April 10, 1980; born Margaret O'Regin, New York, NY). Roman Catholic, of Irish ancestry, Medford was often amused to be cast as a stereotypical Jewish mother. Beginning as a cabaret performer, she hit Broadway at the age of thirty-seven as Cherry in *Paint Your Wagon* (1951). She was also seen in *Mr. Wonderful* (1956); *A Hole in the Head* (1957); *Carousel* (1957); *Bye Bye Birdie* (1960), for which she won the New York Drama Critic's Award; and *Funny Girl* (1964), for which she snagged a Tony as the mother of Fanny Brice; she played Mrs. Brice in the film version as well. *Tony Award:* Best Featured Actress, *Funny Girl*, 1964.

ETHEL MERMAN (January 16, 1908–February 15, 1984; born Ethel Agnes Zimmermann, Astoria, Queens, NY). Beginning with her stage debut in *Girl Crazy* (1930), Merman was the preeminent star of Broadway musical comedy. No one could belt a song like Merman, even with her untrained voice, and no one could sing "There's No Business Like Show Business" as she did. She took her stage name by removing the first three letters and the last letter of her birth name. Married and divorced four times, her last marriage (to actor Ernest Borgnine) lasted thirty-two days. When she published her autobiography in 1978, her description of the marriage consisted of one blank page. When told she had lost the Tony Award to Mary Martin in *The Sound of Music*, she said, "You can't buck a nun." *Tony Awards:* Best Actress in a Musical, *Call Me Madam*, 1951; Special Tony Award for Lifetime Achievement in the Theatre, 1972. *Tony nominations:* Best Actress in a Musical, *Happy Hunting*, 1957; Best Actress in a Musical, *Gypsy*, 1960.

LIZA MINNELLI (March 12, 1946; born Liza May Minnelli, Los Angeles, CA). Daughter of film superstar Judy Garland and movie director Vincente Minnelli, Liza was practically raised in the MGM studios. She has had a long and varied career despite high profile stays at drug-rehabilitation clinics. Minnelli won an Oscar for *Cabaret* in 1972 and a Tony for *Flora, the Red Menace* in 1965. She received a special Tony in 1974 for "adding lustre to the Broadway season." *Tony Award:* Best Actress in a Musical, *Flora, the Red Menace*, 1965. Best Actress in a Musical, *The Act*, 1978. *Tony nomination:* Best Actress in a Musical, *The Rink*, 1984.

PATRICIA NEWAY (September 30, 1919; born New York, NY). An opera singer, Neway also taught voice and choir. She won a Tony for her role as the Abbess to Mary Martin in *The Sound of Music*. *Tony Award:* Best Featured Actress, *The Sound of Music*, 1960.

MOLLY PICON (June 1, 1898–April 5, 1992; born Margaret Pyekoon, New York, NY). Picon was a Yiddish icon who entertained audiences for more than seven decades. Her role as Clara Weiss in *Milk and Honey* (1961) brought her to a far larger audience. *Tony nomination:* Best Actress in a Musical, *Milk and Honey*, 1962.

IRENE RICH (October 13, 1891–April 22, 1988; born Irene Luther, Buffalo, NY). This star of silent films and early talkies had one claim to fame on Broadway; she was the first female U.S. president in Bobby Clark's long-running musical *As the Girls Go* (1948). She retired from screen and stage in 1950.

THELMA RITTER (February 14, 1905–February 5, 1969; born Brooklyn, NY). Known mainly for her film work, she received six Oscar nominations during her career for Best Supporting Actress but never won. She won a Tony, which she shared with costar Gwen Verdon, for *New Girl in Town* (1957). *Tony Award:* Best Actress in a Musical (shared with Verdon), *New Girl in Town*, 1958.

CHITA RIVERA (January 23, 1933; born Dolores Conchita Figueroa del Rivero, Washington, D.C.). Rivera was given a scholarship to the George Balanchine School of American Ballet in 1944; her teachers were Allegra Kent and Maria Tallchief. She landed a role in *Call Me Madam* (1950), which was followed by other such productions as *Guys and Dolls* (1950) and *Can-Can* (1953). But what made her a Broadway star was as the firebrand Anita in *West Side Story* (1957). (Another Puerto Rican, Rita

Moreno, received fame—and an Oscar—for the film version.) In 2003, she played Liliane LaFleur in a revival of *Nine*, which earned her a nomination for Best Featured Actress in a Musical. In the post Golden Age, Rivera won Tonys for Best Actress in a Musical for *The Rink* (1984) and *Kiss of the Spider Woman* (1993). She was nominated for the award five other times for *Chicago* (1976), *Bring Back Birdie* (1976), *Merlin* (1983), *Jerry's Girls* (1986), and *Chita Rivera: A Dancer's Life* (2006). In 2003, she played Liliane LaFleur in a revival of *Nine*, which earned her a nomination for Best Featured Actress in a Musical. *Tony nomination:* Best Featured Actress in a Musical, *Bye Bye Birdie*, 1961.

ROSALIND RUSSELL (June 4, 1907–November 28, 1976; born Waterbury, CT). Russell was known mainly as a film actress, but she toured with *Bell, Book, and Candle* (1951) and won a Tony for *Wonderful Town* two years later (1953). The musical was based on the same source as her film *My Sister Eileen* (1942), for which she received an Oscar nomination for her first of four. *Tony Award:* Best Actress in a Musical, *Wonderful Town*, 1953. She later received a Tony nomination for Best Actress in a Play for *Auntie Mame* (1957).

OLGA SAN JUAN (March 16, 1927–January 3, 2009; born Brooklyn, NY). Limited in films by her heavy accent, San Juan appeared on Broadway as one of the leads in *Paint Your Wagon* (1951).

JEAN STAPLETON (January 19, 1923; born Jeanne Murray, New York, NY). Stapleton (her mother's maiden name) is best known as the long-suffering, devoted wife of Archie Bunker in the television hit sitcom *All in the Family,* for which she won three Emmys. She began her stage career in the Off-Broadway play *American Gothic.* She was also featured in several Broadway productions, including *Damn Yankees* (1955), *Bells Are Ringing* (1956), *Juno* (1959), and *Funny Girl* (1964).

BARBRA STREISAND (April 24, 1942; born Barbara Joan Streisand, Brooklyn, NY). One of the most successful female entertainers in history and one of the all-time best-selling recording artists in the United States, Streisand is a singer, actress, composer, director, and film producer. She has won two Oscars, eight Grammys, four Emmy awards, and a Special Tony. She was inducted as a Kennedy Center honoree in 2008 for her contribution to the performing arts. Streisand made her Broadway debut in *I Can Get It for You Wholesale* (1962) and went on to star in the hit *Funny Girl* (1964). *Tony nominations:* Best Featured Actress in a Musical, *I Can Get It for You Wholesale*, 1961; Best Actress in a Musical, *Funny Girl*, 1964.

PAT SUZUKI (September 23, 1934; born Chiyoko Suzuki, Cressey, CA). Suzuki's family was one of many Japanese American families forced to enter internment camps during World War II. She released her first singing album in 1958, which led to a role in *Flower Drum Song* (1958).

MIYOSHI UMEKI (May 8, 1929–August 28, 2007; born Otarui, Hakkaido, Japan). Umeki traveled with a U.S. Army jazz band in Japan as Nancy Umeki and moved to the United States in 1955. In 1958 she won the Oscar for Best Supporting Actress for *Sayonara*. Her big hit on Broadway was in *Flower Drum Song* (1958) as the demure mail order bride. She recreated the role in the film version in 1961. *Tony nomination:* Best Actress in a Musical, *Flower Drum Song*, 1958. In 1958 she won the Oscar for Best Supporting Actress for *Sayonara*.

GWEN VERDON (January 13, 1925–October 18, 2000; born Gwyneth Evelyn Verdon, Culver City, CA). Verdon, a dancer and film and stage actress, spent her early years in rigid leg braces from a case of rickets. After many jobs in the chorus line, she got the second female lead in *Can-Can* (1953). Considered Broadway's best dancer in the 1950s and 1960s, she is best remembered as Lola in *Damn Yankees* (1955). She was Charity in *Sweet Charity* (1966), choreographed by husband Bob Fosse. She also appeared in *Chicago* (1975) and *Dancin'* (1978). Upon her death from a heart attack in 2000, the lights of Broadway dimmed in tribute. *Tony Awards:* Best Actress in a Musical, *Damn Yankees*, 1956; Best Actress in a Musical, *New Girl in Town* (shared with Thelma Ritter), 1958; Best Actress in a Musical, *Redhead*, 1959. *Tony nomination:* Best Featured Actress in a Musical, *Can-Can*, 1954. Best Actress in a Musical, *Sweet Charity*, 1966; Best Actress in a Musical, *Chicago*, 1976.

NANCY WALKER (May 10, 1922–March 25, 1992; born Anna Myrtle Swoyer, Philadelphia, PA). Although at four feet, ten inches, she was somewhat difficult to cast, Walker was a working actress throughout the 1940s and 1950s, noted for her dry wit. On Broadway she originated the roles of Hildy Eszterhazy in *On the Town* (1944) and Katey O'Shea in *Copper and Brass* (1957). Walker made many televisions appearances through the years, most notably as Valene Harper's mother on *Rhoda*, and received eight Emmy nominations. *Tony nominations:* Best Actress in a Musical, *Phoenix '55*, 1956; Best Actress in a Musical, *Do Re Mi*, 1961.

DIRECTORS

GEORGE ABBOTT (June 25, 1887–January 31, 1995; born George Francis Abbott, Forestville, NY). At the University of Rochester, in New York, Abbott wrote his first play, *Perfectly Harmless*. He wrote *The Head of the Family* for the Harvard Dramatic Club in 1912. He first appeared on Broadway as an actor in *The Misleading Lady* (1913). His theatre credits as director beginning in 1926 include *Lilly Turner* (1932), *High Button Shoes* (1947), *Call Me Madam* (1950), *The Pajama Game* (1954), *Fiorello!* (1959; 1960 Pulitzer Prize for Drama), and *A Funny Thing Happened on the Way to the Forum* (1962). His last production as director was *Music Is* (1976). Abbott was honored at the Kennedy Center in 1982 for his contributions to the performing arts. *Tony Awards:* Best Musical (Book), *The Pajama Game*, 1955; Best Musical (Book), *Damn Yankees*, 1956; Best Musical, *Fiorello!*, 1960; Best Direction of a Musical, *Fiorello!*, 1960; Best Direction of a Musical, *A Funny Thing Happened on the Way to the Forum*, 1963; Lawrence Langer Award, 1976; Special Tony Award on occasion of his 100th birthday, 1987. *Tony nominations:* Best Musical (Book), *New Girl in Town*, 1958, Best Direction of a Play, *Never Too Late*, 1963, Best Direction of a Musical, *How Now Dow Jones*, 1968.

JOSEPH ANTHONY (May 24, 1912–January 20, 1993; born Milwaukee, WI). Of his many Broadway productions, two were during the Golden Age, *The Most Happy Fella* (1956) and *110 in the Shade* (1963). His first Broadway credit was as author of *A Ship Comes In* (1934), and his acting roles include *Lady in the Dark* and *Peer Gynt*. He was six times nominated for a Tony as best director but never won. *Tony nominations:* Best Direction of a Musical, *The Lark*, 1956; Best Direction of a Musical, *The Most Happy Fella*, 1957; Best Direction of a Play, *A Clearing in the Woods*, 1957; Best Direction of a Play, *The Best Man*, 1960; Best Direction of a Play, *Rhinoceros*, 1961; Best Direction of a Musical, *110 in the Shade*, 1964.

PETER BROOK (March 21, 1925; born Peter Stephen Paul Brook, London, UK). Although known mainly for his work in the English theatre, Brook's Broadway musical credits include *House of Flowers* (1954) and *Irma La Duce* (1960). He was nominated three times for Best Director of a Play, winning twice for *The Persecution and Assassination of Marat . . .* (1966) and *A Midsummer Night's Dream* (1971). *Tony nominations:* Best Direction of a Play, *The Visit*, 1959, Best Direction of a Musical, *Irma La Douce*, 1961.

ABE BURROWS (December 18, 1910–May 17, 1985; born Abram Solman Borowitz, New York, NY). Humorist, author, and director for radio and the stage, Burrows hosted his own radio program in 1948. He attributed his eventual success on the stage to his work under legend George S. Kaufman. Among his many credits are *Can-Can* (1953) and *How to Succeed in Business without Really Trying* (1961). He was such a noted script doctor that when a producer got in trouble, the call went out, "Get me Abe Burrows!" His son, James Burrows, has been nominated for more than 40 Emmys, winning 10 for directing and producing such shows as *Taxi*, *Cheers*, *Frasier*, and *Will and Grace*. *Tony Awards:* Best Musical (Book), *Guys and Dolls*, 1951; Best Musical (Book), *How to Succeed in Business without Really Trying*, 1962; Best Author of a Musical, *How to Succeed in Business without Really Trying*; Best Direction of a Musical, *How to Succeed in Business without Really Trying*, 1962.

PETER COE (April 11, 1929–May 25, 1987; born London, England). Coe's career peak was in 1961, when three plays he directed ran simultaneously in London's West End: *The Miracle Worker*, *The World of Suzie Wong*, and *Oliver!* He is best known to American audiences for directing *Oliver!* It opened on Broadway in 1963 and ran for 775 performances at the Imperial and Shubert theatres, before going on a national tour. It reopened at the Martin Beck in 1965 and was revived in 1984 at the Mark Hellinger, again under Coe's direction. In 1981 he received a Tony nomination for best Direction of *Play for a Life*. Coe died in London as the result of an auto accident in 1987. *Tony nomination:* Best Direction of a Musical, *Oliver!*, 1963

MORTON DACOSTA (March 7, 1914–January 29, 1989; born in Philadelphia, PA). DaCosta started his career as a stage actor in 1942 and gained fame as director for *The Music Man*. *Tony nomination:* Best Direction of a Musical, *The Music Man*, 1958.

CY FEUER (January 15, 1911–May 17, 2006; born Seymour Arnold Feuer, Brooklyn, NY). Feuer once worked as a trumpet player in Radio City Music Hall. Winner of four Tonys as a producer, he was also nominated twice for a Tony for best direction. *Tony Awards:* Best Musical, *Guys and Dolls*, 1951; Best Musical, *How to Succeed in Business without Really Trying*, 1962; Best Producer of a Musical, *How to Succeed in Business without Really Trying*, 1962; Special Tony for Lifetime Achievement in the Theatre, 2003. *Tony nominations:* Best Direction of a Musical, *Little Me*, 1963; Best Musical, *Skyscraper*, 1966; Best Direction of a Musical, *Skyscraper*; Best Musical, *Walking Happy*, 1967.

MOSS HART (October 24, 1904–December 20, 1961; born New York, NY). Hart suffered with bouts of depression throughout his adult life. His play *Merrily We Roll Along*, which he cowrote with George S. Kaufman, was adapted into a 1982 Broadway show by Stephen Sondheim. It subsequently received the Laurence Olivier Theatre Award in 2001. Hart's face appeared on a thirty-seven-cent stamp in 2004. The last show he directed was Alan Jay Lerner's and Frederick Loewe's *Camelot* (1960). *Tony Award: Best Direction of a Musical, My Fair Lady*, 1957.

GARSON KANIN (November 24, 1912–March 13, 1999; born Rochester, NY). A noted American writer and director of plays and films, Kanin collaborated with his wife, Ruth Gordon, on many film classics, such as *Adam's Rib* and *Pat and Mike*. He wrote and staged the comedy *Born Yesterday* (1946), which ran for 1,642 performances. He directed *The Diary of Anne Frank* (1955), for which he received a Tony nomination for Best Director, and the Golden Age musical *Funny Girl* (1964). *Tony nominations:* Best Musical (Book), *Do Re Mi*, 1961; Best Direction of a Musical, *Do Re Mi*.

GEORGE S. KAUFMAN (November 16, 1889–June 2, 1961; born Pittsburgh, PA). Kaufman was known as a director, playwright, producer, humorist, and drama critic for the *New York Times*. His Broadway debut was *Someone in the House*, written in 1918 with Larry Evans and W. C. Percival. It was panned; however, from 1921 through 1958, a play written by Kaufman appeared in every Broadway season. He was very successful with two productions, *The Cocoanuts* (1925) and *Animal Crackers* (1928), for the Marx Brothers. Kaufman wrote very few plays alone; his most successful collaborations were with Moss Hart, including *You Can't Take It with You* (1936), which won the Pulitzer Prize for Drama in 1937. His big Broadway success was *Guys and Dolls* (1950), which he directed but did not write. *Tony Award:* Best Direction of a Musical, *Guys and Dolls*, 1951.

WALTER KERR (July 8, 1913–October 9, 1996; born Walter Francis Kerr, Evanston, IL). Best known as a writer for the *New York Times* and a producer, Kerr also directed *Goldilocks* (1958) on Broadway. The theatre on West 48th Street is named for him.

ARTHUR LAURENTS (July 14, 1918; born Brooklyn, NY). Also a playwright, novelist, screenwriter, and librettist, he wrote his first play, *Home of the Brave*, in 1945. His several books for musicals include *West Side Story* (1957), *Anyone Can Whistle* (1964), and *Do I Hear a Waltz?* (1965). Among his film credits are *The Snake Pit* and Alfred Hitchcock's *Rope*. His productions as director include *I Can Get It for You Wholesale* (1962), *La Cage aux Folles* (1983), and the 2009 revival of *West Side Story*. He won for Best Director of a Musical in 1975 for *Hallelujah, Baby!* and in 1984 for the stage adaptation of *La Cage aux Folles* and was twice nominated for Best Director of a Musical for revivals of *Gypsy* in 1975 and 2008. *Tony nominations:* Best Musical (Book), *West Side Story*, 1958; Best Musical (Book), *Gypsy*, 1960.

JOSHUA LOGAN (October 5, 1908–July 12, 1988; born Joshua Lockwood Logan III, Texarkana, TX). A Princeton graduate, Logan began his Broadway career as an actor in *Carry Nation* (1932). After spending time in London and Hollywood, he directed *On Borrowed Time* (1938) on Broadway and later in 1938 directed his first big success, *I Married an Angel*. After World War II, he shared the 1950 Pulitzer Prize for Drama with Richard Rodgers and Oscar Hammerstein II for cowriting *South Pacific* (1955). Somehow his name was omitted, and at first the Pulitzer committee gave the prize only to Rodgers and Hammerstein. In his autobiography in 1976, he admitted to having bipolar disorder. He won three Tonys in 1948 for *Mister Roberts*: Best Direction, Best Play, and Best Author (the latter two shared with Thomas Heggen). He won another Best Director Tony in 1953 for *Picnic*, and received a nomination for Best Play in 1959 by coproducing *Epitaph for George Dillon*. *Tony Awards:* Best Direction of a Musical, *South Pacific*, 1950; Best Musical, *South Pacific*, 1950; Best Producer of a Musical, *South Pacific*; Best Libretto (shared with Oscar Hammerstein), *South Pacific*. *Tony nominations:* Best Direction of a Musical, *All American*, 1962.

HAROLD PRINCE (January 30, 1928; born Harold Smith Prince, New York, NY). Prince is associated with many of the best-known Broadway musicals of the second half of the twentieth century, both as director and producer. He began work as an assistant to director George Abbott and later produced *The Pajama Game* (1954) with him. After a string of failures, he hit success with *Cabaret* (1966) and then joined forces with composer/lyricist Stephen Sondheim, resulting in a string of hits that included *Company* (1970), *A Little Night Music* (1973), and *Sweeney Todd* (1979). Prince's post–Golden Age awards include Best Musical, *Cabaret* (1967), Best Direction of a Musical, *Cabaret* (1967), Best Musical, *Company* (1971), Best Direction of a Musical, *Company* (1971), Best Direction of a Musical, *Follies* (1972), Best Musical, *A Little Night Music* (1973), Best Direction of a Musical, *Candide* (1974), Best Direction of a Musical, *Sweeney Todd* (1979), Best Direction of a Musical, *Evita* (1980), Best Direction of a Musical, *The Phantom of the Opera* (1988), Best Direction of a Musical, *Show Boat* (1995). Prince also received a Special Award for *Candide* (1974) and one for Lifetime Achievement in the Theatre in 2006.

He received nominations for Best Musical, *Zorba* (1967), Best Direction of a Musical, *Zorba* (1969), Best Musical, *Follies* (1972), Best Direction of a Musical, *A Little Night Music* (1973), Best Musical, *Pacific Overtures* (1976), Best Direction of a Musical, *Pacific Overtures* (1976), Best Musical, *Side by Side by Sondheim* (1977), Best Direction of a Musical, *On the Twentieth Century* (1978), Best Musical, *Grind* (1985), Best Direction of a Musical, *Grind* (1985), Best Direction of a Musical, *Kiss of the Spider Woman* (1993), Best Direction of a Musical, *Parade* (1999). *Tony Awards:* Best Producer of a Musical, *The Pajama Game*, 1954; Best Producer of a Musical, *Damn Yankees*, 1955; Best Producer of a Musical, *She Loves Me*, 1963; Best Producer of a Musical, *A Funny Thing Happened on the Way to the Forum*, 1963; Best Musical, *Fiddler on the Roof*, 1965; Best Direction of a Musical, *Fiddler on the Roof*; Best Producer of a Musical, *Fiddler on the Roof*. *Tony nominations:* Best Musical, *West Side Story*, 1958; Best Musical, *New Girl in Town* 1958; Best Musical, *Little Me*, 1964; Best Direction of a Musical, *Little Me*; Best Producer of a Musical, *Little Me*

BRETAIGNE WINDUST (January 20, 1906–March 18, 1960; born Ernest Retaigne Windust, Paris, France). Windust moved to the United States in 1920 and attended Columbia University and Princeton. His first major production as a theatre director was Eugene O'Neill's *Strange Interlude* (1932). His first major hit on Broadway was directing *Life with Father* (1939), which ran for 3,224 performances, a record for many years. Windust's claim to fame in the Golden Age was as director of the much acclaimed *Finian's Rainbow* (1947).

COMPOSERS AND LYRICISTS

RICHARD ADLER (August 3, 1921; born New York, NY). After serving in the U.S. Navy, Adler teamed with Jerry Ross in 1950. Their first major hit was "Rags to Riches," recorded by Tony Bennett. Their first big success on Broadway was *The Pajama Game* (1954), which was followed a year later by another hit, *Damn Yankees* (1955). After Ross's early death in 1955, Adler composed alone and with other partners. His last Broadway musical was *Music Is* (1976). *Tony Awards:* Best Musical, *The Pajama Game*, 1955 (Music and Lyrics with Ross); Best Musical and Lyrics (Music with Ross), *Damn Yankees*, 1956. *Tony nomination:* Best Composer (Music and Lyrics), *Kwamina*, 1962.

LEROY ANDERSON (June 29, 1908–May 18, 1975; born Cambridge, MA). Schooled at the New England Conservatory of Music and a Harvard University graduate, Anderson started his song-writing career in 1946 with

"Sleigh Ride." By 1952, he was established as a noted American composer of light concert music. His one try at musical theatre resulted in *Goldilocks* (1958). The reviews were scathing, but his score was praised.

HAROLD ARLEN (February 15, 1905–April 23, 1986; born Hyman Arluck, Buffalo, NY). A noted composer of twentieth-century popular music, Arlen wrote more than 400 songs for Broadway, films, and the Cotton Club, a popular Harlem night spot in the 1930s. While working in New York in the early 1920s as an accompanist in vaudeville, he changed his name to Arlen. His first well-known song was "Get Happy" (1929), with lyrics by Ted Koehler. In California in 1938, he teamed with lyricist Yip Harburg to write one of the all-time popular tunes, "Over the Rainbow," which won them an Oscar for Best Original Song. Arlen's Broadway contributions include the Golden Age musicals *Bloomer Girl* (1944), *Jamaica* (1957), and *Saratoga* (1959). *Tony nomination:* Best Musical (Music), *Jamaica*, 1957.

IRVING BERLIN (May 11, 1888–September 22, 1989; born Israel Isidore Baline, either in Belarus or Ryumen, Russia). One of America's most prolific songwriters, Berlin wrote both lyrics and music. Composer of more than 3,000 songs, he wrote 17 film scores and 31 scores for Broadway. "Alexander's Ragtime Band" (1911) launched his career. While in the U.S. Army in World War I, he staged a musical revue, *Yip Yip Yaphank*. The song he composed for it, "God Bless America," was not released until years later and became one of the most widely known songs in the country. Besides revues, Berlin wrote book shows as well, such as *The Cocoanuts* (1925) and *Face the Music* (1932). His most successful Broadway production was *Annie Get Your Gun* (1946). He was called in after Jerome Kern died suddenly. This is considered his best theatre score, but he almost left out the showstopper, "There's No Business Like Show Business," because he thought—wrongly—that Richard Rodgers and Oscar Hammerstein II did not like it. His second greatest success was *Call Me Madam* (1950). He won the Academy Award for "White Christmas" and received eight more Oscar nominations, two for Original Story. *Tony nomination:* Best Original Score, *Call Me Madam*, 1951.

LEONARD BERNSTEIN (August 25, 1918–October 14, 1990; born Lawrence, MA). Composer, conductor, author, pianist, and lecturer, Bernstein was a Harvard graduate who is probably best known as the longtime music director of the New York Philharmonic Orchestra and for writing the music for *West Side Story* (1957). He began at the Philharmonic in 1958 and held the post until 1969. His other principal works for the musical theatre include *On the Town* (1944), *Wonderful Town* (1953), *1600 Pennsylvania*

Avenue (1976), *The Madwoman of Central Park West* (1979), and *The Race to Urgo* (1987). In 1969 he received a Special Award Tony. *Tony Award:* Best Musical, *Wonderful Town*, 1953. *Tony nominations:* Best Musical (Music), *Candide*, 1957; Best Musical (Music), *West Side Story*, 1957.

JERRY BOCK (November 23, 1928–November 3, 2010; born Jerrold Lewis Bock, New Haven, CT). Inducted into the Songwriters Hall of Fame in 1972, Bock won four Tonys and was nominated for a Tony for three other productions. He is especially known for the scores of *Fiorello!* and *Fiddler on the Roof*. He received three Tony nominations in 1967 for *The Apple Tree* and another in 1971 as Best Composer and Lyricist for *The Rothschilds*. *Tony Awards:* Best Musical (Music), *Fiorello!*, 1960; Best Musical (Music), *Fiddler on the Roof*, 1965; Best Composer and Lyricist, *Fiddler on the Roof*, 1965. *Tony nominations:* Best Musical (Music), *She Loves Me*, 1964.

SAMMY CAHN (June 18, 1913–January 15, 1993; born Samuel Cohen, New York, NY). Although best known for his film work—Oscars for "Three Coins in the Fountain" (1954) and "All the Way" (1957), among others—songwriter Cahn also had success with the Golden Age production of *High Button Shoes* (1947). He received three Tony nominations for his work after the Golden Age, including *Skyscraper* (1966) and *Walking Happy* (1967), both with Jimmy Van Heusen.

CY COLEMAN (June 14, 1929–November 18, 2004; born Seymour Kaufman, New York, NY). Known for such songs as "Big Spender" and "Hey, Look Me Over," Coleman gave his first piano recital at age six in Town Hall, New York City. He wrote the Broadway scores for *Wildcat* (1960), *Little Me* (1962), and *Sweet Charity* (1966). He received several post-Golden Age nominations, including two for *Sweet Charity* (Best Musical-Music, Best Composer and Lyricist), *Seesaw* (Best Original Score, 1974), *I Love My Wife* (Best Original Score, 1977), two for *Barnum* (Best Musical, Best Original Score, 1980), and three for *The Life* (Best Musical, Best Original Score, Best Book, 1997). He won Best Original Score Tonys for *On the Twentieth Century* in 1978, *City of Angels* in 1990, and *The Will Rogers Follies* in 1991. On November 19, 2004, the lights of Broadway dimmed in his honor. *Tony nominations:* Best Composer, *Little Me*, 1963. Best Musical (Music), *Little Me*, 1963.

BETTY COMDEN AND ADOLPH GREEN (Comden: May 3, 1915–November 23, 2006; born Elizabeth Cohen, New York, NY. Green: December 2, 1914–October 23, 2002; born Bronx, NY). Comden and Green were a famed songwriting team who won seven Tony awards from 1953 to

1991. Their collaboration was so well known and so close that many thought they were married, which they were not. They met in 1938 when Comden was studying drama at New York University. Their first try at Broadway was *On the Town* (1944), for which they were both lyricists and librettists, with Leonard Bernstein as composer. Among their great triumphs are both the Broadway and television Mary Martin versions of *Peter Pan*. Post–Golden Age wins included Best Musical (Lyrics) and Best Composer and Lyricist for *Hallelujah, Baby!*, Best Musical (Book) for *Applause* (1970), Best Book of a Musical and Best Original Score (Lyrics) for *On the Twentieth Century* in 1978, and Best Original Score (Lyrics) for *The Will Rogers Follies* in 1991. The also received nominations for Best Book of a Musical and Best Original Score (Lyrics) for *A Doll's Life* in 1983 and Best Book of a Musical for *Singin' in the Rain* in 1986. They were honored by the Kennedy Center in 1991 for their lifetime contributions to the performing arts. *Tony Award:* Best Musical (Best Lyrics), *Wonderful Town*, 1953. *Tony nominations:* Best Musical (Book), *Bells Are Ringing,* 1957); Best Musical (Lyrics), *Bells Are Ringing*; Best Musical (Lyrics), *Do Re Mi*, 1961.

NOËL COWARD (December 16, 1899–March 26, 1973; born Noël Peirce Coward, Teddington, UK). Noted for his wit and flamboyance, Coward was a playwright, director, actor, and singer, in addition to composer, such as for *Sail Away* (1961) and *The Girl Who Came to Supper* (1963) during the Golden Age. In 1970 he received a Special Award Tony for "his multiple and immortal contributions to the theatre." *Tony nominations:* Best Direction (Musical), *High Spirits*, 1964; Best Author (Musical), *The Girl Who Came to Supper*, 1964.

DUKE ELLINGTON (April 29, 1899–May 24, 1974; born Edward Kennedy Ellington, Washington, D.C.). One of the most influential figures in jazz and one of the twentieth century's best-known African American celebrities, the Duke's only Broadway musical was *Beggar's Holiday* (1946). An award-winning revue, *Sophisticated Ladies* (1981) contained many of the tunes he made famous.

SAMMY FAIN (June 17, 1902–December 6, 1989; born Samuel E. Feinberg, New York, NY). With Irving Kahal, Fain wrote such classic songs as "Let a Smile Be Your Umbrella." His credits on Broadway during the Golden Age include *Flahooley* (1951) and *Ankles Aweigh* (1955).

DOROTHY FIELDS (July 15, 1905–March 28, 1974; born Allenhurst, NJ). Fields wrote more than 400 songs for Broadway and Hollywood. In 1961, she won an Oscar with Jerome Kern for Best Song for "The Way You Look

Tonight." In the 1940s, she teamed with her brother Herbert as librettists for three Cole Porter shows: *Let's Face It!* (1941), *Something for the Boys* (1943), and *Mexican Hayride* (1944). They were also the librettists for *Annie Get Your Gun* (1946). Her biggest success in the 1950s was *Redhead*, which won five Tonys, including Best Musical. She collaborated with Cy Coleman in the 1960s for *Sweet Charity* and then *Seesaw* in 1973. From that came her last great hit, "It's Not Where You Start, It's Where You Finish." She received post–Golden Age nominations for Best Composer and Lyricist (Lyrics) for *Sweet Charity* in 1966 and Best Original Score (Lyrics) for *Seesaw* in 1974. *Tony Award:* Best Lyrics, *Redhead*, 1959; Best Musical (Book), *Redhead*, 1959.

MORTON GOULD (December 10, 1913–February 21, 1996; born Richmond Hill, NY). Recognized early on as a child prodigy, Gould won the 1995 Pulitzer Prize for Drama for *Stringmusic* and was honored by the Kennedy Center in 1994 for his lifetime contributions to the performing arts. His Broadway scores include *Billion Dollar Baby* (1945) and *Arms and the Girl* (1950).

ADOLPH GREEN. *See* **BETTY COMDEN AND ADOLPH GREEN**.

OSCAR HAMMERSTEIN II (July 12, 1895–August 23, 1960; born Oscar Greeley Clendenning Hammerstein II, New York, NY). Half of the famous Rodgers and Hammerstein team on Broadway, Oscar studied law at Columbia University until he left school to join Otto Harbach for his first musical *Always You* in 1921. Hammerstein teamed with many other composers through the years, including Jerome Kern; their biggest hit was *Show Boat* (1927). His first collaboration with Richard Rodgers was the opener for the Golden Age musical *Oklahoma!* (1943). They went on to such great successes as *South Pacific* (1949) and *The King and I* (1951). Hammerstein died of stomach cancer shortly after the opening of *The Sound of Music* (1960). *Tony Awards:* Best Producer of a Musical, *South Pacific*, 1950; Best Libretto, *South Pacific*; Best Musical, *South Pacific*, 1950; Best Musical, *The King and I*, 1952; Best Musical, *The Sound of Music*, 1960. *Tony nominations:* Best Musical, *Pipe Dream*, 1956; Best Musical, *Flower Drum Song*, 1957; Best Lyrics Collaboration, *Flower Drum Song*, 1959; Best Original Score (Lyrics), *State Fair*, 1966.

E. Y. HARBURG (April 8, 1896–March 4, 1981; born Isidore Hochberg, New York, NY). Known as Edgar Yip Harburg, his nickname was Yipsel, shortened to Yip. He is best known for writing the lyrics to *The Wizard of Oz*, for which he won an Oscar with Harold Arlen. His musical Broadway credits include *Bloomer Girl* (1944); the hit *Finian's Rainbow* (1947), which was one of the first Broadway musicals with an integrated chorus line; *Flahooley* (1951); *Jamaica* (1957), featuring Lena Horne; and *The Happiest Girl in the World* (1961). *Tony nomination:* Best Musical, *Jamaica*, 1958.

SHELDON HARNICK (April 30, 1924; born Sheldon Mayer Harnick, Chicago, IL). Inducted into the Songwriters Hall of Fame in 1972 with his partner, Jerry Bock, Harnick won three Tonys and was nominated for five others. *Tony Awards:* Best Musical, *Fiorello!*, 1960; Best Musical (Lyrics), *Fiddler on the Roof*, 1965; Best Composer and Lyricist, *Fiddler on the Roof*, 1965. Along with Bock, he received three Tony nominations in 1967 for *The Apple Tree* and another in 1971 as Best Composer and Lyricist for *The Rothschilds*. He also received a Best Original Score nomination for *Cyrano-The Musical* in 1994. *Tony nominations:* Best Musical (Lyrics), *She Loves Me*, 1964; Best Composer and Lyricist, *Fiddler on the Roof*, 1965.

JERRY HERMAN (July 10, 1931; born Gerald Herman, New York, NY). Herman first became involved in musical productions at a camp in the Berkshires. After graduating from the University of Miami, he moved to New York City and produced an Off-Broadway revue called *I Feel Wonderful*. His Broadway debut came in 1960 with the revue *From A to Z*. His first full musical was *Milk and Honey* (1961). Then came the hits *Hello, Dolly!* (1964) and *Mame* (1966), the latter bringing him nominations for best Musical and Best Composer and Lyricist. These were followed by *Dear World* (1969), *Mack & Mabel* (1974), *The Grand Tour* (1979), and another big hit, *La Cage aux Folles* (1983). *The Grand Tour* brought him nominations for Best Original Score as composer and lyricist, and he won in the same category for *La Cage*. He is the first composer/lyricist with three musicals that ran more than 1,500 performances on Broadway: *Hello, Dolly!*, 2,844; *Mame*, 1,508; *La Cage aux Folles*, 1,761. In 2009 he received a Special Award for Lifetime Achievement. *Tony Awards:* Best Composer and Lyricist, *Hello, Dolly!*, 1964. *Tony Awards:* Best Musical (Music and Lyrics), *Hello Dolly!*, 1964. *Tony nominations:* Best Composer, *Milk and Honey*, 1962; Best Musical (Music and Lyrics), *Milk and Honey*, 1962.

BURTON LANE (February 2, 1912–January 5, 1997; born Burton Levy, New York, NY). Lane composed such popular songs as "How Are Things in Glocca Morra?," from *Finian's Rainbow* (1947), for which he wrote the score. He also composed the score for *On a Clear Day You Can See Forever* (1965), which earned him a nomination for best Composer and Lyricist. He also received a Best Original Score nomination for *Carmelina* in 1979.

JACK LAWRENCE (April 7, 1912–March 16, 2009; born New York, NY). Lawrence wrote the lyrics for "Tenderly," which became one of Rosemary Clooney's trademark songs. His Broadway lyrics include those for *Courtin' Time* (1951) and *I Had a Ball* (1964).

ALAN JAY LERNER AND FREDERICK LOEWE (Lerner: August 31, 1918–June 14, 1986; born New York, NY. Loewe: June 10, 1901–February 14, 1988; born Berlin, Germany). One of Broadway's most respected musical teams, Lerner and Loewe's Broadway musicals include *Life of the Party* (1942), *Brigadoon* (1947), *Paint Your Wagon* (1951), *My Fair Lady* (1956), *Camelot* (1960), and *Gigi* (1973). They also collaborated on the film version of *Gigi* (1958), which won nine Oscars and later earned them a Best Original Score Tony in 1974 for the stage version. The two met in 1942 at the Lambs Club, a hangout for theatre people. *My Fair Lady* was their crowning Broadway achievement. It set a record at the time for the longest original run of any musical production in London or New York City. It was translated into eleven languages, toured the country for several years, and was revived several times. After Loewe's retirement, Lerner collaborated with several other composers on Broadway, such as Burton Lane for *On a Clear Day You Can See Forever* (1965), but never to the level of success he achieved with Loewe. However, Lerner did receive Tony nominations for *On a Clear Day You Can See Forever* (1965), *Coco* (1970), and *Carmelina*, (1979). *Tony Awards:* Best Musical, *My Fair Lady*, 1957.

FRANK LOESSER (June 29, 1910–July 26, 1969; born Frank Henry Loesser, New York, NY). Composer and lyricist, Loesser wrote "Praise the Lord and Pass the Ammunition" (1942), the first time that he wrote both the melody and lyrics. Besides composing for the movies and Tin Pan Alley, Loesser has several musicals to his credit, including *Where's Charley?* (1948), *Guys and Dolls* (1950), *The Most Happy Fella* (1956), *Greenwillow* (1960), *How to Succeed in Business without Really Trying* (1961), and *Pleasures and Palaces* (1965). *Tony Awards:* Best Musical (Music and Lyrics), *Guys and Dolls*, 1951; Best Musical (producer: Frank Productions), *The Music Man*, 1958. *Tony nominations:* Best Musical (Book, Music, and Lyrics), *The Most Happy Fella*, 1957; Best Composer, *How to Succeed in Business without Really Trying*, 1962; Best Musical, *How to Succeed in Business without Really Trying*, 1962.

FREDERICK LOEWE. *See* ALAN JAY LERNER AND FREDERICK LOEWE.

HUGH MARTIN (August 11, 1914; born Birmingham, AL). Best known for his score in the classic 1944 MGM musical *Meet Me in St. Louis*, Martin wrote the music for five Broadway musicals, including *Best Foot Forward* (1941), *Look Ma, I'm Dancin'!* (1948), *Make a Wish* (1951), *High Spirits* (music and lyrics with Timothy Gray, 1964), and *Meet Me in St. Louis* (1989), the last of which earned him a Tony nomination for Best Score. He also appeared on Broadway as a performer in *Where Do We Go from Here* (1938) and *Louisiana Purchase* (1940). *Tony nominations:* Best Musical, *High Spirits*, 1964; Best Composer and Lyricist, *High Spirits*.

JIMMY MCHUGH (July 10, 1893–May 23, 1969; born James Francis McHugh, Boston, MA). McHugh's first Broadway score was for *Blackbirds* (1928), but he later returned to Broadway for *As the Girls Go* (1948). His long Hollywood career produced such memorable tunes as "I'm in the Mood for Love" and "A Lovely Way to Spend an Evening."

BOB MERRILL (May 17, 1921–February 17, 1998; born Henry Levan, Atlantic City, NJ). Merrill's many song hits include "If I Knew You Were Comin' Id've Baked a Cake," and "Love Makes the World Go Round." He made his Broadway debut in 1957 with *New Girl in Town*, but his greatest success was with Barbra Streisand in *Funny Girl* (1964), with the introduction of "People." His Broadway credits include *Take Me Along* (1959) and *Carnival* (1961). Progressively ill in the 1990s, he took his own life in 1998. *Tony nominations:* Best Musical (Music and Lyrics), *New Girl in Town*, 1957; Best Musical (Music) and Lyrics), *Take Me Along*, 1959; Best Musical (Music and Lyrics), *Carnival*, 1962; Best Composer and Lyricist (Lyricist), *Funny Girl*, 1964.

COLE PORTER (June 9, 1891–October 15, 1964; born Cole Albert Porter, Peru, IN). Noted for his sophisticated lyrics and clever rhymes, the name of Yale-educated Cole Porter first appeared on Broadway in the revue *Hands Up* (1915), for which he wrote his first song, "Esmeralda." His first Broadway production, *See America First* (1916), was a flop. In 1928, the musical *Paris* introduced some of his greatest songs, such as "Let's Do It"; however, most consider his greatest score to be that for *Anything Goes* (1934), with such songs as "I Get a Kick Out of You" and "All Through the Night." It was the first Porter show to feature Ethel Merman; she went on to star in five of his musicals. After 1937, a riding accident left his legs crippled, but he continued to be a success on Broadway with such shows as *Panama Hattie* (1940); *Seven Lively Arts* (1944), which featured "Everytime We Say Goodbye"; and his biggest hit show, *Kiss Me, Kate* (1948).

His last original Broadway production was *Silk Stockings* (1955). His life story was immortalized on film twice, first with the sanitized *Night and Day* (1946), with Cary Grant and Alexis Smith, and with the more realistic *De-Lovely* (2004), with Kevin Kline and Ashley Judd. *Tony Award:* Best Musical (Music and Lyrics), Best Composer and Lyricist *Kiss Me, Kate*, 1949.

MARY RODGERS (January 11, 1931; born New York, NY). Daughter of Richard Rodgers, Mary Rodgers was twice nominated for a Tony, in 1960 and 1978 (Best Original score for *Working*). *Tony nomination:* Best Musical (Music), *Once upon a Mattress*, 1960.

RICHARD RODGERS (June 28, 1902–December 30, 1979; born Richard Charles Rodgers [original family name: Rojazinsky], New York, NY). Rodgers was part of Rodgers and Hammerstein, probably the best-known musical team on Broadway. Along with Oscar Hammerstein II, he wrote the scores for such outstanding works as *Oklahoma!* (1943), *Carousel* (1945), *South Pacific* (1949), *The King and I* (1951), *Flower Drum Song* (1958), and *The Sound of Music* (1959). Rodgers's first musical was *Pal Joey* (1940), written with Lorenz Hart. The songs in most Rodgers and Hammerstein musicals were essential to the development of the characters and the story line and could not be removed without damaging both. In addition to their own success, the two produced shows by other writers, such as *Annie Get Your Gun* (1946), by Irving Berlin. Rodgers is one of only two people ever to have won an Oscar, a Grammy, an Emmy, a Tony, and a Pulitzer Prize (Marvin Hamlisch is the other). He won eleven Tonys (including three special awards in 1962, 1972, and 1979), and was inducted into the Songwriters Hall of Fame in 1970. *Tony Awards:* Best Musical (Producer, Music), Best Producer (Musical), Best Original Score, *South Pacific*, 1950; Best Musical (Music), *The King and I*, 1952; Best Musical (Music, Producer), *The Sound of Music*, 1960; Best Composer, *No Strings*, 1962. *Tony nominations:* Best Musical, Best Producer, *Pipe Dream*, 1956; Best Musical, *Flower Drum Song*, 1959; Best Musical (Producer, Music, Lyrics), *No Strings*, 1962; Best Composer and Lyricist (Music), *Do I Hear a Waltz?*, 1965; Best Original Score (Music), *State Fair*, 1996.

HAROLD ROME (May 27, 1908–October 26, 1993; born Hartford, CT). Composer and lyricist, Rome attended Yale and composed songs for a revue entitled *Pins and Needles* (1937), which ran for 1,108 shows. After World War II, he wrote the songs for *Call Me Mister* (1946). His hits include *Wish You Were Here* (1952), *Destry Rides Again* (1959), and *I Can Get It for You Wholesale* (1962). His last Broadway musical was *Zulu and the Zeyda* (1965).

JERRY ROSS (March 9, 1926–November 11, 1955; born Jerold Rosenberg, Bronx, NY). Billed as "boy star" in the Yiddish theatre, composer Ross studied at New York University and collaborated with Richard Adler in the 1950s. They won a Tony for *The Pajama Game* (1954), followed by another hit, *Damn Yankees* (1955). Ross died at age twenty-nine from lung disease; however, during that short time, alone or in collaboration, he wrote more than 250 songs. *Tony Awards:* Best Musical (Music with Adler), *The Pajama Game*, 1955; Best Musical and Lyrics (Music with Adler), *Damn Yankees*, 1956.

ARTHUR SCHWARTZ (November 4, 1900–September 3, 1984; born Brooklyn, NY). A songwriter on Broadway and in Hollywood for decades, Schwartz is best known for his compositions that have become standards, such as "You and the Night and the Music." A graduate of New York University law school, he published his first song in 1923. His songs were heard in his first Broadway show, *The New Yorkers* (1927). He closed his law office the following year and began to collaborate with lyricist Howard Dietz. Their first hit song, "I Guess I'll Have to Change My Plan," was for a 1929 Broadway revue entitled *The Little Show*. Their best Broadway revue was *The Band Wagon*, which marked Fred Astaire's final appearance with his sister Adele and featured their most famous song, "Dancing in the Dark." After time in Hollywood, Schwartz returned to Broadway in 1946. He wrote the songs with Dorothy Fields for *A Tree Grows in Brooklyn* (1951). He resumed his partnership with Dietz in the early 1960s. They are probably best known for what has become the show business standard "That's Entertainment."

STEPHEN SONDHEIM (March 22, 1930; born New York, NY). Sondheim was only in his teens when Richard Rodgers and Oscar Hammerstein had a hit with *Oklahoma!* in 1943, but he had already made up his mind to become a songwriter for the theatre. A graduate of Williams College, he got his first big break writing lyrics for Leonard Bernstein's music in the smash *West Side Story* (1957). His next lyric-writing hit was *Gypsy* (1959). But with *A Funny Thing Happened on the Way to the Forum* (1962), "music and lyrics by Stephen Sondheim" finally appeared on Broadway. He has since written music and lyrics for many hit productions and won Tonys for three post–Golden Age shows. *Tony Award:* Best Musical (Lyrics), *A Funny Thing Happened on the Way to the Forum*, 1963.

CHARLES STROUSE (June 7, 1928; born New York, NY). Strouse's first Broadway musical was the hit *Bye Bye Birdie* (1960), with collaborator Lee Adams, who wrote the lyrics. *Golden Boy* followed (1964), also with Adams. Strouse won Emmy awards for the television adaptations of *Bye Bye Birdie* and *Annie*. *Tony Award:* Best Musical (Music), *Bye Bye Birdie*, 1961.

JULE STYNE (December 31, 1905–September 20, 1994; born Julius Kerwin Stein, London, UK). Styne moved with his family to Chicago at the age of eight and attended Chicago Musical College. While still a teenager, Mike Todd commissioned him to write a song for a musical art show; it was the first of more than 1,500 songs Styne wrote during his career. He collaborated with lyricist Sammy Cahn on many songs for movies, including "Five Minutes More" and the Oscar-winning "Three Coins in the Fountain." His first Broadway score was with Cahn for *High Button Shoes* (1947). Many scores followed with several collaborators, including *Gentlemen Prefer Blondes* (1949), *Peter Pan* (1954), *Bells Are Ringing* (1956), *Gypsy* (1959), *and Funny Girl* (1964). He was honored at the Kennedy Center in 1990 for his contributions to the performing arts.

JIMMY VAN HEUSEN (January 26, 1913–February 7, 1990; born Edward Chester Babcock, Syracuse, NY). Before he moved to New York City in 1933, composer Van Heusen adopted his last name from the men's collar manufacturer. With lyricist Johnny Burke, he wrote such hit tunes for Hollywood as "Moonlight Becomes You," "Swinging on a Star," and "Suddenly It's Spring." Van Heusen received fourteen Oscar nominations, winning four for his film work. He also collaborated on the Broadway productions *Nellie Bly* (1946) and *Carnival in Flanders* (1953).

KURT WEILL (March 2, 1900–April 3, 1950; born Kurt Julian Weill, Dessau, Germany). A leading composer for the stage, Weill's most famous work is *Threepenny Opera*, which opened on Broadway in 1933 and closed after thirteen performances. His most famous song is "Mack the Knife," from that score. Weill won the first Tony given for Best Original Score in 1947. *Tony Award:* Best Original Score, *Street Scene*, 1947.

MEREDITH WILLSON (May 18, 1902–June 15, 1984; born Robert Meredith Willson, Mason City, IA). Willson attended Juilliard (then Damrosch Institute) in New York City and joined the New York Philharmonic Orchestra from 1924 to 1929. He composed symphonies as well as music for radio for many years. He is best known on Broadway for his hit *The Music Man* (1957), which was set in his hometown. Willson said it was, "an Iowan's attempt to pay tribute to his home state." *Tony Award:* Best Musical, *The Music Man*, 1958.

CHOREOGRAPHERS

GOWER CHAMPION (June 22, 1921–August 25, 1980; born Gower Carlyle Champion, Genova, IL). A Tony winner for both directing and choreography, Champion began dancing at age eighteen, when he toured nightclubs with friend Jeanne Tyler. He worked on Broadway as a dancer and choreographer in the late 1930s and 1940s. After Coast Guard duty in World War II, he married Marjorie Belcher, and they became a dance team. He won his first Tony for staging *Lend An Ear* (1948), which introduced Carol Channing to Broadway audiences. In 1964, he had his biggest blockbuster as director with *Hello, Dolly!*, which ran for 2,844 performances. After some failures, including a divorce, in the 1970s, Champion was back in 1980 to choreograph and direct a stage adaptation of the film classic *42nd Street*. The show ran for 3,486 performances, but Champion never got to see any of them, as he died of blood cancer on the day the show opened. *Tony Awards:* Best Choreography, *Lend an Ear*, 1949; Best Direction and Best Choreography, *Bye Bye Birdie*, 1961; Best Choreography, *Hello, Dolly!*, 1964; Best Direction of a Musical, *Bye Bye Birdie*, 1961; Best Direction of a Musical and Best Choreography, *Hello, Dolly!*, 1964; Best Direction of a Musical, *The Happy Time*, 1968. *Tony nominations:* Best Direction of a Musical, *Carnival!*, 1962; Best Direction of a Musical, *I Do! I Do!*, 1967.

JACK COLE (April 27, 1914–February 16, 1974; born New Brunswick, NJ). Cole began his career as a dancer and went on to choreograph both in films and on Broadway, including *Kismet* (1953), *Jamaica* (1957), and *A Funny Thing Happened on the Way to the Forum* (1962). His work was noted for Asian and jazz motifs.

AGNES DE MILLE (September 18, 1905–October 6, 1993; born Agnes George de Mille, Harlem, New York, NY). Born into a family of theatre professionals, de Mille originally wanted to be an actress but turned to dance to help cure her flat feet. One of her earliest jobs was in the movies, choreographing *Cleopatra* (1934); the dances were later cut from the film. Her first major work was *Rodeo* (1942); her final ballet was completed in 1992 (*The Informer*). In between, de Mille had many hits to her credit, including *Oklahoma!* (1943), *Bloomer Girl* (1944), *Carousel* (1945), *Brigadoon* (1947), *Gentlemen Prefer Blondes* (1949), *Paint Your Wagon* (1951), *Goldilocks* (1958), and *110 in the Shade* (1963). She did not fare as well in Hollywood, except for *Oklahoma!*. De Mille was a significant force in the world of the theatre that became the Golden Age. *Tony Awards:* Best

Choreography, *Brigadoon*, 1947. *Tony nominations:* Best Choreography, *Goldilocks*, 1959; Best Choreography, *Kwamina*, 1962.

BOB FOSSE (June 23, 1927–September 23, 1987; born Robert Louis Fosse, Chicago, IL). A choreographer and director, as a young dancer Fosse teamed with Charles Grass as the Riff Brothers, touring theatres in the Chicago area. After a few film appearances, he choreographed his first musical, *The Pajama Game* (1954), followed by *Damn Yankees* (1955). Fosse developed an immediately recognizable jazz style with stylized sexuality, inward knees, and rounded shoulders. He also used props—a la Fred Astaire—such as canes, chairs, and bowler hats. In 1986, he directed, choreographed, and wrote the Broadway production *Big Deal*. He married his third wife, Gwen Verdon, in 1960. *Tony Awards:* Best Choreography, *Redhead*, 1959; Best Choreography, *Little Me*, 1963. *Tony nominations:* Best Choreography, *New Girl in Town*, 1958.

HANYA HOLM (March 3, 1893–November 3, 1992; born Johanna Eckert, Worms, Germany). A member of the Wigman School in Dresden, Germany, she came to New York City in 1931 to open a branch of the dance school. In 1948, she choreographed *Kiss Me, Kate*, which led to other such musicals as *Out of This World* (1950), *My Darling Aida* (1952), *The Golden Apple* (1954), *My Fair Lady* (1956), *Camelot* (1960), and *Anya* (1965). *Tony nomination:* Best Choreography, *My Fair Lady*, 1957.

GENE KELLY (August 23, 1912–February 2, 1996; born Eugene Curran Kelly, Highland Park, PA). Choreographer and director on stage, Kelly is best known for his film work as an actor, dancer, and singer, especially for *Singin' in the Rain* (1952). He was a dominant force in Hollywood from the mid-1940s until the late 1950s, credited with bringing the ballet form of dance to the silver screen. Kelly appeared on Broadway in 1938 as a dancer in *Leave It to Me!* He first danced to his own choreography on stage in *The Time of Your Life* (1939). His leading role in *Pal Joey* (1940) brought him to stardom. After years in Hollywood, he returned to the stage to direct *Flower Drum Song* (1958). He was nominated for an Oscar for Best Actor for *Anchors Aweigh* (1945).

MICHAEL KIDD (August 12, 1915–December 23, 2007; born Milton Greenwald, New York, NY). Kidd was pursuing a career in chemical engineering at the City College of New York when he got a scholarship to the School of American Ballet. Noted for his work both in films and on the stage, he received an honorary Oscar in 1997 for the art of dance on the screen and also won five Tonys. *Tony Awards:* Best Choreography, *Finian's Rainbow*, 1947; Best Choreography, *Guys and Dolls*, 1951; Best Choreography, *Can-Can*, 1954; Best Choreography, *L'il Abner*, 1957; Best Choreography, *Destry Rides Again*, 1960. *Tony nominations:* Best Direction of a Musical: *Destry Rides Again*.

JOE LAYTON (May 3, 1931–May 5, 1994; born Joseph Lichtman, Brooklyn, NY). Both a director and choreographer, Layton began his career as a dancer in *Wonderful Town* (1953). He won an Emmy for *My Name Is Barbra*, introducing Streisand. His Broadway credits include *The Sound of Music* (1959), *No Strings* (1962), *George M!* (1968), and *Two by Two* (1970). *Tony Award:* Best Choreography, *No Strings*, 1962. *Tony nominations:* Best Choreography, *Greenwillow*, 1960; Best Direction of a Musical, *No Strings*, 1962.

JONATHAN LUCAS (August 14, 1922; born Luca Aco Giarraputo, Salaparuta, Sicily). Lucas had a number of stage appearances as a dancer, including in *Of Thee I Sing* (1952), before his first credit as a choreographer for *First Impressions* (1959).

JEROME ROBBINS (October 11, 1918–July 29, 1998; born Jerome Rabinowitz, New York, NY). A choreographer and director, Robbins danced in several Broadway musicals in the late 1930s. He also choreographed several ballets. His musical comedy works include *Billion Dollar Baby* (1945), *High Button Shoes* (1947), and *Look Ma, I'm Dancin'!* (1948), but he is best known for *Peter Pan* (1954) and *West Side Story* (1957), both of which he also directed. In the 1960s, he choreographed *Funny Girl* (1964) and *Fiddler on the Roof* (1964). Robbins is considered by many to be the greatest American choreographer.

HERBERT ROSS (May 13, 1927–October 9, 2001; born Herbert David Ross, Brooklyn, NY). Choreographer, actor, and director, Ross made his stage debut with the touring company of *Macbeth* in 1942. In 1954, he choreographed his first Broadway production, *A Tree Grows in Brooklyn*. His other choreography credits include *Three Wishes for Jamie* (1952), *House of Flowers* (1954), *The Body Beautiful* (1958), *Finian's Rainbow* (1960 revival), *The Gay Life* (1961), *I Can Get It for You Wholesale* (1962), *Tovarich* (1963), *Anyone Can Whistle* (1964), *Do I Hear a Waltz?* (1965), *On a Clear Day You Can See Forever* (1965), and *The Apple Tree* (1965).

HELEN TAMIRIS (April 24, 1903–August 4, 1966; born Helen Becker, New York, NY). Tamiris's Broadway musical career lasted from 1945 to 1957, during which time she choreographed modern dances in eighteen musical comedies, including *Annie Get Your Gun* (1946) and *Fanny* (1954). She began studying dance at the age of eight and founded her own company in 1930. She chose the name Tamiris because it sounded exotic. From 1927 to 1944, she created works for herself and such contemporaries as Martha Graham. For a time, she danced with the Metropolitan Opera. In 1960, she founded the Tamiris-Nagrin Dance Company with her husband, Daniel Nagrin.

ONNA WHITE (March 24, 1922–April 8, 2005; born Inverness, Nova Scotia). From Nova Scotia to the San Francisco Ballet Company led White to her first Broadway performance in *Finian's Rainbow* (1947). In *Guys and Dolls* (1950), she assisted choreographer Michael Kidd and choreographed her first Broadway show, *Carmen Jones*, in 1956. She received one of only two Oscars ever presented for choreography for *Oliver!* (1968). *Tony nomination:* Best Choreography, *The Music Man*, 1958.

THE THEATRES OF BROADWAY

The term *Broadway theatre* refers to thirty-nine professional buildings in New York City that each seat 500 or more patrons. (Forty-three theatres are listed here; however, the New Century was demolished in 1962, the Ziegfeld in 1966, and the George Abbott in 1970; and the Mark Hellinger is now the home of the Times Square Church.) Thirty-eight of the buildings are in the theatre district of Manhattan; the thirty-ninth is the Vivian Beaumont Theatre, regarded as Broadway class, uptown at Lincoln Center. Besides being a key tourist attraction, the theatre district, along with London's West End, is regarded as the highest form of commercial theatre in the English-speaking world.

Most Broadway theatre owners and producers belong to the Broadway League, formerly known as the League of American Theatres and Producers. It is a trade organization that showcases Broadway theatre, coadministers the Tony Awards with the American Theatre Wing, and negotiates contracts with the many theatrical unions. Most theatres on Broadway are either owned or managed by three groups: the Shubert Organization, which owns seventeen theatres; the Nederlander Organization, which has nine theatres; and Jujamcyn, which owns five.

AL HIRSCHFELD (302 W. 45th St., opened 1924 as the Martin Beck, seats 1,292). Designed as the most opulent theatre of its time by architect G. Albert Lansburgh for vaudeville promoter Martin Beck, this was the only Broadway theatre that opened without a mortgage. The opening production on November 11, 1924, was *Madame Pompadour*. Critics claimed that patrons would not cross Eighth Avenue to get to the new theatre, but Beck proved them wrong. Two Pulitzer Prize winners opened at the Martin Beck: *The Teahouse of the August Moon* (October 15, 1953) and *A Delicate Balance* (September 22, 1966). In addition, many well-known actors performed there, including Katharine Cornell, Alfred Lunt and Lynn Fontanne, and Helen Hayes. The theatre was renamed on June 21, 2003, for the caricaturist famous for his drawings of Broadway celebrities. Its reopening production, on November 23, 2003, was a revival of *Wonderful Town*. Other notable shows include *Bye Bye Birdie* (April 14, 1960), *Oliver!* (August 2, 1965), *Kiss Me, Kate* (November 18, 1999), and *Sweet Charity* (May 2, 2005). The theatre has dressing rooms for 200 actors.

Golden Age musicals: As the Martin Beck: *St. Louis Woman*, 3/30/46; *Barefoot Boy with Cheek*, 4/3/47; *Copper and Brass*, 10/17/57; *Beg, Borrow, or Steal*, 2/10/60; *Bye Bye Birdie*, 4/14/60; *The Happiest Girl in the World*, 4/3/61; *Milk and Honey*, 10/10/61; *Café Crown*, 4/17/64; *I Had a Ball*, 12/15/64; *Drat! The Cat!*, 10/10/65

AMBASSADOR (219 W. 49th St., opened 1921, seats 1,088). Designed by architect Herbert J. Krapp for the Shuberts, the theatre's opening show was the musical *The Rose Girl* (February 11, 1921). It starred Mabel Withee and Charles Purcell and ran for ninety-nine performances. This was the first of six theatres built by the Shuberts on 48th and 49th streets. Although the theatre outwardly looks like any other Broadway house, it is built diagonally across the plot to seat as many people as possible. The Shuberts sold the property in 1935. Four years later, it was the launching site for the careers of three notable performers, Imogene Coca, Alfred Drake, and Danny Kaye, who appeared in *Strawhat Revue*. It was used as a movie theatre/television studio until 1956, when the Shuberts repurchased it and made it a legitimate theatre once again. Notable productions include *The Diary of Anne Frank* (February 26, 1957), *The Lion in Winter* (March 3, 1966), and *Chicago: The Musical* (January 29, 2003). The Ambassador is a designated New York City landmark.

AMERICAN AIRLINES (227 W. 42nd St., opened 1918 as the Selwyn, seats 740). The Selwyn was one of three theatres built by the Selwyn brothers and named for producer Arch Selwyn. Its opening production was *Information Please* (October 2, 1918), starring Jane Cowl. The entire 1927 season showcased *The Royal Family*, concerning the Barrymore family (family of Drew Barrymore). Early musicals included Cole Porter's *Wake Up and Dream* (December 30, 1929). Over the next few decades, it was used as a legitimate theatre now and again until the city and state of New York took possession in 1992. Renovated in 1997 to restore its former glamour, it was renamed and reopened with a revival of *The Man Who Came to Dinner* on July 27, 2000.

AUGUST WILSON (245 W. 52nd St., opened 1925, seats, 1,263). Built by the Theatre Guild, the August Wilson was leased as a radio station in 1943 and purchased by the American National Theatre and Academy (ANTA) in 1950. In 1981, Jujamcyn bought it and named it the Virginia. It was renamed in 2005 for a Pennsylvania-born poet of black culture. He is one of seven American playwrights to have won two Pulitzer Prizes. Notable productions at the theatre include revivals of *Shenandoah* (August 8, 1989), *Flower Drum Song* (October 17, 2002), and *Jersey Boys* (November 6, 2005).

    Golden Age musicals: As the ANTA: *Seventh Heaven*, 5/26/55; *Say, Darling*, 4/3/58; *The Conquering Hero*, 1/16/61

BELASCO (111 W. 44th St., opened 1907 as the Stuyvesant, seats 1,907). The opening production in the Stuyvesant on October 16, 1907, was *A Grand Army Man*, with William Warfield and Antoinette Perry (for whom the Tony Award is named). The theatre, built by director David Belasco, contained the most sophisticated lighting system of its day, as well as plush apartments for him and the star actors. In 1910, Belasco renamed the theatre for himself, and it housed his own presentations until he died in 1931. It has remained a legitimate playhouse, except for a brief period in the 1950s when NBC used it as a radio studio.

BERNARD B. JACOBS (242 W. 45th St., opened 1927 as the Royale, seats 1,078). The opening production in the Royale was *Piggy* on January 11, 1927, and it scored a hit in the second season with *Diamond Lil* (April 9, 1928), starring Mae West. Built by the Chanin Brothers, real estate magnates, ownership was transferred to the Shuberts in 1930. Two years later it housed the Pulitzer Prize winner *Both Your Houses* (March 6, 1933). John Golden leased the theatre from 1934 to 1936 and named it for himself. It was back in Shubert hands in 1936, and the name returned to the Royale. As such it was leased to a CBS radio studio until 1940. In 1964, it housed another Pulitzer Prize winner, *The Subject Was Roses* (May 25, 1964). In 2005, the name was changed to honor the former president of the Shubert organization. The Jacobs has been home to many hits, such as Cole Porter's *Du Barry Was a Lady* (October 21, 1940), with Gypsy Rose Lee and Betty Grable; *The Lady's Not for Burning* (November 8,

1950), with John Gielgud and an acclaimed revival of *One Flew Over the Cuckoo's Nest* (April 8, 2001).

Golden Age musical: As the Royale: *The Boy Friend*, 9/20/54

BILTMORE (261 W. 47th St., opened 1925, seats 903). One of the smaller Broadway houses, the Biltmore opened on December 7, 1925, with *Easy Come Easy Go*. From 1952 to 1961, it was leased by CBS as a radio and television studio. An arsonist destroyed the interior of the theatre in 1987, leaving the house vacant for several years. Manhattan Theatre Club bought it in 2001, restoring several sections of the original building. Notable productions at the Biltmore include *Brother Rat* (December 16, 1936), *My Sister Eileen* (December 26, 1940), *Barefoot in the Park* (October 23, 1963), and the rock musical *Hair* (April 29, 1968), which moved uptown from Off-Broadway. The Biltmore is a designated New York City landmark.

BOOTH (222 W. 45th St., opened 1913, seats 766). The Booth was built by Lee Shubert and producer Winthrop Ames to honor actor Edwin Booth (1833–1893), brother of John Wilkes Booth, who assassinated Abraham Lincoln. This was actually the second Booth theatre, the first built in 1869 on 23rd Street and Sixth Avenue by Booth himself. The first production of the second theatre was *The Great Adventure* by Arnold Bennet (October 16, 1913). Many stars have had great success at the Booth, including Shirley Booth in *Come Back, Little Sheba* (February 15, 1950); Henry Fonda and Anne Bancroft in *Two for the Seesaw* (January 16, 1958); Stephen Sondheim and James Lapine in *Sunday in the Park with George* (May 2, 1984), which won the Pulitzer Prize for Drama; and Paul Newman's return to Broadway in *Our Town* (December 4, 2002). Two earlier Pulitzer winners on its stage were *You Can't Take It with You* (December 14, 1936) and *Time of Your Life* (September 23, 1940).

BROADHURST (235 W. 44th St., opened 1917, seats 1,156). Built by the Shuberts in partnership with British-born playwright George Broadhurst, for whom the theatre is named, the first production was a drama, *Misalliance* (September 17, 1917). The theatre's first musical production was *Ladies First* (October 24, 1918). This was not a Gershwin musical, but it was the first time that a song by George and Ira Gershwin ("The Real American Folk Song") was heard on Broadway. Notable productions include the Pulitzer winners *Men in White* (September 26, 1933) and the Golden Age musical *Fiorello!* (November 23, 1959).

Golden Age musicals: *Flahooley*, 5/14/51; *Seventeen*, 6/21/51; *Fiorello!*, 11/23/59; *Sail Away*, 10/3/61; *Bravo Giovanni*, 5/19/62; *110 in the Shade*,

10/24/63; *Oh! What a Lovely War*, 9/30/64; *Kelly*, 2/5/65; *Half a Sixpence*, 4/25/65

BROADWAY (1681 Broadway, opened 1924 as B. S. Moss's Colony, seats 1,761). This theatre is one of only five that are actually on Broadway. (The other four are Marquis, Minskoff, Palace, and Winter Garden.) Originally a film house, its most notable showing was Disney's *Steamboat Willie* (1928). In 1930, it became a legit theatre with its present name. From 1934 until 1940, it was back in the film business, this time offering the Disney premiere of *Fantasia* (1939). From 1940 onward, except for a brief time as a Cinerama movie house, it has showcased live theatre. The first theatrical production was Cole Porter's and Herbert Fields's *The New Yorkers* (December 8, 1930), starring Jimmy Durante. The Broadway has also housed some other notable premieres, including Irving Berlin's *This Is the Army* (July 4, 1942). Sammy Davis Jr. appeared there in *Mr. Wonderful* (March 22, 1956), and Ethel Merman took central stage in *Gypsy* (May 21, 1959).

   Golden Age musicals: *Carmen Jones*, 12/2/43; *Beggar's Holiday*, 12/22/46; *The Body Beautiful*, 1/23/58; *Mr. Wonderful*, 3/22/56; *Shinbone Alley*, 4/13/57; *Gypsy*, 5/21/59; *Kean*, 11/2/61; *Tovarich*, 3/18/63; *The Girl Who Came to Supper*, 12/8/63; *Baker Street*, 2/16/65

BROOKS ATKINSON (256 W. 47th St., opened 1926 as the Mansfield, seats 1,069). Originally called the Mansfield (for actor Richard Mansfield), the theatre's opening production was *The Night Duel* (February 15, 1926), a melodrama starring Marjorie Rambeau and Felix Krembs. According to the *Times* review, the second act bedroom scene was embarrassing, although the audience seemed to enjoy it; however, the show lasted only seventeen performances. One of its notable productions was the 1930 Pulitzer Prize winner *Green Pastures*. In 1950, the theatre was renamed for the famed *New York Times* drama critic but was a television playhouse for the next ten years. It was refurbished in 2000, with the restoration of its original chandelier. The theatre tends to favor dramas, but it does house the occasional musical.

CIRCLE IN THE SQUARE (235 W. 50th St., opened 1972, seats 620). The Circle in the Square, along with the Gershwin, was built after the Uris Brothers tore down the Capitol Movie Theatre to build the Paramount Plaza office tower. Originally, the theatre was the midtown home to the Circle-in-the-Square repertory company in Greenwich Village. *Mourning Becomes Electra* (November 15, 1972) was the first production. The below-level theatre is only one of two legit Broadway houses with a thrust stage (the other at Lincoln Center's Vivian Beaumont). A thrust stage (also called a platform or open stage) extends into the audience on three sides, providing greater intimacy between performer and patron. The Circle-in-the-Square Theatre School is the only accredited training conservatory that is associated with a Broadway theatre. It offers a two-year training program.

CORT (138 W. 48th St., opened 1912, seats 1,082). Architect Thomas Lamb built the Cort for John Cort, a successful theatre operator on the West Coast, copying the Petit Trianon in Versailles, France. The first production was *Peg o' My Heart* (December 20, 1912), with the early 1900s superstar Laurette Taylor. It ran for an unheard-of-at-the-time 603 performances. Except for a short period as a television studio in the late 1960s, the Cort has been a legitimate Broadway theatre, with such performances as Lillian Gish in *Uncle Vanya* (April 15, 1930) and the Tony and Pulitzer winner *The Diary of Anne Frank* (October 5, 1955). It also premiered another two–Pulitzer Prize winner, *The Shrike*, on January 15, 1951.

ETHEL BARRYMORE (243 W. 47th St., opened 1928, seats 1,058). Named for the great lady of the theatre, the Ethel Barrymore's opening production, fittingly enough, starred her in *The Kingdom of God* (December 20, 1928). This is the only legitimate theatre left of those built by Lee and J.J. Shubert for performers with whom they worked. In 1932, Fred Astaire starred in Cole Porter's musical *The Gay Divorcee* (November 29, 1932), appearing without his sister Adele for the first time and in his last Broadway show before heading for Hollywood.

EUGENE O'NEILL (230 W. 49th St., opened 1925 as the Forrest, seats 1,110). Originally named for the international actor Edwin Forrest, the theatre's first production was *Mayflowers* (November 24, 1925). On December 4, 1933, *Tobacco Road* opened at the The Masque but moved to the Forrest in 1934, where it stayed for most of its 3,182 performances. The name was changed to the Coronet in 1945. In November 1959, it was renamed to honor the Nobel Prize–winning playwright, whose works include *The Ice Man Cometh* (1940) and *Long Day's Journey into Night* (1941). Playwright Neil Simon bought the theatre, which enjoyed a string of his hits, beginning with *The Last of the Red Hot Lovers* (December 28, 1969). Simon sold it to Jujamcyn Theatres in 1982. Among its many hits was the revival of *Grease* with Tommy Tune in 1994.

  Golden Age musicals: As the Coronet: *Happy as Larry*, 1/6/50. As the Eugene O'Neill: *Let It Ride*, 10/12/62; *She Loves Me*, 4/23/63; *Something More!*, 11/10/64

GEORGE ABBOTT (152. W. 54th St., opened 1928 as the Craig, seats 1,434). The George Abbott has a long and varied history. It was renamed the Adelphi in 1934, the Radiant Center in 1940, and the Yiddish Arts Theatre in 1943. It became the Adelphi once again in 1944, was renamed the 54th Street in 1958, and was renamed to honor Broadway's George Abbott in 1965. The Hilton chain tore it down in 1970 to expand a hotel.

Golden Age musicals: As the Adelphi: *Allah Be Praised!*, 4/20/44; *On the Town*, 12/28/44; *The Girl from Nantucket*, 11/8/45; *Nellie Bly*, 1/21/46; *The Duchess Misbehaves*, 2/13/46; *Street Scene*, 1/9/47; *Look, Ma, I'm Dancin'!*, 1/29/48; *Portofino*, 2/21/58. As the 54th Street: *Happy Town*, 10/7/59; *13 Daughters*, 3/2/61; *Kwamina*, 10/23/61; *No Strings*, 3/15/62; *What Makes Sammy Run?*, 2/27/64

GEORGE GERSHWIN (222 W. 51st St., opened 1972 as the Uris, seats 1,933). The George Gershwin opened as the Uris with the musical *Via Galactica* (November 18, 1972), starring Raul Julia; however, the show closed after seven performances. The first theatre built in New York City since 1928, it was renamed in 1983 to honor composer George Gershwin and his brother Ira. It is presently the largest theatre on Broadway (the New York State Theatre of Lincoln Center and New York City Center are larger). From 1974 to 1976, it was a concert hall for pop music and jazz performances. The Theatre Hall of Fame is located in the lobby.

GERALD SCHOENFELD (236 W. 45th St., opened 1917 as the Plymouth, seats 1,079). The Shubert brothers leased the theatre to producer Arthur Hopkins, who wanted it to be a showcase for such prominent actors as John and Lionel Barrymore. The opening production was a comedy called *A Successful Calamity* (October 10, 1917), with William Gillette. After Hopkins's death, the property returned to the Shuberts. Designated a New York City landmark in 1987, it was renamed for the chairman of the Shubert Organization in 2005. Its hit shows include *Dial "M" for Murder* (October 29, 1952), *Jekyll & Hyde* (April 28, 1997), *Long Day's Journey into Night* (May 6, 2003 revival), and *A Chorus Line* (October 5, 2006 revival).

Golden Age musicals: As the Plymouth: *Irma La Douce*, 9/29/60; *The Beast in Me*, 5/16/63

HELEN HAYES (240 W. 44th St., opened 1912 as the Little Theatre, seats 595). Designed by architect Harry Creighton Ingalls, the theatre was first called the Little Theatre because of its small size; it sat only 300. Today, it is still the smallest of the Broadway theatres. The opening production was *The Pigeon* (March 12, 1912), by John Galsworthy. The theatre was redesigned in the 1920s to improve the acoustics and enlarge the seating capacity. The *New York Times* bought it in 1931 and turned it into a conference hall, but ABC turned it back into a legitimate theatre in 1958. *The Dick Clark Show* originated from there from 1958 through September 1961. For a brief time in 1964, it was called the Winthrop Ames Theatre, but it reverted to its original name from 1965 through 1983. In that year, the namesake theatre for Helen Hayes, known as the first lady of the American theatre, was demolished, but Hayes was still alive. Due to the unusual event of having someone outlive his or her monument, the Little Theatre became the Helen Hayes. Since 1978, it has been privately owned by Martin Markinson.

HILTON (213 W. 42nd St., opened 1998, seats 1,815). The neighboring Lyric and Apollo theatres were destroyed in 1998 so that Canadian impresario Garth Drabinsky could build the Ford Center for the Performing Arts to launch his new musical, *Ragtime*. Although some gave it critical acclaim, the production foundered mainly due to Drabinsky's financial problems. In 2005, the Hilton Hotels Corporation along with Clear Channel Entertainment changed the name to the Hilton. It was home to a long run of *42nd Street* (May 2, 2001), winner of the 2001 Tony for Best Musical Revival.

IMPERIAL (249 W. 45th St., opened 1923, seats 1,443). The Imperial was built specifically to accommodate musical theatre. It has been home to many musicals, including the opening production of *Mary Jane McKane* (Oscar Hammerstein II and Vincent Youmans, December 25, 1923). Other hit shows include *Annie Get Your Gun* (May 16, 1946), *Fiddler on the Roof* (September 22, 1964), and *Les Misérables* (October 17, 1990). Famous names on its stage include Gertrude Lawrence, Clifton Webb, Ray Bolger, Mary Martin, Zero Mostel, Shelley Winters, and John Lithgow.

   Golden Age musicals: *One Touch of Venus*, 10/7/43; *Annie Get Your Gun*, 5/16/46; *Miss Liberty*, 7/15/49; *Call Me Madam*, 10/12/50; *Wish You Were Here*, 6/25/52; *Silk Stockings*, 2/24/55; *The Most Happy Fella*, 5/3/56; *Jamaica*, 10/31/57; *Destry Rides Again*, 4/23/59; *Carnival*, 4/13/61; *Oliver!*, 1/6/63; *Fiddler on the Roof*, 9/22/64

JOHN GOLDEN (252 W. 45th St., opened 1927 as The Masque, seats 804). The opening production at the Masque was *Puppets of Passion* (February 24, 1927). John Golden bought the theatre ten years later and named it for himself. *Tobacco Road* premiered there on December 4, 1933. In the 1940s and 1950s, it operated as a movie house until the Shuberts took over and returned it to legitimate theatre use. Seventy-six years after its opening, it housed another puppet production, the award-winning *Avenue Q*.

LONGACRE (220 W. 48th St., opened 1913, seats 1,091). The opening production at the Longacre was the comedy *Are You a Crook?* (May 1, 1913). It has been a legitimate theatre, except for a short period in the mid-1940s to early 1950s when it was a television studio. Named for the original name of Times Square, it was built by impresario Harry Frazee. Frazee is far better remembered, however, as the owner of the Boston Red Sox baseball team. When he needed money for his Broadway dealings, Frazee sold Babe Ruth's contract to the New York Yankees. Supposedly, there is a curse on the theatre because of that sale. In William Goldman's book *The Season: A Candid Look at Broadway* (1984), he notes that some producers actually avoid the theatre, fearing a flop; however, there have been many successful productions, including Hal Holbrook in *Mark Twain Tonight!*, for which he won a Tony in 1966; Julie Harris in *The Belle of Amherst*, which garnered a Tony for Harris in 1976; and Diana Rigg in *Medea*, for which she won a Tony in 1994.

LUNT-FONTANNE (205 W. 46th St., opened 1910 as the Globe, seats 1,489). The Globe opened in 1910 for the musicals of Charles Dillingham, with a performance of *The Old Town* (January 10, 1910), starring Fred Stone, Dave Montgomery, and Peggy Wood. Dillington went into bankruptcy in 1933, and the Globe became a movie house. Completely renovated, it reopened in 1958, renamed for the famous Broadway theatre team of Alfred Lunt and Lynn Fontanne, who performed in *The Visit* (May 5, 1958). In the audience that night to watch the famous acting couple were Katharine Cornell, Henry Fonda, Helen Hayes, Beatrice Lillie, Anita Loos, Mary Martin, Laurence Olivier, and Ginger Rogers. Lunt and Fontanne were married in 1922 and acted together on stage twenty-seven times, the last being in 1958. On display in the theatre lobby are photographs from the collection of Lunt and Fontanne.

   Golden Age musicals: *Goldilocks*, 10/11/58; *The Sound of Music*, 11/16/59; *Little Me*, 11/17/62; *Ben Franklin in Paris*, 10/27/64

LYCEUM (149 W. 45th St., opened 1903, seats 922). The Lyceum is the oldest Broadway theatre in continuous use and the first to achieve landmark status. It is also one of the few Broadway houses to operate under its original name. The opening production was *The Proud Prince* (November 2, 1903). An apartment located above the orchestra section serves as the headquarters of the Shubert Archives. In the early years, such stars as Billie Burke, Basil Rathbone, Fanny Brice, Ethel Barrymore, and Miriam Hopkins appeared on its stage. Its notable productions include *Born Yesterday* (February 4, 1946), *Gentlemen Prefer Blondes* (April 10, 1995), and *Macbeth* (April 8, 2008).

MAJESTIC (245 W. 44th St., opened 1927, seats 1,645). Given landmark status in 1987, the Majestic was intended as a musical theatre from the outset and remains a premier Broadway musical house. The opening production was *Rufus Le Maire's Affairs* (March 28, 1927). Built for Irwin Chanin, he lost control during the Depression, and the theatre became the property of the Shuberts. In 1928, John Gielgud made his Broadway debut there in *The Patriot. Carousel* was a hit in 1945. In 1949, Mary Martin and Ezio Pinza enchanted the audience with Pulitzer Prize winner *South Pacific. The Music Man*, with Robert Preston, was the feature in 1957, as was the Tony-winning musical *The Wiz* in 1975. *Phantom of the Opera* began its phenomenal run in 1988.

   Golden Age musicals: *Dream with Music*, 5/18/44; *Carousel*, 4/19/45; *Allegro*, 10/10/47; *South Pacific*, 4/7/49; *Me and Juliet*, 5/28/53; *By the Beautiful Sea*, 4/8/54; *Fanny*, 11/4/54; *Happy Hunting*, 12/6/56; *The Music Man*, 12/19/57; *Camelot*, 12/3/60; *Hot Spot*, 4/19/63; *Jennie*, 10/17/63; *Anyone Can Whistle*, 4/4/64; *Golden Boy*, 10/20/64

MARK HELLINGER (237 W. 51st Street, opened 1930 as the Warner Bros. Hollywood theatre, seats 1,506). Built as a movie house, the stage was large enough for live performances, the first being Martha Raye in *Calling All Stars* (1934). It was renamed the 51st Street Theatre in 1940, and in 1948 it was renamed to honor Broadway journalist Mark Hellinger, who died that year. The biggest smash hit at the Hellinger was *My Fair Lady*, which ran for a total of 2,717 performances (1956–1962). The Nederlander group bought the theatre in 1970, and it continued to showcase musicals, most of which were unsuccessful. The building was sold in 1991 to the Times Square Church, which has kept most of the original interior décor and invites the public for tours.

   Golden Age musicals: *Texas, Li'l Darlin'*, 11/25/49; *Three Wishes for Jamie*, 3/21/52; *Hazel Flagg*, 2/11/53; *The Girl in Pink Tights*, 3/3/54; *Hit the Trail*, 12/2/54; *Plain and Fancy*, 1/27/55; *Ankles Aweigh*, 4/18/55; *My Fair Lady*, 3/15/56; *Fade Out—Fade In*, 5/26/64; *On a Clear Day You Can See Forever*, 10/17/65

MARQUIS (1535 Broadway, opened 1986, seats 1,611). One of Broadway's newer theatres, the Marquis has showcased a series of hit musicals, including *Me and My Girl* (August 10, 1986), *Gypsy* (April 28, 1991), *Damn Yankees* (March 3, 1994), *Peter Pan* (November 23, 1998), and *Thoroughly Modern Millie* (April 18, 2002). It is located inside the Marriott Marquis Hotel.

MINSKOFF (1515 Broadway, opened 1973, seats 1,597). Broadway producer Jerome Minskoff joined the real estate firm of his father, Sam

Minskoff, and in 1966, the company bought the old Astor Hotel in Times Square. A fifty-four-story office tower was erected on the site, and in 1973, the Minskoff opened in the building. Its first production was a hit revival of *Irene* (March 13, 1973), with Debbie Reynolds.

MUSIC BOX (239 W. 45th St., opened 1921, seats 1,009). The Music Box was built for Irving Berlin's *Music Box Revues*, the first production being *Music Box Revue of 1921*. The revues continued until 1924, with Robert Benchley making his stage debut in 1923. The theatre was given landmark status in 1987. The team of George S. Kaufman and Moss Hart had a string of hits in this theatre in the 1930s. *Of Thee I Sing* (December 26, 1931) was the first musical to win the Pulitzer Prize, and it helped to keep the theatre alive during the Depression years. In the 1950s, William Inge enjoyed success with *Picnic* (February 19, 1953), *Bus Stop* (March 2, 1955), and *The Dark at the Top of the Stairs* (December 5, 1957). *Side by Side by Sondheim* was featured there in 1977, and Christopher Plummer won a Tony for *Barrymore* in 1997.

   Golden Age musical: *Lost in the Stars*, 10/30/49

NEDERLANDER (208 W. 41st St., opened 1921 as the National, seats 1,232). Over the years, this theatre has been known as the National, the Billy Rose, and the Trafalgar. Since 1980, it honors the name of the well-known theatre family. In its list of successful productions are *Cyrano de Bergerac* (November 1, 1923), *Julius Caesar* (March 1, 1938), *King Lear* (December 25, 1950), *Who's Afraid of Virginia Woolf?* (October 13, 1962), and *Private Lives* (December 4, 1969). Lena Horn won a Special Tony Award for her role in *The Lady and Her Music* (May 12, 1981, 333 performances).

   Golden Age musicals: As the National: *The Day before Spring*, 11/22/45; *Hold It!*, 5/5/48; *Courtin' Time*, 6/13/51; *Maggie*, 2/18/53. As the Billy Rose: *A Family Affair*, 1/27/62

NEIL SIMON (250 W. 52nd St., opened 1927 as the Alvin, seats 1,445). This musical comedy house was built for producers Alex Aarons and Vinton Freedly, hence the "Al" and "Vin" that made up the original name. Its opening production featured Fred and Adele Astaire in *Funny Face* (November 22, 1927). After the owners lost control in the Depression year of 1932, the theatre was used as a radio studio by CBS until the mid-1940s, when it returned to legitimate use. It was bought by the Shubert Organization in 1975 and renamed in 1983 for the playwright during the production of his *Brighton Beach Memoirs* (March 27, 1983). The theatre was designated a landmark in 1985. Among its memorable performances are Ethel Merman singing "I've Got Rhythm" in 1930; Alfred Lunt and Lynn Fontanne in the Pulitzer Prize winner *There Shall Be No Night* in 1940; Andy Griffith in *No Time for Sergeants* in 1955; Beatrice Lillie in her last Broadway show, *High Spirits*, in 1964; and a revival of *The King and I* in 1996.

Golden Age musicals: As the Alvin: *Jackpot*, 1/13/44; *Sadie Thompson*, 11/16/44; *Billion Dollar Baby*, 12/21/45; *A Tree Grows in Brooklyn*, 4/19/51; *The Golden Apple*, 3/11/54; *House of Flowers*, 12/30/54; *Rumple*, 11/6/57; *Oh Captain!*, 2/4/58; *First Impressions*, 3/19/59; *Greenwillow*, 3/8/60; *Wildcat*, 12/16/60; *A Funny Thing Happened on the Way to the Forum*, 5/8/62; *High Spirits*, 4/7/64; *Flora, the Red Menace*, 5/11/65

NEW AMSTERDAM (214 W. 42nd St., opened 1903, seats 1,745). The New Amsterdam is one of Broadway's oldest surviving legitimate theatres, achieving landmark status in 1982. The opening production was *Midsummer Nights Dream* (November 2, 1903). From 1913 through 1927, Florenz Ziegfeld staged his follies at the theatre, as well as other reviews. In 1937, the building was converted into a movie house. The house was bought by the Nederlander Organization, but plans to return it to theatre use were constantly delayed. In 1992, the state of New York bought the New Amsterdam and sold it to the Walt Disney Company for $29 million. It was finally reconstructed in 1997. One of its greatest hits was *The Lion King*, which opened in 1998.

NEW CENTURY (932 Seventh Ave., opened as Jolson's 59th Street Theatre, seats 1,700). Originally named by the Shuberts, the theatre underwent several name changes over the years, including the Shakespeare and the Molly Picon. It was twice restored to its original name before becoming the New Century in 1944. Used for live television programs in the early 1950s, it was closed in 1954 and torn down in 1962.

Golden Age musicals: As the 59th St. Theatre: *Buttrio Square*, 10/14/52. As the New Century: *Follow the Girls*, 4/8/44; *Are You with It?*, 11/10/45; *Louisiana Lady*, 6/2/47; *High Button Shoes*, 10/9/47; *Heaven on Earth*, 9/16/48; *Kiss Me, Kate*, 12/30/48; *Carnival in Flanders*, 9/8/53

PALACE (1564 Broadway, opened 1913, seats 1,740). In the early years of Broadway, with its policy of just two shows a day, it was supposedly every variety actors dream to "play the Palace." It meant he or she had reached the top. Built by Martin Beck, it was for many years the preeminent vaudeville theatre in the country. Ed Wynn headlined the opening performance on March 24, 1913, and Ethel Barrymore appeared later in the year. Kate Smith had an eleven-week run in 1931. The highlight of the 1950s was the appearance of Judy Garland on its stage. The Nederlanders turned it into a legitimate theatre in 1965, and since then the who's who of the entertainment world have appeared there. Joel Grey starred in *George M!* in 1968, and Gene Barry in *La Cage aux Folles* had a run of 1, 176 performances in 1983. In the 1980s, a huge hotel was built over the theatre, so that today only its marquee is visible. The Palace also has an infamous side. Nearly every seat in its enormous second balcony has an obstructed view.

RICHARD RODGERS (226 W. 46th St., opened 1924 as Chanin's 46th Street Theatre, seats 1,319). The opening production was *Greenwich Village Follies* (December 24, 1924). Owner Irwin Chanin leased the building to the Shuberts soon after its opening. The Shuberts bought it in 1931 and called it the 46th Street Theatre. Its long-running productions include *Du Barry Was a Lady* (December 6, 1939), *Finian's Rainbow* (January 10, 1947), *Guys and Dolls* (November 24, 1950), and *Damn Yankees* (May 5, 1955). The Nederlander Organization bought it in 1982 and renamed it in honor of the great Broadway composer on March 27, 1990. This theatre was the first to use Chanin's so-called democratic seating plan. In earlier years, patrons who bought expensive seats had a different entrance from those who bought the cheap seats. Now, everyone entered through the same door. Among other notable productions are *How to Succeed in Business without Really Trying* (October 14, 1961), *Chicago* (June 3, 1975; November 14, 1996), *Footloose* (October 22, 1998), and *Movin' Out* (October 24, 2002).

    Golden Age musicals: As the 46th Street: *Finian's Rainbow*, 1/10/47; *Love Life*, 10/7/48; *Guys and Dolls*, 11/10/50; *Damn Yankees*, 5/5/55; *New Girl in Town*, 5/14/57; *Redhead*, 2/5/59; *Tenderloin*, 10/17/60; *Donnybrook!*, 5/18/61; *How to Succeed in Business without Really Trying*, 10/14/61; *Do I Hear a Waltz?*, 3/18/65; *Pickwick*, 10/4/65

SAM S. SHUBERT (225 W. 44th St., opened 1913, seats 1,460). Named after one of the three brothers of the theatrical producing family, it opened on October 21, 1913, with a series of Shakespeare's plays. The theatre shares a façade with the adjoining Booth, which connects to it by a private sidewalk known as Shubert's Alley. The top floor of the building is home to the Shubert Organization offices. The Shubert is a New York City landmark; its auditorium and murals were restored in 1996. The theatre has been home to many hits through the years, its most spectacular being *A Chorus Line*, which began on July 25, 1975, and ran for fifteen years for 6,137 performances.

    Golden Age musicals: *Bloomer Girl*, 10/5/44; *Park Avenue*, 11/4/46; *Paint Your Wagon*, 11/12/51; *Can-Can*, 5/7/53; *The Roar of the Greasepaint—The Smell of the Crowd*, 5/16/55; *Pipe Dream*, 11/30/55; *Bells Are*

Ringing, 11/29/56; *Whoop-Up*, 12/22/58; *Take Me Along*, 10/22/59; *The Gay Life*, 11/18/61; *I Can Get It for You Wholesale*, 3/22/62; *Stop the World—I Want to Get Off*, 10/3/62; *Here's Love*, 10/3/63; *Bajour*, 11/23/64

ST. JAMES (246 W. 44th St., opened 1927 as the Erlanger, seats 1,623). Built by producer Abraham L. Erlanger on the site of the original Sardi's restaurant, the theatre's first production was *The Merry Malones* (September 25, 1927). After Erlanger's death in 1930, control went to the Astor family, who actually owned the land under the building, and it was given its present name. William McKnight got it in 1957 after winning an antitrust case. It was renovated and reopened in 1958. Among its notable productions are *L'il Abner* (November 15, 1956), *Hello, Dolly!* (January 16, 1964), *Barnum* (April 30, 1980), and *Gypsy* (March 27, 2008). On March 31, 1943, *Oklahoma!* began its string of 2,212 performances. It was the first Richard Rodgers and Oscar Hammerstein musical on Broadway, the first Broadway show for choreographer Agnes de Mille, and the first Broadway musical for Celeste Holm.

   Golden Age musicals: *Oklahoma!*, 3/31/43; *Sleepy Hollow*, 6/3/48; *Where's Charley?*, 10/11/48; *The King and I*, 3/29/51; *The Pajama Game*, 5/13/54; *L'il Abner*, 11/15/56; *Flower Drum Song*, 12/1/58; *Do Re Mi*, 12/26/60; *Subways Are for Sleeping*, 12/27/61; *Mr. President*, 10/20/62; *Hello, Dolly!*, 1/16/64

STEPHEN SONDHEIM (124 W. 43rd St., opened 1918 as Henry Miller's, seats 1,055). Originally named for actor-producer Henry Miller, it was the first air-conditioned theatre in Manhattan. The first hit show was Noel Coward's *The Vortex* (September 16, 1925). From then until the 1960s, such stars as Helen Hayes, Lillian Gish, and Douglas Fairbanks appeared on stage. Sold in 1968, it became a porn theatre, then a discotheque, and returned to a legitimate theatre as the Kit Kat Club in 1998. With the opening of *Urinetown* on September 20, 2001, it was once again named for Henry Miller. It closed in 2004 and given a new interior. In March 2010, it was named to honor composer and lyricist Stephen Sondheim.

   Golden Age musical: As Henry Miller's: *The Nervous Set*, 5/12/59

VIVIAN BEAUMONT (Lincoln Center, 150 W. 65th St., opened 1965, seats 1,080). The only Broadway-class theatre not in the theatre district, it is named for Vivian Beaumont Allen, former actress and heiress to the May Department Stores. It differs from most other Broadway theatres because of its thrust stage (one of only two legit Broadway houses with a thrust stage, the other being at the Circle at the Square) and amphitheatre configuration. Operated by Lincoln Center Theater since 1985, it was the site of such notable productions as the 1994 Tony Award revival of *Carousel* (March 24, 1994) and the 2008 revival of *South Pacific* (April 3, 2008).

WALTER KERR (219 W. 48th St., opened 1921 as the Ritz, seats 945). The building was constructed in 1921 in a record sixty days, built by the Shuberts as a sister theatre to the Ambassador on West 49th. It opened with Clare Eames on March 21, 1921, in John Drinkwater's *Mary Stuart*. Katherine Cornell appeared in 1923 in *The Enchanted Cottage* (March 31, 1923) and Claudette Colbert in *The Kiss in a Taxi* (August 25, 1925). That decade ended with the appearance of a young actress named Bette Davis in *Broken Dishes* (November 5, 1929). Soon afterward, David left for Hollywood. From that time onward, the theatre was occasionally used for live radio shows but went completely legitimate in 1971 with a rock opera called *Soon* (January 12, 1971). The Ritz underwent a major renovation and reopened in May 1983. In 1990, it was renamed for Broadway theatre critic and writer Walter Kerr (1913–1996). The opening production was *The Piano Lesson* (April 16, 1990), which won August Wilson Pulitzer and New York Drama Critics awards for best play.

WINTER GARDEN (1634 Broadway, opened 1911, seats, 1,526). The fourth New York venue to be called the Winter Garden, it opened with Jerome Kern's *La Belle Paree* (March 10, 1911). It was originally built by William Vanderbilt in 1896, who wanted it as the American Horse Exchange. The Shuberts leased it in 1911 as a legitimate theatre, and it was completely remodeled in 1922. From 1928 through 1933, it was used as a movie studio, but after that it remained a live theatre house. In 2002, it was renamed the Cadillac Winter Garden, but the name was changed back to its present one in 2007. The longest-running show in the Winter Garden was *Cats*, which ran for 7,485 performances over a span of almost nineteen years, beginning October 7, 1982. To accommodate a junkyard scene, the entire auditorium had to be gutted. After the show closed, the auditorium was restored to its 1920s appearance.

    Golden Age musicals: *Mexican Hayride*, 1/28/44; *As the Girls Go*, 11/13/48; *Great to Be Alive*, 3/23/50; *Make a Wish*, 4/18/51; *Top Banana*, 11/1/51; *My Darling Aida*, 10/27/52; *Wonderful Town*, 2/25/53; *Peter Pan*, 10/20/54; *The Vamp*, 11/10/55; *Shangri-La*, 6/13/56; *West Side Story*, 9/26/57; *Juno*, 3/9/59; *Saratoga*, 12/7/59; *The Unsinkable Mollie Brown*, 11/3/60; *Nowhere to Go but Up*, 11/10/62; *Sophie*, 4/15/63; *Funny Girl*, 3/26/64

ZIEGFELD (141 W. 54th St., opened 1927, seats 1,660). Named for impresario Florenz Ziegfeld, the theatre opened on February 2, 1927, with

Rio Rita, to be followed by the landmark musical *Show Boat*, which opened on December 27, 1927. During the Depression, the building was also a movie house and later a television studio. It was torn down in 1966 to make room for a skyscraper. The box taken from the cornerstone is in the New York Public Library's Billy Rose Theater Collection.

Golden Age musicals: *Brigadoon*, 3/13/47; *Magdalena*, 9/20/48; *Gentlemen Prefer Blondes*, 12/8/49; *Kismet*, 12/3/53; *Foxy*, 2/16/64

⑦

THE AWARDS OF BROADWAY

To recognize and reward excellence in the theatre, a number of awards are given each year in several categories including Best Musical, Best Actor or Actress, Best Direction, and more. Some honor Broadway productions and some cite Off-Broadway or touring companies and other categories.

DRAMA DESK. Created in 1955, the Drama Desk Awards recognize Broadway productions as well as those produced Off-Broadway, Off-Off-Broadway, and in legitimate not-for-profit theatres. They were originally known as the Vernon Rice Awards named for the theatre critic of the *New York Post*. The name was changed in 1963. This award is often a boost to stardom, as was the case for Sada Thompson (*Misanthrope*, 1957) and Dustin Hoffman (*Eh?*, 1966). After receiving the award, such productions as *Driving Miss Daisy* and *Steel Magnolias* gained international spotlight. The Drama Desk is made up of theatre critics, editors, and writers. The award is given each year at LaGuardia Concert Hall at Fiorello H. LaGuardia High School of Music and Art and Performing Arts in Lincoln Center.

NEW YORK DRAMA CRITICS' CIRCLE. The oldest American theatre award, after the Pulitzer Prize for Drama, this annual citation honors the best play of the season, with added awards for musicals and foreign plays. It carries with it a cash prize of $2,500 to the playwright. The New York Drama Critics' Circle is made up of twenty-two drama critics from newspapers, magazines, and wire services based in New York City, excluding critics from the *Times*, who are nonvoting members. The organization was founded in 1935 at the Algonquin Hotel by a group including Brooks Atkinson and Walter Winchell. It honored as best musical *Carousel* in 1946, *Fiorello!* in 1960, and *Hairspray* in 2003.

Citation for Best Musical of the Golden Age: 1946–1947: *Brigadoon*; **1948–1949:** *South Pacific*; **1950–1951:** *Guys and Dolls*; **1952–1953:** *Wonderful Town*; **1953–1954:** *The Golden Apple*; **1955–1956:** *My Fair Lady*; **1956–1957:** *The Most Happy Fella*; **1957–1958:** *The Music Man*; **1959–1960:** *Fiorello!*; **1960–1961:** *Carnival*; **1961–1962:** *How to Succeed in Business without Really Trying*; **1963–1964:** *Hello, Dolly!*; **1964–1965:** *Fiddler on the Roof*

OBIE. The *Village Voice* newspaper annually bestows this award to Off-Broadway and Off-Off-Broadway artists, similar to the Tony Awards for on Broadway. First given in 1956 and initiated by Edwin Fancher, *Village Voice* publisher, they included only Off-Broadway but were later expanded to Off-Off-Broadway. There are no fixed categories and no listed nominations and not every category is awarded each year.

PULITZER PRIZE FOR DRAMA. Since 1917, Columbia University, in New York City, has awarded annual prizes for achievement in American journalism, letters, and music. The prizes were originally endowed with a $500,000 gift from newspaper editor and publisher Joseph Pulitzer (1847–1911). Since 1918, a Pulitzer Prize has been awarded for drama.

Golden Age winners: 1950: *South Pacific*; **1960:** *Fiorello!*; **1962:** *How to Succeed in Business without Really Trying*

THEATRE WORLD. Since the 1945–1946 season, the Theatre World Award recognizes actors in outstanding Broadway and Off-Broadway productions. The winners are chosen by a committee of New York–based critics, including writers for New York newspapers and *Playbill*. The awards are traditionally presented annually by former winners, including Carol Channing, Grace Kelly, Meryl Streep, Richard Burton, Laurence Harvey, and Anthony Perkins. The award itself is a bronze sculpture known as Janus after the Roman god of entrances, exits, and all beginnings.

Golden Age winners: 1944–1945: Betty Comden, *On the Town*; Bambi Linn and John Raitt, *Carousel*. **1945–1946:** Patricia Marshall, *The Day Before Spring*. **1946–1947:** Marion Bell, George Keane, and James Mitchell, *Brigadoon*; Ann Crowley, *Carousel*; Ellen Hanley, *Barefoot Boy with Cheek*; Dorothea MacFarland, *Oklahoma!*; David Wayne, *Finian's Rainbow*. **1947–1948:** Mark Dawson, *High Button Shoes*; Patricia Wymore, *Hold It!*. **1948–1949:** Mary McCarty, *Sleepy Hollow*; Allyn

Ann McLerie and Byron Palmer, *Where's Charley?* **1949–1950:** Marcia Henderson, *Peter Pan.* **1950–1951:** Isabel Bigley, *Guys and Dolls*; Russell Nype, *Call Me Madam.* **1951–1952:** Tony Bavaar, *Paint Your Wagon*; Peter Conlow, *Courtin' Time*; Dick Kallman and Helen Wood, *Seventeen.* **1952–1953:** Edie Adams, *Wonderful Town*; Sheree North, *Hazel Flagg*; Gwen Verdon, *Can-Can.* **1953–1954:** Joan Diener, *Kismet*; Carol Haney, *The Pajama Game*; Jonathan Lucas, *The Golden Apple.* **1954–1955:** Julie Andrews, *The Boy Friend*; Shirl Conway, Barbara Cook, and David Daniels, *Plain and Fancy.* **1955–1956:** Susan Johnson, *The Most Happy Fella*; John Michael King, *My Fair Lady.* **1956–1957:** Sydney Chaplin, *Bells Are Ringing*; Peter Palmer, *L'il Abner.* **1957–1958:** Eddie Hodges and Wynne Miller, *The Music Man*; Carol Lawrence, *West Side Story*; Jacqueline McKeever, *Oh Captain!*; Robert Morse, *Say, Darling.* **1958–1959:** Pat Suzuki, *Flower Drum Song.* **1959–1960:** Carol Burnett, *Once Upon a Mattress*; Lauri Peters, *The Sound of Music.* **1960–1961:** Nancy Dussault, *Do Re Mi*; Robert Goulet, *Camelot*; Ron Husmann, *Tenderloin*; Bruce Yarnell, *The Happiest Girl in the World.* **1961–1962:** Elizabeth Ashley, *Take Her, She's Mine.* **1962–1963:** Dorothy Louden, *Nowhere to Go but Up*; Swen Swenson, *Little Me.* **1963–1964:** Alan Alda, *Fair Game for Lovers.* **1964–1965:** Joyce Jillson, *The Roar of the Greasepaint—The Smell of the Crowd*; Victor Spinetti, *Oh! What a Lovely War.* **1965–1966:** John Cullum, *On a Clear Day You Can See Forever*; John Davidson, *Oklahoma!*; Leslie Ann Warren, *Drat! The Cat!*.

TONY (Antoinette Perry Awards for Excellence in Theatre). The Tony Awards, founded in 1947, are the American theatre's highest honor, similar to the Academy Awards for motion pictures and the Olivier Award in British theatre. They recognize achievement in live American theatre and are presented annually. They honor Broadway productions and performances, and, in addition, there are Special Tony Awards (including Lifetime Achievement) and Tony Honors for Excellence in the Theatre. The Tonys are named after Antoinette Perry, actor, director, producer, and wartime leader of the American Theatre Wing, which, along with the Broadway League, presents the awards. The award itself is a medallion. The first awards ceremony was held on April 6, 1947, at the Waldorf Astoria hotel in New York City, but the medallion was not actually given to winners until the third ceremony, in 1949.

The American Theatre Wing, originally part of the World War II Allied Relief Fund, was founded in 1939 by a group of theatrical women, including Perry, who were theatre actors and/or patrons. They were dedicated to supporting excellence and education in the theatre. The American Theatre Wing also established the Stage Door Canteen to entertain U.S. servicemen during World War II.

A panel of some 700 judges from all areas of the entertainment industry and press selects Tony winners. The awards, only for productions in the thirty-nine Broadway theatres, cover twenty-seven categories from Best Play to Best Performance by a Leading Actor to Best Choreography to Best Costume Design to Best Sound Design of a Musical (added in 2008). To be eligible, a production must open within the dates specified each year by the Management Committee. For example, the cutoff date for the 2007–2008 season was May 7, 2008. To win a Tony, a "new" play or musical must not have previously been produced on Broadway; however, shows recently transferred from Off-Broadway are regarded as new productions, as are those based closely on films. The rules for the awards are contained in the Rules and Regulations of The American Theatre Wing's Tony Awards. They apply only to the current season.

Top Golden Age winners: 1949: Musical: *Kiss Me, Kate*; Actor: Ray Bolger, *Where's Charley?*; Actress: Nanette Fabray, *Love Life*; Music/Lyrics: Cole Porter, *Kiss Me, Kate*; Choreography: Gower Champion, *Lend an Ear* (a revue). **1950:** Musical: *South Pacific*; Actor: Ezio Pinza, *South Pacific*; Actress: Mary Martin, *South Pacific*; Music: Richard Rodgers, *South Pacific*; Lyrics: Oscar Hammerstein II, *South Pacific*; Choreography: Helen Tamiris, *Touch and Go*. **1951:** Musical: *Guys and Dolls*; Actor: Robert Alda, *Guys and Dolls*; Actress: Ethel Merman, *Call Me Madam*; Music/Lyrics: Frank Loesser, *Guys and Dolls*; Choreographer: Michael Kidd, *Guys and Dolls*. **1952:** Musical: *The King and I*; Actor: Phil Silvers, *Top Banana*; Actress: Gertrude Lawrence, *The King and I*. Choreographer: Robert Alton, *Pal Joey*. **1953:** Musical: *Wonderful Town*; Actor: Thomas Mitchell, *Hazel Flagg*; Actress: Rosalind Russell, *Wonderful Town*; Music: Leonard Bernstein, *Wonderful Town*; Choreographer: Donald Saddler, *Wonderful Town*. **1954:** Musical: *Kismet*; Actor: Alfred Drake, *Kismet*; Actress: Dolores Gray, *Carnival in Flanders*; Music: Aleksandr Borodin, *Kismet*; Choreographer: Michael Kidd, *Can-Can*. **1955:** Musical: *The Pajama Game*; Actor: Walter Slezak, *Fanny*; Actress: Mary Martin, *Peter Pan*; Music/Lyrics: Richard Adler and Jerry Ross, *The Pajama Game*; Choreographer: Bob Fosse, *The Pajama Game*. **1956:** Musical: *Damn Yankees*; Actor: Ray Walston, *Damn Yankees*; Actress: Gwen Verdon, *Damn Yankees*; Music/Lyrics: Richard Adler and Jerry Ross, *Damn Yankees*; Choreographer: Bob Fosse, *Damn Yankees*. **1957:** Musical: *My Fair Lady*; Actor: Rex Harrison, *My Fair Lady*; Actress: July Holliday, *Bells Are Ringing*; Music: Frederick Loewe, *My Fair Lady*; Lyrics: Alan Jay Lerner, *My Fair Lady*; Choreographer: Michael Kidd, *Lil Abner*. **1958:** Musical: *The Music Man*; Actor: Robert Preston, *The Music Man*; Actress: Thelma Ritter and Gwen Verdon (tie), *New Girl in Town*; Music/Lyrics: Meredith Willson, *The Music Man*. **1959:** Musical: *Redhead*; Actor: Richard Kiley, *Redhead*; Actress:

Gwen Verdon, *Redhead*; Music: Albert Hague, *Redhead*; Choreographer: Bob Fosse, *Redhead*. **1960:** Musical: *Fiorello!* and *The Sound of Music* (tie); Actor: Jackie Gleason, *Take Me Along*; Actress: Mary Martin, *The Sound of Music*; Music: Jerry Bock, *Fiorello!*, and Richard Rodgers, *The Sound of Music* (tie); Choreographer: Michael Kidd, *Destry Rides Again*. **1961:** Musical: *Bye Bye Birdie*; Actor: Richard Burton, *Camelot*; Actress: Elizabeth Seal, *Irma la Douce*; Music. **1962:** Musical: *How to Succeed in Business without Really Trying*; Actor: Robert Morse, *How to Succeed in Business without Really Trying*; Actress: Anna Maria Alberghetti, *Carnival*, and Diahann Carroll, *No Strings* (tie); Music: Richard Rodgers, *No Strings*; Choreographers; Agnes de Mille, *Kwamina*, and Joe Layton, *No Strings*. **1963:** Musical: *A Funny Thing Happened on the Way to the Forum*; Actor: Zero Mostel, *A Funny Thing Happened on the Way to the Forum*; Actress: Vivien Leigh, *Tovarich*; Music/Lyrics: Lionel Bart, *Oliver!*; Choreographer: Bob Fosse, *Little Me*. **1964:** Musical: *Hello, Dolly!*; Actor: Bert Lahr, *Foxy*; Actress: Carol Channing, *Hello, Dolly!*. **1965:** Musical: *Fiddler on the Roof*; Actor: Zero Mostel, *Fiddler on the Roof*; Actress: Liza Minnelli, *Flora, the Red Menace*; Music, Lyrics: Jerry Bock and Sheldon Harnick, *Fiddler on the Roof*; Choreographer: Jerome Robbins, *Fiddler on the Roof*.

TOURING BROADWAY. Previously known as the National Broadway Theatre Awards, they celebrate excellence in touring Broadway by recognizing both the productions and artists that perform in as many as 140 cities across North America. They are the only national awards for touring shows from Broadway. The award is chosen annually by fans of Broadway.

APPENDIX OF SHOW TUNES

Title	Musical
Abbondanza	The Most Happy Fella
The A.B.C. Song	Stop the World—I Want to Get Off
Abracadabra	Mexican Hayride
Addie's at It Again	I Had a Ball
Adelaide's Lament	Guys and Dolls
Adventure	Do Re Mi
Affable Balding Me	Texas, Li'l Darlin'
After All, It's Spring	Seventeen
Ain't It the Truth	Jamaica
All American	Stop the World—I Want to Get Off
All at Once You Love Her	Pipe Dream
Allegro	Allegro
All 'er Nothin'	Oklahoma!
All for Him	Paint Your Wagon
All for You	Tovarich
All I Need Is the Girl	Gypsy
All in the Cause of Economy	Half a Sixpence
All Kinds of People	Pipe Dream
All of My Life	Do Re Mi
All of You	Silk Stockings
All the Time	Oh Captain!
All You Need Is a Quarter	Do Re Mi
Almost	I Had a Ball
Almost Like Being in Love	Brigadoon

Alone Too Long
Always, Always You
Always True to You (in My Fashion)
Ambition
America
American Cannes
Anatevka
And This Is My Beloved
An English Teacher
Anna Lilla
Another Autumn
Another Hot Day
Another O'p'nin, Another Show
Anyone Who's Who
Anyone Would Love You
The Apaches
Aren't You Glad?
Are You Ready, Gyp Watson?
Are You Sure?
Are You with It?
Arm in Arm
The Army of the Just
Artificial Flowers
Asking for You
As the Girls Go
As Long as He Needs Me
As on Through the Seasons We
   Sail
As Simple As That
At the Spotlight Canteen
The Audition

Baby
Baby June and Her Newsboys
Bad Companions
Bad Timing
Bajour
Bali Ha'i
Ballad of the Garment Trade
Ballad of the Gun
A Balloon Is Ascending
Bamboo Cage
Bargaining
The Battle
Baubles, Bangles, and Beads
Be a Performer
Be a Santa

By the Beautiful Sea
Carnival
Kiss Me, Kate
Do Re Mi
West Side Story
As the Girls Go
Fiddler on the Roof
Kismet
Bye Bye Birdie
New Girl in Town
Paint Your Wagon
110 in the Shade
Kiss Me, Kate
Happy Hunting
Destry Rides Again
Can-Can
The Most Happy Fella
Destry Rides Again
The Unsinkable Molly Brown
Are You with It?
Here's Love
Tenderloin
Tenderloin
Do Re Mi
As the Girls Go
Oliver!
Silk Stockings

Milk and Honey
Follow the Girls
Mr. Wonderful

Bye Bye Birdie
Gypsy
Goldilocks
Billion Dollar Baby
Bajour
South Pacific
I Can Get It for You Wholesale
Destry Rides Again
Ben Franklin in Paris
House of Flowers
Do I Hear a Waltz?
Peter Pan
Kismet
Little Me
Subways Are for Sleeping

The Beast in You
Beatnik Love Affair
Beat Out Dat Rhythm on a Drum
Beautiful Candy
The Beautiful Land

Be Back Soon
Been a Long Day

Before I Gaze at You Again
Before the Parade Passes By
The Begat
Behave Yourself
Be Kind to Your Parents
Bells Are Ringing
Belly Up to the Bar
Be My Host
Benvenuta
The Best Thing for You Would
   Be Me
Better Get Out of Here
Better Than a Dream
Bianca
The Bicycle Song
The Big Black Giant
Big D
Big Mole
The Big Movie Show in the Sky
Bikini Dance
A Bird of Passage
Bird Watchers Song
Birthday Party
Birthday Song
Bless This Land
Blondo
Bloody Mary
Blow High
Bonjour
Boom Boom
Bottleneck
Boy for Sale
The Boy Friend
A Boy Like That
Boys, Boys, Boys
The Bridge of Caulaincourt
Brigadoon
Bright College Days

Goldilocks
Sail Away
Carmen Jones
Carnival
The Roar of the Greasepaint—The
   Smell of the Crowd
Oliver!
How to Succeed in Business
   without Really Trying
Camelot
Hello, Dolly!
Finian's Rainbow
Redhead
Fanny
Bells Are Ringing
The Unsinkable Molly Brown
No Strings
The Most Happy Fella
Call Me Madam

Where's Charley?
Bells Are Ringing
Kiss Me, Kate
High Spirits
Me and Juliet
The Most Happy Fella
Lost in the Stars
Texas, Li'l Darlin'
Happy Hunting
Lost in the Stars
High Button Shoes
Little Me
Fanny
Tenderloin
Goldilocks
South Pacific
Carousel
The Unsinkable Molly Brown
Little Me
Destry Rides Again
Oliver!
The Boy Friend
West Side Story
I Had a Ball
Irma La Douce
Brigadoon
Wish You Were Here

Brighten Up and Be a Little Sunbeam	As the Girls Go
Bring Me My Bride	A Funny Thing Happened on the Way to the Forum
Broadway Blossom	Billion Dollar Baby
Brotherhood of Man	How to Succeed in Business without Really Trying
Brunette	Goldilocks
Brush Up Your Shakespeare	Kiss Me, Kate
The Bugle	Here's Love
The Bum One	Fiorello!
Bums Opera	Pipe Dream
A Bushel and a Peck	Guys and Dolls
But	Irma La Douce
Button Up with Esmond	Gentlemen Prefer Blondes
But Yours	Take Me Along
Bye Bye Baby	Gentlemen Prefer Blondes
Call Me Savage	Fade Out—Fade In
Calypso	The Golden Apple
Camelot	Camelot
Camp Karefree	Wish You Were Here
Can-Can	Can-Can
Can It Be Possible?	I Had a Ball
Can't You Just See Yourself in Love with Me?	High Button Shoes
Can't You See It?	Golden Boy
Can You Use Any Money Today?	Call Me Madam
Captain Henry St. James	Oh Captain!
Carino Mio	Paint Your Wagon
Carlotta	Mexican Hayride
Carnival Ballet	Carnival
The Carnival Song	Say, Darling
Carried Away	On the Town
Castle Walk	High Button Shoes
Certain Individuals	Wish You Were Here
C'est Magnifique	Can-Can
Charleston	Billion Dollar Baby
Charlie Welch	Mr. Wonderful
The Chase	Brigadoon
Chess and Checkers	New Girl in Town
Chick-a-Pen	The Unsinkable Molly Brown
Chief of Love	Say, Darling
Children's Ballet	Allegro
Chin Up, Ladies	Milk and Honey
Chop Suey	Flower Drum Song

Christmas Child
Christopher Street
The Church Social
Cinderella Darling

Circe, Circe
City Mouse, Country Mouse
Climb Every Mountain
Close Harmony
Cockeyed Optimist
Cocoanut Sweet
The Code
Coffee Break

Cold, Clear World
Cold Cream Jar Song
Colorful
Come Along, Boys
Come Along with Me
Come and Be My Butterfly
Come Back to Me

Comedy Tonight

Come Home
Comes Once in a Lifetime
Come to Me
Come to Me, Bend to Me
Come Up to My Place
The Company Way

Coney Island Boat
Coney Island, U.S.A.
Conga!
Conquering New York
Consider Yourself
Conversation Piece
Cool
Coquette
Corduroy Road
Cornet Man
Could Be
The Country's in the Very Best
    Hands
Count Your Blessings
Cry the Beloved Country

Irma La Douce
Wonderful Town
The Golden Apple
How to Succeed in Business
    without Really Trying
The Golden Apple
Plain and Fancy
The Sound of Music
Fade Out—Fade In
South Pacific
Jamaica
Ankles Aweigh
How to Succeed in Business
    without Really Trying
Baker Street
Fanny
Golden Boy
The Golden Apple
Can-Can
Hello, Dolly!
On a Clear Day You Can See
    Forever
A Funny Thing Happened on the
    Way to the Forum
Allegro
Subways Are for Sleeping
Sail Away
Brigadoon
On the Town
How to Succeed in Business
    without Really Trying
By the Beautiful Sea
I Had a Ball
Wonderful Town
Wonderful Town
Oliver!
Wonderful Town
West Side Story
Gentlemen Prefer Blondes
Wildcat
Funny Girl
Wish You Were Here
L'il Abner

Mexican Hayride
Lost in the Stars

Cry Like the Wind — Do Re Mi

Dainty June and Her Farmboys Dance — Gypsy
The Dance at the Gym — West Side Story
Dance Only with Me — Say, Darling
Dancing — Hello, Dolly!
The Dangerous Age — Fade Out—Fade In
Dat's Love — Carmen Jones
Dat's Our Man — Carmen Jones
The Day Before Spring — The Day Before Spring
The Day I Do — Wildcat
Days Gone By — She Loves Me
Dear Friend — She Loves Me
Dear Friend — Tenderloin
De Cards Don't Lie — Carmen Jones
Deep Down Inside — Little Me
The Denver Police — The Unsinkable Molly Brown
The Departure of Rhododendron — The Golden Apple
Dere's a Café on de Corner — Carmen Jones
Diamonds Are a Girl's Best Friend — Gentlemen Prefer Blondes
Diane Is — Ben Franklin in Paris
Did You Close Your Eyes? — New Girl in Town
Dimples — Little Me
Direct from Vienna — Carnival
Dis-Donc — Irma La Douce
Dis Flower — Carmen Jones
Distant Melody — Peter Pan
Dites-Moi, Pourquoi? — South Pacific
Does He Know? — Fanny
Dog Is a Man's Best Friend — Top Banana
Do I Hear a Waltz? — Do I Hear a Waltz?
Doin' What Comes Naturally — Annie Get Your Gun
Do It Yourself — Bells Are Ringing
Don Jose — Wish You Were Here
Don't Be Afraid of Romance — Mr. President
Don't Cry — The Most Happy Fella
Don't Forget 127th Street — Golden Boy
Don't Like Goodbyes — House of Flowers
Don't Marry Me — Flower Drum Song
Don't Rain on My Parade — Funny Girl
Don't Tamper with My Sister — On a Clear Day You Can See Forever

Don't Tell Me — Happy Hunting
Don't Turn Away from Love — Sail Away
Doomed, Doomed, Doomed — The Golden Apple
Do-Re-Me — The Sound of Music

Down in the Valley
Down on MacConnachy Square
Do You Love Me?
Dreams Come True
Dr. Brock
Dr. Freud
Drop That Name

Eager Beaver
Eagle and Me
Eat a Little Something
Economics
Elegance
Elevator Song
Eleven O'Clock Song
El Sombrero
The Embassy Waltz
Empty Pockets Filled with Love
Erbie Finch's Twitch
Essie's Vision
Ethel, Baby
Evelina
Everybody Likes You
Everybody Loves Everybody
Everybody Ought to Have a Maid

Everybody's Got a Home but Me
Every Man Is a Stupid Man
Every Once in a While
Every Street's a Boulevard in Old
    New York
Everything Beautiful Happens at
    Night
Everything's Coming Up Roses
Everything's Great
The Exorcism
Expect Things to Happen
Extra, Extra

Fade Out—Fade In
Fair Warning
Fairyland
Faith
Falling Out of Love Can Be Fun
Family Fugue
Family Way
Fancy Forgetting

Texas, Li'l Darlin'
Brigadoon
Fiddler on the Roof
Billion Dollar Baby
Tenderloin
I Had a Ball
Bells Are Ringing

No Strings
Bloomer Girl
I Can Get It for You Wholesale
Love Life
Hello, Dolly!
Top Banana
Ankles Aweigh
Wildcat
My Fair Lady
Mr. President
Redhead
Redhead
Mr. Wonderful
Bloomer Girl
Carnival
Wish You Were Here
A Funny Thing Happened on the
    Way to the Forum
Pipe Dream
Can-Can
Destry Rides Again
Hazel Flagg

110 in the Shade

Gypsy
Golden Boy
High Spirits
Here's Love
Miss Liberty

Fade Out—Fade In
Destry Rides Again
Carnival
I Had a Ball
Miss Liberty
Stop the World—I Want to Get Off
I Can Get It for You Wholesale
The Boy Friend

Fanny

Fan Tan Fannie

Far from the Home I Love

The Farmer and the Cowman

Farmer's Daughter

Faster Than Sound

Fate

Father's Day

Fear

Fear!

Feeling Good

A Fella Needs a Girl

Femininity

Fickle Finger of Fate

The Fiddler and the Fighter

Fie on Goodness!

The Fight

Finaletto

Finding Words for Spring

Find Yourself a Man

Fireworks

The First Lady

Five More Minutes in Bed

Flash Bang Wallop

Flattery

Flings

Follow the Fold

Follow the Girls

Follow Your Heart

Food, Glorious Food

Foolish Heart

Forever and a Day

For Every Fish

For Love or Money

For Sweet Charity

Four O'Clock

Free

The Freedom of the Seas

Freshman Dance

Fresno Beauties

The Friendliest Thing

Friends to the End

From a Prison Cell

From This Day On

Fanny

Flower Drum Song

Fiddler on the Roof

Oklahoma!

Bloomer Girl

High Spirits

Kismet

As the Girls Go

Fade Out—Fade In

Lost in the Stars

The Roar of the Greasepaint—The

   Smell of the Crowd

Allegro

Oh Captain!

I Had a Ball

Fade Out—Fade In

Camelot

Golden Boy

How to Succeed in Business

   without Really Trying

Baker Street

Funny Girl

Do Re Mi

Mr. President

Are You with It?

Half a Sixpence

Wish You Were Here

New Girl in Town

Guys and Dolls

Follow the Girls

Plain and Fancy

Oliver!

One Touch of Venus

High Spirits

Jamaica

Happy Hunting

Take Me Along

Lost in the Stars

A Funny Thing Happened on the

   Way to the Forum

Irma La Douce

Allegro

The Most Happy Fella

What Makes Sammy Run?

The Day Before Spring

Irma La Douce

Brigadoon

Fugue for Tinhorns   Guys and Dolls
A Funny Thing Happened   I Can Get It for You Wholesale

Gaby's Comin'   On the Town
The Game   Damn Yankees
The Game of Love   Happy Hunting
Gary, Indiana   The Music Man
Gee, Officer Krupke   West Side Story
The Gentleman Is a Dope   Allegro
Gentleman Jimmy   Fiorello!
Gentlemen Prefer Blondes   Gentlemen Prefer Blondes
Geraniums in the Winder   Carousel
Gesticulate   Kismet
Get Away for a Day in the Country   High Button Shoes
Get Me to the Church on Time   My Fair Lady
Getting to Know You   The King and I
A Gift Today   I Can Get It for You Wholesale
Gimme Some   Golden Boy
Girls   Mexican Hayride
Girls Like Me   Subways Are for Sleeping
The Girl That I Marry   Annie Get Your Gun
Give It All You Got   Oh Captain!
Give the Little Lady   Goldilocks
Give a Little Whistle   Wildcat
Glad to Be Home   Mr. President
Gliding Through My Memoree   Flower Drum Song
Glorious Russian   Stop the World—I Want to Get
                                               Off
God Bless the Human Elbow   Ben Franklin in Paris
God's Green World   The Day Before Spring
Go Home Train   Fade Out—Fade In
Go into Your Trance   High Spirits
Golden Boy   Golden Boy
Gonna Build a Mountain   Stop the World—I Want to Get
                                               Off
Goodbye, Georg   She Loves Me
Goodbye, Old Girl   Damn Yankees
Good Clean Fun   Tenderloin
Good Morning, Good Day   She Loves Me
Goodnight Ladies   The Music Man
Goodnight, My Someone   The Music Man
Good Time Charlie   By the Beautiful Sea
Goona-Goona   The Golden Apple
Go Slow, Johnny   Sail Away
The Gossips   Where's Charley?
Gotta Dance   Look, Ma, I'm Dancin'!
Grand Imperial Cirque de Paris   Carnival

Grand Knowing You
Grand Old Ivy

Grant Avenue
Green-Up Times
Growing Pains
Guarantees
Guenevere
Guys and Dolls

The Haggie
Hail, Bibinski
Half the Battle
Half a Sixpence
Hand Me Down That Can O Beans
The Happiest House on the Block
Happily Ever After
Happy Birthday, Mrs. J. J. Brown
Happy Habit
Happy Hunting
Happy Talk
Happy to Be
Happy to Keep His Dinner Warm

Has I Let You Down?
Have I Told You Lately?
Havin' a Time
Headin' for the Bottom
Heart
Heart of Stone
The Heather on the Hill
Hector's Song
He Had Refinement
Helen Is Always Willing
Hello, Dolly!
Hello, Hazel
Hello, Hello There!
Hello, Mazurka
Hello, Young Lovers!
Henry Street
Here I Go Again
Here I'll Stay
Here's Love
Here's to Dear Old Us
Here's to Us
Here We Are Again
Her Face

Seventeen
How to Succeed in Business
     without Really Trying
Flower Drum Song
Love Life
A Tree Grows in Brooklyn
Bajour
Camelot
Guys and Dolls

Bajour
Silk Stockings
Ben Franklin in Paris
Half a Sixpence
Paint Your Wagon
Pipe Dream
Once Upon a Mattress
The Unsinkable Molly Brown
By the Beautiful Sea
Happy Hunting
South Pacific
The Most Happy Fella
How to Succeed in Business
     without Really Trying
House of Flowers
I Can Get It for You Wholesale
Billion Dollar Baby
Ankles Aweigh
Damn Yankees
Goldilocks
Brigadoon
The Golden Apple
A Tree Grows in Brooklyn
The Golden Apple
Hello, Dolly!
Hazel Flagg
Bells Are Ringing
Bells Are Ringing
The King and I
Funny Girl
Are You with It?
Love Life
Here's Love
Ankles Aweigh
Little Me
Do I Hear a Waltz?
Carnival

Her Is	The Pajama Game
Hernando's Hideaway	The Pajama Game
The Heroes Come Home	The Golden Apple
He's in Love	Kismet
He's a VIP	Do Re Mi
He Tried to Make a Dollar	High Button Shoes
Hey, Look Me Over	Wildcat
Hey Madame	Oh Captain!
Hey There	The Pajama Game
Hic Haec Hoc	Ben Franklin in Paris
The Highest Judge of All	Carousel
The Hills of Ixopo	Lost in the Stars
His and Hers	Ankles Aweigh
His Love Makes Me Beautiful	Funny Girl
Ho, Bill, O!	Love Life
Holiday in the Country	As the Girls Go
Home Again	Fiorello!
Homesick Blues	Gentlemen Prefer Blondes
Home Sweet Heaven	High Spirits
Homework	Miss Liberty
Honestly Sincere	Bye Bye Birdie
Honest Man	Bajour
Honey Bun	South Pacific
Honeymoon	Ankles Aweigh
Hook's Waltz	Peter Pan
Hoop-de-Dingle	Destry Rides Again
Hooray for George the Third	By the Beautiful Sea
Hootin' Owl Trail	Texas, Li'l Darlin'
Horseshoes Are Lucky	Texas, Li'l Darlin'
The Hosier Way	Seventeen
The Hostess with the Mostest on the Ball	Call Me Madam
House of Flowers	House of Flowers
The House of Marcus Lycus	A Funny Thing Happened on the Way to the Forum
House on Rittenhouse Square	Gentlemen Prefer Blondes
How Are Things in Glocca Morra?	Finian's Rainbow
How Beautiful the Days	The Most Happy Fella
How Can I Wait?	Paint Your Wagon
How Can Love Survive?	The Sound of Music
How Can You Describe a Face?	Subways Are for Sleeping
How Do You Do, Miss Pratt?	Seventeen
How Do You Raise a Barn?	Plain and Fancy
How Do You Speak to an Angel?	Hazel Flagg
How Laughable It Is	Ben Franklin in Paris
How Long?	Pipe Dream
How Lovely to Be a Woman	Bye Bye Birdie

How the Money Changes Hands   Tenderloin
How Much I Love You   One Touch of Venus
How Sad   No Strings
How To   How to Succeed in Business
                                       without Really Trying
How to Handle a Woman   Camelot
Humming   Carnival
A Hundred Million Miracles   Flower Drum Song
Hungry Men   110 in the Shade
Hurry! It's Lovely Up Here!   On a Clear Day You Can See
                                       Forever
The Husking Bee   Say, Darling
Hymn for a Sunday Evening   Bye Bye Birdie
A Hymn to Him   My Fair Lady
Hymn to Hymie   Milk and Honey

I Ain't Down Yet   The Unsinkable Molly Brown
I Am Ashamed That Women Are   Kiss Me, Kate
  so Simple
I Am Going to Like It Here   Flower Drum Song
I Am in Love   Can-Can
I Believe in You   How to Succeed in Business
                                       without Really Trying
I Can   Bajour
I Can't Be in Love   Goldilocks
I Can't Say No   Oklahoma!
Icecream   She Loves Me
I Could Be Happy With You   The Boy Friend
I Could Get Married Today   Seventeen
I Could Have Danced All Night   My Fair Lady
I'd Do Anything   Oliver!
I'd Do It Again   Baker Street
I Don't Know His Name   She Loves Me
I Don't Think I'll End It All Today Jamaica
I'd Rather Wake Up By Myself   By the Beautiful Sea
I Enjoy Being a Girl   Flower Drum Song
I Feel Humble   What Makes Sammy Run?
I Feel Like I'm Gonna Live   Hazel Flagg
  Forever
I Feel Like I'm Not Out of   On the Town
  Bed Yet
I Feel Pretty   West Side Story
If Ever I Would Leave You   Camelot
If a Girl Isn't Pretty   Funny Girl
If I Can't Take It with Me   Goldilocks
If I Gave You   High Spirits

If I Had My Druthers — L'il Abner
If I Knew — The Unsinkable Molly Brown
If I Loved You — Carousel
If I Were a Bell — Guys and Dolls
If I Were a Rich Man — Fiddler on the Roof
If Momma Was Married — Gypsy
If'n — Happy Hunting
I Fought Every Step of the Way — Top Banana
If the Rain's Got to Fall — Half a Sixpence
If That Was Love — New Girl in Town
If This Isn't Love — Finian's Rainbow
If We Only Could Stop the Old Town Clock — Seventeen

If You Haven't Got a Sweetheart — A Tree Grows in Brooklyn
If You'll Be Mine — Look, Ma, I'm Dancin'!
If You Loved Me Truly — Can-Can
I Get Embarrassed — Take Me Along
I Get a Kick Out of You — Mexican Hayride
I Got Everything I Want — I Had a Ball
I Got Lost in His Arms — Annie Get Your Gun
I Go to Bed — Tovarich
I Got a Song — Bloomer Girl
I Had a Ball — I Had a Ball
I Hate Him — Carnival
I Hate Him — Destry Rides Again
I Hate Men — Kiss Me, Kate
I Have Dreamed — The King and I
I Have a Love — West Side Story
I Have to Tell You — Fanny
I Invited Myself — Ben Franklin in Paris
I Just Can't Wait — Subways Are for Sleeping
I Just Heard — Fiddler on the Roof
I Know about Love — Do Re Mi
I Know the Feeling — Tovarich
I Know How It Is — The Most Happy Fella
I Know It Can Happen Again — Allegro
I Know What I Am — Half a Sixpence
I Know Your Heart — High Spirts
I Know Your Kind — Destry Rides Again
I Like You — Fanny
I'll Buy You a Star — A Tree Grows in Brooklyn
I'll Go Home with Bonnie Jean — Brigadoon
I'll Know — Guys and Dolls
I'll Never Be Jealous Again — The Pajama Game
I'll Never Say No — The Unsinkable Molly Brown
I'll Show Him — Plain and Fancy
I'll Try — Redhead

Ilona | She Loves Me
I Love a Cop | Fiorello!
I Loved You Once in Silence | Camelot
I Loved You This Morning | The Day Before Spring
I Love the Ladies | Ben Franklin in Paris
I Love Paris | Can-Can
I Love What I'm Doing | Gentlemen Prefer Blondes
I Love You | Little Me
I Love You | Mexican Hayride
I'm Back in Circulation | Redhead
I'm Calm | A Funny Thing Happened on the
 | Way to the Forum
I Met a Girl | Bells Are Ringing
I'm the First Girl | Look, Ma, I'm Dancin'!
I'm a Funny Dame | Happy Hunting
I'm Glad I'm Leaving | Hazel Flagg
I'm Going Back | Bells Are Ringing
I'm Gonna Get Him | Mr. President
I'm Gonna Leave off Wearing My | House of Flowers
 Shoes |
I'm Gonna Wash That Man Right | South Pacific
 Outta My Hair |
I'm the Greatest Star | Funny Girl
I'm in London Again | Baker Street
I'm in Love with a Wonderful Guy | South Pacific
I'm Just Taking My Time | Subways Are for Sleeping
I'm Like a New Broom | A Tree Grows in Brooklyn
I'm Not at All in Love | The Pajama Game
I'm Not So Bright | Look, Ma, I'm Dancin'!
I'm On the Way | Paint Your Wagon
I'm an Ordinary Man | My Fair Lady
I'm Past My Prime | L'il Abner
Impossible | A Funny Thing Happened on the
 | Way to the Forum
I'm a Stranger Here Myself | One Touch of Venus
I'm Sure of Your Love | Billion Dollar Baby
I'm a Tingle, I'm a Glow | Gentlemen Prefer Blondes
I'm Tired of Texas | Look, Ma, I'm Dancin'!
I'm with You | Fade Out—Fade In
I'm You're Man | Love Life
I'm Your Girl | Me and Juliet
In Between | Paint Your Wagon
Independence Day Hora | Milk and Honey
Indians! | Peter Pan
I Never Has Seen Snow | House of Flowers
I Never Know When | Goldilocks
In a Little While | Once Upon a Mattress

In Our Cozy Little Cottage of Tomorrow — Are You with It?

In Our Hideaway — Mr. President

Intermission Talk — Me and Juliet

Introducin' Mr. Paris — The Golden Apple

Introduction Tango — Tovarich

Iowa Stubborn — The Music Man

I Put My Hand In — Hello, Dolly!

I Remember It Well — Love Life

I Resolve — She Loves Me

Irma La Douce — Irma La Douce

I Said It and I'm Glad — Subways Are for Sleeping

I Say Hello — Destry Rides Again

I See Something — What Makes Sammy Run?

I Shall Miss You — Baker Street

I Shall Scream — Oliver!

Is He the Only Man in the World — Mr. President

I Sing of Love — Kiss Me, Kate

Is It a Crime? — Bells Are Ringing

Is It Him or Is It Me — Love Life

Is It Really Me? — 110 in the Shade

Is That My Prince? — A Tree Grows in Brooklyn

I Still Get Jealous — High Button Shoes

I Still See Elisa — Paint Your Wagon

I Talk to the Trees — Paint Your Wagon

Italy — Ankles Aweigh

It Feels Good — Me and Juliet

It Gets Lonely in the White House — Mr. President

It Isn't Enough — The Roar of the Greasepaint—The Smell of the Crowd

It Only Takes a Moment — Hello, Dolly!

It's All Right with Me — Can-Can

It's a Chemical Reaction — Silk Stockings

It's a Darn Campus — Allegro

It's Delightful Down in Chile — Gentlemen Prefer Blondes

It's Doom — Say, Darling

It's a Fine Life — Oliver!

It's the Going Home Together — The Golden Apple

It's Good to Be Alive — New Girl in Town

It's Good to Be Back Home — Fade Out—Fade In

It's Good to Be Here — Happy Hunting

It's Great to Be Alive — Texas, Li'l Darlin'

It's a Helluva Way to Run a Love Affair — Plain and Fancy

It's High Time — Gentlemen Prefer Blondes

It's Legitimate — Do Re Mi

It's Like a Beautiful Woman — Happy Hunting

It's Love	Wonderful Town
It's a Lovely Day Today	Call Me Madam
It's Me	Me and Juliet
It's More Fun Than a Picnic	As the Girls Go
It's Never Quite the Same	Oh Captain!
It's Never Too Late to Fall in Love	The Boy Friend
It's a Perfect Relationship	Bells Are Ringing
It's a Scandal! It's an Outrage!	Oklahoma!
It's the Second Time You Meet that Matters	Say, Darling
It's a Simple Little System	Bells Are Ringing
It's So Simple	Baker Street
It's You	Mr. Wonderful
It Takes a Woman	Hello, Dolly!
It Takes a Woman to Get a Man	As the Girls Go
It Used to Be	Tovarich
It Was a Glad Adventure	The Golden Apple
It Was Good Enough for Grandma	Bloomer Girl
It Wonders Me	Plain and Fancy
I Understand	On the Town
I've Already Started In	The Unsinkable Molly Brown
I've Been There and I'm Back	Oh Captain!
I've Been Too Busy	Mr. Wonderful
I've Come to Wive It Weathily in Padua	Kiss Me, Kate
I've Got the President's Ear	As the Girls Go
I've Got to Be Around	Mr. President
I've Got to Find a Reason	Carnival
I've Got Your Number	Little Me
I've Grown Accustomed to Her Face	My Fair Lady
I've Never Been in Love Before	Guys and Dolls
I Wanna Get Married	Follow the Girls
I Want to Be Rich	Stop the World—I Want to Get Off
I Want to Be Seen with You Tonight	Funny Girl
I Want to Be with You	Golden Boy
(I Was Born Under a) Wandrin' Star	Paint Your Wagon
I Was a Shoo-in	Subways Are for Sleeping
I Whistle a Happy Tune	The King and I
I Will Follow You	Milk and Honey
I Wish I Was Dead	On the Town
I Wonder What the King is Doing Tonight	Camelot

I Won't Grow Up	Peter Pan
I Would Die	Take Me Along
Jacques D'Iraq	Mr. Wonderful
Jazz	Look, Ma, I'm Dancin'!
Jeannie's Packing Up	Brigadoon
The Jester and I	Once Upon a Mattress
Jet Song	West Side Story
Jewelry	Baker Street
Joey, Joey, Joey	The Most Happy Fella
John Paul Jones	Follow the Girls
The Joker	The Roar of the Greasepaint—The
	Smell of the Crowd
Josephine	Silk Stockings
Joseph Taylor Jr.	Allegro
Jubilation T. Cornpone	L'il Abner
The Judgment of Paris	The Golden Apple
A Jug of Wine	Damn Yankees
The Juke Box Hop	Do Re Mi
June Is Busting Out All Over	Carousel
Just Another Guy	Happy Hunting
Just Beyond the Rainbow	Are You with it?
Just for Once	Redhead
Just in Time	Bells Are Ringing
Just a Kiss Apart	Gentlemen Prefer Blondes
Just One Way to Say I Love You	Miss Liberty
Just You Wait	My Fair Lady
Kansas City	Oklahoma!
Katie Went to Haiti	Mexican Hayride
Keep a Hoppin'	The Unsinkable Molly Brown
Keeping Cool with Coolidge	Gentlemen Prefer Blondes
Keep It Gay	Me and Juliet
Keep It Simple	Oh Captain!
Kiss Me and Kill Me with Love	Ankles Aweigh
Kiss Me, Kate	Kiss Me, Kate
Kiss Me No Kisses	What Makes Sammy Run?
Kukla Katusha	Tovarich
Lady in Waiting	Goldilocks
La Festa	Ankles Aweigh
The Late, Late Show	Do Re Mi
Later Than Spring	Sail Away
Laugh It Up	Mr. President
Laura De Maupassant	Hazel Flagg
Lazy Afternoon	The Golden Apple
Lazy Moon	Goldilocks

Leadville Johnny Brown	The Unsinkable Molly Brown
Leave the Atom Alone	Jamaica
Leave It to Us, Gov	Baker Street
Le Grisbi Is le Root of le Evil in Man	Irma La Douce
Let Me Entertain You	Gypsy
Let's Do It	Mexican Hayride
Let's Go Back to the Waltz	Mr. President
Let's Not Waste a Moment	Milk and Honey
Let's Take an Old Fashioned Walk	Miss Liberty
Letters	Baker Street
Lichtenburg	Call Me Madam
Lida Rose	The Music Man
Life Does a Man a Favor	Oh Captain!
A Life with Rocky	Billion Dollar Baby
Lift 'Em Up and Put 'Em Down	Carmen Jones
Like a God	Flower Drum Song
Like a Young Man	Milk and Honey
Lila Tremaine	Fade Out—Fade In
Lites—Camera—Platitude	What Makes Sammy Run?
Little Biscuit	Jamaica
A Little Bit of Love	Wonderful Town
The Little Boy Blues	Look, Ma, I'm Dancin'!
A Little Brains	Damn Yankees
A Little Fish in a Big Pond	Miss Liberty
A Little Girl from Little Rock	Gentlemen Prefer Blondes
The Little Gray House	Lost in the Stars
Little Green Snake	Take Me Along
Little Me	Little Me
A Little More Heart	Hazel Flagg
Little Old New York	Tenderloin
The Little Ones' ABC	Sail Away
A Little Red Hat	110 in the Shade
Little Tin Box	Fiorello!
Live and Let Live	Can-Can
Living Simply	Bajour
Liza Crossing the Ice	Bloomer Girl
Lizzie's Coming Home	110 in the Shade
Loads of Love	No Strings
The Lonely Gotherd	The Sound of Music
Lonely Room	Oklahoma!
Lonely Town	On the Town
Long Ago	Half a Sixpence
Long Before I Knew You	Bells Are Ringing
A Long Time Ago	The Most Happy Fella
Look at 'Er	New Girl in Town

Look at That Face

Look for Small Pleasures
Look, Little Girl
Look No Further
Look to the Rainbow
Look Who's Dancing
Look Who's in Love
A Lopsided Bus
Lorna's Here
Lost in the Stars
A Lot of Livin' to Do
Lottie Gibson Specialty
Love and Kindness
Love Come Take Me Again
Love, Don't Turn Away
Love from a Heart of Gold

Love Hell
Love, I Hear

Love in a Home
Love Is a Chance
Love Is the Reason
Love Is a Very Light Thing
Lovelier Than Ever
Love-Line
Love Look Away
Lovely

A Lovely Girl
Love Makes the World Go
Love Me, Love My Dog
The Love of My Life
Love Song
Luck Be a Lady
Lucky in the Rain
Lucky to Be Me
Lullaby
Lumbered
The Lusty Month of May
L. Z. in the Quest of His Youth

Madame Rose's Toreadorables
Madame ZuZu
Magic, Magic

The Roar of the Greasepaint—The
    Smell of the Crowd
Ben Franklin in Paris
Here's Love
No Strings
Finian's Rainbow
A Tree Grows in Brooklyn
Redhead
Pipe Dream
Golden Boy
Lost in the Stars
Bye Bye Birdie
By the Beautiful Sea
The Most Happy Fella
Here's Love
110 in the Shade
How to Succeed in Business
    without Really Trying
Oh Captain!
A Funny Thing Happened on the
    Way to the Forum
L'il Abner
Bajour
A Tree Grows in Brooklyn
Fanny
Where's Charley?
Bajour
Flower Drum Song
A Funny Thing Happened on the
    Way to the Forum
Billion Dollar Baby
No Strings
Texas, L'il Darlin'
Brigadoon
Love Life
Guys and Dolls
As the Girls Go
On the Town
Once Upon a Mattress
Stop the World—I Want to Get Off
Camelot
Fade Out—Fade In

Gypsy
Love Life
Carnival

Maidens Typical of France	Can-Can
Maine	No Strings
Make a Friend	Tovarich
Make the Man Love Me	A Tree Grows in Brooklyn
Make a Miracle	Where's Charley?
Make the People Cry	Hazel Flagg
Make Someone Happy	Do Re Mi
Mama, Mama	I Can Get It for You Wholesale
Mamie Is Mimi	Gentlemen Prefer Blondes
A Man and a Woman	110 in the Shade
A Man Doesn't Know	Damn Yankees
Man for Sale	Bloomer Girl
The Man I Used to Be	Pipe Dream
Man of the Year This Week	Top Banana
Man to Man Talk	Once Upon a Mattress
The Man Who Has Everything	No Strings
Many Moons Ago	Once Upon a Mattress
Many a New Day	Oklahoma!
The Marathon Dance Faithless	Billion Dollar Baby
The Marathoners	Billion Dollar Baby
Mardi Gras	House of Flowers
Maria	The Sound of Music
Maria	West Side Story
Marion the Librarian	The Music Man
Marriage Type Love	Me and Juliet
A Married Man	Baker Street
Marrying for Love	Call Me Madam
Marry the Man Today	Guys and Dolls
Matchmaker, Matchmaker	Fiddler on the Roof
The Matrimonial Stomp	L'il Abner
Maybe Some Other Time	What Makes Sammy Run?
May We Entertain You	Gypsy
Me and My Bundle	Miss Liberty
Meat and Potatoes	Mr. President
Meet Miss Blendo	Top Banana
Meilinki, Meilchick	Stop the World—I Want to Get Off
Melinda	On a Clear Day You Can See
	Forever
Melisande	110 in the Shade
Merely Marvelous	Redhead
Miami	Mr. Wonderful
The Midas Touch	Bells Are Ringing
Milk and Honey	Milk and Honey
Million Dollar Smile	Billion Dollar Baby
Mine Next Monday	A Tree Grows in Brooklyn
Mine 'Til Monday	A Tree Grows in Brooklyn

The Minstrel
Minstrel Parade
Mira
Miracle of Miracles
Miss Liberty
Miss Marmelstein
Mix and Mingle
Mona from Arizona
Money Isn't Everything
Money to Burn
Monkey in the Mango Tree
Monsoon
A Month of Sundays
Montmartre
Moon in My Window
More I Cannot Wish You
More Love Than Your Love
The Morning Music of
    Montmartre
The Most Expensive Statue in the
    World
The Most Happy Fella
Motel Kamzoil
Mother Hare's Prophecy
Mother Hare's Seance
Motherhood
Mother's Getting Nervous
Move Over, America
Move Over, New York
Mr. Goldstone
Mr. Livingstone
Mr. Right
Mrs. Sally Adams
Mr. Wonderful
Mu-Cha-Cha
Mumbo Jumbo
Murder in Parkwold
The Music That Makes Me Dance
Must It Be Love?
Mutual Admiration Society
My Darlin' Eileen
My Darling, My Darling
My Favorite Things
My First Love Song

My Fortune Is My Face

Once Upon a Mattress
Love Life
Carnival
Fiddler on the Roof
Miss Liberty
I Can Get It for You Wholesale
Wish You Were Here
By the Beautiful Sea
Allegro
Half a Sixpence
Jamaica
What Makes Sammy Run?
Texas, Li'l Darlin'
Can-Can
Do I Hear a Waltz?
Guys and Dolls
By the Beautiful Sea
Oh Captain!

Miss Liberty

The Most Happy Fella
Fiddler on the Roof
The Golden Apple
The Golden Apple
Hello, Dolly!
Love Life
Bajour
Bajour
Gypsy
Happy Hunting
Love Life
Call Me Madam
Mr. Wonderful
Bells Are Ringing
Stop the World—I Want to Get Off
Lost in the Stars
Funny Girl
Bajour
Happy Hunting
Wonderful Town
Where's Charley?
The Sound of Music
The Roar of the Greasepaint—The
    Smell of the Crowd
Fade Out—Fade In

My Gentle Young Johnny	Tenderloin
My Girl Is Just Enough Woman for Me	Redhead
My Heart Belongs to Daddy	Mexican Hayride
My Home Is in My Shoes	Top Banana
My Home Town	What Makes Sammy Run?
My Joe	Carmen Jones
My Kind of Night	Love Life
My Lord and Master	The King and I
My Love Is a Married Man	The Day Before Spring
My Love Is on the Way	The Golden Apple
My Miss Mary	Tenderloin
My Mother's Weddin' Day	Brigadoon
My Name	Oliver!
My Name Is Samuel Cooper	Love Life
My Own Brass Bed	The Unsinkable Molly Brown
My Picture in the Papers	The Golden Apple
My State	Here's Love
Mysterious Lady	Peter Pan
My Time of Day	Guys and Dolls
My Way	The Roar of the Greasepaint—The Smell of the Crowd
My White Knight	The Music Man
My Wish	Here's Love
Nag! Nag! Nag!	Stop the World—I Want to Get Off
Namely You	L'il Abner
The Name's LaGuardia	Fiorello!
Napoleon	Jamaica
Near to You	Damn Yankees
Necessity	Finian's Rainbow
The Neighborhood Song	I Had a Ball
Never Give Anything Away	Can-Can
Neverland Waltz	Peter Pan
Never, Never Be an Artist	Can-Can
Never Too Late for Love	Fanny
Never Was Born	Bloomer Girl
New Art Is True Art	One Touch of Venus
The New Ashmolean Marching Society and Students' Conversatory Band	Where's Charley?
A Newfangled Tango	Happy Hunting
The New Look	Look, Ma, I'm Dancin'!
A New Pair of Shoes	What Makes Sammy Run?
A New Town Is a Blue Town	Pajama Game
New York, New York	On the Town
The Next Time It Happens	Pipe Dream

Next to Texas, I Love You — High Button Shoes
Night of My Nights — Kismet
Night Song — Golden Boy
Nine O'Clock — Take Me Along
Nitchevo — Tovarich
Nobody Ever Died for Dear Old Rutgers — High Button Shoes

Nobody's Heart but Mine — As the Girls Go
Nobody Told Me — No Strings
No More — Golden Boy
No More Candy — She Loves Me
No! No! No! — Tovarich
No One'll Ever Love You — Goldilocks
No Other Love — Me and Juliet
Normal American Boy — Bye Bye Birdie
Normandy — Once Upon a Mattress
No Strings — No Strings
Not Guilty — Destry Rides Again
Nothing at All — Ankles Aweigh
Nothing Can Replace a Man — Ankles Aweigh
Nothing Ever Happens in Angel's Roost — The Golden Apple

Nothing in Common — Here's Love
Not Since Nineveh — Kismet
No Understand — Do I Hear a Waltz?
No Way — The Sound of Music
Now I Have Everything — Fiddler on the Roof
Nutmeg Insurance — Are You with It?

The Ocarina — Call Me Madam
Octopus Song — Fanny
Ode to Lola — Seventeen
Oh Happy Day — L'il Abner
Ohio — Wonderful Town
Oh, My Feet — The Most Happy Fella
Oh, Please — Take Me Along
Oh, What a Beautiful Mornin' — Oklahoma!
O.K. for TV — Top Banana
Oklahoma! — Oklahoma!
Old Devil Moon — Finian's Rainbow
Old Enough to Love — By the Beautiful Sea
The Oldest Established — Guys and Dolls
Old Fashioned Mothers — Ankles Aweigh
Old Maid — 110 in the Shade
The Old Military Canal — Half a Sixpence
Oliver! — Oliver!
The Olive Tree — Kismet

Omm-Pah-Pah

Oliver!

Once in the Highlands

Brigadoon

Once in a Lifetime

Stop the World—I Want to Get Off

Once in Love with Amy

Where's Charley?

Once Knew a Fella

Destry Rides Again

Once a Time Today

Call Me Madam

Once a Year Day

The Pajama Game

On a Clear Day You Can See Forever

On a Clear Day You Can See Forever

One Boy

Bye Bye Birdie

One Day We Dance

Wildcat

One Foot, Other Foot

Allegro

One Hand, One Heart

West Side Story

One Hundred Easy Ways

Wonderful Town

One Man Ain't Quite Enough

House of Flowers

One Touch of Venus

One Touch of Venus

One-Track Mind

Billion Dollar Baby

On the Farm

New Girl in Town

The Only Dance I Know

Mr. President

Only For Americans

Miss Liberty

Only If You're in Love

Top Banana

The Only One

Tovarich

Only Time Will Tell

Destry Rides Again

On the Side of the Angels

Fiorello!

On the S.S. Bernard Cohn

On a Clear Day You Can See Forever

On the Street Where You Live

My Fair Lady

On a Sunday by the Sea

High Button Shoes

OO-OOO-OOO, What You Do to Me

Seventeen

An Opening for a Princess

Once Upon a Mattress

An Orthodox Fool

No Strings

The Other Generation

Flower Drum Song

The Other Half of Me

I Had a Ball

Other Hands, Other Hearts

Fanny

The Other Side of the Tracks

Little Me

O Tixo, Tixo, Help Me!

Lost in the Stars

Our Language of Love

Irma La Douce

Out for No Good

Follow the Girls

Out of My Dreams

Oklahoma!

Oysters, Cockles, and Mussels

Fanny

Paint a Rainbow

What Makes Sammy Run?

Pajama Dance

Look, Ma, I'm Dancin'!

The Pajama Game

The Pajama Game

Panisse and Son

Fanny

Papa, Won't You Dance with Me?
The Parade
Paris Loves Lovers
Paris Original

Paris Wakes Up and Smiles
The Party's on the House
The Party's Over
The Party That We're Gonna Have
    Tomorrow Night
The Passenger's Always Right
Pass the Football
Payday
People
People of Denver
People Will Say
Perfectly Lovely Couple
Perfect Young Ladies
Pernambuco
Perspective
The Persuasion
Piano Lesson
Pickalittle
Pick-Pocket Tango
The Picture of Happiness
Pigtails and Freckles
Pine Cones and Holly Berries
Pity the Sunset
Plain We Live
The Plastic Alligator
Pleasant Beach House
Plenty of Pennsylvania
Poker Polka
The Policemen's Ball
Politics
Politics and Poker
Poor Little Hollywood Star
Poor Little Me
Poor Little Pierrette
Pore Jud
Postage Stamp-Principality
The Pow-Wow Polka
The Practice Scherzo
Pretty Little Picture

The Prince's Farewell
Progress

High Button Shoes
Take Me Along
Silk Stockings
How to Succeed in Business
    without Really Trying
Miss Liberty
Half a Sixpence
Bells Are Ringing
Pipe Dream

Sail Away
Wonderful Town
A Tree Grows in Brooklyn
Funny Girl
The Unsinkable Molly Brown
Oklahoma!
Do I Hear a Waltz?
The Boy Friend
Where's Charley?
She Loves Me
Camelot
The Music Man
The Music Man
Redhead
Tenderloin
Mr. President
Here's Love
Jamaica
Plain and Fancy
Here's Love
Take Me Along
Plain and Fancy
110 in the Shade
Miss Liberty
Texas, Li'l Darlin'
Fiorello!
Little Me
Are You with It?
The Boy Friend
Oklahoma!
Happy Hunting
Peter Pan
Gentlemen Prefer Blondes
A Funny Thing Happened on the
    Way to the Forum
Little Me
Love Life

Progress Is the Root of All Evil

Promise Me a Rose

A Proper Gentleman

Pursuit

The Pussyfoot

Put 'em Back

Put on a Happy Face

Put on Your Sunday Clothes

A Puzzlement

Quadrille

Quiet

A Quiet Girl

Racing with the Clock

Rag Offen the Bush

Rahadlakum

The Rain in Spain

The Rain Song

Rakish Young Man with the
  Wiskuhs

Rat-Tat-Tat-Tat

Raunchy

Ready Cash

Real Live Girl

Reciprocity

Red-Blooded American Boy

The Red Blues

Reform

Relax

Respectability

Restless Heart

Reviewing the Situation

Rhymes Have I

Ribbons Down My Back

The Rich

Ride 'em, Cowboy

Ride Through the Night

Right as the Rain

The Right Finger on My Left Hand

Ring Out the Bells

Rita's Audition

The Road Tour

Rock Island

Rock, Rock, Rock

L'il Abner

Take Me Along

Half a Sixpence

Baker Street

Goldilocks

L'il Abner

Bye Bye Birdie

Hello, Dolly!

The King and I

Can-Can

Once Upon a Mattress

Wonderful Town

The Pajama Game

L'il Abner

Kismet

My Fair Lady

110 in the Shade

Bloomer Girl

Funny Girl

110 in the Shade

Ankles Aweigh

Little Me

Seventeen

I Had a Ball

Silk Stockings

Tenderloin

Wish You Were Here

Destry Rides Again

Fanny

Oliver!

Kismet

Hello, Dolly!

Carnival

Texas, Li'l Darlin'

Subways Are for Sleeping

Bloomer Girl

Redhead

On a Clear Day You Can See
  Forever

Mr. Wonderful

Golden Boy

The Music Man

As the Girls Go

Roll Yer Socks Up   New Girl in Town
A Romantic Atmosphere   She Loves Me
Roof Space   Baker Street
A Room in Bloomsbury   The Boy Friend
A Room without Windows   What Makes Sammy Run?
Rosabella   The Most Happy Fella
Rosemary   How to Succeed in Business
                                          without Really Trying
Rose's Turn   Gypsy
Rosie   Bye Bye Birdie
The Royal Bangkok Academy   The King and I
Rumson   Paint Your Wagon
Runyonland   Guys and Dolls

Sabbath Prayer   Fiddler on the Roof
The Sadder-But-Wiser Girl   The Music Man
Sadie, Sadie   Funny Girl
Safety in Numbers   The Boy Friend
Sail Away   Sail Away
The Sailing   Fanny
Salzburg   Bells Are Ringing
The Sandwich Man   High Spirits
Sans Souci   Top Banana
Santa's Lullaby   Bells Are Ringing
Satin and Silk   Silk Stockings
Satin Gown and Silver Shoe   Bloomer Girl
Savannah   Jamaica
Save a Kiss   Goldilocks
Say, Darling   Say, Darling
Say You'll Stay   Tovarich
Scylla and Charybdis   The Golden Apple
The Search   Lost in the Stars
A Secretary Is Not a Toy   How to Succeed in Business
                                          without Really Trying
The Secret Service   Mr. President
Security   High Button Shoes
Send Us Back to the Kitchen   Are You with It?
Senorita Dolores, Dolores   On the Town
Sensitivity   Once Upon a Mattress
Serenade with Asides   Where's Charley?
7½ Cents   The Pajama Game
The Seven Deadly Virtues   Camelot
Seventy-Six Trombones   The Music Man
The Sewing Bee   The Golden Apple
The Sew-Up   Bajour
Shall I Take My Heart and Go?   Goldilocks

Shall I Tell You What I Think of   The King and I
   You?
Shall We Dance?   The King and I
Shalom   Milk and Honey
Shauny O'Shay   Look, Ma, I'm Dancin'!
She Hadda Go Back   Here's Love
She Is Never Far Away   Allegro
She Loves Me   She Loves Me
Shepherd's Song   Milk and Honey
She's Got the Lot   Irma La Douce
She's Just Another Girl   Happy Hunting
She's My Love   Carnival
She's Not Enough Woman for Me   Redhead
She's Too Far Above Me   Half a Sixpence
She Wasn't You/He Isn't You   On a Clear Day You Can See
                                             Forever
Shipoopi   The Music Man
Shoeless Joe from Hannibal, Mo   Damn Yankees
Shopping Around   Wish You Were Here
Show Me   My Fair Lady
The Shriners Ballet   Bye Bye Birdie
The Shunning   Plain and Fancy
Shy   Once Upon a Mattress
Siberia   Silk Stockings
Sid, Ol' Kid   Take Me Along
Silk Stockings   Silk Stockings
The Simple Joys of Maidenhood   Camelot
Simple Little Things   110 in the Shade
The Simpson Sisters   Redhead
Sincere   The Music Man
Sing to Me Guitar   Mexican Hayride
Sit Down, You're Rockin' the Boat   Guys and Dolls
Six Months Out of Every Year   Damn Yankees
1617 Broadway   Mr. Wonderful
Skip the Buildup   Ankles Aweigh
A Sleeping Bee   House of Flowers
Sleep-Tite   The Pajama Game
Slide, Boy, Slide   House of Flowers
Slightly, Slightly   Are You with It?
Slogan Song   Top Banana
A Small Cartel   Tovarich
Small Walk   The Pajama Game
Small World   Gypsy
Social Director   Wish You Were Here
Society Party   L'il Abner
So Far   Allegro
So in Love   Kiss Me, Kate

So Long, Baby

So Long, Dearie

So Long, Farewell

Somebody, Somewhere

Some Days Everything Goes
    Wrong

Some Enchanted Evening

Someone Like You

Someone Nice Like You

Someone Woke Up

Some Other Time

Some People

Something Is Coming to Tea

Something's Always Happening on
    the River

Something's Coming

Something Sort of Grandish

Something Tells Me

Something to Dance About

Something to Live For

Something Very Strange

Something Wonderful

Somewhere

Song of Love

Sons of France

Soon

The Sound of Money

The Sound of Music

Sounds While Selling

Spanish Panic

Spanish Rose

Speaking of Pals

Speak Low

A Special Announcement

Square Dance

Standing on the Corner

Stan' Up and Fight

Station Rush

Stay

Staying Young

Stay Well

Steam Heat

Sterophonic Sound

Stick Around

Store-Bought Suit

Strange Duet

Stranger in Paradise

On the Town

Hello, Dolly!

The Sound of Music

The Most Happy Fella

What Makes Sammy Run?

South Pacific

Do I Hear a Waltz?

Stop the World—I Want to Get Off

Do I Hear a Waltz?

On the Town

Gypsy

High Spirits

Say, Darling

West Side Story

Finians' Rainbow

High Spirits

Call Me Madam

What Makes Sammy Run?

Sail Away

The King and I

West Side Story

Once Upon a Mattress

Irma La Douce

Bajour

I Can Get It for You Wholesale

The Sound of Music

She Loves Me

Once Upon a Mattress

Bye Bye Birdie

Million Dollar Baby

One Touch of Venus

Stop the World—I Want to Get Off

Texas, Li'l Darlin'

The Most Happy Fella

Carmen Jones

Subways Are for Sleeping

Do I Hear a Waltz?

Take Me Along

Lost in the Stars

The Pajama Game

Silk Stockings

Golden Boy

The Golden Apple

Subways Are for Sleeping

Kismet

Strip Flips Hip	Follow the Girls
Stuck with Each Other	Tovarich
Subway Directions	Subways Are for Sleeping
Subway Incident	Subways Are for Sleeping
Subways Are for Sleeping	Subways Are for Sleeping
Success	Do Re Mi
Sue Me	Guys and Dolls
Summer Afternoon	Wish You Were Here
A Summer Incident	High Button Shoes
Summertime Is Summertime	Seventeen
Sunday	Flower Drum Song
Sunday in Cicero Falls	Bloomer Girl
Sunrise, Sunset	Fiddler on the Roof
Sunshine	Gentlemen Prefer Blondes
Sunshine Girl	New Girl in Town
Sur La Page	The Boy Friend
Surprise	Oh Captain!
The Surrey with the Fringe on Top	Oklahoma!
Suzy Is a Good Thing	Pipe Dream
Swamps of Home	Once Upon a Mattress
The Sweetest Sounds	No Strings
Sweet Thursday	Pipe Dream
Swing!	Wonderful Town
Swing Your Projects	Subways Are for Sleeping
Sword, Rose, and Cape	Carnival
The Tailor	Fiddler on the Roof
Take Back Your Mink	Guys and Dolls
Take a Crank Letter	Texas, Li'l Darlin'
Take It Slow, Joe	Jamaica
Take a Job	Do Re Mi
Take Me Along	Take Me Along
Take the Moment	Do I Hear a Waltz?
Take Your Time and Take Your Pick	Plain and Fancy
Taking No Chances	Love Life
The Taking of Rhododendrun	The Golden Apple
Talking to You	High Spirits
Talk to Him	Mr. Wonderful
Talk to Me	Bye Bye Birdie
Tall Hope	Wildcat
Tango Tragique	She Loves Me
Tanz Mit Mir	Carnival
Taunting	West Side Story
The Telephone Hour	Bye Bye Birdie
The Tenderloin Celebration	Tenderloin
The Tender Spot	What Makes Sammy Run?
Texas, Li'l Darlin'	Texas, Li'l Darlin'

Thanks for a Lousy Evening   Follow the Girls
Thank You, Madam   She Loves Me
Thank You So Much   Do I Hear a Waltz?
That Dirty Old Man   A Funny Thing Happened on the
                                       Way to the Forum
That Face   Tovarich
That Great Come and Get It Day   Finian's Rainbow
That'll Show Him   A Funny Thing Happened on the
                                       Way to the Forum
That Man Over There   Here's Love
That Ring on the Finger   Destry Rides Again
That's a Crime   Irma La Douce
That's for Sure   Top Banana
That's Him   One Touch of Venus
That's How I Am Sick of Love   One Touch of Venus
That's How It Goes   A Tree Grows in Brooklyn
That's How It Starts   Take Me Along
That's the Way It Happens   Me and Juliet
That's What It Is to Be Young   The Roar of the Greasepaint—The
                                       Smell of the Crowd
That's Your Funeral   Oliver!
That Was Yesterday   Milk and Honey
Then You May Take Me to the   Camelot
   Fair
There   Mr. Wonderful
There Ain't No Flies on Me   New Girl in Town
There But for You Go I   Brigadoon
There I'd Be   Billion Dollar Baby
There Is Nothing Like a Dame   South Pacific
There Is Only One Paris for That   Irma La Douce
There Must Be Someone for Me   Mexican Hayride
There Never Was a Woman   Goldilocks
There Once Was a Man   The Pajama Game
There's a Coach Comin' In   Paint Your Wagon
There's No Business Like Show   Annie Get Your Gun
   Business
There's No Getting Away from You   As the Girls Go
There's No Reason in the World   Milk and Honey
There's Nothing Like a Model T   High Button Shoes
There's Nothing Nicer Than   Wish You Were Here
   People
They Call the Wind Maria   Paint Your Wagon
They Like Ike   Call Me Madam
They Love Me   Mr. President
They Say It's Wonderful   Annie Get Your Gun
They Talk a Different Language   Texas, Li'l Darlin'

They Won't Know Me
Things Are Gonna Hum This
    Summer
Things to Remember

Think Beautiful
Thinkin'
Thinking
Think of the Time I Save
The Thirties
This Dream

This Is All Very New to Me
This Is a Great Country
This Is the Life
This Is the Life
This Is My Beloved
This Is My Holiday
This Is What I Call Love
This Much I Know
This Nearly Was Mine
This Time of the Year
This Was Just Another Day
This Was a Real Nice Clambake
This Week Americans
Those Were the Good Old Days
The Thought of You
Thousands of Miles
Three Paradises
Three Letters
Throw the Anchor Away
The Tide Pool
Till There Was You
Till Tomorrow
Tiny Room
Tippy Toes
The Tirade
T'Morra', T'Morra'
Today Will Be Yesterday
    Tomorrow
Together Wherever We Go
To Life
Tom Cat
Tommy, Tommy
Tomorrow Morning
To My Wife
Tonight at Eight

Wish You Were Here
Seventeen

The Roar of the Greasepaint—The
    Smell of the Crowd
I Had a Ball
Pipe Dream
Do I Hear a Waltz?
The Pajama Game
Fade Out—Fade In
The Roar of the Greasepaint—The
    Smell of the Crowd
Plain and Fancy
Mr. President
Golden Boy
Love Life
Are You with It?
The Day Before Spring
Happy Hunting
Happy Hunting
South Pacific
Finian's Rainbow
Seventeen
Carousel
Do I Hear a Waltz?
Damn Yankees
Fanny
Lost in the Stars
Oh Captain!
She Loves Me
By the Beautiful Sea
Pipe Dream
The Music Man
Fiorello!
Look, Ma, I'm Dancin'!
Wildcat
The Golden Apple
Bloomer Girl
Follow the Girls

Gypsy
Fiddler on the Roof
Goldilocks
Tenderloin
Destry Rides Again
Fanny
She Loves Me

Too Bad	Silk Stockings
Too Charming	Ben Franklin in Paris
Too Close for Comfort	Mr. Wonderful
Too Darn Hot	Kiss Me, Kate
Too Soon	I Can Get It for You Wholesale
Top Banana	Top Banana
To the Ship	Peter Pan
Tosy and Cosh	On a Clear Day You Can See Forever
Tradition	Fiddler on the Roof
The Train	Miss Liberty
Train to Johannesburg	Lost in the Stars
A Tree That Grows in Brooklyn	Follow the Girls
The Trial	Tenderloin
Tripping the Light Fantastic	Wish You Were Here
A Trip to the Library	She Loves Me
Trouble	The Music Man
Trouble Man	Lost in the Stars
The Trouble with Women	One Touch of Venus
The Truth	Little Me
Try Me	She Loves Me
Try to Love Me	Say, Darling
Tunnel of Love Chase	I Had a Ball
Turtle Song	House of Flowers
Twelve Days to Christmas	She Loves Me
Twelve O'Clock and All Is Well	Follow the Girls
Twin Soliloquies	South Pacific
Two Faces in the Dark	Redhead
Two Ladies in the Shade	House of Flowers
Two Lost Souls	Damn Yankees
The Two of Us	Look, Ma, I'm Dancin'!
Two Years in the Making	Goldilocks
Typically English	Stop the World—I Want to Get Off
Ugg-a-Wugg	Peter Pan
Uh-Oh!	Tovarich
Ulysses Soliquey	The Golden Apple
The Uncle Sam Rag	Redhead
Unfair	Fiorello!
Up Where the People Are	The Unsinkable Molly Brown
Useful Phrases	Sail Away
The Usher from the Mezzanine	Fade Out—Fade In
Valse Milieu	Irma La Douce
Ven I Valse	New Girl in Town
The Very Next Man	Fiorello!
A Very Nice Man	Carnival

A Very Proper Town | Oh Captain!
A Very Proper Week | Oh Captain!
Very Soft Shoes | Once Upon a Mattress
A Very Special Day | Me and Juliet
The Villain Always Gets It | Ankles Aweigh
V.I.P. | Do Re Mi

The Waiters' Gallop | Hello, Dolly!
Waitin' | House of Flowers
Waitin' for My Dearie | Brigadoon
Waiting, Waiting | Do Re Mi
Wait 'Til We're Sixty-Five | On a Clear Day You Can See Forever

Walk Like a Sailor | Ankles Aweigh
Warm All Over | The Most Happy Fella
Washington Square Dance | Call Me Madam
The Washington Twist | Mr. President
Was I Wazir? | Kismet
Was She Prettier Than I? | High Spirits
Way Out West in Jersey | One Touch of Venus
The Way Things Are | I Can Get It for You Wholesale
Weatherbee's Drugstore | Seventeen
The Wedding | Billion Dollar Baby
The Wedding | Milk and Honey
Wedding of the Year | What Makes Sammy Run?
Wedding of the Year Blues | Happy Hunting
We Deserve Each Other | Me and Juliet
We Kiss in a Shadow | The King and I
Welcome Hinges | Bloomer Girl
Welcome Home Fanny | Fanny
Welcome to Sludgepool | Stop the World—I Want to Get Off
Welcome to Sunvale | Stop the World—I Want to Get Off
Well Man | I Can Get It for You Wholesale
Wells Fargo Wagon | The Music Man
We Loves Ya, Jimey | Redhead
We Love You, Conrad! | Bye Bye Birdie
Wendy | Peter Pan
We Open in Venice | Kiss Me, Kate
We're Gonna Be Alright | Do I Hear a Waltz?
We're Home | Take Me Along
We're Not Children | Oh Captain!
Were Thine That Special Face | Kiss Me, Kate
We Sail the Seas | Ben Franklin in Paris
Western People Funny | The King and I
West Wind | One Touch of Venus
What Are They Doing to Us Now? | I Can Get It for You Wholesale
What Became of Old Temple | Ben Franklin in Paris

What a Crazy Way to Spend
   Sunday

What Did I Ever See in Him?

What Did I Have That I Don't
   Have?

What Do I Have to Do to Get My
   Picture Took?

What Do We Do? We Fly!

Whatever Lola Wants

What Good Does It Do?

What in the World Did You Want?

What Is a Friend For?

What Is This Feeling in the Air?

What Is This Thing?

What Kind of Fool Am I?

What a Man!

What a Night This Is Going to Be

What's Goin' on Here?

What's Good for General
   Bullmoose

What's in It for Me?

What's in It for You?

What's New at the Zoo?

What's the Use of Wond'rin

What Takes My Fancy?

What a Waste

When the Boys Come Home

When the Children Are Asleep

When Did I Fall in Love

When Gemini Meets Capricorn

When a Good Man Takes to
   Drink

When I Dance with the Person I
   Love

When the Idle Poor Become the
   Idle Rich

When I Marry Mister Snow

When I'm Being Born Again

When I'm Not Near the Girl I
   Love

When You Want Me

Where Are You?

Where Did the Night Go?

Mexican Hayride

Bye Bye Birdie

On a Clear Day You Can See
   Forever

Miss Liberty

Do I Hear a Waltz?

Damn Yankees

Jamaica

High Spirits

House of Flowers

Subways Are for Sleeping

Mexican Hayride

Stop the World—I Want to Get
   Off

The Roar of the Greasepaint—The
   Smell of the Crowd

Baker Street

Paint Your Wagon

L'il Abner

I Can Get It for You Wholesale

Tenderloin

Do Re Mi

Carousel

Wildcat

Wonderful Town

Bloomer Girl

Carousel

Fiorello!

I Can Get It for You Wholesale

Are You with It?

Ben Franklin in Paris

Finian's Rainbow

Carousel

On a Clear Day You Can See
   Forever

Finian's Rainbow

Sail Away

Follow the Girls

Wish You Were Here

Where Is the Life That Late I Led?	Kiss Me, Kate
Where Is Love?	Oliver!
Where Is the Man I Married?	High Spirits
Where Is the Tribe for Me?	Bajour
Where's Charley?	Where's Charley?
Where Shall I Find Him?	Sail Away
Where's My Wife?	The Day Before Spring
Where's My Shoe?	She Loves Me
Where Would You Be without Me?	The Roar of the Greasepaint—The Smell of the Crowd
Whichaway'd They Go?	Texas, Li'l Darlin'
While the City Sleeps	Golden Boy
Whizzin' Away Along de Track	Carmen Jones
Who Are You Now?	Funny Girl
Who Can I Turn To (When Nobody Needs Me)?	The Roar of the Greasepaint—The Smell of the Crowd
Who Is Mr. Big?	Do Re Mi
Who Is Samuel Cooper?	Love Life
Who Knows?	I Can Get It for You Wholesale
Who Knows What Might Have Been?	Subways Are for Sleeping
Who'll Buy?	Lost in the Stars
Whoop'in' and a-Hollerin'	Texas, Li'l Darlin'
Whoop-Ti-Ay!	Paint Your Wagon
Who's Been Sitting in My Chair?	Goldilocks
Who's the Bravest?	Hazel Flagg
Who's Gonna Be the Winner	Billion Dollar Baby
Who's Got the Pain?	Damn Yankees
Who Taught Her Everything?	Funny Girl
Who Will Buy?	Oliver!
Why Can't the English?	My Fair Lady
Why Can't You Behave?	Kiss Me, Kate
Why Do the Wrong People Travel?	Sail Away
Why Not Katie?	Plain and Fancy
Why Shouldn't I?	Mexican Hayride
Wildcat	Wildcat
Wilkes-Barre, PA	Tovarich
Will He Like Me?	She Loves Me
Will I Ever Tell You?	The Music Man
Windflowers	The Golden Apple
The Winters Go By	Allegro
Wish You Were Here	Wish You Were Here
With All Due Respect	The Roar of the Greasepaint—The Smell of the Crowd
With a Little Bit of Luck	My Fair Lady
Without Love	Silk Stockings

Without You — My Fair Lady
Without You, I'm Nothing — Mr. Wonderful
The Woman in His Room — Where's Charley?
Women's Club Blues — Love Life
Wonderbar — Kiss Me, Kate
A Wonderful Day Like Today — The Roar of the Greasepaint—The Smell of the Crowd

Wonderful Music — 110 in the Shade
Won't You Charleston with Me? — The Boy Friend
Word a Day — Top Banana
Words, Words, Words — Bajour
Workout — Golden Boy
The World Is Beautiful Today — Hazel Flagg
Wouldn't It Be Loverly? — My Fair Lady
Wreck of a Mec — Irma La Douce
Wrong Note Rag — Wonderful Town

Ya Got Me — On the Town
Yankee Dollar — Jamaica
Yatata, Yatata, Yatata — Allegro
The Years Before Us — Where's Charley?
Yer My Friend, Aintcha? — New Girl in Town
Yes, My Heart — Carnival
Yesterday I Loved You — Once Upon a Mattress
The Yo Ho Ho — How to Succeed in Business without Really Trying

You Are Beautiful — Flower Drum Song
You Are Sixteen — The Sound of Music
You Are Woman — Funny Girl
You Can Have Him — Miss Liberty
You Can't Get a Man with a Gun — Annie Get Your Gun
You Can Trust Me — What Makes Sammy Run?
You'd Better Get a Gimmick — Gypsy
You'd Better Love Me — High Spirits
You Deserve Me — I Had a Ball
You Don't Dance — Follow the Girls
You Don't Know — Here's Love
You Don't Know Him — Oh Captain!
You Don't Tell Me — No Strings
You Don't Want to Play with Me Blues — The Boy Friend
You Haven't Changed at All — The Day Before Spring
You Help Me — What Makes Sammy Run?
You'll Make an Elegant Butler — Tovarich
You'll Never Get Away from Me — Gypsy
You'll Never Walk Alone — Carousel
You Love Me — Tovarich

You Mustn't Be Discouraged	Fade Out—Fade In
You Need a Hobby	Mr. President
Younger Than Springtime	South Pacific
You're Gonna Dance with Me, Willie	Hazel Flagg
You're in Paris	Ben Franklin in Paris
You're Just in Love	Call Me Madam
You're a Liar	Wildcat
You're a Long, Long Way from America	Sail Away
You're My Boy	High Button Shoes
You're My Girl	High Button Shoes
You're No Good	What Makes Sammy Run?
You're Not Foolin' Me	110 in the Shade
You're Perf	Follow the Girls
You're a Queer One, Julie Jordan	Carousel
You're So Beautiful That—	Top Banana
You're So Right for Me	Oh Captain!
You Say the Nicest Things, Baby	As the Girls Go
You Say You Care	Gentlemen Prefer Blondes
You Talk Just Like My Maw	Carmen Jones
You've Come Home	Wildcat
You've Got to Be Carefully Taught	South Pacific
You've Got to Do It	Bells Are Ringing
You've Got to Pick a Pocket or Two	Oliver!
Yum Ticky	Carnival

BIBLIOGRAPHY

Bordman, Gerald. *American Musical Comedy*. New York: Oxford University Press, 1982.

Citron, Stephen. *The Musical from the Inside Out*. Chicago: Dee, 1992.

Henderson, Mary C. *The City and the Theatre*. Clifton, N.J.: White, 1973.

Hughes, Glenn. *A History of the American Theatre, 1700–1950*. New York: French, 1951.

Kernodle, George, Portia Kernodle, and Edward Pixley. *Invitation to the Theatre*. New York: Harcourt, 1967.

Laufe, Abel. *Broadway's Greatest Musicals*. New York: Funk & Wagnells, 1977.

Rodgers, Richard. *Musical Stages*. New York: Random House, 1975.

Suskin, Steven. *More Opening Nights on Broadway*. New York: Schirmer, 1997.

PLAYBILLS

All American, March 19, 1962

Allah Be Praised!, April 20, 1944

Allegro, October 10, 1947

Ankles Aweigh, April 18, 1955

Annie Get Your Gun, May 16, 1946

Anyone Can Whistle, April 4, 1964

Are You with It?, November 10, 1945
As the Girls Go, November 13, 1948
Bajour, November 23, 1964
Baker Street, February 16, 1965
Barefoot Boy with Cheek, April 3, 1947
The Beast in Me, May 16, 1963
Beg, Borrow, or Steal, February 10, 1960
Beggar's Holiday, December 22, 1946
Bells Are Ringing, November 29, 1956
Ben Franklin in Paris, October 27, 1964
Billion Dollar Baby, December 21, 1945
Bloomer Girl, October 5, 1944
The Body Beautiful, January 23, 1958
The Boy Friend, September 20, 1954
Bravo Giovanni, May 19, 1962
Brigadoon, March 13, 1947
Buttrio Square, October 14, 1952
By the Beautiful Sea, April 8, 1954
Bye, Bye, Birdie, April 14, 1960
Café Crown, April 17, 1964
Call Me Madam, October 12, 1950
Camelot, December 3, 1960
Can-Can, May 7, 1953
Carmen Jones, December 2, 1943
Carnival, April 13, 1961
Carnival in Flanders, September 8, 1953
Carousel, April 19, 1945
The Conquering Hero, January 16, 1961
Copper and Brass, October 17, 1957
Courtin' Time, June 13, 1951
Damn Yankees, May 5, 1955
The Day Before Spring, November 22, 1945
Destry Rides Again, April 23, 1959
Do I Hear a Waltz?, March 18, 1965
Donnybrook!, May 18, 1961
Do Re Mi, December 26, 1960
Drat! The Cat!, October 10, 1965
Dream with Music, May 18, 1944
The Duchess Misbehaves, February 13, 1946
Fade Out—Fade In, May 26, 1964
A Family Affair, January 27, 1962
Fanny, November 4, 1954

Fiddler on the Roof, September 22, 1964
Finian's Rainbow, January 10, 1947
Fiorello!, November 23, 1959
First Impressions, March 19, 1959
Flahooley, May 14, 1951
Flora, the Red Menace, May 11, 1965
Flower Drum Song, December 1, 1958
Follow the Girls, April 8, 1944
Foxy, February 16, 1964
Funny Girl, March 26, 1964
A Funny Thing Happened on the Way to the Forum, May 8, 1962
The Gay Life, November 18, 1961
Gentlemen Prefer Blondes, December 8, 1949
The Girl from Nantucket, November 8, 1945
The Girl in Pink Tights, March 3, 1954
The Girl Who Came to Supper, December 8, 1963
The Golden Apple, March 11, 1954
Golden Boy, October 20, 1964
Goldilocks, October 11, 1958
Great to be Alive, March 23, 1950
Greenwillow, March 8, 1960
Guys and Dolls, November 10, 1950
Gypsy, May 21, 1959
Half a Sixpence, April 25, 1965
The Happiest Girl in the World, April 3, 1961
Happy as Larry, January 6, 1950
Happy Hunting, December 6, 1956
Happy Town, October 7, 1959
Hazel Flagg, February 11, 1953
Heaven on Earth, September 16, 1948
Hello, Dolly!, January 16, 1964
Here's Love, October 3, 1963
High Button Shoes, October 9, 1947
High Spirits, April 7, 1964
Hit the Trail, December 2, 1954
Hold It!, May 5, 1948
Hot Spot, April 19, 1963
House of Flowers, December 30, 1954
How to Succeed in Business without Really Trying, October 14, 1961
I Can Get It for You Wholesale, March 22, 1962
I Had a Ball, December 15, 1964
Irma La Douce, September 29, 1960

The Jackpot, January 13, 1944
Jamaica, October 31, 1957
Jennie, October 17, 1963
Juno, March 9, 1959
Kean, November 2, 1961
Kelly, February 6, 1965
The King and I, March 29, 1951
Kismet, December 3, 1953
Kiss Me, Kate, December 30, 1948
Kwamina, October 23, 1961
Let It Ride, October 12, 1962
L'il Abner, November 15, 1956
Little Me, November 17, 1962
Look, Ma, I'm Dancin'!, January 29, 1948
Lost in the Stars, October 30, 1949
Louisiana Lady, June 2, 1947
Love Life, October 7, 1948
Lute Song, February 6, 1946
Magdalena, September 20, 1948
Maggie, February 18, 1953
Make a Wish, April 18, 1951
Me and Juliet, May 28, 1953
Mexican Hayride, January 28, 1944
Milk and Honey, October 10, 1961
Miss Liberty, July 15, 1949
The Most Happy Fella, May 3, 1956
Mr. President, October 20, 1962
Mr. Wonderful, March 22, 1956
The Music Man, December 19, 1957
My Darling Aida, October 27, 1952
My Fair Lady, March 15, 1956
Nellie Bly, January 21, 1946
The Nervous Set, May 12, 1959
New Girl in Town, May 14, 1957
No Strings, March 15, 1962
Nowhere to Go But Up, November 10, 1962
Oh Captain!, February 4, 1958
Oh! What Lovely War, September 30, 1964
Oklahoma!, March 31, 1943
Oliver!, January 6, 1963
On a Clear Day You Can See Forever, October 17, 1965
On the Town, December 28, 1944

Once Upon a Mattress, May 11, 1959
110 in the Shade, October 24, 1963
One Touch of Venus, October 7, 1943
Out of This World, December 21, 1950
Paint Your Wagon, November 12, 1951
The Pajama Game, May 13, 1954
Park Avenue, November 4, 1946
Peter Pan, October 20, 1954
Pickwick, October 4, 1965
Pipe Dream, November 30, 1955
Plain and Fancy, January 27, 1955
Portofino, February 21, 1958
Redhead, February 5, 1959
The Roar of the Greasepaint—The Smell of the Crowd, May 16, 1955
Rumple, November 6, 1957
Sadie Thompson, November 16, 1944
Sail Away, October 3, 1961
Saratoga, December 7, 1959
Say Darling, April 3, 1958
Seventeen, June 21, 1951
Seventh Heaven, May 26, 1955
Shangri-La, June 13, 1956
She Loves Me, April 23, 1963
Shinbone Alley, April 13, 1957
Silk Stockings, February 24, 1955
Sleepy Hollow, June 3, 1948
Something More!, November 10, 1964
Sophie, April 15, 1963
The Sound of Music, November 16, 1959
South Pacific, April 7, 1949
St. Louis Woman, March 30, 1946
Stop the World—I Want to Get Off, October 3, 1962
Street Scene, January 9, 1947
Subways Are for Sleeping, December 27, 1961
Take Me Along, October 22, 1959
Tenderloin, October 17, 1960
Texas, L'il Darlin', November 25, 1949
13 Daughters, March 2, 1961
Three Wishes for Jamie, March 21, 1952
Top Banana, November 1, 1951
Tovarich, March 18, 1963
A Tree Grows in Brooklyn, April 19, 1951

The Unsinkable Molly Brown, November 3, 1960
The Vamp, November 10, 1955
West Side Story, September 26, 1957
What Makes Sammy Run?, February 27, 1964
Where's Charley?, October 11, 1948
Whoop-Up, December 22, 1958
Wildcat, December 16, 1960
Wish You Were Here, June 25, 1952
Wonderful Town, February 25, 1953

INDEX

Note: Bold page numbers denote biographies.

ABOUT THE AUTHOR

Corinne J. Naden is a former children's book editor in New York City and the author of more than 100 titles for children and adults. She spent four years as a journalist in the U.S. Navy and lives in Tarrytown, New York.

Breinigsville, PA USA
18 January 2011
253481BV00002B/2/P